The Power of the Periphery

What is the source of Norway's culture of environmental harmony in our troubled world? Exploring the role of Norwegian scholar-activists of the late twentieth century, Peder Anker examines how they portrayed their country as a place of environmental stability in a world filled with tension. In contrast with societies dirtied by the hot and cold wars of the twentieth century, Norway's power, they argued, lay in the pristine, ideal natural environment of the periphery. Globally, a beautiful Norway came to be contrasted with a polluted world and fashioned as an ecological microcosm for the creation of a better global macrocosm. In this innovative, interdisciplinary history, Anker explores the ways in which ecological concerns were imported via Rachel Carson's Silent Spring in 1962, then to be exported from Norway back to the world at the Earth Summit in Rio de Janeiro in 1992. This title is also available as Open Access on Cambridge Core.

PEDER ANKER is Associate Professor at The Gallatin School of Individualized Study, New York University. He is also Professor II in History of Science at the University of Oslo. He is on Twitter @pederanker.

Studies in Environment and History

Editors

J. R. McNeill, *Georgetown University*
Ling Zhang, *Boston College*

Editors Emeriti

Alfred W. Crosby, *University of Texas at Austin*
Edmund P. Russell, *Carnegie Mellon University*
Donald Worster, *University of Kansas*

Other Books in the Series

Peder Anker *The Power of the Periphery: How Norway Became an Environmental Pioneer for the World*
David Moon *The American Steppes: The Unexpected Russian Roots of Great Plains Agriculture, 1870s–1930s*
James L. A. Webb, Jr. *The Guts of the Matter: A Global Environmental History of Human Waste and Infectious Intestinal Disease*
Maya K. Peterson *Pipe Dreams: Water and Empire in Central Asia's Aral Sea Basin*
Thomas M. Wickman *Snowshoe Country: An Environmental and Cultural History of Winter in the Early American Northeast*
Debjani Bhattacharyya *Empire and Ecology in the Bengal Delta: The Making of Calcutta*
Chris Courtney *The Nature of Disaster in China: The 1931 Yangzi River Flood*
Dagomar Degroot *The Frigid Golden Age: Climate Change, the Little Ice Age, and the Dutch Republic, 1560–1720*
Edmund Russell *Greyhound Nation: A Coevolutionary History of England, 1200–1900*
Timothy J. LeCain *The Matter of History: How Things Create the Past*
Ling Zhang *The River, the Plain, and the State: An Environmental Drama in Northern Song China, 1048–1128*
Abraham H. Gibson *Feral Animals in the American South: An Evolutionary History*
Andy Bruno *The Nature of Soviet Power: An Arctic Environmental History*
David A. Bello *Across Forest, Steppe, and Mountain: Environment, Identity, and Empire in Qing China's Borderlands*
Erik Loomis *Empire of Timber: Labor Unions and the Pacific Northwest Forests*
Peter Thorsheim *Waste into Weapons: Recycling in Britain during the Second World War*

(continued after index)

The Power of the Periphery

How Norway Became an Environmental Pioneer for the World

PEDER ANKER
New York University

CAMBRIDGE
UNIVERSITY PRESS

University Printing House, Cambridge CB2 8BS, United Kingdom

One Liberty Plaza, 20th Floor, New York, NY 10006, USA

477 Williamstown Road, Port Melbourne, VIC 3207, Australia

314–321, 3rd Floor, Plot 3, Splendor Forum, Jasola District Centre,
New Delhi – 110025, India

79 Anson Road, #06–04/06, Singapore 079906

Cambridge University Press is part of the University of Cambridge.

It furthers the University's mission by disseminating knowledge in the pursuit of education, learning, and research at the highest international levels of excellence.

www.cambridge.org
Information on this title: www.cambridge.org/9781108477567
DOI: 10.1017/9781108763851

© Peder Anker 2020

This work is in copyright. It is subject to statutory exceptions and to the provisions of relevant licensing agreements; with the exception of the Creative Commons version the link for which is provided below, no reproduction of any part of this work may take place without the written permission of Cambridge University Press.

An online version of this work is published at doi.org/10.1017/9781108763851 under a Creative Commons Open Access license CC-BY-NC-ND 4.0 which permits re-use, distribution and reproduction in any medium for non-commercial purposes providing appropriate credit to the original work is given. You may not distribute derivative works without permission. To view a copy of this license, visit https://creativecommons.org/licenses/by-nc-nd/4.0

All versions of this work may contain content reproduced under license from third parties. Permission to reproduce this third-party content must be obtained from these third-parties directly.

When citing this work, please include a reference to the DOI 10.1017/9781108763851

First published 2020

A catalogue record for this publication is available from the British Library.

ISBN 978-1-108-47756-7 Hardback

Cambridge University Press has no responsibility for the persistence or accuracy of URLs for external or third-party internet websites referred to in this publication and does not guarantee that any content on such websites is, or will remain, accurate or appropriate.

– Europe's Tibet, heavenly high, silent
And almost infinite, as thinking.
                    Rolf Jacobsen, "The Alternative Nation"

Contents

List of Figures		*page* ix
Acknowledgments		xi
	"We Are As Gods"	1
1	The Power of the Periphery	9
	The Allure of Life Lost	9
	Chasing Paradise	14
	The Return to the Wild	20
	Learning from the People of Swat	23
	The Fisherman-Peasant	26
2	The Ecologists	30
	The High Mountain Ecology Research Station	30
	Rachel Carson's Silent Spring	32
	The First Lectures in Ecology by Biologists	34
	International Biological Program	37
	A Steady-State Nation	40
3	The Ecophilosophers	45
	True Weltanschauung	45
	The Last Messiah	50
	The Nation's Philosopher	53
	Mastering the Mountains	59
	The Mardøla Demonstrations	63
	The Ecophilosophy Group	69
4	The Deep Ecologists	75
	Environmental Orientalism and the Critique of the West	75
	The Referendum on the European Community	79

	Deep Ecology in Bucharest	85
	Marxist Attack	88
5	Environmental Studies	92
	Ecology, Community, and Lifestyle	94
	The Case against Science	101
	Education in Ecological Dogmatism	106
6	The Call for a New Ecoreligion	118
	Deep Ecology and Religion	120
	Ecological Debate within the Church	126
	Ecoreligion on the Syllabus	133
	The Greening of the Church	137
7	The Sustainable Society	143
	The Limits to Growth Report	144
	The Call for a Golden Age in Equilibrium	149
	Leading the Sustainable Effort	153
	The Sustainable Society in Bucharest	159
	The Limits to Growth in Norway	165
	The Resource Policy Group	169
8	The Acid Rain Debate	174
	Power-Socialism and the Social Function of Science	176
	The Power-Socialism of the Labor Party	182
	The Case against Environmentalism	185
	Labor Party Environmentalism	188
	The Acid Rain Debate	195
9	Our Common Future	202
	The Alta Demonstrations	203
	The End of Deep Ecology in Norway	206
	Deep Ecology Goes Global	210
	Our Common Future	216
	The World's "Pioneer Country"	220
	A Sustainable Climate	225
	The Alternative Nation	230

Bibliography 241
Index 279

Figures

1 The High Mountain Ecology Research Station, Finse, emblem, 1972. Courtesy of the University of Oslo Archive. *page* 31
2 Arne Næss on vacation with the Norwegian Alpine Club in Pakistan, 1950. Unknown photographer. Courtesy of Gyldendal. 49
3 Today (left) and tomorrow? (right). From the exhibition *And after Us* ... (1970) with the polluted society of New York to the left and the future ecological self-sufficient society in Norway to the right. Courtesy of the Norwegian Society for the Conservation of Nature. 64
4 Sigmund Kvaløy being taken away by the police at Mardøla, 1970. Photo: NTB. Courtesy of Scanpix. 68
5 The front-page of the Ecophilosophical Reader used in the Nature and Humans course. Drawing by Sigmund Kvaløy, 1973. Courtesy of the University of Oslo Archive. 110
6 Sustainable effort as Jørgen Randers saw it in the manuscript "The Lifecycle of a Movement" from November 1972. Courtesy of Jørgen Randers. 157
7 The lifecycle of a social movement as Jørgen Randers saw it in November 1972. Courtesy of Jørgen Randers. 158
8 The Minister of the Environment, Gro Harlem Bruntland, answering the world press about the major "Bravo" oil spill in the North Sea, 1977. Photo: NTB. Courtesy of Scanpix. 201
9 Demonstrators blocking the road to the Alta hydropower construction site. The writing on the rocks reads "LA ELVA LEVE" (Let the river live). September 1979. Photo: Erik Thorberg. Courtesy of NTB Scanpix. 205

Acknowledgments

This book grew out of debates I have had with students, friends, and colleagues, both in Oslo and in New York, who share my sense of helplessness in facing our global environmental crisis. Is it possible for a single, unheard-of scholar or for a tiny group of middle-of-the-road researchers at non-prestigious universities to reach an international audience? Is it feasible for students speaking an odd, non-academic language or for unknown thinkers from the world's periphery to raise global environmental debates? Judging from the story I am about to tell, the answer is yes. And that above all is what motivates this book. In revisiting Norwegian environmental debates from the 1970s, I have been awed, amused, bewildered, appalled – and have even burst out laughing – at the various ways in which activists and scholars of the period managed to reach an audience with their environmental concerns. Yet I have never stopped being impressed by the various ways in which they took Karl Marx's famous thesis to heart: "The philosophers have only interpreted the world in various ways; the point however is to change it."[1]

My first round of thanks therefore goes to all the people I write about in this book, most of whom I have met, and many of whom I have had the pleasure of sharing my thoughts with over the years. As a child I came to witness one of Helge Ingstad's stunning lectures. Then as a young environmental activist (and faithful ecophilosopher), subsequently as a critic, and finally as a historian of science, I have benefited from conversing with Per Ariansen, Ottar Brox, Nils Faarlund, Dagfinn Føllesdal, Harold

---

[1] Karl Marx, "Theses on Feuerbach" (1888). In D. McLellan (eds.), *Karl Marx: Selected writings* (New York: Oxford University Press, 1977), p. 158.

Glasser, Ola Glesne, Hjalmar Hegge, Thor Heyerdahl, Paul Hofseth, Helge Høibraaten, David R. Klein, Ivar Mysterud, Arne Næss, Kit-Fai Næss, Siri Næss, Jørgen Randers, Nils Roll-Hansen, David Rothenberg, Sigmund Kvaløy Setreng, Gunnar Skirbekk, Nils Christian Stenseth, Randi Veiberg, Lars Walløe, and Jon Wetlesen. I owe a warm shout-out to Høibraaten from whom I have borrowed the title.[2] A special thanks to Hofseth for access to his personal archive, to Hans Eirik Aarek who gave me some impossible-to-get-hold-of books, and to Hegge for giving me his press archive and hard-to-find articles. I have never met Oddvar Skre and Erik Steineger, but I have had the opportunity to communicate with them in writing. These people do not necessarily agree with my reading of the events. Indeed, it should be stated, this book is not "their" story, though I have benefited enormously from their various accounts and pointed to them in the footnotes.

My previous colleagues at the Forum for University History, University of Oslo, offered their time for intellectual discussions. I am particularly grateful to its former leader John Peter Collett, and to fellow Norwegian historians Edgeir Benum, Vidar Enebakk, Robert Marc Friedman, Jorunn Sem Fure, Magnus Gulbrandsen, Kim Helsvig, Eirinn Larsen, Johannes Løvhaug, Jon Røyne Kyllingstad, Jan Eivind Myhre, Fredrik W. Thue, and Bent Sofus Tranøy for their support. They helped ensure the publication of a much abbreviated Norwegian account of this book, as well as two articles on the topic for an English-speaking audience.[3] Fellow Norwegians Kristin Asdal, Thomas Hylland Eriksen, Erling Kagge, Thorgeir Kolshus, Yngve Nilsen, Hallvard Notaker, Tarjei Rønnow, Lars Fr. H. Svendsen, Karen Victoria Lykke Syse, Terje Tvedt, Nina Witoszek, and Knut Olav Åmås have also inspired me in various ways to move on with the project.

I am also grateful to The Department of Archeology, Conservation, and History at the University of Oslo who generously included me institutionally, and to the Norwegian Non-Fiction Writers and Translators Association for funding. Frøydis Brekken Elvik assisted me with initial

---

[2] Helge Høibraaten, "Norway in 1968 and its aftermath; Maoism, the power of the periphery and the cultural upper class of the sixty-eighters," in Guri Hjeltnes (ed.), *Universitetet og studentene* (Oslo: Forum for universitetshistorie, 1998), pp. 184–91.
[3] Peder Anker, "Den store økologiske vekkelsen som har hjemsøkt vårt land." In *Universitetet i Oslos historie*, vol. 7 (Oslo: Unipub, 2011), pp. 103–71, 461–79; "The call for a new EcoTheology in Norway," *Journal for the Study of Religion, Nature and Culture*, 7, no. 2 (2013), 187–207; "Science as a vacation: A history of ecology in Norway," *History of Science*, 45 (2007), 455–79.

archival searches in Norway, and Kjetil Korslund, Rachel Stern, and Barbara Wilson have done invaluable editorial work. I am also thankful for two generous anonymous reviews and the fine work of Cambridge University Press's editorial team Rachel Blaifeder, John McNeill, and Ling Zhang.

Over the years I have had the pleasure of discussing aspects of this book with Ken Alder, Nina Edwards Anker, Stephen Bocking, Andrew Brennan, Graham Burnett, Jimena Canales, Deborah Coen, Eugene Cittadino, Stephen Duncombe, Paul Forman, Peter Galison, Jeanne Haffner, Myles Jackson, Mitchell Joachim, James Lovelock, Gregg Mitman, Daniel Kevles, Rachel Rothschild, Hashim Sarkis, James C. Scott, Sverker Sörlin, Alistair Sponsel, Matthew Stanley, and Jennifer Telesca. Generous colleagues at the Gallatin School of Individualized Study at New York University have also provided invaluable help and support, including our amazing Dean Susanne Wofford. My gratitude also goes to the munificent students of my History of Ecology and Environmentalism course at New York University who endured the process of me turning research into a book. It is my sincere hope that it will empower them to think that it is indeed possible to reach a global audience and perhaps even change the course of our unfolding environmental crisis for the better.

Finally, there is an element of self-reflection in this book, as I grew up in Oslo where I also attended environmental study and philosophy seminars at the University of Oslo. I spent much of my spare time at many of the peripheral sites discussed, including going cross-country skiing and hiking at Hemsedal, Hardangervidda, Finnmark, Finse, and Ustaoset. I have climbed the Hallingskarvet peak, visited Budalen, sailed at Vesterålen, admired the Vøringsfossen waterfall, and spent my life's happiest moments in the beautiful Larvik fjord and at Tjøme. More recently I have brought my two incredible boys, Lukas and Theo, to these places so that they too, perhaps, may be inspired to care for the natural world. It is in that spirit that I dedicate the book to them.

"We Are As Gods"

"It is the Noah's Ark for securing biological diversity for future generations," Norway's Prime Minister Jens Stoltenberg told a freezing audience of world dignitaries, including the European Commission President José Manuel Barroso.[1] The occasion was the opening of the Svalbard Global Seed Vault in February 2008, a vault constructed to secure the world's food crops against climate change, wars, and environmental disasters. The Vault was to be a safe deposit box for the world's genetic material, secured in eternal permafrost high above the coastline to protect against climate-change-induced sea level rise. In this icy arctic facility, national seed banks from all over the world could deposit their genetic heritage under Norwegian protection. After unlocking the Vault, the 2004 Nobel Peace Prize winner Wangari Maathai of Kenya made the first deposit: a box of her nation's rice seeds.

"Doomsday Seed Vault" and "Noah's Seed Ark" were the nicknames suggested to the press by the Norwegian government. They were told that Norway had financed and built the Vault simply "as a service to the world community."[2] The opening ceremony became a major news item in media outlets around the world, often as front-page news, with Norwegians portrayed as virtuous guardians of the world's biological heritage. These articles had a Biblical ring to them: The oceans were rising and Stoltenberg was depicted as the world's Noah securing at least two seeds of every

---

[1] Doug Mellgren, "'Doomsday' Seed Vault Opens in Arctic," *NBC News*, Feb. 27, 2008.
[2] Svalbard Global Seed Vault, "'Doomsday Seed Vault' to Open in Arctic Circle on February 26th," Croptrust Archive. Marte Qvenild, "Svalbard Global Seed Vault: a 'Noah's Ark' for the world's seeds," *Development in Practice*, 18, no. 1 (2008), 110–16.

living species in his ark. The dramatic architectural design of the Vault entrance provided a perfect setting for a photo shoot, with a large perpetually glowing crystal-window in a landscape engulfed in the arctic dark. The Vault shone like a star in the polar night, and Norwegians were portrayed as the good citizens of the world providing a safe haven for the world's common genetic heritage. For countries in the Global South it was especially important that deposits in the Vault could only be accessed by the seeds' owners, as they were acutely aware of a legacy of seed industries that had reaped the benefits of their nations' genetic heritage without consent.[3] Norway was to be on the good side of such conflicts, Stoltenberg assured the audience, by constructing the Vault to protect the vulnerable, rather than enrich the strong. In effect, Norwegians assumed the role of bank vault executives for the economy of nature.

Norway had an underlying political interest in building a presence on Svalbard. Since the archipelago was annexed back in 1920 in the context of the nation's imperial ambition, Norway has done its very best to confirm its sovereignty. Today most countries in the northern hemisphere have signed the Spitsbergen Treaty of 1920, which established Norwegian hegemony, while those in the Global South have not. Indeed, only forty-four out of a total of a hundred and ninety-five countries in the world had signed the treaty by 2008. Kenya, for example, is not among the signatories. The backdrop of building the Seed Vault at Spitsbergen was thus to showcase to the world – especially to the Global South – the virtue of Norwegian dominion over the archipelago. Yet it would be to miss the point to argue that the purpose of the Vault was only to strengthen Norwegian sovereignty. Stoltenberg also genuinely wanted to do something good for the world, and the Vault was a way of doing exactly that.

The act of doing something good was the cultural Archimedean point from which Norwegians tried to move the Earth in a new and, to them, more environmentally sound direction. This cultural point has, as the Seed Vault illustrates, taken the form of a self-confident, do-gooding gaze toward the rest of the world. Indeed, the official foreign policy has been to establish "Norway as a humanitarian super power" and "as a peace nation" in the world.[4] There are numerous examples of Norwegians being

---

[3] Hanne Svarstad and Shivcharn S. Dhillion (eds.), *Responding to Bioprospecting* (Oslo: Spartacus, 2000).

[4] Quotes by Jan Egeland (1985) and Jonas Gahr Støre (2006), respectively Norway's State Secretary and Minister of Foreign Affairs, in Øyvind Østerud, "Lite land som humanitær stormakt?" *Nytt norsk tidsskrift*, 4 (2006), 303–16, quote p. 303. Helge Pharo, "Norway's peace tradition spanning 100 years," *Scandinavian Review*, 93 (2005), 15–23.

engaged in this enterprise, most notably in Africa, the Middle East, and Asia. The so-called Oslo Accord of 1995 between Palestine and Israel may serve as an illustration of this.[5] This agenda of being global peacemakers has been reinforced by the fact that the world's dignitaries come to Oslo every year to witness the ultimate peace fest, hosted by the Permanent Secretariat of the Nobel Peace Prize and celebrated at the Nobel Peace Center. Being elected to the Nobel Peace Prize Committee is widely seen as the highest honor among Norwegians, who follow and debate every step the Committee makes. For those not elected to the Committee, the career path for a successful Norwegian politician or diplomat often leads to a leadership position within an international peacemaking organization, such as the United Nations, Amnesty International, the Red Cross, or Human Rights Watch. According to the principal historian of Norwegian foreign policy, Olav Riste, the nation's diplomatic mantra can be captured with the phrase "Saving the Globe."[6] As a consequence, Oslo has become a hub for international peace initiatives, some of which are very visible and others only known as rumors that circulate in a fairly transparent city of only 600,000 people. During the Cold War, Norway was particularly well situated, both geographically and politically, to play this mediating role in a divided world, and the United Nations became an important arena in which Norway's mission of becoming the world's "humanitarian super power" played out. Terje Tvedt, the leading historian of Norwegian developmental aid, has shown that this gaze of goodness has been a hallmark for the nation's foreign policy, serving as a disguise for sociopolitical self-criticism and reflection.[7]

At first glance Norway seems an unlikely place for worldly self-confidence. Its citizens speak a non-academic language and are educated at ordinary universities in the academic periphery. A tiny country with a small population like Norway may look like a no-impact-land at the mercy of events larger than itself. Yet, as this book will show, Norwegians put forward a set of policies and philosophies that detailed how to approach our global environmental crisis through innovative thinking about ecophilosophy, eco-politics, eco-religion, sustainability, sustainable development, climate economics, and much more. It was all formulated in

---

[5] Edward W. Said, "How do you spell Apartheid? O-s-l-o," *Ha'aretz*, Oct. 11, 1998.
[6] Olav Riste, *Norway's Foreign Relations: A History*, 2nd ed. (Oslo: Universitetsforlaget, 2005), 268–73.
[7] Terje Tvedt, *Angels of Mercy or Development Diplomats?* (Oxford: James Curry, 1998); *Det internasjonale gjennombruddet* (Oslo: Dreyer, 2017).

the context of a culture of self-confident well-wishing for a troubled world. What was the source of this environmental gaze?

The title of the book – *The Power of the Periphery* – is meant to express the ways in which Norwegian environmentalists found nature in the periphery as morally superior and the source of everything good. To spend real or imagined time in the high mountains or on vacation in remote cottages was the norm. Such outdoor life and research in beautiful and pristine environments were considered to be superior to work done in central academic institutions where scientists taught and wrote. The power of the periphery was that of a pristine natural environment contrasted with the dirty center in need of change. At the local level that could be the forest outside the city, a mountain high above the town that sits down in the valley, or farmers or fishermen working everyday within nature in contrast to office workers that were detached from it. At the global level it became the beautiful, peaceful Norway contrasted with the polluted, troubled world. The power of the periphery was a social construction and a system of belief which allowed the environmentalist's self-confident gaze of goodness.

The power of the periphery allowed scholars and politicians alike to showcase Norway as an alternative environmentally sound nation compared with the rest of the world. Norway was fashioned by Norwegian scholar-activists as a microcosm for a better macrocosm. The North Pole, as historian Michael Bravo has shown, has for centuries served as a place of idealized dreams in contrast to the problematic socio-political realities around the world.[8] In a similar vein, Norway sought to be an alternative loadstar for a world in need of an alternative environmental direction. For this reason it was important to Norwegian scholar-activists to maintain the distinction between local and global as a way of resisting the destructive powers of globalization. Abroad, Norwegians met a receptive audience, especially among North American scholars and activists on the progressive left admiring everything Scandinavian. Typically, when US Congresswoman Alexandria Ocasio-Cortez promoted socialism and a Green New Deal in a 2019 interview for CBS' "60 Minutes," she pointed to Scandinavia and Norway.[9] In doing so she appealed to deep-seated longings for the politics of this region among her audience.

---

[8] Michael Bravo, *North Pole: Nature and Culture* (London: Reaction Books, 2019). Michael Bravo and Sverker Sörlin (eds.), *Narrating the Arctic: A Cultural History of Nordic Scientific Practices* (Canton, MA: Science History Pub., 2002).

[9] Anderson Cooper, "Alexandria Ocasio-Cortez on 60 Minutes," *CBS*, Jan. 6, 2019. Bill McKibben, *Falter: Has the Human Game Begun to Play Itself Out?* (New York: Henry Holt and Co., 2019), pp. 116, 193.

As a contribution to the field of history of science, this book will focus on the scientific and intellectual side of environmental debate by placing the well-meaning scholar-activist at the center of focus. In terms of timing, the book spans thirty years of Norwegian history, beginning with the translation of Rachel Carson's *Silent Spring* into Norwegian in 1962 and ending with Norwegian scholars attending the Earth Summit in Rio de Janeiro in 1992. The chief focus in terms of archival sources, however, lies in the 1970s, which the book spends a good amount of time unpacking. It tells the story of the ways in which ecological concerns were imported into Norway via Carson's work and, thirty years later, exported from Norway to the world at the Rio conference in the language of "sustainable development." During this period Norwegian environmentalists attempted to navigate the tense relations of the Cold War by adopting a middle-ground position that could be embraced by both sides. While Stalinists, Leninists, Maoists, and other intellectual hooligans on the left fought capitalist Vietnam warmongers on the right, Norwegian peacemakers and environmentalists alike took the high middle ground by developing alternative visions that could be embraced by both sides. The Norwegian ecologists provided a vision of harmony and stability in a world of tension and instability. This middle ground reflected the interdisciplinary nature of ecological debate in Norway, which was hardly divided by the "two cultures" in academia of humanists and scientists.[10] The social interactions were particularly intense between ecologists and philosophers, as the formative years of Deep Ecology took place in this period.

The subtitle of the book – *How Norway Became an Environmental Pioneer for the World* – is meant to capture the ways in which the environmental researchers anchored their global solutions in a particular Norwegian culture of being good to the world. As will be shown, a telling illustration of the worldliness of ecological reasoning is the way ecology was first introduced to Norwegians. It happened in 1956 through a Cambridge University study of a remote village in north-west Pakistan carried out by the young Norwegian social anthropologist Fredrik Barth. This event will, together with studies conducted by the ocean explorer Thor Heyerdahl, and the archeologists Helge Ingstad and Anne Stine Ingstad who found Viking settlements in the United States, form the first chapter of the book. The formation of the biological field of ecology in Norway is the topic of the next chapter, which describes the ecologists'

---

[10] Charles P. Snow, *The Two Cultures and the Scientific Revolution* (Cambridge: Cambridge University Press, 1959).

contribution to the International Biological Program. The subsequent four chapters follow the Deep Ecology movement among scholars in Norway, particularly in the circle that congregated around the philosopher Arne Næss and the peace researcher Johan Galtung. Their antagonists were the "shallow" ecologists, namely the Norwegian co-author of *The Limits to Growth* (1972), Jørgen Randers, and the Chair of the World Commission on Environment and Development, Gro Harlem Brundtland, discussed in Chapter 7 and 8. The last chapter tells the tale of how Brundtland, with the help of Stoltenberg's climate economics, envisioned Norway to be *"et foregangsland"* (a pioneer country) for the world. An aspiration she would later carry with her as Director-General for the World Health Organization (1998–2003). And besides creating the Seed Vault, Stoltenberg is also known for his work as the United Nations Special Envoy on Climate Change and as the Secretary General of NATO.

Each chapter in this book addresses environmental debates within different fields of academia starting with (1) anthropology and archeology, followed by (2) ecology, (3) philosophy, (4) politics, (5) environmental studies, (6) theology, (7) managerial sciences, (8) geology, and finally ending with (9) economics. Through the lens of social history of sciences, the chapters place people at the core of the narrative, especially the scholar-activists who were integral to these stories. Chapter 1 will untangle the peculiar Norwegian culture of nature that may be foreign to non-Norwegians. Chapters 2 through 6 are mostly about the Deep Ecologists, who dominated Norwegian environmental debates in the 1970s, while Chapters 7 through 9 explain the reaction to them at home and abroad from more mainstream scholars and politicians. What people described in this book have in common is that they sought to create a green vision for the world. How did these scholars and environmental politicians manage that?

Though secular in spirit, the environmental agenda of improving the world harkens back to a missionary history enforced by the country's all-dominating pietistic Lutheran religion. The ecologically inspired scholar-activists were not particularly religious, but nevertheless assumed the power of gods in their gaze from the periphery. Though perhaps shocking to our secular ears, it is worth recalling that assuming the power of a god was a popular exercise within the counterculture. It was famously advocated for by the British anthropologist Edmund Leach, who told his BBC listeners in a 1967 radio lecture that we "have become like gods. Isn't it about time that we understood our divinity? Science offers us total mastery over our environment and over our destiny, yet instead of rejoicing we feel deeply afraid. Why should this be? How might these fears be resolved?"[11] His answer was that people should take charge of their own destiny by acting as if they were "like gods," using science for constructive purposes and thereby intervening positively in the course of history. Leach's idea would go viral after Stewart Brand adopted it in his opening motto for *The Whole Earth Catalogue* (1968): "We are as gods and might as well get good at it." The *Catalogue* would provide tools and aid the "power of the individual to conduct his own education, find his own inspiration, shape his own environment, and share his adventure with whoever is interested."[12] In the subsequent decade, Brand's adaptation of Leach's lecture became one of the most quoted lines among his generation, serving as a sort of hallmark for counterculture thinking. This assumption of divine power gave many of the characters mentioned in this book a ring of charismatic authority. In terms of personality, they often came across as being on a mission, driven by their own environmental goodness. Fortunately, the Norwegian scholars in the cultural studies of religion have already deciphered the religious bearings of the nation's environmentalism, which is most notable in the work of Tarjei Rønnow.[13] This book will continue these discussions of the role of Lutheranism in Norwegian environmentalism in Chapters 6 and 7.

In behaving like a good god, an activist or scholar assumed distinctive god-like abilities in their gaze from the periphery. The Norwegian scholar would often assume an argument to be valid at all places on Earth, for example, ignoring the world's diversity of cultures and traditions. Research was done with the prime objective of letting the world know what it had to learn from Norway. The scholar-activists were also pursuing the right course against the evils of the world, and they framed environmental problems in the binary of good and bad by first locating the evil. They would then place the blame where they saw evil and mobilize a feeling of guilt around it. This was then followed by offering a path of awakening, salvation, and finally redemption. The scholar-activists longed for endless power so that they could solve all the problems of the world, as well as gain endless knowledge. Through their

---

[11] Edmund Leach *A Runaway World?* (New York: Oxford University Press, 1968), p. 1.
[12] Stewart Brand (eds.), *The Whole Earth Catalogue* (San Francisco: Point Foundation, 1968), p. 2. Andrew G. Kirk, *Counterculture Green: The Whole Earth Catalog and American Environmentalism* (Lawrence: University Of Kansas Press, 2007).
[13] Tarjei Rønnow, "Takk gode Gud for moder jord, hun gjør oss ett med alt som gror: Religiøsitet og miljøengasjement i Norge," *Norsk antropologisk tidsskrift*, 15 (2004), 18–31.

epistemological lens the scholar-activists assumed they were capable of answering most questions relevant to the environment. Naturally, there was much more to be learned and many new things the sciences could and should figure out. Yet the epistemological apparatus and scientific modus operandi were stable factors in the life of the scholar-activist. Indeed, the environmentalists discussed in this book would rarely admit to having made a false argument or advanced an erroneous opinion. Public self-scrutiny was not on the horizon. And finally, the scholar-activist perspective on time would often entail a narrative of the deep past reaching into the far future. It was a grand story of an environmentally harmonious past, followed by environmental havoc, which, thanks to the environmental awakening of the scholar and his or her followers, would eventually lead to the restoration of a new harmonious future for the world. To be sure, Norwegian scholar-activists did not think of themselves literally as gods. More precisely, they thought of themselves as having the right answer to environmental issues, and they brought it upon themselves to inform the world about their good news. In short, they were environmental do-gooders with a worldly gaze.

The idea of assuming the power of a god has old intellectual roots in Norway. According to ancient Nordic mythology, Ragnarök will one day befall upon us, and it will be in the form of a series of environmental disasters. At that time the god Heimdall will blow his Gjallarhorn to call upon all the gods to leave their heavenly Asgardr. From the periphery of Valhalla, Thor and an army of immortal Viking warriors and beautiful Valkyries will cross the Bifrost-bridge, and enter the natural world in order to protect the tree of life, Yggdrasil, which encompasses the entire world. This book will revisit a group of Norwegian scholar-activists, who, like those gods, rushed to save the tree of life from an impending environmental Ragnarök. Though the ethical aspiration of their efforts can indeed be traced back to ancient Norse values and the teachings of Edda,[14] the focus of this book will be on more recent events, starting in the 1960s.

---

[14] Nina Witoszek, *Norske naturmytologier: fra Edda til økofilosofi* (Oslo: Pax, 1998).

I

The Power of the Periphery

THE ALLURE OF LIFE LOST

In the 1960s the homes of the vanishing class of hardworking Norwegian fjord fishermen and mountain peasants were bought by vacationers seeking to fill their leisure-time with country-style activities of the past. This trend was part of a boom in outdoor recreation in the nation's most scenic places, which turned nature from a place of work into a place of leisure. Thousands of cottages were built in the mountains and by the fjords to satisfy back-to-nature lovers seeking harmony with their holiday environment. By 1970 fifteen percent of a total 3.7 million Norwegians had their own private vacation place, totaling 190,000 cottages. And the numbers were growing radically, as twenty-five percent of these places were built after 1965. The overwhelming majority did not have their own vacation home, but surveys show that they either borrowed or rented a cottage, or stayed in hospices, or sports hotels.[1] Indeed, in 1970, only sixteen percent of the population did not participate in some sort of outdoor recreation, and this group consisted mostly of the elderly.

Despite imagined and real historical precursors, this cult of the outdoors was a new phenomenon, reflective of the growing wealth of the nation.[2] Norwegians had for decades – perhaps centuries – discussed environmental issues, including pollution and landscape degradation.

---

[1] Statistics Norway, *Holiday House Survey* (Oslo: Statistics Norway, 1970); *Outdoor Life* (Oslo: Statistics Norway, 1974); *Holiday Survey* (Oslo: Statistics Norway, 1968).

[2] Bredo Berntsen, "Nasjonalparker," *Naturen*, 96 (1972), 195–204. Bredo Berntsen, *Naturvernets historie i Norge: Fra klassisk naturvern til økopolitikk* (Oslo: Grøndahl, 1977). Olav G. Henriksen (ed.), *Kvinner i fjellet* (Lom: Norsk fjellmuseum, 2002). Gunnar Repp,

A series of legal bills, such as *Lov om naturfredning* (The preservation of nature law) from 1910, *Jaktloven* (The hunting law) from 1951, *Lov om naturvern* (The conservation of nature law) from 1954, and the oil pollution law (1955), point to a rich history of environmental protection in Norway. Yet the most important of these legal milestones for environmentalism was *Friluftsloven* (The free-air-law) of 1957. The Norwegian word for outdoor life, *friluftsliv* (free-air-life), captures the sense of freedom when vacationing in spectacular natural environments. The free-air-law granted an *allemannsrett* (everyone's right) for cross-country skiing, walking, camping, and harvesting wherever one wants, including on private properties. For sure, there are some restrictions in the law with regards to farming, commercial berry picking, hunting, and fishing. A tent, for example, has to be set up at least 150 meters (492 feet) from a private home. On government-owned land (and most land in Norway is owned by the government), one has to pay a reasonable fee to go fishing, and have a license to hunt, while fishing and hunting are restricted on private land. Yet, despite these minor restrictions, the "free-air-law" has not been undermined over time. Indeed, it has a status of an untouchable holy grail in Norwegian political culture. The freedom to roam, walk, cross-country ski, and set up a tent wherever you want is as ingrained in Norwegians as, say, the right to freedom of speech is among people from the United States. "Norwegians walk, run, creep into nature to get rid of whatever represses them and contaminates the air, not only the atmosphere," a devoted "free-air-life" enthusiast noted: "They don't talk about going *out*, but *in* and *into* nature. There they find themselves, who they are, what they stand for."[3]

It is also there, in the wild, Norwegians would find the source of all things good, and problems would as a consequence have to be solved in better contact with the natural. Thanks to this sentiment and the free-air-law, outdoor vacationing grew into a sizable industry with its own

---

"Norwegian relationships to nature through outdoor life," in *Outdoor Activities*, Jan Neuman, Ivar Mytting, and Jiri Brtnik (eds.) (Lüneburg: Edition Erlebnispädagogik, 1996), pp. 32–42. Oskar Solenes, "Friluftsliv og klassekamp: To sider av samme sak?" *Arbeiderhistorie*, 21 (2007), 7–25. Alf-Inge Jansen, *Makt og miljø: En studie av utformingen av den statlige natur og miljøvernpolitikken* (Oslo: Universitetsforlaget, 1989), pp. 51–101. Eivind Dale, Hilde Jervan, Atle Midttun, Jan Eivind Myhre, Dag Namtvedt, *Ressursforvaltningens historie* (Oslo: Resource Policy Group, 1984), pp. 35–84. Ulf Hafsten, *Naturvernets århundre* (Oslo: Norges Naturvernforbund, 1977).

[3] Arne Næss, "The Norwegian roots of deep ecology," *The Trumpeter*, 21, no. 2 (2005), 38–41, quote p. 38. Næss's emphasis.

interest groups defending the environment as a place of leisure. The political battles to create national parks, which grew in intensity between when the first park was created in 1962 and when a series of parks were established in 1971, bear witness to the growing power of the environmental tourism business. This post-war turn toward outdoor life, and tent and cabin vacationing, would frame much of the environmental debate in Norway.

Outdoor life emerged in the context of Labor Party politics, which was the dominating political party with a majority vote in the Parliament from 1945 to 1963. The promotion of outdoor life by the Labor Party was an integral part of a policy of fashioning Norway as a healthy socialist welfare state with a solid democratic footing. Though several political parties would compete for power to their left and right, the Labor Party became so dominating that political historians of Norway describe the post-war Norway as a one-party-state.[4] Few would question the dogmas of the welfare state, namely free healthcare and education for all, and easy recreational access to the environment, along with a series of social security services that made sure no one would starve, or lack housing and other basic needs. After the war, Norwegians would take comfort in that the State would take care of you, no matter what. However, the policy was accompanied by melancholic voices of protest from the wealthy seeing their fortune distributed accordingly.

The Labor Party politicians regarded themselves as being part of a larger international movement echoing Marx's famous slogan: "Workers of the world, unite!" Though they were not communists, they used every opportunity to participate in international politics with the aim of helping those in need. This aspiration would, as will be apparent, also apply to environmental affairs. Empowered by pristine Norwegian nature in the remote, science-activists and environmental politicians alike would envision the nation as an ecological standard for the world to admire. The worldly outlook had its historical legacy in Norway's Lutheran missionary legacy: the country has had more missionaries per capita than any other European country. The long crocked coastline has plenty of excellent harbors for Norway's fishing industries and, as a consequence, a significant history of shipping merchants. Indeed, at the time period of this book the nation had the fourth largest merchant navy in the world.

---

[4] Jens Arup Seip, *Fra embedsmannsstat til ettpartistat og andre essays* (Oslo: Universitetsforlaget, 1963).

To work on a ship sailing the seven seas was for many Norwegians a way of seeing the world.

The welfare state was partly possible because Norway has a relatively small population of about four million people (reaching five million by 2012). Despite – or perhaps because of – a long crooked coastline facing the Atlantic, numerous high mountains, long fjords, and deep valleys, the population has been fairly homogeneous, socially, ethnically, and spiritually. Though the historical homogeneity of Norwegians may be a factual myth, it was an ideal during the post-war period for the Labor Party which sought to modernize and industrialize the nation. The two communities that stuck out, the Sámi and the Romani, have been subject to harsh policies of rectification (i.e. being punished for speaking their own language). Being gay was illegal until 1972, as was women's right to abortion until 1978. More generally, simply being different – in whatever fashion that might be – was not socially helpful. To give an example, Norwegians love cross-country skiing. When schools arranged competitions in the sport, the aim was generally not to be the fastest, but to be the one who is closest to the "ideal time" (the mean average of all the competitors). To compete, to excel, to win would cause suspicion within a culture in which the tall poppy syndrome (Law of Jante) prevails.

The Norwegian mountain environment with its numerous rivers and waterfalls was seen as a place for social recreation and healthy vacationing. Yet that did not hinder the Labor Party in seeing the environment a natural resource for hydropower developments, which, in the post-war period, enabled electrification of the country and its industries. Indeed, the chief political doctrine of the Labor Party was *kraftsosialisme* (power-socialism), which meant turning as many waterfalls in the high mountains into hydropower as possible. In the lower land, the post-war policy was intensive forestry and farming. The homogeneous culture of Norwegian people would translate into homogeneous use of the land. After the war, agricultural politics were focused on making sure forests were planted with the same trees, fields with the same wheat, grassland with the same grass, and that farms would breed the same animals. A diverse stock of locally bred cows, for example, were engineered into one homogeneous race, the *Norsk rødt fe* (Norwegian Red Cow), which provided the nation with one standardized milk from one nationalized state-owned dairy.[5]

---

[5] Torben Hviid Nielsen, Arve Monsen, and Tore Tennøe, *Livets tre og kodenes kode: Fra genetikk til bioteknologi, Norge 1900–2000* (Oslo: Gyldendal Akademisk, 2000), pp. 124–50.

When Norwegians were vacationing, they were vacationing from this standardized society. Yet the mode of vacationing was pretty standard. The longing for a primitive lifestyle that so many Norwegians pursued during their vacations and contact with pristine environments was a reaction to the rapid modernization of the country. Vacationing in remnants of old mountain homes or fjord farms was alluring because it suggested a life lost and spoke to the way of life of the peasants and fishermen that the vacationers had replaced. For the growing counterculture, these peasants and fishermen would gradually come to represent both the origin of and future for Norway. The vacationers imagined that these first citizens had lived in self-sufficient harmony with their environments, and they thus became heroes of future environmentally friendly lifestyles. At the same time these peasants and fishermen served as a contrast to the unhealthy and polluted life in the cities, especially Oslo, which was believed to be corrupted by material lifestyle and lack of direct contact with clean environments.

The admiration for peasants and fishermen among the environmentalists did not come solely from vacationing in their remnant homesteads. Many – perhaps most – city dwellers and academics would have direct family relationships with rural communities. Having grandparents, aunts, or uncles in some remote part of the country was the norm, as the transfer from an agricultural to industrial driven society happened later in Norway than in other European nations. As will be argued, environmental concerns among activists and radicals often blended visions for an ecologically sound future with both imagined and real relationships with the land of the recent past. "Scratch a Norwegian, and you'll generally find a peasant, even if he lives in Oslo [...] at least if he calls himself radical," Helge Høibraaten rightly points out.[6]

Yet, despite the admiration for the peasants and fishermen, personal family, such as grandparents, aunts, or uncles still living on small farms, were rarely used as idols of sound environmentalism. They were too close for comfort and not ideologically reliable. They were corrupted by the advancement of modern goods, such as electricity, hot showers, cars, and so forth. Instead, faraway people and environments from the other side of the world would serve as vehicles for defending the true values of returning to nature by living as mountain peasants and costal fishermen. These faraway places were of such social and geographical distance that

---

[6] Høibraaten, "Norway in 1968 and its aftermath," p. 191.

the way of life there could more easily serve as ideals for reimagining Norway's past and environmental future.

Three scholars in the field of archeology and anthropology were prime movers in setting the stage for this reimagining of Norwegian identity: Thor Heyerdahl, Helge Ingstad, and Fredrik Barth. Their explorations and research into life on the Pacific island of Fatu-Hiva, hunter-gatherers living in North America, Viking settlements in Newfoundland, and the ecological order of the people of Swat in Pakistan allowed a larger reflection about what one could learn from the Norwegian heritage.

CHASING PARADISE

"Back to nature? Farewell to civilization? It is one thing to dream of it and another to do it. I tried it. Tried to return to nature. Crushed my watch between two stones and let my hair and beard grow wild. Climbed the palms for food. Cut all the chains that bound me to the modern world. I tried to enter the wilderness empty-handed and barefoot, as a man at one with nature."[7] So began Thor Heyerdahl his 1974 account of his move to the remote island of Fatu-Hiva in the Pacific in 1937.

Heyerdahl (1914–2002) grew up in the picturesque town of Larvik, south-west of Oslo. Though small in size it had a global orientation with an active shipbuilding industry that over the years had built some of the best seafaring boats in Norway. This included supplying the nation's booming whaling industry. The pride of the town was *Fram* (1892), designed by Colin Archer (1832–1921), and used in various Arctic and Antarctic expeditions between 1893 and 1912. It was most famously used by Fridtjof Nansen (1861–1930) in his quest to reach the North Pole and by Roald Amundsen (1871–1928) in his successful journey to reach the South Pole. Though the era of such wooden boats was over when Heyerdahl grew up, ocean expeditions were still very much an integral part of the town's identity, as was the Larvik fjord with its archipelago of beautiful islands. Its "[n]ature became to me in early childhood what a church was to many of the adults in my town," he would say. He consequently decided to learn more about it, and enrolled to study zoology and geography at the University of Oslo in 1933. He was set for disappointment. Supervised by the zoology professors Kristine Bonnevie and Hjalmar Broch, Heyerdahl sliced up intestines of animals

---

[7] Thor Heyerdahl, *Fatu-Hiva: Back to Nature* (Garden City, New York: Doubleday, 1974), p. 1.

and looked at them under a microscope, which did not fit his idea of exploring wilderness. What he did learn at the university was the importance of evolution, along with diffusionist ideas of how species' traveling habits could explain their evolutionary development.

It was a friend of his father, the wine merchant Bjarne Kroepelin (1890–1966), who first told him about the importance of traveling to explain human evolution. In Oslo he gave Heyerdahl access to what was known to be the world's largest library collection on the topic of the Polynesian islands. The young man immersed himself in this 5,000-volume collection, and came out convinced that he had to buy a "ticket to paradise" and leave Norway and the modern world for good.[8] Like a voluntary Robinson Crusoe he soon found himself in the remote island of Fatu-Hiva in 1937, accompanied by his newlywed wife Liv Heyerdahl (Coucheron Torp, 1916–69). Here they would build a primitive hut, begin gathering food, swim in pristine waters, and enjoy the beautiful environment. Yet this return to nature was not as easy or pleasant as expected, as the couple was soon troubled by tropical rain and diseases. Even more problematic was the growing hostility from the local Polynesians, whom Heyerdahl portrays as already having been corrupted by the modern world. After only one year they abandoned Fatu-Hiva. Back in Oslo, Heyerdahl wrote a charming account of their attempt to return to primitive life in *På jakt efter paradiset* (Chasing Paradise, 1938), which received little attention.[9]

That would most certainly change when Heyerdahl rewrote the book in 1974 and published it in several languages as *Fatu-Hiva: Back to Nature*. Heyerdahl was, by now, an international celebrity and his striking account of life on a remote tropical island appealed to a younger audience who shared his longing to leave modernity in favor of a life in harmony with the natural world. He rose to world fame, as the historian Axel Andersson has shown, thanks to his ability to re-invent the meaning of expeditions within the culture of the Cold War. Most famously in the Kon-Tiki expedition, but also in the Ra 1 and Ra 2 expeditions, Heyerdahl spoke up, not only against archeological and scientific dogmatism but, more importantly, against the bipolar political culture of the Cold War. His basic message was that the world was united. By showing that travel between two distant places could have happened in the historical

---

[8] Heyerdahl, *Green Was the Earth*, pp. 33, 36. Snorre Evensberget, *Thor Heyerdahl: The Explorer* (Oslo: Stenersens Forlag, 1994).
[9] Thor Heyerdahl, *På jakt efter paradiset: Et år på en sydhavsø* (Oslo: Gyldendal, 1938).

past, he also nurtured a dream of unity between distant political ideologies and nations of his own time. "Borders? I have never seen one. But I have heard they exist in the minds of some people" is a quote attributed to him that certainly reflects his thinking, though it has been impossible to trace it.

In *Fatu-Hiva: Back to Nature,* Heyerdahl reframes his 1937 voyage as a travel back in time to a pre-civilized harmonious natural society, which is juxtaposed to the evils of modern environmental degradation. The revisions are substantial when compared to the 1938 edition. One telling example is the introduction of the remote island of Motane (or Mohotane), which they visited for a day during their trip back to Norway. It was not a pleasant place. "Scattered everywhere were bleached bones and complete skeletons: twisted horns of rams, animal craniums, ribs, and leg bones," among windswept stones on a dry and vegetation-less earth.[10] The inhabitants of the island had gone or died for unknown reasons, and left behind an unchecked population of sheep, which had multiplied and eaten up everything green. When the boat party arrived, they found only a handful of starved animals (which they slaughtered and ate). Heyerdahl saw in the island a larger story. "The whole island was [to him] an arena, or battleground, where modern man had beaten up nature." Confronted by "his own shadow," Heyerdahl saw in Motane a possible environmental disaster for the Earth as a whole.[11] What was once a fertile tropical forest had, thanks to the sheep, turned into an "Island of Environmental Holocaust," which would haunt Heyerdahl for the rest of his life as "a terrifying example of what would happen if nature was titled out of balance."[12]

The same was true for Fatu-Hiva. The fact that Heyerdahl and his wife were forced to leave Fatu-Hiva only proved how hard it was for modernized people to return to nature's harmony. Yet the possibility of returning to Eden appealed to an audience of environmentalists longing for a harmonious ecology for the future. At the same time, the exotic natural beauty of Fatu-Hiva, contrasted with the environmental disaster of the Motane, became opposing images of two different environmental paths for the world. For Christian cultures, including that of Norway, these two islands had the sotto voce of Heaven and Hell for the environmentally inclined reader to reflect on.

---

[10] Heyerdahl, *Fatu-Hiva*, p. 186. [11] Heyerdahl, *Fatu-Hiva*, pp. 186–9.
[12] Heyerdahl, *Green Was the Earth*, pp. 161, 170.

One of these readers was Erik Dammann (1931), who, in 1974, founded The Future in Our Hands, an organization devoted to environmental and developmental issues. Dammann had taken his own family on a similar trip, living for a year in a palm hut in the Pacific in 1967.[13] This back-to-nature experience had convinced him that we all should search for a less materialistic and more environmentally friendly lifestyle.

As an amateur archeologist, Heyerdahl was known for hyperdiffusion, or the theory that "a single common cradle of all civilizations" once existed from which all other cultures have diffused.[14] He tried to prove in his spectacular expeditions that all cultures had their origin in ancient Mesopotamia and that its people had then diffused to other cultures. "Man hosted sail before he saddled a horse," he would typically say.[15] Humans and their know-how had travelled by boat from Samaria to the Red Sea and Egypt (the Tigris expedition), from Egypt to Latin America (the Ra expeditions), from Peru to the Pacific islands (the Easter Island and the Kon-Tiki expeditions), and so forth. Ancient knowledge (such as how to build a pyramid) was thus passed from one civilization to another, most importantly by sea. Implicitly, the traveling of the white-culture-bearing race was an integral part of his vision.[16] Many – if not most – archeologists would disagree, and Heyerdahl would, as a consequence, not enjoy the respect he thought he deserved in scholarly communities.

Theories of ancient history aside, his hyperdiffusionist view became important for his understanding of the environmental problems. The link between the Edenic ecological past and the ecological havoc of Heyerdahl's own time was, to him, explainable by diffusion. It was not only humans who traveled, but also their livestock and, most problematically, their pollution. It was humans who had diffused sheep by boat to Motane, and they were thus responsible for its destruction. This came to the forefront of his attention in the summer of 1969. He was in

---

[13] Erik Dammann, *Med fire barn i palmehytte* (Oslo: Aschehoug, 1968); *Ny livsstil – og hva så? Om samfunnsutviklingen fra en ny og bedre livsstil til en ny og bedre verden* (Oslo: Gyldendal, 1976).
[14] Thor Heyerdahl, "Isolationist or diffusionist?" in Geoffrey Ashe (ed.), *The Quest for America* (New York: Praeger, 1971), 115–54, quote p. 115.
[15] Thor Heyerdahl, *Early Man and the Ocean* (Carden City, NY: Doubleday, 1979), p. 3.
[16] Axel Andersson, *A Hero for the Atomic Age: Thor Heyerdahl and the Kon-Tiki Expedition* (Oxford: Peter Lang, 2010). Thor Heyerdahl and Per Lillieström, *Jakten på Odin: På sporet av vår tapte fortid* (Oslo: Stenersen, 2001).

the midst of the Atlantic Ocean with his first Ra expedition when he and his team discovered pollution in the form of clumps of oil. This he would tell in his daily radio reports to journalists covering the voyage. Likewise to the United Nations, which was a formal patron of the expedition by lending its flag to the boat. "Whatever be the cause, this pollution is so widespread that it calls for a planned investigation and explanation," Heyerdahl pointed out in a summary of his findings for the journal Biological Conservation in the spring of 1970.[17] The issue caught the attention of U Thant, the General Secretary of the United Nations, who personally asked Heyerdahl to do another round of pollution sampling over the Atlantic during the second Ra expedition of that summer. The result came in an equally troubling report, which was also published in Biological Conservation, where Heyerdahl found pollution in the water on forty-three out of fifty-seven days they were sailing. He concluded that the Atlantic Ocean was about to become a major "dumping ground" for asphalt-like material, plastic, and other garbage.[18]

In the early 1970s, in his numerous public appearances, Heyerdahl would remind his audiences of the growing problem of ocean pollution. This included addressing the United Nations committee on the Convention on the Law of the Sea and committees within the United States Congress and Senate, lecturing at the USSR Academy of Sciences, and so on. The ocean was contested Cold War territory, and in talking about oceanic pollution Heyerdahl saw an opportunity not only to better the environment but also to bring people of the world together. Humanity had, in the ancient past, shared a common harmonious Edenic origin, he argued, and now was the time to unite the people of the world again in joint pursuit for a green common environmental future.

This, at least, was the message Heyerdahl gave to the United Nations Conference on the Human Environment in Stockholm in June 1972. Upon entering the rostrum at the Mirror Ballroom at the Grand Hotel he began by saying:

---

[17] Thor Heyerdahl, "Atlantic Ocean pollution observed by Expedition Ra," *Biological Conservation*, 2, no. 3 (Apr. 1970), 221–2. Ragnar Kvam, *Mannen og havet* (Oslo: Gyldendal, 2005), p. 357.

[18] Thor Heyerdahl, "Atlantic Ocean pollution and biota observed by the 'Ra' expeditions," *Biological Conservation*, 3, no. 3 (Apr. 1971), 164–7, quote p. 167.

"At least five thousand years ago man started to rebel against the nature that had bred him, and successfully nourished him for perhaps a million years or more. It has been five thousand years of technological progress and a continued series of victories for the human rebel, the only mutineer among the descendants of nature. Nature has yielded, tree by tree, acre by acre, species by species, river by river, while man has triumphed."[19]

However, this opening heroic narrative was soon tempered by Heyerdahl's account of all the environmental ills the human "rebel" had caused throughout history. People had once diffused from their shared origin across the ocean, he argued, and now was the time for people of the world to recognize that common origin and come together again. "Let us hope they bear in mind that the ocean currents circulate with no regard for political borderlines, and that nations can divide the land, but the revolving ocean, indispensable and yet vulnerable, will forever remain a common heritage."[20]

Numerous scholars and activists talked at various venues in Stockholm. Heyerdahl's lecture, however, was one of only seven given a semi-official blessing by the United Nations (together with talks by Barbara Ward, René Dubos, Gunnar Myrdal, Carmen Miró, Solly Zuckerman, and Aurelio Peccei). The lectures were organized by the International Institute for Environmental Affairs in cooperation with the Population Institute, both of which were think tanks that reported directly to General Secretary U Thant.

It was not only Heyerdahl's fame as an explorer that appealed to the UN leadership. He had, over the years, actively endorsed the organization by sailing his ships with the UN flag as the official flag. Heyerdahl was an active leader in the World Federalist Movement that tried to improve international cooperation during the Cold War and saw a more powerful United Nations as a vehicle for bettering the world. To Heyerdahl, ocean pollution was an example illustrating the necessary importance of world-cooperation in solving shared problems. The UN leadership agreed, of course, and Heyerdahl soon found himself on the UN selection committee for its Environmental Protection Prize.

After 1972 Heyerdahl would continue raising environmental concerns.[21] In an article from 1985 he stated: "With respect to environmental

---

[19] Thor Heyerdahl, "How vulnerable is the ocean?" in Barbara Ward (et al. eds.), *Who Speaks for Earth?* (New York: Norton, 1973), pp. 45–63, quote p. 45. Barbara Ward and René Dubos, *Only One Earth: The Care and Maintenance of a Small Planet* (New York: Norton, 1972).
[20] Heyerdahl, "How vulnerable is the ocean?" p. 63.
[21] Frank Dehli, "Heyerdahl om miljøvern," *NRK Dagsrevyen*, June 5. 1982. Online archive of the Norwegian Broadcasting Corporation.

issues we must all collaborate across national boundaries and go beyond national disagreements. Wind and ocean currents do not know national boundaries, it makes us inseparable. We are all passengers on the same round globe in outer space."[22] In this spirit he became involved in the World Wildlife Fund International, which was known among the more hardcore environmentalists in Norway as anything but radical. In this capacity, in 1987, he managed to enrage Norwegian conservationists by giving an interview for BBC TV near the controversial hydropower dam of the Alta-Kautokeino River where he talked about the beauty of local wildlife, but did not condemn on the destruction of the river.[23] The interview marginalized him among activists. Nevertheless, in 1993, he made a moving plea for protecting the environment as the keynote speaker at the 5th World Wilderness Congress at the University of Tromsø.[24]

Despite this it would be an overstatement to say that Heyerdahl was a devoted environmentalist. His chief concern was ancient history and archeology. He does not portray himself as an environmentalist in his autobiography, for example, nor do his biographers.[25] Among the activists and scholars he was regarded as either a larger-than-life genius or an arrogant fool. In either case he was detached from the nitty-gritty details of environmental politics. Yet his vision of a shared human globe, his longing for a harmonious Edenic past, and his plea to nations to unite through the United Nations in order to solve dire ecological problems all rang true to Norwegian friends and foes.

THE RETURN TO THE WILD

Another explorer who rose to fame within the Norwegian culture of outdoor life was Helge Ingstad (1899–2001). He was a prominent nature writer, and also an eminent lecturer, who in his numerous public appearances showed slides and documentary films from his travels at a time when these mediums were still uncommon.

At the age of twenty-five, Ingstad decided to leave the modern world and settle among the Athabasca Chipewyan First Nation people in

---

[22] Thor Heyerdahl, "Mennesker og miljø i romfartsalderen." In Arne Fjørtoft, Jahn Otto Johansen, Thor Heyerdahl (eds.), *Befolkningsbomben: overbefolkning, krig og fred* (Oslo: Cappelen, 1985), pp. 89–110, quote p. 90.
[23] Thor Heyerdahl, "Altademningen og norsk dyreliv," *Norsk natur* 1 (1987), 28.
[24] Thor Heyerdahl, "The creative wilderness," in Børge Dahle (ed.), *Nature: The True Home of Culture* (Oslo: NIH, 1994), pp. 9–13.
[25] Thor Heyerdahl, *I Adams fotspor: En erindringsreise* (Oslo: Gyldendal, 2006).

northern Canada. He had just finished his law degree in the city of Bergen, and was thus most certainly not trained for a life in wilderness as a hunter-gatherer. Yet he felt that a law degree and modern society could not offer much of an adventure. After three years of stinging frostbite, wolf howls, and arctic weather, Ingstad returned to Norway to write his book, *Land of Feast and Famine* (1931).[26] It was an instant success and bestseller, and has since been regarded as a must-read for any Norwegian aspiring to think and talk about the wild.

The book is a story of how the arctic climate builds one's disposition and manhood, and how much one has to learn from the wisdom of First Nation people living in these harsh environments. It is also a book that questions the modern world's distance from basic survival knowledge of how to live in the arctic wilderness. Ingstad would tell his readers that there were many things that needed to be learned from the Chipewyans, a point he would reiterate again and again in subsequent lectures in Norway and abroad, such as at the Explorers Club in New York.

Being trained in law and also having the ability to thrive in harsh weather conditions made Ingstad an ideal candidate for the job of the Norwegian Governor of East Greenland, which he accepted in 1932. The status of the area would soon become topic of a heated legal battle, which ended in the International Court of Justice in The Hague where Denmark won its claim on the entire Greenland landmass. These events unfolded despite the fact that Indigenous Inuit saw the land as theirs. To Ingstad East Greenland was very much Erik the Red's Land in reference to the Norwegian Viking who once settled and named the landmass "Greenland."[27] Ingstad's action was ultimately moved by evidence in the Viking sagas, pride in his country as caretakers of the land, and his connection to its natural environment.

The verdict in The Hague put an end to Norwegian imperialism, and a restless Ingstad went to the United States where he worked as a cowboy (among other things). He then traveled with the Apaches, with whom he lived for over a year at the San Carlos Apache Indian Reservation. Upon his return to Norway he wrote a moving book about the Apaches, hailing their wisdom and ability to live in the wild, while at the same time maintaining a careful distance between the Apaches and

---

[26] Helge Ingstad, *Pelsjegerliv blandt Nord-Kanadas Indianere* (Oslo: Gyldendal, 1931); *Land of Feast and Famine* (London: V. Gollancz, 1933).

[27] Helge Ingstad, *Øst for den store bre* (Oslo: Gyldendal, 1935); *East of the Great Glacier* (New York: Knopf, 1937).

Norwegians in the language that he used, discussing how "they" have more wisdom than "us."[28]

The year with the Apaches would remain with him in the subsequent years as he pondered if the Vikings had ever met Indigenous Americans. As a popular author, playwright, novelist, and lecturer, Ingstad became fascinated with the saga of the Viking Leif Erikson and his Vinland Colony. To make a long story short: with his wife, the archeologist Anne Stine (Moe, 1918–97), they discovered a Viking settlement in North America. They made their initial discovery at the L'Anse aux Meadows, Newfoundland, in 1960, after which they would undertake yearly archeological excavations until 1968 under the leadership of Anne Stine. By this point they finally found hard evidence for their thesis, specifically a bronze ring-headed pin that only Vikings could have made.[29] The fact that Norwegian Vikings, not Christopher Columbus and his men, were the first Europeans to arrive in America was the key point Ingstad would stress again and again in his many public appearances.[30]

It is important to point out that this was not a Eurocentric, but a patriotic Norwegian point of view. In the early 1970s Ingstad joined hands with the anti-European Community organizers mobilizing against Norwegian membership in the Community in a national referendum scheduled for the fall of 1972. Here he would unite with most of the environmentalists mentioned in this book, including the ecologists and the ecophilosophers. Ingstad's name and fame was most welcome to the activists who saw him as a powerful ally from the conservative side of Norwegian politics. At this time, it was the importance of Norwegian self-determination and agricultural self-support that motivated Ingstad's political stance, and not necessarily environmental issues.[31]

This would gradually change during the 1970s when Ingstad became more and more involved with environmental affairs, particularly with hydropower developments. His stance came to the forefront of his many public appearances with the proposed hydropower development at the Alta-Kautokeino River, which is located at the heart of where Sámi

---

[28] Helge Ingstad, *Apache-indianerne: jakten på den tapte stamme* (Oslo: Gyldendal, 1939).
[29] Helge Ingstad, *Westward to Vinland* (New York: St. Martin's Press, 1969); *Land under the Pole Star* (New York: St. Martin's Press, 1966).
[30] Helge Ingstad, "Norse explorers," in Geoffrey Ashe (ed.), *The Quest for America* (New York: Praeger, 1971), pp. 96–112. Ralph Maud, *The Man Who Discovered America* (Montreal: National Film Board of Canada, 1981).
[31] Frode Skarstein, *Helge Ingstad: En biografi* (Oslo: Spartacus, 2010). Benedicte Ingstad, *Oppdagelsen: En biografi om Anne Stine og Helge Ingstad* (Oslo: Gyldendal, 2009).

people live and work. The Sámi, it is worth noting, had been living for centuries in the northern part of Norway, Sweden, Finland, and Russia under various degrees of political and cultural oppression. Ingstad would, at the age of eighty, go on a lecture tour around the country, discussing Sámi civil rights and the importance of learning from them in order to save a shared environment. Drawing upon his experiences with the Chipewyans and the Apaches, he pointed to the ancient wisdom of the Sámi relationship to nature from which modern society had so much to learn.

To the environmentalists, Ingstad was a living legend whose lectures on Vikings and life in the wild easily filled the largest auditorium. Yet his age and conservative leaning would set him apart socially from younger scholars and activists. What they admired in him was his Rousseau-style argument of the human "savage" being a source of inspiration for a noble environmental future. Many found his discussions of ancient Vikings along with Chipewyans, Apaches, and the Sámi appealing when searching for a way out of the modern world's eco-disaster. The fact that long-gone Vikings had once settled America was intriguing to Norwegians with global aspirations, as was his idea that arctic climate and outdoor life would help to build a nobler disposition.

LEARNING FROM THE PEOPLE OF SWAT

The social anthropologists were the first to agree with both Heyerdahl and Ingstad on the importance of studying tribes and people who had not been tainted by modernity. And first among Norwegian anthropologists was Fredrik Barth (1928–2016). He was not interested in environmental issues, nor was he particularly concerned about the rights or social status of the Indigenous Sámi living in Norway. His importance lay in his theoretical and descriptive anthropology, though, as will be argued, he also encouraged his students to engage the world politically. But perhaps most importantly, he was the first academic to introduce the science of ecology to the Norwegian scholarly community.

He was the son of the geologist Thomas Barth, who, in 1946, took his son along to the University of Chicago where he gave a guest lecture. The young Barth soon enrolled, and he graduated in 1949 with a Master of Arts in paleoanthropolgy and archaeology. It was during his graduate studies that he, as part of the course requirements, came to read the work of the ecologist Warder Clyde Allee. As the historians of ecology Gregg Mitman and Eugene Cittadino have shown, the University of Chicago was, at the time, a hotbed for animal, social, and human ecology.[32] It was not only Allee's ecological research that caught Barth's attention, but also Marjorie and Allee's daughter Mary ("Molly") (1925–98) with whom he fell in love and married in 1949. After their marriage, the couple moved to Norway, where Allee would visit them in 1950.[33] The bond with the Allee family provided Barth with firsthand knowledge of ecology, which he used as an analytical tool to understand human behavior, an example of which is present in his famous study "Ecological Relationships of Ethnic Groups in Swat, North Pakistan" (1956).

Barth was not the only Norwegian academic to visit this tribal region of Pakistan. The Norwegian Alpine Club arranged a trip to the area in 1950 accompanied by the philosopher and climber Arne Næss, the events of which will be discussed later in this book (Chapter 3). Also, the renowned professor of linguistics at the University of Oslo, Georg Morgenstierne, had been there frequently and knew the tribal languages and dialects by heart.[34] It was Morgenstierne who taught Barth how to speak Pashto so that he could understand the language spoken in this green mountain region of Pakistan. With a point of departure in the ecology that he had learned from Allee, Barth analyzed the ecological division of labor (or niche) among the people of Swat, arguing that the region's political structure reflected its natural environmental conditions. The ecological niches of the tribes in Swat were "analogous to that of different animal species in a habitat," Barth argued, and relationships between them were both stable and static just as in the ecology of animals.[35] The ways in which the landowner, the tenant farmer, the commodity dealer, and so forth engaged with each other, he argued, depended on a semi-annual harvest and other static environmental

---

[32] Warder C. Allee, Alfred E. Emerson, Orlando Park, Thomas Park, and Karl P. Schmidt, *Principles of Animal Ecology* (Philadelphia: W. B. Saunders Co., 1949). Gregg Mitman, *The State of Nature: Ecology, Community, and American Social Thought, 1900–1950* (Chicago: The University of Chicago Press, 1992). Eugene Cittadino, "The failed promise of human ecology," in Michael Shortland (ed.), *Science and Nature* (Oxford: BSHS Monographs, 1993), pp. 252–83; "A 'marvelous cosmopolitan preserve': The dunes, Chicago, and dynamics ecology of Henry Cowles," *Perspectives on Science* 1 (1993), 520–59.

[33] Karl Patterson Schmidt, *Warder Allee 1885–1955* (Washington: National Academy of Sciences, 1957), p. 24. Thomas Hylland Eriksen, *Fredrik Barth: En intellektuell biografi* (Oslo: Universitetsforlaget, 2013).

[34] Nils Johan Ringdal, *Georg Valentin von Munthe af Morgenstiernes forunderlige liv og reiser* (Oslo: Aschehoug, 2008).

[35] Fredrik Barth, "Ecologic relationships of ethnic groups in Swat, North Pakistan," *American Anthropologist, New Series*, 58, no. 6 (Dec. 1956), 1079–89, quote p. 1079.

conditions. In short, what he described as occurring in the Swat communities resembled traditional Norwegian costal fishing and mountain farming communities.

The ecologically informed research in Swat and related work was done under supervision of the British anthropologist Edmund Leach at Cambridge University, from where Barth received a PhD in 1957. Barth subsequently became a lecturer at the University of Oslo where he began lecturing on using the field of ecology as a novel approach to anthropology and ethnology. These were the first lecture series about ecology in Norway. An article from this period by one of his students, for example, would credit Barth with introducing ecology to the study of humans in Norway by focusing on human adaptability to different environments.[36]

Despite having a significant audience in Oslo, Barth would not stay long as he accepted a professorship at the University of Bergen in 1961. In Bergen he would establish ecologically informed social anthropology as the way forward, which, after his divorce from Molly in 1972, would move gradually away from ecology toward economics as a methodological reference. Following Leach's famous call for humans to "become like gods," Barth advised his students to actively engage the world and assume the power to change it. In pursuing "a dynamic study of society," he argued that rather than understa the social structure that enables human action, one should focus on what action people are actually taking.[37] In his work, he would adapt from ecology the idea of the search for the universal, in particular when studying people's behavior in remote places that occupied the world's periphery. The task of social anthropology, he would say, was to investigate the local so that one could get "a deeper understanding of the human condition."[38]

Instead of subscribing to a functionalistic model of society, Barth encouraged his students to investigate how people as individuals or as groups act to understand social processes. As a charismatic professor in Bergen in the 1960s, he came to inspire a new generation of students with his ecological approach. The fact that ecology was introduced to the

---

[36] Helge Kleivan, "Økologisk endring i Labrador," *Naturen* 86 (1962), 200–13, note 1. Lecture by Kleivan given in Oslo in the spring of 1961.
[37] Fredrik Barth, "Preface," in Fredrik Barth (ed.), *The Role of the Entrepreneur in Social Change in Northern Norway* (Bergen: Universitetsforlaget, 1963), 3; "Moral og miljøkrise," in Svein Gjerdåker, Lars Gule, and Bernt Hagtvet (eds.), *Den uoverstigelige grense* (Oslo: Cappelen, 1991), pp. 149–53.
[38] Fredrik Barth and Colin Turnbull, "On responsibility and humanity: Calling a colleague to account," *Current Anthropology*, 15, no. 1 (1974), 99–103, quote p. 99.

Norwegian academic community by a social anthropologist, and not by the biologists, may explain why the field never narrowed to only focus on one type of subject matter. Thanks to Barth, humans would remain a key factor in ecological debates. Barth also thought that many Norwegians could learn from Indigenous people living in the periphery (such as farmers in Swat) to understand and envision humanity in general.

THE FISHERMAN-PEASANT

One particularly important student of Barth was Ottar Brox (b. 1932). Born in the remote village of Torsken in Troms in the North of Norway, he has a soft-spot for rural life. Formally he was a trained agronomist, though his first work of importance came in an article in the anthology *The Role of the Entrepreneur in Social Change in Northern Norway* (1963), edited by Barth and containing papers written by his first group of Norwegian students.

At the heart of the anthology was the concept of the willing human agent – the entrepreneur – trying to adapt to his or her ecological niche. The entrepreneur was, to both Barth and Brox, someone who mobilized a niche in an ecological system, and thus came to change the system as a result. Brox's description of the relationship between the herring boss, crew, and merchant may serve as an example: "The herring boss and his crew exploit the same niche, but their interaction is symbiotic rather than competitive, they are dependent upon each other for survival." The herring merchant, on the other hand, is changing the stable symbiotic system, for the worse. He is "an exploiter who is extracting profit from the clientele, i.e. 'eating' the fisherman, ecologically speaking."[39]

Though Barth would keep himself separate from the politics of trying to halt such ecological exploitation, he actively encouraged his students to engage in local communities, while, at the same time, thinking about the world as a whole. Inspired by his teacher, Brox would turn his anthropological investigations of fishermen into action on behalf of the ecologically oppressed. As he saw it, social anthropologists should not only understand the world, but also change it for the better. His questioning of economic growth, technocracy, and industrialism was, from now on, informed by populist agrarian socialism, which placed greater value on

---

[39] Ottar Brox, "Three types of north Norwegian entrepreneurship," in Fredrik Barth (ed.), *The Role of the Entrepreneur in Social Change in Northern Norway* (Oslo: Universitetsforlaget, 1963), pp. 19–32, quote p. 25.

rural communities and traditional lifestyles. This he expressed in the *Hva skjer i Nord Norge?* (What's happening in North of Norway? 1966). It became a phenomenal success and a must-read within the growing Norwegian counterculture. It's a book that reflects the bipolar Cold War world, in which the evils of centralized "technocratic assumption of power" should be fought in order to protect the virtues of seasonal fishermen-peasants living in harmony with their environments in the country's most pristine regions.[40] There was ancient wisdom in the ways of life of people in the coastal region of the North, Brox argued. His book was a call to action to defend rural communes from centralized urbanization efforts. He would soon enjoy wide support from an emerging group of radical ecologists, ecophilosophers, and environmentalists, who also pinpointed economic growth and industrialization as the root cause of the ecological crisis.

In the wake of his book's enthusiastic reception, Brox would, in the academic year of 1966/1967, visit Newfoundland to explore and learn about its fisheries and subsistence production, making numerous comparisons between rural Newfoundland and the north of Norway, including an allusion to Ingstad's work on Norwegian Vikings who had "rediscovered the island."[41]

Brox had an impact, especially, on the young leftist activist Hartvig Sætra (1933–2004), who, inspired by Brox, became somewhat of a celebrity among environmentalists, thanks to his 1971 book *Populismen i norsk sosialisme* (Populism in Norwegian Socialism), later reissued in 1973 as *Den økopolitiske sosialismen* (The Ecopolitical Socialism). He dreamed of a steady-state, ecologically informed society, with zero population growth, modest use of technology, recirculation of natural resources, and decentralization of political power, and initiated a call to arms against technocracy, centralized power, and exploitation of natural resources. Ecology was at the heart of his thinking: "It's through biology that we will get the best arguments for introducing socialism."[42] Following Brox, Sætra argued that true socialists should bring to an end their longing for the blue-collar worker adored by Marxists. Instead, socialists should find home in emulating the rural

---

[40] Ottar Brox, *Hva skjer i Nord-Norge?* (Oslo: Pax, 1966), p. 23.
[41] Ottar Brox, *Newfoundland Fishermen in the Age of Industry* (Newfoundland: Memorial University of Newfoundland, 1972), p. 1.
[42] Hartvig Sætra, *Den økopolitiske sosialismen*, 3rd ed. (Oslo: Pax, 1973), p. 45. Odd Gaare,"Hartvig Sætra: Økopolitisk sosialist," *Prosa*, 2 (2019), 50–7.

fishermen-peasants, who lived in steady-state harmony with the natural world. The coastal fishermen-peasants were threatened by the industrial society generating, among other things, carbon dioxide pollution that inevitably would cause "climate change," Sætra warned, causing "the ocean to rise several meters all over the world."[43] At the heart of this concern was not carbon dioxide pollution, however, but capitalism itself with economic growth threatening the steady-state society. Instead of capitalism, Sætra imagined a world in which one would not consume more resources than nature could produce, where there would be modest use of technology, decentralized decision making, no growth in human population, and biodiversity built upon recirculation of resources. This was not armchair theory to Sætra, who ended up settling in the municipality of Gratangen in the north of Norway where he tried to live according to his own teachings.

Though his main target was capitalism, the book caused tension among the socialists. What was the source of revolution? Was it the industrial factory workers or rural fishermen-peasants? Sætra would look to Chinese agrarian communism for inspiration, arguing, "China under Mao Tse-tung practices a more conscious ecopolitics than other countries."[44] As will be argued, Sætra was not the only one among ecologically informed academics who found events in China inspiring. That did not go down well with socialists, who argued that the revolution would come from factory workers (and not fishermen-peasants), such as was the case in the Soviet Union.

One of Sætra's stern opponents was the left-leaning German intellectual Hans Magnus Enzensberger (b. 1929). He spoke Norwegian as he had lived in Norway between 1956 and 1964 at the beautiful island of Tjøme in the Oslo fjord. After that, he would, for the next thirty years, visit his rural picturesque farm in Valdres during his summer vacations. What he saw in rural Norway was not a steady-state ecological future, but instead a charming agrarian "anachronism." Norway did not harbor any revolutionary potential due to its large fishing-dependent and agrarian population, Enzensberger argued. Instead, the country had fallen out of step with the evolving dialectics of European history. This he would state in no uncertain terms. To him, Sætra was just a "low-voiced Berserker" and "a real pent-up lone wolf," who did not comprehend the true teachings of Karl Marx. "With a rage bordering on self-hatred

[43] Sætra, *Den økopolitiske sosialismen*, p. 71.
[44] Sætra, *Den økopolitiske sosialismen*, p. 103.

he demands merciless consequence, a forced restriction on consumption, [and] an ecological dictatorship," Enzensberger pointed out.[45]

Sætra was radical, but not a "Berserker." The ecological steady-state society was to him "not an herbal-tea party," but a revolutionary break with industrial growth.[46] The revolution was to come from the fishermen-peasants, revolting against the ecological evils of capitalism, after which they would establish an environmentally harmonious, steady-state communist society. To Brox and Sætra, the allure of this lost way of life represented a new possible environmentally friendly beginning for Norway and the world. They were not alone. To many Norwegians the peripheral nature of mountain peasants' and coastal fishermen's cabins that were bought up in the 1960s as vacation homes for outdoor life enthusiasts came to represent something more than just a beautiful place to relax. Such vacationing was a partial return to the nation's origin and gave people pristine places from which to reflect on a possible new beginning. As will be argued, the ecologically informed steady-state society that Brox and Sætra promoted was based on support from a growing number of ecologists (Chapter 2) as well as philosophers (Chapter 3).

The next chapter will visit Finse where the High Mountain Ecology Research Station was located. This was also the site for exciting archaeological excavations of Stone Age-era hunter-gatherer culture. To ecologists, as well as laymen vacationers, the site came to represent the ability of a pre-industrial society to live self-sufficiently. As one nature writer observed, outdoor life was a "partial return to the state of nature" in which vacationers with modern houses choose to "cook in the open air" and live in "tents for weeks" in order to reconnect with the Stone Age abilities that they have lost.[47]

---

[45] Hans Magnus Enzensberger, "Norwegische anachronismen," published as *Norsk utakt*, Lasse Tømte (trs.) (Oslo: Universitetsforlaget, 1984), pp. 77–8.
[46] Hartvig Sætra, *Jamvektssamfunnet er ikkje noko urtete-selskap* (Oslo: Samlaget, 1990).
[47] Nils Borchgrevink, "Naturfølelse og naturvern," *Samtiden* 77 (1968), 360–6, quotes pp. 360, 361. Arne B. Johansen, "Hardangervidda skal utforskes: Et prosjekt for tverrvitenskaplig kulturforskning i gang fra 1970," *Forskningsnytt*, 14 (1969), 26–9. Anders Hagen, "Fra Hardangerviddas historie," *Forskningsnytt*, 15 (1970), 31–5.

2

The Ecologists

THE HIGH MOUNTAIN ECOLOGY RESEARCH STATION

The chief place ecologists would meet, train their students, and explore the environment was The High Mountain Ecology Research Station, established at Finse in 1965. Finse is a railroad station halfway between Oslo and Bergen, located at the very heart of outdoor recreational activities. As will be apparent, the Finse environment would set the standard as a "reference" from which to evaluate other environments. Here, turn-of-the-century dwellings of navvy railroad maintainers were turned into high-end vacation homes, side by side with a well-known sports hotel, a large hospice owned by the Norwegian Trekking Association, and numerous new private cabins. At Finse thousands of vacationers would enjoy one of the most beautiful mountain regions of Norway. The formative years of ecological research in Norway took place in these types of environments and during the summer period, and the way ecologists came to understand the environment would reflect their experience of nature as a place of recreation. It was Arne Semb-Johansson (1919–2001) and Eivind Østbye (1935–2014) who created the Research Station with initial funds from University of Oslo. Following the trend of the area, they turned an outdated power station into a cabin for research and graduate study.[1]

---

[1] Eivind Østbye, "Høyfjellsøkologisk forskningsstasjons historie," in Lauritz Sømme og Eivind Østbye (eds.), *Finse: Et senter for høyfjellsforskning* (Finse: Høyfjellsøkologisk forskningsstasjon, 1997), pp. 3–9; *Bibliography of the Finse Area 1781–1996* (Finse: The High Mountain Ecology Research Station, 1997). Finn R. Jørstad, *Historien om Finse* (Bergen: Nord 4, 1998).

2 The Ecologists

FIGURE 1 The High Mountain Ecology Research Station, Finse, emblem, 1972.
Courtesy of the University of Oslo Archive

The summer excursions to the scenic mountains of Finse were highly popular, as they gave students and scholars alike a sense of doing something useful and pleasant during their summer recess. Field research in this mountainous peripheral space, under supervision of Semb-Johansson and Østbye, brought significant momentum to the field of ecology, as it was easier to teach and study the relatively uncomplicated biotic relations of the mountains than those of the more complicated lowland environments.[2] Though it is hard to determine the personal motivation of ecologists, it is safe to say that most students entering the field had a passion for outdoor recreation. Typically, membership in the Trekking Association, the nation's largest owner of cottages with over 60,000 members, was, to most of them, a matter of course. Over 800 days of research were carried out by students and scholars at the Research Station between 1965 and 1970. Most of them were involved in the Norwegian division of the International Biological Program, and a few of them lived at Finse on a yearly basis to study the ecology of harsh winter conditions (captured on film in the Hoth battle scenes of *Empire Strikes Back* [1979], which were shot there). In 1970 the Norwegian Parliament allocated enough funds to build a new 700 m² (7,535 ft²) building to be owned by both the Universities of Oslo and Bergen (Figure 1). When finished in 1972 it was, perhaps, the largest and most expensive ecological research station in Europe. It could house large courses, which were usually given in August.

---

[2] Eivind Østbye, "Aktuell forskning i enkle økosystemer, med særlig henblikk på høyfjellsforskning i Norge," *Forskningsnytt*, 4 (1967), 70–3.

The historian of science Robert E. Kohler has, in his study of fieldwork in the USA, noted that "[t]he most widespread form of underwriting [of field work] was the summer vacation, which all academics and most government and museum employees enjoyed. Vacations afforded not money but time."[3] This was also very much the case for the Finse ecologists, whose long summer recess enabled them to do their fieldwork, as the natural environments in question were easily accessible during this period. This scientific vacationing was not necessarily relaxing, though anecdotal evidence suggests that, for some, it was that too. Hardworking or not, fieldwork was the highlight of the year as it enabled ecologists to spent time in places they appreciated and associated with outdoor life.

RACHEL CARSON'S SILENT SPRING

The picturesque research station at Finse was idyllic in comparison to the ecological destruction described in a growing body of environmental literature. Indeed, the prospect of ecological depletion was at the heart of the ecologists' concerns and daily debate. These worries first surfaced with the publication of Rachel Carson's famous warning against pesticides in *Silent Spring*, published for the first time in Norwegian in 1962.[4] It was an important moment in the nation's environmental debate as, from then on, these concerns were framed as *ecological*, while they previously had only been seen as mostly aesthetic. Ecological concerns in Norway were thus imported from abroad. This meant an empowerment of the small but radically growing community of ecologists.

The publication of Carson's book marks a shift, not only toward ecology, but also toward a belief that scientists had something extra to offer in answering the question of how to best protect the environment. *Silent Spring* raised eyebrows and introduced Norwegians not only to ecology, but also to a more integrated approach to environmental issues. Scientists had, of course, been involved in environmental management, such as agriculture, forestry, and fishery management, yet they had hardly been active in nature conservation. What was new with Carson was the

---

[3] Robert E. Kohler, *All Creatures: Naturalists, Collectors, and Biodiversity, 1850–1950* (Princeton: Princeton University Press, 2006), p. 92.

[4] Ragnhild Sundby, "Globalforgiftning," *Naturen*, 89 (1965), 3–11. Rachel Carson, *Silent Spring* (Greenwich: Fawcett Crest, 1962); *Den tause våren*, Torolf Elster (trs.) (Oslo: Tiden, 1962).

2 The Ecologists

turn toward scientific experts, specifically ecologists, as the source for information on how to go about protecting the natural world.

The initial Norwegian reaction to Carson's book came in reviews of the original English edition in Norwegian newspapers. The fact that a foreign book was considered deserving of space was unusual. What brought the editors' attention was her ecological analysis of "the elixir of death," namely DDT.[5] Her book would subsequently surface in Norwegian debates as a rhetorical device and a measurement for environmental success. It was used politically to compare clean Norway to the environmentally problematic United States and Japan.[6] It was used by scientists to promote the new entomological approach in agriculture.[7] It was used by activists to show that, while birds where no longer threatened in the United States (due to legislation against DDT), Norwegian birds (such as the auk) were more threatened than ever due to PCB pollution.[8] Finally, it was used in the ongoing national sport of bantering with the Swedes. When Swedes were busy preparing for the United Nations Conference on the Human Environment in Stockholm in 1972, a Norwegian journalist noted that it was ironic that a city harboring the Royal Swedish Academy of Sciences, who gave Paul Müller, the inventor of DDT, the Nobel Prize in 1948, would now look to Rachel Carson as a source of inspiration.[9] Most commonly, *Silent Spring* was looked to as evidence of the importance of research and science in the ongoing effort to address environmental issues.[10]

Though Carson's warning against pesticides in *Silent Spring* raised eyebrows and inspired Norwegians to adopt an ecological perspective, it should be noted that she was not the only foreign environmentalist in the press. A translation of Marston Bates's classic *Man in Nature* (released in 1961 and revised in 1964) received attention, as Bates addressed issues related to pollution, ecology, and human population growth.[11] Essays about the technological standardization of human life and nature by the philosopher Georg Henrik von Wright and the sociologist Herbert

---

[5] Asbjørn Barlaup, "Rachel Carson," *VG*, Oct. 6 1962, RA. Sara Mjåland, "Dødseleksirer," *VG*, Nov. 7 1962, RA. Anonymous," Dødens eliksir," *VG*, Oct. 18, 1963, RA.
[6] Hj. Munthe-Kaas Lund, "Fugler i fare!" *VG*, Sept. 14, 1964, RA.
[7] Asbjørn Barlaup, "Entomologene lurer naturen," *VG*, Apr. 30, 1966, RA.
[8] Sjur Sandberg, "Fra taus til klangfugl," *VG*, May 29, 1974, RA.
[9] Per-Aslak Ertresvåg, "Miljøvernkonferansen i Stockholm," *VG*, Feb. 9 1972, RA.
[10] Anonymous, "Langsom, snikende – farlig," *VG*, Mar. 23, 1971, RA.
[11] Marston Bates, *Menneskets plass i naturen*, Brynjulf Valum (trs.) (Oslo: Cappelen, 1966).

Marcuse were also significant, as they were both translated into Norwegian after the two men men visited Oslo.[12] These texts, along with the writings of Jacques-Yves Cousteau, were all received with open arms by both ecologists and philosophers.[13] These scholars would have a growing concern with respect to globalization of pollution, the damaging aspect of industrialization, human population growth, and the need to base environmentalism on an ecological footing.[14]

Thus, concerns about an ecological crisis in Norway were largely imported from abroad. Around the same time, conservative parties managed, in 1963 and again between 1965 and 1971, to form a coalition that overthrew the Labor Party government that had been in power since 1945. This shift generated much scrutiny across the political spectrum, and, in this process, environmental degradation emerged as a key issue the Labor Party had failed to address.

THE FIRST LECTURES IN ECOLOGY BY BIOLOGISTS

Though the ecologists were concerned about environmental issues, they were, at least initially, not particularly radical. Indeed, the first lectures in ecology by biologists were by well-respected citizens. It was Semb-Johansson who gave the first lectures at the University of Oslo in 1962, and subsequently Eilif Dahl (1916–93) at the Norwegian Agricultural College in 1963. These courses were devoted to energy circulations in nature as was described by the American ecologist Eugene P. Odum (1913–2002).[15] This methodology dominated Norwegian ecological research, which came to focus on the energy balance between species.

Ecology was, at the time, a new discipline among biologists in Norway, even though it had most likely been known as a methodological approach for a while in intramural debates. For example, the botanist and co-founder of the Natural History Museum in Oslo, Nordal Willie,

---

[12] Herbert Marcuse, *Det en-dimensjonale menneske: Studier i det avanserte industrielle samfunns ideologi*, Thomas Krogh (trs.) (Oslo: Pax, 1968); *One Dimensional Man: Studies in the Ideology of Advanced Industrial Society* (London: Routledge, 1964). Georg Henrik von Wright, "Essays om naturen, mennesket og den vitenskapelig-tekniske revolusjon," *Naturen*, 91 (1967), 155–80.

[13] Jaques-Yves Cousteau, "Er klokken blitt tolv?" *Naturen*, 94 (1970), 411–20.

[14] Sigmund Huse, "Naturvern på økologisk grunnlag," *Norsk natur*, 1 (1965), 4–7. Harald M. Thamdrup, *Naturens husholdning* (Oslo: Aschehoug, 1966).

[15] Eilif Dahl [with Oddvar Skre], *Forelesninger i økologi* (Ås: Norges Landbrukshøgskole, 1967). Eugene P. Odum, *Fundamentals of Ecology*, 2nd ed. (Philadelphia: Saunders Co., 1959).

corresponded with the British ecologist Arthur Tansley on related topics as early as 1903.[16] And there is also a discussion of ecological matters in an esoteric book about the need for social and mental reforms from 1929.[17] Yet it has not been possible to trace much interest or any publications based on ecological methodology among biologists in Norway before *Silent Spring* and Semb-Johansson and Dahl's lectures.

Semb-Johansson gave his first lectures in ecology at the age of forty-three, and as a relatively new professor of zoology. He got his appointment in 1959, the same year he finished his PhD in insect physiology and neuroendocrinology, which was well received, as he became a member of the Norwegian Academy of Science and Letters the following year.[18] Although he submitted his thesis at the Laboratory of Zoology and the University of Oslo, it was actually written under supervision of Berta Scharrer at the University of Colorado where Semb-Johansson enjoyed a stipend from 1954 to 1956. It was during this period that he read the Odum brothers' *Fundamentals of Ecology* in its first edition of 1953.[19] After having presented his thesis, he decided to use his professorial position to build the field of biology at the university, and he realized that the broad interdisciplinary methodology of ecology was better suited for the job than his highly specialized field of neuroendocrinology. In Oslo Semb-Johansson would, in his first decade as a professor, graduate about ten master students in ecology, of which Østbye was perhaps most influential as a teaching fellow for Semb-Johansson's ecology courses and as a subsequent researcher and activist.[20] Semb-Johansson had considerable clout in political circles and among members of the larger public, as an active advocate for better funding of science, particularly biology, which culminated with him serving as the President of the Academy for a decade from 1975 to 1985. What gained him initial respect from the larger public was his involvement in the resistance during the Second World War. He was a courier of the Central Command of the Norwegian resistance movement, Milorg, and for his work there, he received high

---

[16] Arthur George Tansley to Nordal Wille, May 4 and June 12, 1903, OA Br. s. 97, NB.
[17] Dybwad Bertram Brochmann, *Mentalitet og livsskjæbne* (Bergen: Det frie samfunds forlag, 1929), pp. 81–106.
[18] Arne Semb-Johansson, *Relation of Nutrition to Endocrine-Reproductive Functions in the Milkweed Bug Oncopeltus fasciatus (Dallas) (Heteroptera: Lygaeidae)*, PhD thesis (Oslo: University of Oslo, 1958).
[19] Eugene P. Odum, *Fundamentals of Ecology* (Philadelphia: Saunders Co., 1953).
[20] Eivind Østbye, *En undersøkelse over nivale carabiders økologi, særlig innen slekten Nebria Latr*, MA thesis (Oslo: University of Oslo, 1963).

honors, including the Norwegian Defense Medal and the British King's Medal for Courage.

Dahl was also a war hero. He was active in the ultra covert military intelligence organization XU, which was under a veil of total secrecy until 1988. The abbreviation XU stood for unknown (X) undercover (U) agents, and most of them were recruited from within a closed circle of young science students at the University of Oslo, who knew and trusted each other from their student years in the late 1930s.[21] Many of the group would continue to work at the university after the war, including the philosopher Arne Næss and the geologist Ivan Th. Rosenqvist, whose contributions to the environmental debate will be discussed later in this book. It is likely that former XU members in Oslo knew about each other, or at least had informed opinions about other possible members of the organization that were entirely unknown to the public. The bonding experience of war makes it also likely that its members kept a protective eye on each other throughout their lives. In any case, in 1943, Dahl had to flee to Sweden where he worked at the Embassy, before moving to London where he would serve as an officer in the Norwegian Army for the rest of the war.

His interest in botany came at a young age when, at the age of only twenty-one, he was able to participate in an expedition to Spitsbergen in 1937 to study lichen. This became a life-long interest for Dahl, first in his master thesis of 1942 about lichens of Southwest Greenland, and later in various publications where four species were named after him. Was lichen a remnant of a warmer period that had survived the last Ice Age by being on mountaintops? Dahl believed so, and saw it as a possible origin for the subsequent evolution of some of the Norwegian flora. This and other topics he would discuss as a research fellow at the University of Oslo from 1951, which allowed him to visit the universities of Cambridge, Yale, and Michigan. All of this led to a PhD in botany, in 1957, on the subject of vegetation in the Norwegian mountain region of Rondane. It was well received if one is to judge by the fact that the Norwegian Academy of Science and Letters elected him as a member that same year. In 1959 he became a senior lecturer in botany at the Norwegian Agricultural College, and a full professorship followed in 1965.

After the war Dahl became a member of the Labor Party and was active in politics. He was, for several periods, an elected member of the township of Ås, outside Oslo, where the college is located (1964–67,

---

[21] Jorunn Sem Fure, *Universitetet i kamp*. In *Universitetet i Oslos historie*, vol. 4 (Oslo: Unipub, 2011), pp. 169–73.

1968–71, 1990–93), as well as a member of *landsstyre* (The Labor Party's National Board) from 1964 to 1971. As will be argued, his wartime achievements and these positions gave him a significant say on the Labor Party's environmental politics. As a member of *Rådet for utviklingshjelp* (The Council for Development) (1963–82) and as Chair of the Board for the Norwegian Institute of International Affairs (1978–86), Dahl also took great interest in the nation's foreign policy. In his lectures as well as political appearances, he would tell party members, engineers, or students about the importance of ecology, healthy living, and the value of non-instrumental reasoning.[22]

Both Semb-Johansson and Dahl were well established, but still relatively young, scientists when *Silent Spring* was first published in Norwegian, and they would use the book for all its worth to build the science of ecology by actively recruiting students to the field through their lecture series, as well as through new undergraduate and graduate programs. Moreover, they were socially and politically well respected, which was important when they began mobilizing for a Norwegian branch of the International Biological Program (IBP).

INTERNATIONAL BIOLOGICAL PROGRAM

The International Biological Program was initiated in 1960 by members of the International Union of Biological Sciences and the International Council of Scientific Unions. Its main concerns were problems related to food production and management of natural resources in light of a rapidly increasing human population and widespread malnutrition in the world. It was a Big Science project and of key importance to the promotion of systems ecology driven by the image of the world as a manageable self-governing machine.[23] At the helm sat the British ecologist Edgar Worthington, who had spent most of his early career defending the British Empire in the name of better environmental management and protection.[24]

---

[22] Eilif Dahl, *Økologi for ingeniører og arkitekter* (Oslo: Universitetsforlaget, 1969). Eilif Dahl, "Globale ressursproblemer," *Samtiden*, 82 (1973), 257–67.

[23] Chunglin Kwa, "Representations of nature mediating between ecology and science policy: The case of the International Biological Programme," *Social Studies of Science*, 17 (1987), 413–42. Edgar B. Worthington (ed.), *The Evolution of IBP* (Cambridge: Cambridge University Press, 1975).

[24] Edgar B. Worthington, *The Ecological Century: A Personal Appraisal* (Oxford: Oxford University Press, 1983). Peder Anker, *Imperial Ecology: Environmental Order in the British Empire, 1895–1945* (Cambridge: Harvard University Press, 2001).

The worldly managerial benefit of ecological research was, at least initially, at the heart of the Norwegian branch of the International Biological Program. One of its early promoters was Rolf Vik (1917–99), who had just finished his PhD in zoology at the University of Oslo. He argued that ecologists could provide answers to environmental problems described by Carson and von Wright if they were provided with enough funding. "The key word is in fact money!" he told the politicians.[25] There were reasons to worry about food supply, because of the increasing population, both at home and abroad. The ecologists pledged to deliver "methods that enable us to predict the consequences of today's actions and tomorrow's world" with respect to the utilization of the land.[26] It was "a matter of continuing human existence" to research the ecology of the mountains as future "production and recreation areas" for Norwegians.[27] The world may face starvation, so production of food in the mountains was of key importance to the process of making the country self-sufficient. One should therefore train more ecologists, the Parliament was told, with the ability to deal with problems of productivity, food production, and rational management of the nation's natural resources. The study of the mountain regions was especially important, since more than half the country is situated above the tree line. With authorities such as Semb-Johansson and Dahl pushing the cause, and with the prosperity of the nation at stake, the Parliament voted in favor of a generous budget to train ecologists in scientific tools for landscape management.

Receiving funding directly through the Parliament was unusual and it caused tensions between ecologists and biologists, as applications were supposed to go through the Norwegian Research Council. Knut Fægri (1909–2001), a botanist at the University of Bergen, for example, complained that ecology had become "a nice word that rumbles well in pretty reports to the Parliament and other authorities. But do they have a clue

---

[25] Rolf Vik, "Hvor står biologene i teknikkens århundre?" *Naturen*, 91 (1967), 259–69, quote p. 269.
[26] Rolf Vik, *International Biological Programme: Final Report Scandinavian Countries* (Oslo: Scandinavian National Committees of the International Biological Programme, 1975), 7; *International Biological Programme, IBP i Norge: Årsrapport* (Oslo: IBP, 1968–1974). Frans-Emil Wielgolaski, "Fenologi, produksjonsøkologi og andre kjente eller ukjente økologiske begreper," *Naturen*, 92 (1968), 179–84.
[27] Rolf Vik and Frans-Emil Wielgolaski, "Det Internasjonale Biologiske Program i 1969," *Forskingsnytt*, 15 (1970), 14–20, quotes pp. 14, 16.

about what they are doing?"²⁸ What worried Fægri was funding at the expense of taxonomy, and whether or not the ecologists could deliver what they promised. His concerns were not without merit, as taxonomy from now on would take a backstage role.

The International Biological Program would provide a significant boost to ecological research. It was initially promoted by Semb-Johansson and Dahl, though its Chairman became Vik, who in the process also got a professorship in 1965 at the University of Oslo. He became a devoted ecologist and organizer of the Program, which was active between 1964 and 1974, though only fully in effect between 1967 and 1972. Nationally, altogether 221 students and scholars were connected to this Program. They were typically involved for two to four years, and they worked, for the most part, on ecological topics.

Housing all the new scientists was an issue, and the Parliament allocated enough funds to build a new Department of Biology at the University of Oslo. When it was finished in 1971, it was one of the largest buildings ever built by the Norwegian state covering 25,000 m² (269,000 ft²). This was part of a larger state commitment to science, as the average scientific research budget in Norway increased nominally 119 percent between 1963 and 1969. The biologists' share was a 186 percent increase, plus new buildings, all of which is evidence of the substantial political support for the biological sciences.²⁹

When it came to the scientific research done by the International Biological Program scholars, the initial focus on managerial tools and food production became less important. The importance of environmental conservation became instead the imperative, especially among the largest group of scholars working on the ecology on the mountains. The official title of their research project was "Production of Terrestrial Communities" and "Use and Management of Biological Resources," but most of them were critical of the utilitarian perspective these titles suggested. Vik stressed that ecologists were "working *with* nature and not *against* it."³⁰ Similarly, Dahl saw a difference between "*product science* and

---

[28] Knut Fægri, "Den klassiske biologis stilling i moderne naturvitenskap," *Naturen*, 90 (1966), 528–546, quote p. 540. Nils Roll-Hansen, *Det Internasjonale Biologiske Program (IBP) i Norge* (Oslo: Institute for Studies in Research and Higher Education, 1982).
[29] Torstein Engelskjøn, *Biologisk forskning i Norge: En analyse med spesiell vekt på grunnforskningens ressurser, organisasjon og innhold* (Oslo: Institute for Studies in Research and Higher Education, 1972), 7–8, 39–40.
[30] Rolf Vik, "Naturvern er menneskevern," *Naturen*, 90 (1966), 195–205, quote p. 195. Vik's emphasis.

environmental science." Science that produces "products to live on" should be contrasted with research on "a good environment to live in" as in places suitable for "recreation," he argued.[31] To him the difference between "to research on" and "to live in" the environment signified technocratic versus ecological ways of thinking. In their research, ecologists would thus emphasize non-economic values. Typically, an intramural research report about reindeer would stress "the aesthetic importance of these animals to walkers in the area."[32] Such comments should be understood in the context of the culture of mountaineering and outdoor-life from which most ecologists emerged. As the professor of botany and Minister of Agriculture, and soon to be the world's first Minister of the Environment, Olav Gjærevoll (1916–94) argued:

"The increasing urbanization and heavy traffic creates a major need for areas in which humans can find rest, recreation, peace and nature experience. This will demand a significant adjustment in our entire way of thinking about area planning. Thriving-areas must be chosen after a quality evaluation of nature. In our legislation we must draw the conclusion that these thriving-areas must be protected. Any Norwegian must admit that our most important thriving-areas are the beaches and the mountains."[33]

A STEADY-STATE NATION

The ecologists involved with the International Biological Program became powerful lobbyists in favor of large-scale national parks in the nation's periphery or "thriving-areas." They would frequently argue that being in proximity of untouched nature was necessary for health. Dahl, for example, saw urban social problems as a result of the lack of contact with nature in the mountains. Humans have an emotional "need to thrive," he argued, which can only be satisfied through "meetings with nature."[34] Many of his colleagues agreed. Life without outdoor life could lead to

---

[31] Eilif Dahl quoted in Anonymous (eds.), *Working Meeting on Analysis of Ecosystems: Tundra Zone* (Ustaoset: IBP Norway, 1968), 7. Dahl's emphasis. Similarly in Arne Semb-Johansson, "Samspillet i naturen." In Ragnar Frislid and Aren Semb-Johansson (eds.), *Norges Dyr* (Oslo: Cappelen, 1971), vol. 5, pp. 44–58.
[32] Eilif Dahl quoted in Anonymous (eds.), *Working Meeting*, 32.
[33] Olav Gjærvoll, "Forord," in Nalle Valtiala, *Mennesket – et skadedyr?* Brynjulf Valum (trs.) (Oslo: Cappelen, 1970), pp. 7–8.
[34] Eilif Dahl, *Økopolitikk og økologi* (Oslo: The Royal Norwegian Society for Development, 1971), 9. Gunnar Lid, "Om dyrelivet i den foreslåtte nasjonalparken på Hardangervidda," *Norsk natur*, 1 (1966), 66–71.

dangerous urban "ghetto" cultures, since humans "demand recreation, and increasingly, recreation in contact with nature."[35] Pure nature in the periphery could secure healthy life for the contaminated urban centers.

The idea that facts tainted by value judgments were of lesser scientific value was also accepted by Oslo ecologists, who put in a lot of effort trying to describe plants, animals, and their relationships to each other and to the environment in neutral terms. Nevertheless, ecological research questions, researchers, and research results were far from neutral as they all explicitly pointed toward nature conservation and recreational values of outdoor life.[36]

Recreation was a way in which humans could be energized through outdoor life in the steady-state of nature's energy circulation. This was especially important to urban dwellers who lived without direct contact to nature. To protect this possibility, recreation took the center stage as an ecologically sound alternative to large scale plans for hydropower developments of water systems that would run from the high mountains deep down to the fjords. For example, when such plans were proposed for a large mountain plateau, Hardangervidda, near Finse, in 1968, they were met with head-on resistance from ecologists who used these rivers to determine the steady-state of the plateau.[37] As ecology was defined as the study of relations, one thus had to protect the entire area as an untouched reference environment: "Hardangervidda is one unit, and should thus be preserved as one unit," they argued.[38] In May 1969, local planners called them in as scientific experts, and established a procedure that guaranteed ecologists would have a say in future developments. To Vik, this represented "a new chapter in the history" of environmental debate.[39] Ecology as applied science, with ecologists as scholar-activists and counter-experts to engineers, also caught the attention of young

---

[35] Thor Larsen, "Økologi og sunn fornuft," *Norsk natur* 7 (1971), 40–1.
[36] Eivind Østbye (et al.), "Hardangervidda, Norway," *Ecological Bulletins*, 20 (1975), 225–64.
[37] Anonymous, "'Aksjon Hardangervidda' i gang," *Norsk natur*, 6 (1970), 122–4. Jan Økland, "Naturviten og naturbruk: Om dyreliv og miljøforhold I norske vassdrag," *Naturen*, 91 (1967), 387–97.
[38] Olav R. Skage, *Hardangervidda: Naturvern – Kraftutbygging* (Oslo: Universitetsforlaget, 1971), 91. Based on unpublished reports by Arne Semb-Johansson, A. Løvlie, K. Elgmor, Ivar Mysterud, and Eivind Østbye, "Vitenskapelige interesser og vassdragsreguleringer på Hardangervidda," *Forskningsnytt*, 1 (1972), 35–45; "The Future of Hardangervidda," *Research in Norway*, 1 (1973), 57–68.
[39] Rolf Vik, "Forord," in Rolf Vik (ed.) *Vassdrag og samfunn* (Oslo: Universitetsforlaget, 1971), 11; "Vårt miljø og biologenes ansvar," *Samtiden*, 78 (1969), 67–79.

environmentalist philosophers who saw them as allies in the philosophers' fight against the "technocratic politics" they associated with positivist philosophy.[40] In the end, most of the hydropower plans for Hardangervidda were either scaled down or abandoned, and the plateau was instead designated for ecological research and vacationing. The success gave the ecologists, as one of them pointed out, "aim and meaning in life" in a secularized world.[41]

One of the ecologists questioning hydropower developments was the zoologist Ivar Mysterud (b. 1938). He was also in the midst of the environmental debate and was instrumental in incorporating an ecological perspective into it. He wrote several introductory articles that were widely read among environmentalists, philosophers, and students of ecology alike. Most important, perhaps, were his lectures and seminars in which he and series of his colleagues explained, in non-technical terms, the nature of ecology and pollution to a broad audience. Though not best sellers, his publications became standard references and would frame debates about pollution in terms of steady-state and ecological energy circulation, for at least a decade.[42]

Despite all the efforts, Mysterud felt in 1969 that there was not enough time to understand the ecosystems, before the industrial society – like a "cancer abscess" – would destroy them.[43] 1970 was the European Year for Conservation of Nature which, according to Mysterud, developed into a "*national championship* in oral environmentalism." Frustrated by lack of action, he decided with his friend, Magnar Norderhaug (1939–2006), to turn the talking "towards deeper social issues," such as

---

[40] Hans Skjervheim, "Naturvern og politick," in Rolf Vik (ed.), *Vassdrag og samfunn* (Oslo: Universitetsforlaget, 1971), pp. 180–8, quote p. 181. Øyvind Østerud, "Naturverdier og samfunn – en ideologisk skisse," in Rolf Vik (ed.), *Vassdrag og samfunn* (Oslo: Universitetsforlaget, 1971), pp. 189–210. Gunnar Skirbekk, "Distrikshøgskolar, motekspertise og populisme," in Rolf Vik (eds.), *Vassdrag og samfunn* (Oslo: Universitetsforlaget, 1971), pp. 213–34. Per S. Enger, "Hva nå med norsk biologi?" in Nils Roll-Hansen og Hans Skoie (eds.), *Forskningspolitiske spørsmål i norsk biologi* (Oslo: Institute for Studies in Research and Higher Education, 1974), pp. 86–96.

[41] Rasmus Lyngnes, "Kan biologisk kunnskap gjeve dei unge mål og meining med livet?" *Naturen*, 96 (1972), 392–8. Ministry of the Environment, *Bruken av Hardangervidda* (Oslo: Universitetsforlaget, 1974).

[42] Ivar Mysterud (ed.), *Forurensning og biologisk miljøvern* (Oslo: Universitetsforlaget, 1971). Ivar Mysterud, *Noen økologiske grunnbegreper* (Oslo: Universitetet i Oslo, 1973). Ivar Mysterud, "Endringer i miljø og fauna," in Ragnar Fris Lid and Arne Semb-Johansson (eds.), *Norske dyr*, vol. 5. (Oslo: Cappelen, 1971), pp. 412–28.

[43] Ivar Mysterud, "En kommentar til økologisk forskning," *Forskningsnytt*, 14 (1969), 18–25, quote p. 24.

2 The Ecologists

the questioning of economic growth.[44] Politics should be put on a secure ecological footing, they argued, and suggested the term "eco-politics" to distance phony environmentalism from the real thing. The term was quickly adopted, not only by fellow ecologists, but also by a series of scholars, activists, and students questioning technocracy and industrialism. Much of this criticism had, since the mid-1960s, been informed by Ottar Brox and Hartivg Sætra's populist agrarian socialism (discussed in the previous chapter), which, thanks to Mysterud and Norderhaug, continued under the new label "eco-politics" from 1970 and onwards.[45] Unlike the socialists, however, Mysterud and Norderhaug sought an "eco-politics" founded on science, as our common future depended on the development of a "steady-state" social economy that would mirror the steady-state balance of the economy of nature at Hardangervidda.[46] They saw no technical solutions to the eco-crisis, as this depended on uncontrollable economic growth. Instead they searched for an alternative technology in tune with ecological principles of zero-growth and steady-state.[47]

One of many students inspired by their steady-state reasoning was the young graduate Nils Christian Stenseth (b. 1949), who later became a key figure in international ecological research. His first article, published when he was twenty-three years old, was about eco-politics. "Based on their knowledge," he argued, "all biologists should work for a *steady-state society* in replacement of the *growth society*," and one should limit the human population growth to zero.[48] To Stenseth, ecological modeling

---

[44] Ivar Mysterud and Magnar Norderhaug, "Økopolitikk – naturvernets nye dimensjon," *Norsk natur*, 7 (1970), 24–7, quote p. 25. Their emphasis.

[45] Birgit Wiggen, *Debatten omkring populisme/økopolitikk i Norge 1966–1976*, MA thesis (Oslo: The Norwegian Library School, 1976). Brox, *Hva skjer i Nord-Norge*. Sætra, *Den økopolitiske sosialismen*.

[46] Ivar Mysterud and Magnar Norderhaug, "Koblingen mellom økologi og politikk," *Norsk natur*, 8 (1972), 6–11. Kenneth E. Boulding, "The economics of the coming spaceship Earth," in Henry Jarrett (ed.), *Environmental Quality in a Growing Economy* (Baltimore: John Hopkins University Press, 1966), pp. 3–14; *Beyond Economics* (Ann Arbor: University of Michigan Press, 1968). Herman E. Daly, "Toward a stationary-state economy," in J. Harte and R. Socolow (eds.), *The Patient Earth* (New York: Holt, Rinehart, and Winston, 1971), pp. 226–44; (ed.), *Toward a Steady-State Economy* (San Francisco: Freeman, 1973).

[47] Ivar Mysterud and Magnar Norderhaug, "Teknisk-økonomiske løsninger på den økologiske krise?" *Norsk natur*, 8 (1972), 12–16; "Et samfunn i likevekt," Lecture at the Student Union, The Norwegian School of Technology, Trondheim, Apr. 15, 1972, 13 pages, PA; "Mirakeløkonomi og vekstsyke i Japan," *Norsk natur*, 8 (1972), 4–6.

[48] Nils Chr. Stenseth, "En oppfordring til biologene om å utforme en økopolitikk," *Naturen*, 96 (1972), 118–26, quote p. 118. Stenseth's emphasis.

represented the way forward, as simulation models could determine the exact nature of when and how to achieve a steady-state. He was well aware of the practical and theoretical problems in construing such a representation of the world, and therefore devoted his PhD to the topic. He was not alone, as computer modeling was "about to become an independent ecological branch of research" in this period.[49]

The ecologists at Finse could hike and visit the philosopher Arne Næss, who had a keen interest in their research and lived long periods of the year at his mountain cabin at the top of the Hallingskarvet peak. Others would take courses in the practical know-how and philosophy of outdoor life taught by Nils Faarlund at The Norwegian Mountaineering School in nearby Hemsedal. The next chapter will discuss the importance of these philosophers in more detail.

---

[49] Mysterud, "En kommentar til økologisk forskning," 25. Nils Chr. Stenseth, "Matematisk modellbygging i økologisk forskning," *Forskningsnytt*, 19 (1974), 28–34; *Theoretical Studies on Fluctuating Populations: An Evolutionary Approach*, PhD thesis (Oslo: Zoological Institute, 1977).

3

The Ecophilosophers

TRUE WELTANSCHAUUNG

In 1942 the philosopher Arne Næss (1912–2009) decided to build something unusual: a tiny boxlike shed at the very peak of Hallingskarvet, which is one of the highest mountains in Norway. It was hard to construct so he mobilized his mountaineer friends to help with the job. Conquering mountaintops had been a chief passion in his life, and the decision to build a shed on the very summit came as a natural extension of his interests. The first attempt to build it failed. He envisioned the shed overhanging the abyss from the peak's cliff with an entrance from below through a hatch in the floor, but this entailed a complicated and dangerous construction process. His friend Boss Walther died in the attempt to build this, and Næss decided to draw the shed back a bit to make it safer. When it was finished, he named it "Skarveredet" ("The mountain's nest," derived from what locals call "Skarven" – short for Hallingskarvet).[1] The only possible access to the shed is either by steep, almost impossible, hiking routes or by technical climbing. Skarveredet offers a secure place for climbers as protection from wind, rain, and snow. From the window the philosopher could look out on the world and truly think like a mountain. In his own words: "The only dignified way of life would be to remain on the mountain, not to descend. [...] from here you have the proper perspective on the human being. The mountain is a symbol of the wide and deep perspective."[2]

---

[1] Arne Næss, *Det gode lange livs far* (Oslo: Damm, 1995), pp. 67–9.
[2] Næss quoted in David Rothenberg, *Is It Painful to Think? Conversations with Arne Naess* (Minneapolis: University of Minnesota Press, 1992), p. 60.

Indeed, it is from this elevated, cold, and windy dwelling place he would later come up with the main principles of his ecophilosophy and environmental ethic of how to be good to the world.

From Skarveredet he would climb down to his somewhat larger cottage called Tvergastein, built in 1937 on a ledge directly below the shed. At this cottage, Næss explains, "I did all I could to educate myself to love everything here, to achieve the most love: the storms, the tiny flowers, the strong winds, and gray days."[3] Næss hired some local mountain-peasants to build Tvergastein based on his own drawings. They worked extremely hard to carry no less than sixty-two loads of material to this remote location way above tree level. Two horses nearly died before a third horse managed to finish the job so that his mountaineer life could be satisfied. The larger cabin was for living and writing while Skarveredet was a climbing destination and a place for reflection.

Tvergastein was, along with Skarveredet, built to fulfill his desire for escaping from society into nature. The environmental philosophies of Næss and his followers, this chapter argues, reflected the periphery of this remote dwelling place, which offers an extraordinarily deep panoramic *weltanschauung*. Their reflections on the proper ethical relation between the individual and the environment are based on their experience of looking out on the scenery from this tiny shed. Their argument in environmental ethics about the importance of place, belonging, and identification with all species derives from their personal experience at Tvergastein and Skarveredet. Indeed, much of Næss's later thinking around the balance of nature comes out of his experience of technical climbing, a sport where balance is everything.[4]

Just less than a two-hour hike from Tvergastein, in the valley below, one finds a tourist resort called Ustaoset, where Næss used to get his supplies at the local grocery store. From its railroad station he would take a four-hour train ride to Oslo. At this resort, the well-heeled families of Norway enjoy a vacation spot with numerous weekend cottages supplied with electricity, roads, cars, and a monstrous hotel. The hotel was originally built in 1909 and, with its numerous additions, has evolved into a colossal cross-country ski-resort abode for the wealthy. Among those who enjoyed the hotel's amenities was Næss's close family, who had their

---

[3] Næss quoted in Rothenberg, *Is It Painful to Think?* p. 61.
[4] Silviya Serafimova, "Whose mountaineering? Which rationality? The role of philosophy of climbing in the establishment of 20th century Norwegian ecophilosophies," *Balkan Journal of Philosophy*, 8, no. 1 (2016), 61–70.

own vacation cottage at Ustaoset. On his way down from Tvergastein, Næss walked past all these dwellings, which, to him, represented a shallow relationship with nature, and also the social milieu he sought to escape from.

Indeed, Næss was born in 1912 into a wealthy and well-known shipping family who provided him with a modest personal trust fund so that he could pursue his interests without economic worries. His early life can be understood as an attempt to run away from this background, and he succeeded fully in his escape at the age of twenty-five when he built Tvergastein so that he could have more time to enjoy nature and practice technical climbing.[5] He lived in his mountain home at Hallingskarvet for about ten years, and he would, for the rest of his life, continue to spend as much time as possible there. At the cabin he began gathering his own natural history collection of stones in order to emphasize the importance of science to himself and his visitors. Among them was his first wife Else (born Hertzberg, 1911–87). They went to the cabin on their honeymoon in the winter of 1937. Næss recalls:

> We stayed for more than three months, and had storms we had never imagined were possible! ... [T]he walls were just standing up into the air, and when we had the northern wind, the walls would bend so that when we had ink bottles, they would then rush all over the table. The wall was pushing the ink, the table, and the bottles all over. This was February, or March. And it looked as if – yes – the roof separated from the walls here, so you could look out onto the landscape. Hastily, I gathered all heavy things, and loaded down the roof so that it wouldn't collapse. If the roof had lifted just a little more, the wind would have taken all of it. We kept a heap of stones in the middle of the room here, so that if the roof went away, it wouldn't also take away the floor. We would hold onto all those stones, and try to somehow manage to live.[6]

While holding on to the stones, Næss also worked on a regular basis as a philosopher at the University of Oslo. He explains in his own words: "I was made a full professor [in the autumn of 1939], with tremendous responsibilities. I managed to place all my responsibilities, including lectures, from Tuesday evening to before dinner Wednesday. So I could go by train to the mountains Wednesday and come back to the city on Tuesday the following week."[7] In this way he made himself a sanctuary for serious thinking to evade the stress of administrative duties, teaching,

---

[5] Arne Næss and Inga Bostad, *Inn i filosofien: Arne Næss' ungdomsår* (Oslo: Universitetsforlaget, 2002). Truls Gjefsen, *Arne Næss: Et liv* (Oslo: Cappelen Damm, 2011).
[6] Næss quoted in Rothenberg, *Is It Painful to Think?* p. 63.
[7] Næss quoted in Rothenberg, *Is It Painful to Think?* p. 62.

debates, and polemics of the University. Consequently, Tvergastein soon attained a mythic status among Norwegian philosophers, since this is where they all had to travel to receive serious attention from their colleague or advisor. His cottage was a crucial tool in Næss's self-fashioning as a sage, and, as a result, countless famous and not-so-famous celebrities, students, intellectuals, writers, and philosophers went on pilgrimages to the mountain guru.

Over the years they came home from the philosopher's cabin with an almost endless stream of stories and anecdotes about the lively and eccentric professor, and some of these were noted down in mountaineering essays by his fellow technical climber, close friend, and student of philosophy Peter Wessel Zapffe (1899–1990). They were both prominent members of the Norwegian Alpine Club, which today regards them as their chief patrons. Conquering mountaintops was, until the early 1970s, their chief passion in life, and Næss's closest friends were members of the Alpine Club. When Tvergastein was built, he was already the club's most legendary member, having ascended 106 of the highest mountains in Norway before his eighteenth birthday. The club's *bon mot*: "Climbing to other sports is like champagne to bock beer" – flaunted by Zapffe – captures the spirit of this upper crust fraternity. The club members, including Næss and Zapffe, would climb and conquer peaks, mostly in mountain-rich Norway. Having been at Skarveredet was a *rite de passage* for new club members, who were elected through a long and secretive vetting process.

The Alpine Club would arrange challenging climbing vacations for its members at home and abroad. One of Næss's most pleasurable climbing memories after the war was a trip to the north-west tribal region of Pakistan in 1950 (Figure 2). The Alpine Club organized the "expedition" so that its members could climb the mountain Tirich Mir and provide friends at home with thrilling accounts of how they, after much struggle, had managed to be the first climbers in the world to reach the top of this mountain. The Norwegian Geographical Society garnished the journey with some scientific activity by sponsoring the twenty-two-year-old botany student Per Wendelbo (1927–81), who later published an impressive study of the region's flora.[8] Judging from the travel accounts,

---

[8] Anonymous (eds.), *Tirich Mir: The Norwegian Himalaya Expedition*, Sölvi and Richard Bateson (trs.) (London; Hodder and Stoughton, 1952). Per Wendelbo, "Plants from Tirich Mir: A contribution to the flora of Hindukush," *Nytt magasin for botanikk*, 1 (1952), 1–70.

3 The Ecophilosophers

FIGURE 2 Arne Næss on vacation with the Norwegian Alpine Club in Pakistan, 1950.
Unknown photographer. Courtesy of Gyldendal

however, climbing was the all-dominating focus, besides participating in polo matches organized by local officials who went out their way to entertain the Norwegian tourists. In 1964 they repeated the success with another climbing vacation to Tirich Mir, which resulted in a book-length account of the achievement written by Næss. In it he would explain his ability to thrive as a technical climber as a mixture of pain and excitement in mathematical terms as $T = G^2/(L_S + Å_S)$ where T *trivsel* (thriving) equaled G^2 *glød i annen potens* (excitement squared) divided by L_S *legemlige smerter* (bodily pains) plus $Å_S$ *åndelige smerter* (spiritual pains). The formula would later reemerge in his deep ecology inspired Ecosophy T, with the "T" being short for "thriving."[9]

The Alpine Club and Næss's mountaintop view suggests seeing both nature and society from above. Skarveredet and Tvergastein were located as far as possible from the social realm, yet close enough to suggest various household schemes for management of nature and society.

---

[9] Arne Næss, *Opp stupet: til østtoppen av Tirich Mir* (Oslo: Gyldendal, 1964), 126. Geir Grimeland, *En historie om klatring I Norge, 1900–2000* (Oslo: Fagbokforlaget, 2004), 75–81.

The deep view from Skarveredet differs from the shallow view acquired by his family and their wealthy friends down in the valley bellow. Being situated above everybody else environmentally, socially, and intellectually resulted in a bipolar philosophy in which the good environmental life on the mountaintop and Tvergastein were juxtaposed with the evils of Ustaoset and urban life in general. This contrast would, as subsequent chapters will show, evolve in Næss's and his friends' thinking into a more general contrast between the clean and environmentally healthy Norway and a contaminated and unhealthy globe in need of Norwegian environmental wisdom. The high mountains represented what was clean, while the city was dirty and polluted, both literally and morally. Living simply on the mountain was crucial to the philosophers' aesthetic and moral image. Tvergastein served Næss and his ecophilosophy friends as a material representation and manifestation of a rich life with simple means. First among these friends was Zapffe.

THE LAST MESSIAH

"The mark of annihilation is written on thy brow. How long will ye mill about on the edge? But there is one victory and one crown, and one salvation and one answer: Know thy selves; be unfruitful and let there be peace on Earth after thy passing." This was the dramatic conclusion in Zapffe's essay, "The Last Messiah" (1933). Written in a poetic and somewhat archaic Norwegian, he argued that we humans are "a noble vase in which fate has planted an oak."[10] As he saw it, humans are, with our ability to reason, the only species to be reflective enough to realize that the earth would be better off without us and that we consequently should be unfruitful and voluntarily cease to exist as a species. Our ability to reason was an accidental mutation gone wrong; it was an overdeveloped skill, and it made us unsuitable for our environment. As the earth will never satisfy human needs, hopes, and desires, we might as well leave it, instead of destroying it further. Or so was the revelation of the Earth's last Messiah.

Zapffe's deeply pessimistic view on the human condition was informed by a "biospheric" perspective he developed in the 1930s as a doctoral student of Næss. The result was Zapffe's thesis, *Om det tragiske* (On the

---

[10] Peter W. Zapffe, "The Last Messiah" (1933), in Peter Reed and David Rothenberg (eds. trs.), *Wisdom in the Open Air* (Minneapolis: University of Minnesota Press, 1993), 40–52, quotes pp. 52, 39. Zapffe's emphasis. *The Bible*, Isaiah 61, 1–3.

Tragic), published in 1941 when he was forty-two years old. Næss was, at the time, a full professor in philosophy, and only three years younger than his most talented student. Today Zapffe is almost unknown to the English-speaking community, but read by "everybody" in Norway. His works (sold in numerous editions) includes poems, philosophy, fairy tales, plays, and accounts from his mountaineering life. As an eminent storyteller, humorist, critic, iconoclast, and passionate environmentalist, his pessimist voice was taken seriously. Indeed, having read and marveled at his captivating essays was the secret handshake of environmental thinkers in Norway, who would rarely quote them but constantly reflect on them.

If one were not to follow Zapffe's advice to be unfruitful and die out, what was then the human place in the environment? What was the human condition on Earth? Over the years, Zapffe himself would follow the various answers to such questions from ecologists, fellow philosophers, sociologists, and others from the academic sideline. He did not actively pursue university positions, but worked instead as an adjunct in philosophy. Yet, as an esteemed mountaineer, well-known technical climber, poetic writer, and environmentalist, he was the grandfather figure of philosophizing about nature. His argument – that we should leave Earth alone and die out – was not only the most radical, but also the best-articulated position in the room. And this was not a theoretical stand, as Zapffe refused to have children himself. He could not be ignored. As will be shown, Næss was greatly influenced by his student, as his thinking about ecology can be understood as an answer to Zapffe's pessimism. Indeed, the history of Norwegian ecophilosophy can be understood as an ongoing reflection on how to address Zapffe's arguments. The outdoor seminars at the remote Stetind Mountain in the north of Norway, which have been regular events since the mid-1960s, may serve as an example of this.

Though Zapffe certainly had a close circle of admirers among technical climbers in the 1930s, it was not until the late 1960s that his writings were canonized as required readings for outdoor enthusiasts, culminating with his 70th birthday in 1969. Compilations of his essays, a book-length philosophical introduction to his thinking, and a bestselling anthology about outdoor life entitled *Barske glæder* (Harsh Pleasures, 1969) would hit the bookstores. Using the metaphor of archeology, a reviewer in one of the nation's largest newspapers noted that a "philosophical son of the wild [has been] dug up" by publishers from obscure and forgotten journals.[11]

---

[11] Rolf Gudevold, "Filosofisk villmarkssønn graves frem," VG, Dec. 19, 1969, 30, RA. Peter W. Zapffe, *Essays og epistler* (Oslo: Gyldendal, 1967); *Barske glæder og andre*

While the larger public would muse on Zapffe's cunning reflections on the deeper meaning of sleeping bags, a new generation of young nature philosophers would take his academic work very seriously.[12] Two of them, to whom this chapter will turn shortly, were the philosopher Sigmund Kvaløy (1934–2014), who was the editor who "dug op" the essays in *Barske glæder*, and Nils Faarlund (b. 1937) who saluted Zapffe by asking: "Why waste your time on Marcuse and Habermas? Zapffe has already addressed the essential."[13]

First formulated in the early 1930s, Zapffe's thinking can in its modus operandi be compared to Oswald Spengler's *Der Untergang des Abendlandes* (*The Decline of the West*, 1918–23). By making analogies to the evolution of organisms, Spengler argued that the Western world had reached its last stage in life, and that the European civilization was at its decline. Zapffe would not make such sweeping generalizations about civilizations, but would place his pessimistic view of human future on a similar organismic footing. Næss was, while serving as his advisor in the late 1930s, committed to the Vienna school of positivism, and he consequently told Zapffe that he had to provide a scientific base for his thinking. Following this advice, Zapffe turned to Estonian-born German biologist Jakob von Uexküll's work on the ways in which different species experience and react to their *Umwelt* (environment). In a similar manner, Zapffe analyzed the human condition within the environment and concluded that our "tragedy" was that our mental capacities made us overqualified to live in our *Umwelt*, the Earth.[14]

In 1961 he restated his pessimistic stance on humanity in a "biosophic perspective" in which he would, for the first time in Norwegian philosophical debate, introduce ecology as one of the keys to understanding the human condition. The "survival of the fittest and the luckiest" captures well the biological drama of human life in the natural world, he argued. Yet the tragedy is that our inner metaphysical aspirations do not match

---

temaer fra et liv under åpen himmel, Sigmund Kvaløy (ed.) (Oslo: Gyldendal, 1969). Guttorm Fløistad and Per Fredrik Christiansen (eds.), *Peter Wessel Zapffe: Dikt og drama* (Oslo: Universitetsforlaget, 1970). Guttorm Fløistad (ed.), *Peter Wessel Zapffe* (Oslo: Pax, 1969).

[12] Sigmund Kvaløy, "Peter Wessel Zapffe og verdien av utemmet natur," in Guttorm Fløistad and Per Fredrik Christiansen (eds.), *Peter Wessel Zapffe: Dikt og drama* (Oslo: Universitetsforlaget, 1970), pp. 252–65.

[13] Nils Faarlund, "Peter Wessel Zapffe 70 år," *Mestre fjellet*, 1 (1970), 19.

[14] Peter W. Zapffe, *Om det tragiske* (Oslo: Gyldendal, 1941). Oswald Spengler, *The Decline of the West* (New York: Oxford University Press, 1991).

our ecological condition.[15] The fact that our aspirations will never be satisfied on Earth, did not entitle us, Zapffe argued, to carry on with ecological destruction. Indeed, in the late 1950s he published what became some of the best-known – and certainly best articulated – prose in defense of nature conservation that exists in the Norwegian language. He wrote a very moving "funeral hymn" to the Gaustad Mountain, for example, when NATO built a trolley inside it for military purposes.[16] All of this made Zapffe the most prominent philosopher of nature and most famous advocate of nature conservation and outdoor life in the late 1960s. The fact that he operated outside academia made him even more attractive to a new generation of counterculture students suspicious of accredited philosophizing.

Zapffe and Næss were close friends as members of the Alpine Club, yet over time their friendship would run aground. They had different personalities: Zapffe was not particularly lighthearted, while Næss was playful and easygoing. "Sickness enters the body 'by the kilo' and has to be fought back 'gram by gram'," Zapffe would say, noting that "longstanding friendships often end because of a trifle."[17] The "trifle" that ended their friendship was the fact that Næss would not endorse Zapffe's book *Den logiske sandkasse* (The Logical Sandbox, 1966) for the syllabus for core courses in logic, and instead favored his own *Endel elementære logiske emner* (Some Elementary Logical Topics, 1941–75).[18] Having limited sources of income, Zapffe was in need of the royalties that Næss, in effect, denied him. This tension between them would place Zapffe in the margin of university life at the very moment that his thinking rose to the forefront of environmental philosophy and activism.

THE NATION'S PHILOSOPHER

Næss was also marginalized in the late 1960s by a new generation of students engaged in social and environmental affairs. At the time he very

---

[15] Peter W. Zapffe, "Biosofisk perspektiv" (1961), in Jan Brage Gundersen (ed.) *Essays* (Oslo: Aventura, 1992), pp. 141–68, quote p. 149.
[16] As in Zapffe's "Avskjed med Gausta" (1958) or "Farvell Norge" (1958), both in *Barske glæder* (Oslo: Cappelen Damm, 2012), 127–8, 129–35.
[17] Zapffe, "Biosofisk perspektiv," p. 149.
[18] Gjefsen, *Arne Næss*, 254–6. Jørgen Haave, *Naken under kosmos: Peter Wessel Zapffe, en biografi* (Oslo: Pax, 1999). Arne Næss, *En del elementære logiske emner* (Oslo: Universitetsforlaget, 1941–1985). Peter W. Zapffe, *Den logiske sandkasse: elementær logikk for universitet og selvstudium* (Oslo: Pax, 1966).

much represented the older generation and the old way of doing things, and thus he felt he urgently needed to refashion himself as a philosopher of current affairs.

How did this come about? Back in the 1930s, Næss would not reflect on environmental issues. Instead, he devoted his thinking to epistemological and logical positivism. Before building Tvergastein, he had visited Vienna as a student to attend the famous logic seminar arranged by Moritz Schlick in the academic year of 1934/1935. He stayed in the city for fourteen months, and during this time he attended daily sessions of psychological therapy with Edward Hitschmann, a student of Sigmund Freud, as a part of a program to study psychology. Upon returning to Norway he went straight back to his parent's cabin at Ustaoset where he wrote his PhD thesis on philosophy of science, which is clearly inspired by the Vienna Circle.[19] It got modest attention.[20] He then wrote a treatise on the meaning of the word "truth" as it was conceived of by those who are not professional philosophers, specifically based on semantic surveys of high-school students.[21] It was an untraditional way of pursuing philosophy, to say the least. Later in his life, the treatise would hurt his reputation, especially after Willard Van Orman Quine pointed to it as an example of "unimaginative" philosophy.[22]

After finishing the treatise on truth, in the academic year of 1938/1939, Arne and Else Næss went to the University of California to study behaviorism with Edward C. Tolman. Arne recalls studying the psychology of rats by tracking their movements and behavior in specially made labyrinths. Though there is only evidence of him giving a philosophical lecture in Tolman's archives,[23] Næss apparently worked on a manuscript about

---

[19] Arne Næss, *Erkenntnis und wissenschaftliches Verhalten* (Oslo: Vitenskapsakademiet, 1936).
[20] Except for a lukewarm review in the journal *Theoria*, I have not found any references to Næss among followers of the school of logical positivists of the period. Hendrik Josephus Pos, "Erkenntnis und wissenschaftliches Verhalten," *Theoria*, 3 (1937), 117–24.
[21] Arne Næss, *"Truth" as Conceived by Those Who Are Not Professional Philosophers* (Oslo: Vitenskapsakademiet, 1938).
[22] Willard Van Orman Quine, "Methodological reflections on current linguistic theory," *Synthese*, 21 (1970), 386–98, quote p. 392. Quine refers misleadingly to Arne Næss, *Interpretation and Preciseness* (Oslo: Dybwad, 1953). Anonymous, "Too high a price?" *Times Literary Supplement*, June 5, 1969, 616.
[23] Letter from Nancy K. Innis to the author, Mar. 12, 2001, PA. Arne Næss "Abstract of Professor Hull's Informal Seminar," May 25, 1939, Archives of the History of American Psychology, Special Collections, University of Akron.

3 The Ecophilosophers

the rat experiments (which is lost) based on research he did with Kurt Lewin.[24] In any case, Næss returned to Norway as a behaviorist.

"I have learned as much from my rats as I have learned from Plato," Næss told a competitor for the vacant position in philosophy at the University of Oslo, who had an interest in platonic metaphysics. The Platonist did not answer.[25] A debate arose at the time between those in favor of philosophy in the tradition of German *geisteswissenschaft*, and those who favored empirical philosophy inspired by the Vienna Circle. Of the three applicants Næss was the only empiricist, and, as the committee had a bias in that direction, he got the position at the young age of twenty-seven. His opponents saw his appointment as evidence of a problematic instrumental, material, rational, and reductive view of humanity taking hold on the field of philosophy.[26]

With the onslaught of war, Næss became involved in the secret intelligence unit XU of the resistance movement, along with other science students, such as the radio-chemist Ivan Th. Rosenqvist and the botanist Eilif Dahl (discussed elsewhere in this book).[27] While working for XU, some of his students (who were involved in other aspects of the resistance) had to cover for him, by making it look as if he was working while he was actually out delivering secret documents. This, at least, could possibly explain why the book *Oppgavesamling i logikk* (Set of Exercises in Logic, 1942*)*, written by one of his students, Mia Berner (1923–2009), was published with Næss's name on the cover.[28] Whatever the motive, Næss would subsequently often get help from students in the production of teaching material and textbooks, thus blurring the boundary between authorship and assistantship.

After the war Næss published his major work *Interpretation and Preciseness* (1953), which became the foundation for the "Oslo group"

---

[24] Neither Tolman nor Lewin mention Næss in their books or articles. Arne Næss, *Notes on the Foundation of Psychology as a Science* (Oslo: Universitetets studentkontor, 1948), 1.
[25] Næss quoted in Rothenberg, *Is It Painful to Think?* p. 48. The remark came in a conversation with Andreas H. Winsnes.
[26] Jorunn Sem Fure, *Inni forskningsalderen, Universitetet i Oslos 1911–1940* (Oslo: Unipub, 2011), 278. Fredrik W. Thue, *Empirisme og demokrati* (Oslo: Universitetsforlaget, 1997), 46–9.
[27] Einar Sæter and Svein Sæter, *XU – i hemmeleg teneste 1940–1945* (Oslo: Det Norske Samlaget, 1995), 33–7, 50, 77, 133. Ragnar Ulstein, *Etterretningstjenesten i Norge 1940–45* (Oslo: Cappelen, 1989–1990), vol 1: 170–9, vol 2: 97–9. Kristian Ottosen, *Liv og død: Historien om Sachsenhausenfagene* (Oslo: Aschehoug, 1990).
[28] Arne Næss, *Oppgavesamling i logikk med kommentarer* (Oslo: Universitetets studentkontor, 1943). Mia Berner, "Min debut," *Prosa*, 1 (2006), 48.

in semantics, which, despite recognition at home,[29] failed to gain influence internationally due to a series of harsh reviews,[30] of which an evaluation by Benson Mates from the University of California, may serve as an example. A major point in Næss's treatise was a formal procedure on how to generate precise interpretations of texts by developing alternative readings. Mates created a telling illustration of the procedure to readers of the prestigious *Philosophical Review* by using two interpretations of the statement "He yawned," which were "He yawned voluntarily" and "He yawned involuntarily."[31] The problem with Næss's semantics was not that they were incorrect, but that they were boring.

Yet some people did find the Oslo group interesting, most notably the biologist Julian Huxley, who, in his capacity as the Director-General for the United Nations Educational, Scientific and Cultural Organization (UNESCO), hired Næss to study the semantics of the ambivalent word "democracy" as it was used in different political systems. It was an effort to find a unified language in a world of increasing bipolar Cold War tensions. Næss was, to Huxley, an example of a positivist philosopher who took science seriously. Under UNESCO's patronage, and with the assistance of his student Stein Rokkan (1921–79), who later became a well-known sociologist, Næss consequently surveyed professors and leading intellectuals from around the world about the semantic meaning and different interpretations of the word "democracy." The result was a fine contribution to objective political *science* about what democracy *is* while avoiding unscientific suggestions about what democracy *should be*.[32]

---

[29] Thue, *Empirisme og demokrati*, 1997.
[30] Georg Henrik von Wright, "Symbolsk logikk," *Journal of Symbolic Logic*, 14 (1949), 185. Arne Næss, *Symbolsk logikk* (Oslo: Univeristetets studentkontor, 1948). Karl Egil Aubert, "En del elementære logiske emner," *Journal of Symbolic Logic*, 17 (1952), 288. Frithjof Fluge, "Interpretation and preciseness," *Journal of Philosophy*, 45 (1948), 502–3. Anders Wedberg, "Interpretation and preciseness," *Journal of Symbolic Logic*, 14 (1949), 54–5. Anders Wedberg, "Interpretation and preciseness," *Journal of Symbolic Logic*, 15 (1950), 73–4. Anders Wedberg, "Interpretation and preciseness," *Journal of Symbolic Logic*, 15 (1950), 204. Carl G. Hempel, "Toward a theory of interpretation and preciseness," *Journal of Symbolic Logic*, 15 (1950), 154. Stephen Toulmin, "An empirical study," *Philosophical Review*, 65 (1956), 116–18.
[31] Benson Mates, "Interpretation and preciseness," *Philosophical Review*, 67 (1958), 546–53, quote p. 552.
[32] Richard McKeon (ed.), *Democracy in a World of Tensions* (Chicago: University of Chicago Press, 1951), 447–512. The monograph got the most damaging reviews, see Ferdinand A. Hermens, "Democracy in a world of tensions," *Review of Politics*, 13 (1951), 375–81. Frank K. Klingberg, "Democracy in a world of tensions," *Western Political Quarterly*, 4 (1951), 337–8. Vidar Enebakk, "UNESCO og vitenskapshistoriens relevans," in John Peter Collett, Jan Eivind Myhre, and Jon Skeie (eds.), *Kunnskapens*

3 The Ecophilosophers

To many delegates of the United Nations, it was rather shocking to read about Stalinism as one possible semantic interpretation of democracy, and despite a large amount of interest UNESCO never reprinted the report. To scholarly critics, the study and a follow-up done by the Oslo group were seen as "merely another useless addition to such compendia of semantic jiu-jitsu covering this field of definitions and re-definitions."[33]

Næss had more on his mind than semantic jiu-jitsu, which is apparent in his first popular philosophy book. Mahatma Gandhi's teaching of non-violence came to the forefront of his thinking after his first visit to Pakistan with the Alpine Club in 1950. Back in Oslo he gave a lecture series about Gandhi's political ethics, which resulted in a book co-authored with the young sociologist Johan Galtung (b. 1930), published in 1955.[34] Gandhi's teachings, they argued, could be helpful in finding a peaceful transition away from the Cold War deadlock. In 1960 Næss followed up with a shorter version, which was translated into English and published as *Gandhi and the Nuclear Age* in 1965. Here he argued that people from the West had much to learn from Gandhi, given the threat of nuclear Armageddon. The book became Næss's first international success with favorable reviews in academic as well as popular journals.[35] What was especially encouraging with *Gandhi and the Nuclear Age* was its appeal to young students. This was much welcomed, as his previously published books and articles had been generally ill received or ignored.[36]

Næss also had to deal with the intellectual and social jiu-jitsu of teaching and maintaining the *Examen philosophicum* courses at the

---

betingelser. Festskrift til Edgeir Benum (Oslo: Vidarforlaget, 2009), pp. 124–45. Anker, *Imperial Ecology*, 233.

[33] Joseph S. Roucek, "Democracy in a world of tensions," *American Sociological Review*, 16 (1951), 425–6. L. Jonathan Cohen, "Democracy, ideology and objectivity," *Mind*, 67 (1958), 411–13. Arne Næss, Jans A. Christophersen, and Kjell Kvaløe, *Democracy, Ideology and Objectivity: Studies in Semantics and Cognitive Analysis of Ideological Controversy* (Oslo: Oslo University Press, 1956).

[34] Johan Galtung and Arne Næss, *Gandhis politiske etikk* (Oslo: Tanum, 1955). Arne Næss, "Gandhis lære og situasjonen i dag," *Forskningsnytt*, 5 (1960), 2–4; *Gandhi og atomalderen* (Oslo: Universitetsforlaget, 1960).

[35] Arne Næss, *Gandhi and the Nuclear Age*, Alistair Hannay (trs.) (Totowa, NJ: Bedminster Press, 1965). P. F. Power, "Gandhi and the nuclear age," *Annals of American Academics*, 368 (1967), 201. Mulford Q. Sibley, "Gandhi and the nuclear age," *Political Science Quarterly*, 82 (1967), 144–5. D. Dalton, "Gandhi and the nuclear age," *Political studies*, 15 (1967), 251–2. Anonymous, "Gandhi and the nuclear age," *Choice*, 3 (1967), 364. Lore L. Kopp, "Gandhi and the nuclear age," *Kyklos*, 19 (1966), 764–5. H. Arthur Steiner, "Gandhi and the nuclear age," *Western Political Quarterly*, 19 (1966), 547–8.

[36] Peder Anker, "Arne Næss sett utenfra," *Samtiden*, 4 (2002), 4–19.

University. All students entering universities in Norway were required to take a preliminary set of core courses designed to introduce them to the academic culture and methodology, which meant studying logic and the history of philosophy for one semester. As higher education was (and still is) cost free in Norway, and as most studies were open to all, the chief social function of the tests was to filter out unsuitable candidates. Thus, for many, these tests would be their only academic experience. The tests have a rich history reaching back to the founding of the University of Oslo in 1811 and even further back to antecedents of preliminary exams of 1675 taken at the University of Copenhagen. Much of the identity of Norwegian academic life was built around these courses: they served as a model to other universities in the nation, as a demarcation of inclusion in and exclusion from academia, and would consequently cause a continuous stream of public debates.[37]

The preliminary courses were important to the philosophers who put much energy into maintaining their social position. The courses were a key for recruitment of both students and faculty to the field, they meant employment opportunities for graduate students, and the syllabus provided the professors with healthy royalties from textbooks. Næss was in the focal point of these courses, as the only tenured professor in philosophy until 1967 (when the student of Quine, Dagfinn Føllesdal (b. 1932), was called upon and given a full professorship by the President of the University).

Næss was the author of a textbook on the history of philosophy and a textbook on logic, which were both required readings, not only in Oslo, but at most institutions of higher education in Norway.[38] These textbooks gave him a public persona as most scholars and students in Norway would read them at some point in their lives. Moreover, most students at the University of Oslo (with the exception of students in medicine) would have heard his lectures, usually given in the University's largest auditorium. This gave him not only royalties (which he used to hire assistants), but also an important platform to spread his thinking. For at least three decades his philosophy of semantics and interpretations were part of the required curriculum and the subject of intricate exam questions for freshman students with absolutely no interest in the topic. Yet the art of semantic precession when providing an interpretation of a

---

[37] John Peter Collett, *Historien om Universitetet i Oslo* (Oslo: Universitetsforlaget, 1999).
[38] Arne Næss, *Filosofiens historie*, 2 vol., various editions (Oslo: Universitetsforlaget, 1961–2001); *En del elementære logiske emner*.

text was of paramount importance in order to stay on campus, as a forty percent failure rate on the exams was not uncommon.

With the number of students at the University of Oslo growing from about 6,000 in 1946 to more than 16,000 in 1970, teaching and managing *Examen philosophicum* became a daunting task for Næss and his growing cohort of teaching assistants and adjuncts. More and more time was spent in Oslo, and less and less in the mountains at his beloved Tvergastein. In his personal life, his wife, Else, had divorced him back in 1946. In 1955 he married the psychology student Siri (born Blom, 1927), which prevented him from seeing his children, but not from having to pay dependency allowances into the 1960s. His salary was a necessity to keep these commitments, though Siri became financially independent after her studies. By 1969 Næss was fifty-seven years old, had paid his family dues, and was craving the personal freedom and the simpler mountaineer life he had once had at Tvergastein. As a professor, "I am only functioning instead of living," he said, and – to everyone's surprise – he resigned.[39]

MASTERING THE MOUNTAINS

His desire for freedom and longing for outdoor life was not the only reason Næss quit. When he signed his resignation letter in January he did not do so in his office, as it was occupied by radical leftists and followers of Mao. Indeed, the entire Department of Philosophy was in turmoil due to a weeklong occupation of all its facilities by students demanding a new curriculum, which in effect meant abandoning the syllabus arranged by Næss. He represented decidedly the old guard with his Vienna Circle-inspired philosophies of semantics, interpretations, definitions, and empiricisms. This was not an asset to students who thought of positivism as another word for the administrative nihilism they associated with the technocratic military complex of the Vietnam War.[40] Besides, technical climbing and bourgeois mountaineering did not prepare the mind for a revolution. If Næss wanted to leave his professorship, so much the better.

---

[39] Arne Næss, "Hvorfor fratre som professor?" note, 1969, AN.
[40] Per Fredrik Christiansen and Helge Vold, *Kampen om universitetet: Boken fra filosofistudentenes aksjonsuke* (Oslo: Pax, 1969). Fredrik W. Thue and Kim G. Helsvik, *1946–1975 Den store transformasjonen*, vol. 5, *Universitetet i Oslo 1811–2011* (Oslo: Unipub, 2011), pp. 331–42.

Not all the students would throw themselves upon the treasure troves of Lenin, Stalin, and Mao's philosophies. Some of the more sophisticated criticism of Næss's positivism began with the essay *Objectivism and the study of man* (1959) written by Hans Skjervheim (1926–99). In it he criticized the unity of science doctrine of logical empirisism from Næss's early work, arguing that it led to a society in which nature, humans, and society could be treated as objects for social management.[41] In 1969 Skjervheim's criticism of Næss was applied to environmental issues in a seminar, and he continued with a series of papers that later emerged in the anthology *Vassdrag og samfunn* (Watercourse and Society, 1971), edited by the ecologist Rolf Vik. Here Skjervheim would lash out against "technocratic politics" in which "one would plan and execute things over people's heads" when implementing hydropower projects.[42] The young sociologist Øyvind Østerud (b. 1944) and the philosopher Gunnar Skirbekk (b. 1937) followed suit with similar criticisms.[43] To them hydropower politics illustrated the pitfalls of the managerial politics of power-socialism that emerged in the context of Næss's positivist thinking. The fact that one possible interpretation of positivism would endorse hydropower development and exploitation of nature must have been a wakeup call to Næss, as he would soon agree with his critics.

Two people who were consistently loyal to Næss through this period were Sigmund Kvaløy and Nils Faarlund. Kvaløy was a thirty-five-year-old former student of Næss, who had grown up in the picturesque mountain village of Lom. He later moved to Eidsvold to attend high school, where he became friends with Faarlund, and he subsequently became an air mechanic for the Norwegian Air Force. His chief interests were philosophy and jazz, while he also, along with Næss, Zapffe, and Faarlund, pursued mountaineering interests as an active member of the Alpine Club and was a regular visitor at Tvergastein.

Faarlund was not a student of Næss but shared his interests. He had a graduate degree in engineering and biochemistry, and had been trained in landscape architecture and ecology in Hannover, Germany. As an active

---

[41] Hans Skjervheim, *Objectivism and the Study of Man* (Oslo: Universitetsforlaget, 1959). Rune Slagstad, *Positivisme og vitenskapsteori* (Oslo: Universitetsforlaget, 1979).
[42] Skjervheim, "Naturvern og politikk," p. 181; "Økologi og normalpolitikk." In, Svein Gjerdåker, Lars Gule, and Bernt Hagtvet (eds.), *Den uoverstigelige grense* (Oslo: Cappelen, 1991), pp. 85–101.
[43] Østerud, "Naturverdier og samfunn." Skirbekk, "Distriktshøgskolar." Øyvind Østerud, *Konflikt og administrasjon: en studie i norsk kraftutbygging*, MA thesis (Oslo: Department of Political Science, University of Oslo, 1970).

member of the Alpine Club he too had interests that drifted toward the field of philosophy. In 1967 he founded his own school, the Norwegian Mountaineering School, located in the mountain village of Hemsedal, while he also lectured in the art and practice of outdoor life at the Norwegian School of Sport Sciences in Oslo from the time of its inauguration, in 1968, onwards. His lectures became legendary among environmentalists seeking a combination of philosophical training and practical experience in dealing with the wild, and his tiny Mountaineering School evolved into a hub for practical and philosophical reflections on how to live within the environment. Many of these reflections were published in the school's journal *Mestre fjellet* (Mastering the Mountains, 1968–99), which was devoted mostly to cross-country skiing in the mountains, glacier hiking, and technical climbing. Faarlund was the chief editor and a regular contributor, and there were contributions from his outdoor-life friends and fellow alpinists, including his childhood friend Kvaløy, who would regularly contribute articles on the existential experience of wilderness while climbing, and the pitfalls of mass tourism.[44]

Faarlund saw "outdoor life as a means to pursue scientific research," and ecologists took him seriously by sending students – in need of courses in everything from tenting and outdoor cooking to survival strategies for harsh winter climates – to his school.[45] This type of knowledge was important for carrying out research in the field. Along with the practical know-how came an ethic of "using without consuming" nature and ecological reflections about the Earth being like a giant spaceship.[46] To Faarlund, being "outside" was actually being "inside," as nature was the only true human home. Following this line of reasoning, he formulated his own philosophy of "free-air-life" of the "free-air-person," thinking which inspired not only Næss, but the inner circle of Norway's most devoted young mountaineers and environmentally concerned ecologists.[47]

---

[44] Sigmud Kvaløy, "Klatring og naturopplevelse," *Mestre fjellet*, 2 (1968), 11–12; "Kommersiell turisme – informasjonsmengde null?" *Mestre fjellet*, 3–4 (1968), 29.

[45] Nils Faarlund, *Friluftsliv: hva – hvorfor – hvordan* (Oslo: Norges idrettshøyskole, 1974, 11. Nils Faarlund, "Hva mener vi med friluftsliv?" *Mestre fjellet*, 15 (1973), 4–6.

[46] Nils Faarlund, "Vi må lære å bruke naturen – uten å forbruke den," *Mestre fjellet*, 1 (1968), 5–8; "Jorden – et lite romskip i det golde universet," *Mestre fjellet*, 1 (1970), 5–6.

[47] Næss, "The Norwegian roots of deep ecology." Faarlund, "Hva mener vi med friluftsliv?" "Friluftsliv – a way home," in Børge Dahle (ed.), *Nature: The true home of culture* (Oslo, 1994), pp. 21–6. Sigmund Kvaløy Setreng, "Inside nature," in Børge Dahle (ed.), *Nature: The True Home of Culture* (Oslo, 1994), pp. 29–37.

Kvaløy worked as an assistant to Næss in 1961, and he submitted an MA thesis under his supervision in 1965 on the philosophy of music communication. Both Næss and Kvaløy were passionate about music, the former of classical piano and the latter of jazz, which raised the question of how to "talk about music" within Næss's philosophy of semantics.[48] Kvaløy's thesis is decidedly an alternative piece of scholarship for which Zapffe's biosophy would serve as the underlying methodology, while Kvaløy, at the same time, tried to be more empirical than his advisor. He would, for example, substitute page numbers with a metric system of measuring text. In any case, the thesis led to a lectureship in philosophy starting in 1967, and subsequently to a fellowship at the Institute of Biology where he would have his office next to the ecologist Ivar Mysterud, who became a close friend.[49] Mysterud would over the years engage not only Kvaløy but also Næss in numerous discussions. It was through these conversations that many of the Oslo philosophers and other non-biologists learned about ecological concepts and terms.

Though Næss had resigned in early 1969, for practical reasons he still had to remain in his position until the end of the year. However, he did not stay on campus. In his office he left Kvaløy in charge with "a pile of the Department's letter-paper with Arne's signatures – in the middle, further down, and at the bottom" so that Kvaløy could expedite things as he thought best.[50] He also left his seminar "Nature and Humans" in Kvaløy's hands, which enabled Kvaløy to use Næss's name as he saw fit and to organize the seminar according to his own mind.

Kvaløy did not stay put in the office, but instead invited Næss to drive what was known as the "Hippie Trail" from Oslo to Varanasi, along with Galtung in his Peugeot station wagon. As they left in January 1969, the trip marked Næss's newfound freedom, while for Kvaløy and Galtung it was an attempt to heal the wounds inflicted by the students' occupation of the Philosophy Department. Judging from Kvaløy's charming flashback,

---

[48] Sigmund Kvaløy, *Musikk-kritikk og kommunikasjon*, MA thesis (Oslo: Department of Philosophy, University of Oslo, 1965), n.p. cm. 30. Nils Faarlund, "Sigmund 70 år!" *Tindeposten*, 4 (2004), 16–19.

[49] Sigmund Kvaløy Setreng, "Ivar Mysterud, inspirator og medarbeider – hvordan økofilosofien ble til," in *Med lua i hånden* (Oslo: Department of Biosciences, 2008), 37–9.

[50] Sigmund Kvaløy, "To økosofier i Norge; deres begynnelse og en del til," *Norsk filosofisk tidsskrift*, 37 (2002), 117–25, quote p. 122.

the eighteen-day road trip undoubtedly created some of his very fondest memories.[51] Upon arrival in Varanasi, they celebrated Gandhi's centenary with a month of peace researching at the Gandhi Institute. They then went on a vacation in Nepal, where they climbed to the top of the mountain Nagarkot, north of Katmandu, before flying back to Norway where Næss would continue to enjoy the mountains at Tvergastein. To Kvaløy the trip was like a "pilgrimage" to pristine beautiful mountains. He would, on his way home, travel through Iran and climb Mount Damavand together with Stein Jarving (1945–2005), who, taken with Kvaløy's thinking, went home to found an ecologically inspired steady-state peasant community.[52]

THE MARDØLA DEMONSTRATIONS

Upon his return to Oslo, Kvaløy saw the exhibition, *Og etter oss ...* (And after us ...), created by students of the Oslo School of Architecture in June 1969. They drew attention to the possibility of children "after us" having no environment to live in.[53] Built in specially designed tent structures and placed at the University Square at Karl Johansgate in the center of the city, it was seen by 80,000 people in Oslo alone. It was a travelling exhibition of ecological doom and gloom inspired by Vik's popular writings about the eco-crisis and sponsored by the Norwegian Society for the Conservation of Nature.[54] With the help of dramatic graphic design, the architects crystallized a clear message about the world "after us" being either a disaster or a harmoniously balanced ecosystem. The self-sufficient ecological harmony of tomorrow was depicted as a remote picturesque Norwegian landscape, while the epicenter of environmental problems of

---

[51] Kvaløy, "To økosofier i Norge." Anonymous, "Norske vitenskapsmenn på biltur til India," *VG*, Jan. 9., 1969, RA.
[52] Sigmund Kvaløy, "Nagarkot og Damavand – to pilgrumsturer vinteren 1969," *Mestre fjellet*, 2 (1969), 5–6, 16; "Forord," in Stein Jarving, *Likevektssamfunn* (Karlsøy: Regnbuetrykk, 1976), 6–7.
[53] Anonymous (eds.), *Og etter oss ...* (Oslo: Norges Naturvernforbund, 1970); "Og etter oss," *Norsk Natur*, 5 (1969), 34–9. Erling Amble and Henning Hansen, *Det kapitalistiske boligproblemet* (Oslo: Arkitekthøgskolen i Oslo, 1970). Erling Amble, *Avfallsbehandling og planlegging* (Oslo: Arkitekthøgskolen i Oslo, 1973).
[54] Rolf Vik, "Kjenner vi vårt miljø? – Tar vi vare på det?" in anonymous (ed.), *Fem på tolv: En bok av vitenskapsmenn om vår mulige fremtid* (Oslo: Gyldendal, 1968), pp. 125–54; "Trusselen mot miljøet," in Anonymous (ed.),*Verden i dag* (Oslo: Gyldendal, 1969), pp. 79–92. Eilif Dahl, *Økologi for ingeniører og arkitekter* (Oslo: Universitetsforlaget, 1969).

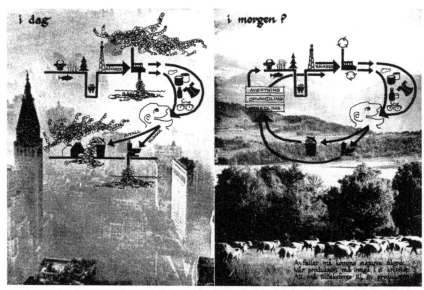

FIGURE 3 Today (left) and tomorrow? (right). From the exhibition *And after Us ...* (1970) with the polluted society of New York to the left and the future ecological self-sufficient society in Norway to the right.
Courtesy of the Norwegian Society for the Conservation of Nature

today was at the Madison Square Park in New York City (Figure 3). This either/or dichotomy between the polluted city or the clean remote countryside, a future of industrial doom or ecological bliss, came to dominate the environmental debate in Norway thanks to Kvaløy and the emerging group of ecophilosophers.

Kvaløy was very impressed with the exhibition, and invited the architects to join hands with students of ecology, philosophy, and members of the Alpine Club, to create *Samarbeidsgruppa for natur- og miljøvern* (Co-working Group for the Protection of Nature and the Environment), known in the English-speaking community as the Deep Ecologists. Those with a philosophical bent met at the Nature and Humans Seminar at the University of Oslo, which was a subsection of the association. In the fall semester of 1969 they turned Næss's seminar into a hub for students and scholars who were both seeking deeper philosophical answers and questioning how humans should (and should not!) relate to the natural world. With the formal termination of Næss's professorship at the end of the semester, they would continue to meet at the Department of Zoology where Ivar Mysterud worked. In the spring of 1970 they became known

3 The Ecophilosophers

as the Ecophilosophy Group. Though the ecophilosophers were to have an equal say, Kvaløy would actually set the agenda of the seminar. His mountaineering interests from the Alpine Club would initially dominate with his philosophizing on the aesthetic and recreational quality of the environment in general, and mountains and waterfalls in particular. As a consequence, the historian of science Nils Roll-Hansen accused the ecophilosophers of favoring an "escape from the daily reality to the vacation paradise" of untouched nature.[55]

Kvaløy and the Co-working Group quickly gained a significant following of students seeking radicalism within the acceptable sociopolitical boundaries of the Cold War. Soon the Co-Working Group grew into "Groups" as new subsections formed in Oslo, Bergen, and beyond. Ecophilosophy was not the only active group. Some chose to focus on coordinating the logistics of the broad-spanning association, while others chose to study hydropower and its alternatives, and others again chose to read aesthetics.[56] A significant number would gather to read Gandhi and study non-violence, inspired by Galtung and Næss's book, and discuss whether or not direct action was a possible way to save pristine nature.[57] The groups were allied with neither the left nor the right, and thus were non-threatening in the bipolar political terrain. "What we stand for may seem archconservative and at the same time extremely radical," Kvaløy argued. "We will therefore strike in both directions, and we will be attacked from all sides."[58] They became an effective hard-hitting association attacking hydropower developments in particular.

The Co-working Groups were indeed "attacked from all sides" in their dramatic attempt to save the Mardøla river from hydropower development during the summer and early fall of 1970. The Mardøla Waterfall was Norway's highest waterfall (and the 4th highest in the world). One of the activists, the technical climber and novelist Finn

---

[55] Nils Roll-Hansen, "Naturvern eller menneskevern?" *Dagbladet*, 20. Apr. 1970, RA; "Hva slags natur ønsker vi?" *Samtiden*, 82 (1973), 285–95.
[56] Sigmund Kvaløy, "Samarbeidsgruppen for Natur og Miljøvern: Mini historikk og aktualia," *Mestre fjellet*, 1 (1970), 7–8, 17.
[57] Guttorm Larsen, "Naturvern og ikkevold," *Mestre fjellet*, 3–4 (1969), 11, 16.
[58] Sigmund Kvaløy, 30 Oct. 1969, quoted in Finn Alnæs, *Svart snø eller samvern: Dokumentarbok fra en brytningstid* (Oslo: Aschehoug, 1976), 1. Bredo Berntsen, "Radikal, liberal, konservativ – en grenseoppgang," *Samtiden*, 81 (1972), 178–85. Paul Hofseth, "Fra estetikk til økopolitikk," in Bredo Berntsen (ed.), *Fra blomsterfredning til økopolitikk: Østlandske Naturvernforening 1914–1974* (Oslo: Østlandske Naturvernforening, 1975), pp. 44–50. Frode Gundersen, "Utviklingstrekk ved miljøbevegelsen i Norge," *Sosiologi i dag*, 2 (1991), 12–35.

Alnæs, would climb up right beside the waterfall and take dramatic pictures of it, which he later published in a booklet.[59] Though the demonstrators had support from the neighborhood peasants who would lose their water, they got no sympathy from local workers in the neighboring valley, who could not care less about the waterfall and saw nature more as a resource for securing their jobs. They threatened the activists with violence and displayed banners, such as: "HIPPIES GO HOME – IF YOU HAVE ONE" and "TRY SOMETHING NEW – WHAT ABOUT A JOB?"[60] Most of the demonstrators had jobs. The underlying issue at stake was instead how to understand nature. Was it a resource to be used to secure jobs, a scenic place in which to enjoy country-life vacations, or an environment in which humans should learn to live in a different way? Thanks to well-organized Co-Working Groups, the demonstration evolved into a dramatic – yet still strictly non-violent – civil disobedience sit-in with more than 150 protesters blocking the construction site, followed by 50 journalists covering the story. In the end the demonstrators left voluntarily or, as in the case of Kvaløy and Næss, were carried away by the police. The whole event was made into an innovative documentary film, *Kampen om Mardøla* (The Battle for Mardøla, 1972), in which cameras were hand-held, creating a visual language of authenticity (as opposed to the official newsreels by the Norwegian national television).[61] For more than a decade the Mardøla demonstration was the defining event for environmentalism in Norway, in which taking a stand on this or other hydropower developments would distinguish friends from foes.

The demonstrators failed to save the waterfall, but managed to create an intense public debate around the nature of democracy and the importance of nature conservation. Though there were sympathies in the press for nature conservation, the confrontational mode of the Co-Working Groups caused general head shaking. There is not much of a tradition in

---

[59] Alnæs, *Svart snø eller samvern*.
[60] Jon Grepstad (eds.), *Mardøla: Dokumentasjon og perspektiv* (Oslo: Samarbeidsgruppa for natur og miljøvern, 1971), 24. Nils Petter Gleditsch, Åke Hartmann, and Jon Naustalslid, *Mardøla-aksjonen* (Oslo: Institute for Peace Research, 1971). Sigmund Kvaløy, "Mardøla, miljøvern og maktspill," in Brunjulf Valum (ed.), *Øko-katastrofe* (Oslo: Grøndahl, 1971), pp. 153–62; "Mardøla, Masi: Vår egen tid" (interview), in Magnar Mikkelsen, *Masi, Norge* (Oslo: Cappelen, 1971), pp. 97–111. Ketil Lehland,"Mardøla etc., især det siste," *Samtiden*, 79 (1970), 517–22. Fredrik H. Moe (et al. eds.), *Miljøvern og kraftutbygging* (Oslo: Aschehoug, 1970).
[61] Oddvar Einarson, *Kampen om Mardøla*, 90 minutes (Oslo: Elinor Film, Apr. 1972).

3 The Ecophilosophers

Norway for civil disobedience, so this method of engaging the public became a topic of debate. One of the demonstrators, the philosopher Hjalmar Hegge (1920–2003), would take the lead, using much ink defending it as a way of protecting the nation against majority rule, technocratic bureaucracy, and the excesses of a representative democracy.[62] It is also clear from the press cuttings that the Co-Working Groups got either the credit or blame for what happened at Mardøla, and that Kvaløy was seen as the groups' leader.

Perhaps the best articulated rhetorical defense of Kvaløy and the Co-Working Groups came from Zapffe and his wife Berit. In a long feature article, "At the Crossroad," they would give "Sigmund Kvaløy and his collaborators our warmest thanks" for their heroic fight against "the moral pollution of government services with their bulldozer souls." They then juxtaposed the defenders of nature's *"egenverdi"* (inherent values) with those who were willing to sell the land so that we would all end up "chewing aluminum" (a chief product of hydropower electricity).[63] In their rage against hydropower, philosophical nuances were lost. With the question being whether or not to build a dam, the environmentalists got all the praise, while defenders of a dam were labeled in derogatory terms. This black and green way of thinking would, from now on, continue in the soon-to-be-written ecophilosophies of both Kvaløy and Næss. Kvaløy had edited Zapffe's *Barske glæder*, he had used Zapffe's biosophic perspective as a methodology in his master thesis, and he knew him personally through a common interest in technical climbing. Yet getting this kind of public endorsement from the old and much-respected philosopher, who was most certainly not known for scattering praise, must have been most heartwarming.

Næss did not participate in organizing the Mardøla demonstration, nor did he take much interest in environmental issues before the summer of 1970. He had published a short statement on the importance of creating a national park in 1965, and that was about it.[64] He was brought to Mardøla by Kvaløy in the last dramatic week of the demonstration, so that his fame in Norwegian intellectual life could bring momentum and attention to the cause (Figure 4).

---

[62] Hjalmar Hegge, "Mardøla-demonstratene og demokratiet," *Morgenbladet*, Aug. 11, 1970, HH; "Parlamentarismen som avgud," *Morgenbladet*, Aug. 21, 1970, HH.
[63] Berit and Peter Zapffe, "På skilleveien," *Morgenbladet*, Sept. 3, 1970, HH.
[64] Arne Næss, "Naturen ebber ut," in *Innerdalen bør bli nasjonalpark* (Oslo: Grøndahl, 1965), pp. 8–9.

FIGURE 4 Sigmund Kvaløy being taken away by the police at Mardøla, 1970. Photo: NTB. Courtesy of Scanpix

A photo of the nation's philosopher being taken away by the police was published twice in the press (and over time it has become perhaps the best known image of him) though only one journalist asked Næss questions while he was at Mardøla.[65] Instead it was Kvaløy who did most of the talking. Yet Næss's sense of being involved with the young became a formative experience for him, given the occupation of the Department of Philosophy only one year earlier. He would, from now on, devote himself to the environmental cause, and thereby refashion himself as a philosopher of current affairs.

Unlike his resignation letter and newspaper interviews from 1969 – which are all about being liberated from the professional duties of a professor – he would now claim that he resigned so that he could devote himself to saving the environment. This, at least, is what he said on the book jacket of his next book, *The Pluralist and Possibilist Aspect of the*

---

[65] Imange first printed in Anonymous, "Mardøla-aksjonen innendørs," *VG*, Sept. 14, 1970, 27, HH; Anonymous, "Mardøla–forøk i ikke-vold" *A-Magasinet*, Sept. 1970, HH. Næss interviewd by Halvor Elvik, "Mardøla-aksjonen følges ikke av nye demonstrasjoner," *Dagbladet*, Aug. 13, 1970, HH.

Scientific Enterprise (1972). His critics, who gave the book the most damaging reviews,[66] took it as an admission of philosophical failure: "Many philosophers have been led to the conclusion that philosophy is futile, but few have taken their own arguments seriously enough to act on them. On the book jacket we read that Arne Næss resigned from this Chair of Philosophy at Oslo in order to devote himself more fully to the urgent environmental problems facing man."[67] Though it is true that Næss did not resign to devote himself to the environmental problems, in retrospect he probably wished he had or thought he had actually done so, as Næss after the summer of 1970 would spend the rest of his life thinking about the deeper meaning of ecology and spend his time arguing in favor of environmentalism. And he would pick up the philosophical ammunition to do so from the Ecophilosophy Group.

THE ECOPHILOSOPHY GROUP

The Mardøla experience would energize and radicalize the philosophy students attending Næss's former Nature and Humans Seminar. This was especially the case in the thinking of Kvaløy, the charismatic seminar leader. The fall of 1970 would prove to be their most active and productive semester. Why had they been unable to save the Mardøla waterfall? The majority of Norwegians were in favor of the hydropower development and opposed to the demonstrations. A survey from the time shows that fifty-seven percent of Norwegians thought the non-violent civil disobedience practiced at Mardøla was wrong.[68] Yet the activists thought they had done the right thing and that history would judge them differently. At the seminar it was time for soul searching.

The attendees were both students and faculty members with an interest in philosophy, and most of them had been at Mardøla that summer. Besides Kvaløy, Faarlund, and Næss, these participants included: Finn Alnæs, Reidar Eriksen, Per Garder, Jon Godal, Jon Grepstad, Hjalmar Hegge, Paul Hofseth, Oddmund Hollås, Karl Georg Høyer, Johan Marstrander, Ivar Mysterud, Sven Erik Skønberg, Ragnhild Sletelid,

---

[66] Arne Næss, *The Pluralist and Possibilist Aspect of the Scientific Enterprise* (London: George Allen and Unwin, 1972). R. P. M., "The pluralist and possibilist aspect," *Review of Metaphysics*, 27 (1974), 804–5. Ervin Laszlo, "The pluralist and possibilist aspect," *Philosophical and Phenomenological Research*, 34 (1973), 279–80.
[67] Noretta Koertge, "The pluralist and possibilist aspect," *British Journal for the Philosophy of Science*, 24 (1973), 313–16, concluding quote.
[68] Nils Faarlund, "Expertokrati eller demokrati," *Mestre fjellet*, 1 (1971), 3.

Svein Smelvær, Erna Stene, Arne Vinje, Jon Wetlesen, and probably many more.[69] Some of these attendees would, in subsequent years, shape Norwegian environmental academic, political, and bureaucratic institutions. At the seminar they read texts and discussed topics ranging from ecology to psychology of perception, social psychology, anthropology, nature philosophy, pedagogy, information theory, thermodynamics, and cybernetics. This was all done in an effort to understand the state of national and global environmental problems as revealed from the periphery of Mardøla.

The debate would gradually swing from aesthetic appreciation of scenic nature and waterfalls to broader ecological concerns about the harmony of nature as expressed by Mysterud and other ecologists. What started with reflections about the recreational quality of mountains would thus lead to social criticism concerning industrialism's lack of steady-state and ecologically informed thinking about the human status within the environment. It was not a shift without tensions. In the end, broader eco-political ideas for a steady-state society came to dominate the discussion. The alternative vision that would gradually emerge was that of a self-supporting nation in equilibrium inspired by fishermen-peasants who had once lived in harmony with Mardøla's ecological balance. This alternative nation could then be the model for the world to admire. The Western consumer society and mentality, along with population growth, was at the heart of the environmental problem, and life at Mardøla was the remedy.[70]

Kvaløy would cast the Mardøla conflict as being that of a reckless industrial society destroying a harmonious nature. As he saw it, the natural ecological complexities of the environment were broken down by the industrial society, and the task of the environmentalist was to stop the process by non-violent means.[71] After the Mardøla experience, he adopted from ecology the idea that complex ecosystems are more robust than a simple one. Inspired by Herbert Marcuse, he argued that a complex human society would have a better chance of surviving the environmental crisis than the "one dimensional man" of the industrial society.[72]

---

[69] Sigmund Kvaløy Setreng, "Økokrise – glimt fra det norske økofilosofiske forsøket," in *Den uoverstigelige grense* (Oslo: Cappelen, 1991), pp. 102–16.
[70] J. Chr. Keller, "Naturfilosofi – en omvurdering av moral," *Mestre fjellet*, 4 (1970), 4.
[71] Sigmund Kvaløy, "Mardøla – samvær som kampform," *Mestre fjellet*, 1 (1971), 5–13.
[72] Sigmund Kvaløy, "Økologi – vannkraft – samfunn," *Norsk natur*, 6 (1970), 150–62. Marcuse, *One Dimensional Man*. Hjalmar Hegge, "Økonomisk vekst eller økologisk likevekt," *Samtiden*, 81 (1972), 74–81.

What living in an ecological steady-state society entailed was rather unclear, though it implied some sort of agrarian "green lung" away from industrial and urban pollution.[73]

Despite his resignation, Næss would stay on campus in the fall of 1970 in order to participate in the seminar. This is evidence of Næss taking a sincere interest, as he was known to be impatient with long meetings. He was intrigued by the questioning of the way in which humans treat the environment, and began taking notes for a possible publication. The first result of this came in a short article in which he questioned the ethics of the Alpine Club, including the "conquest" of mountains.[74] Næss also kept his office on the condition that teaching assistants to the *Examen philosophicum* course also could use it. In the fall of 1970 one of them was the philosopher Thomas Krogh (b. 1946). He challenged Næss to rethink his philosophy of science, and he must have been quite successful at it, as Næss would, from then on, give up much of his positivist informed thinking and come to agree with his opponents.

This turnaround came about when Næss co-wrote a preliminary textbook about the philosophy of science with Krogh, which was meant for the University's core courses. Krogh had Marxist sympathies and encouraged Næss to analyze the social relations of science, including "the dark sides of the gigantic science apparatus of our century."[75] In working with Krogh, Næss was confronted with the writings of John Bernal and other socialist critics of the role of science in society. As a result he came to agree with the critiques that the good things science can do are overshadowed by an abuse of science, which has led and will lead to a dehumanized society and environmental degradation of the planet.

As an alternative, Krogh and Næss pointed to the way "a scientific field's general ecology" or "ecosophy" addressed environmental problems in an interdisciplinary fashion, as "ecosophy" was understood by

---

[73] Sigmund Kvaløy, "Eikesdal-Grytten i naturvernåret – utbyggernes glansnummer," *Norsk natur*, 6 (1970), 69 (quote); "Mardøla, miljøvern og maktspel," *Senit*, 3 (1970), 4–11; "Mardøla – samvær som kampform," *Mestre fjellet*, 1 (1971), 5–13; "Mangfold er livsstyrke!" *Byggekunst*, 53 (1971), 126–8.
[74] Arne Næss, "'Conquest of mountains': A contradiction?" *Mestre fjellet*, 1 (1970), 13, 17; "De forskjellige holdningene til fjell opp gjennom tidene," *Mestre fjellet*, 2–3 (1970), 19, 22.
[75] Arne Næss with Thomas Krogh, *Vitenskapsfilosofi: utvalgte emner til innledning* (Oslo: Universitetsforlaget, 1971), 1.

Wetlesen (at the time a graduate student of Næss and attendee of the seminar).[76] Unfortunately, there is no other record of what Wetlesen meant by "ecosophy" in what is probably the first appearance of this term in Norwegian (and international) literature. Næss would soon adopt it as his own term in formulating his own environmental ethic. Krogh and Næss argued that the ecological sciences could offer a constructive alternative to the pitfalls of its competing disciplines. "We are all 'thrown into' our cosmic, social and individual existence," they noted. "It is impossible to resign from the ecological context."[77] Thus, it was imperative to develop a new interdisciplinary mode of research that addressed shared ecological needs and existence.

By the spring semester of 1971, the Nature and Humans Seminar was simply known as the Ecophilosophy Group. According to Mysterud's recollections, Næss was one of the few who took notes at the meetings, and he would transform them into a couple of lectures entitled *Økologi og filosofi 1* (Ecology and Philosophy 1), which he gave at the Student Association's meeting at the University of Tromsø in May the same year. In them he introduced, for the first time, his "ecosophy":

[It is] a type of philosophy, which takes an identification with all life as its point of departure in this life-giving environment. It establishes in a way a classless society within the entire biosphere, a democracy in which we can talk about a justice not only for humans, but also for animals, plants, and minerals. And life will not be conceived as an antagonism to death, but as being in interaction with surroundings, the life-giving environment. This represents a very strong emphasis on everything hanging together and the idea that we are only *fragments* – not even parts.[78]

The eco-centric notion of humans as fragments of a larger whole was inspired not only by the ecological view of species as fragments in nature's energy-circulation patterns, but also by Chinese social philosophy. The politics of Mao were popular with those young philosophers who had occupied Næss's former department, and Mao's collected poetry had just been translated into Norwegian. They include a rich body of metaphors concerning nature's harmony, which caught Næss's attention. Mao's poem "In Praise of the Winter Plum Blossom" may serve as an example:

---

[76] Næss with Krogh, *Vitenskapsfilosofi*, p. 2.
[77] Næss with Krogh, *Vitenskapsfilosofi*, p. 55.
[78] Arne Næss, *Økologi og filosofi 1* (Oslo: Department of Philosophy, 1971), p. 54. Næss's emphasis.

> Spring disappears with rain and winds
> and comes with flying snow.
> Ice hangs on a thousand feet of cliff
> yet at the tip of the topmost branch the plum blooms.
>
> The plum is not a delicious girl showing off
> yet she heralds spring.
> When mountain flowers are in wild bloom
> she giggles in all the color.[79]

Næss would read this as an analogy of the individual's relationship to society and the ecosystem. In China, he claimed, "the human being is not in the foreground, but instead an entire 'ecological system,' in which humans take part as fragments. Mao has perhaps kept a part of the classical Chinese outlook. In his political poetry, animals, plants, minerals, and landscape elements have a place that seems ludicrous to rough Western observers."[80] The harmony of nature Mao endorsed, it is worth noting, was tough on both nature and humans, treating them indeed as fragments. Yet Næss would, like many of his contemporaries, fail to see this. Eager to gain acceptance, he wrote a sympathetic booklet about Mao, and included Mao's thinking in a revised edition of his history of philosophy textbook in which he went out of his way to appeal to young radicals, as it was required reading for *all* the students at the University. The textbook had, for a while, a portrait of Mao on its front cover.[81]

Næss's adaptation of Mao's thinking should be understood as an opportunistic attempt to gain acceptance among students and not as a sincere endorsement of Maoism. Moreover, the Mao quotes are taken from a first "preliminary edition" that in its physical shape looks more like a manuscript for circulation within the Ecophilosophy Group than a real publication. Though there are some references to Barry Commoner and Paul Ehrlich, American nature philosophers such as Aldo Leopold are notably absent from the analysis and did not enter Norwegian ecophilosophical debate until the 1980s (as discussed in Chapter 9). Moreover, as will be argued in Chapter 4, by 1973, Mao would fade away from Næss's

---

[79] Mao Tsetung, "In praise of the winter plum blossom," *The Poems of Mao Tse-tung* (New York: Harper and Row, 1972), 107. Mao Tsetung, *Mao Tsetungs dikt*, Kjell Heggelund and Tor Obrestad (trs.) (Oslo: Gyldendal, 1971).

[80] Næss, *Økologi og filosofi 1*, p. 59.

[81] Arne Næss, *Mao Tsetung: massene filosoferer* (Oslo: Universitetsforlaget, 1974); *Filosofiens historie*, 6 eds., vol. 2 (Oslo: Universitetsforlaget, 1980). Judith Shapiro, *Mao's War against Nature: Politics and the Environment in Revolutionary China* (Cambridge: Cambridge University Press, 2001).

ecophilosophical writings and would be replaced by Gandhi. Indeed, the academic year of 1970–71 was, for the ecophilosophers, a period of asking questions rather than coming up with well-thought-out and articulated answers. A comprehensive "eco-philosophy" addressing the environmental crisis, Kvaløy noted in his orientation to the seminar in May 1971, "has not yet been formulated." It was still in "the sketching stage."[82] That would soon change, as the next chapter will show, as the ecophilosophers and activists from Mardøla would formulate a platform for what was soon to become known as the Deep Ecology movement.

---

[82] Sigmund Kvaløy, *Øko-filosofi: Litteraturliste og orientering til studenter og andre interesserte* (Oslo: Samarbeidsgruppa for natur og miljøvern, May 1971), 10 pages, quote p. 1. Bjørn L. Hegseth, *Miljøkunnskap – miljøvern: Forsøk på en oversikt* (Trondheim: NTH-trykk, 1970).

4

The Deep Ecologists

ENVIRONMENTAL ORIENTALISM AND THE CRITIQUE OF THE WEST

In the summer of 1971 the three Norwegian ecophilosophers Sigmund Kvaløy, Arne Næss and Nils Faarlund traveled to the periphery, to the faraway mountains of Nepal. It was a transformative experience for them. In the lives of the Sherpa, they saw an alternative environmentally friendly way of living. Upon their return to Norway they wrote about Sherpa life as an Oriental harmony juxtaposed with the harsh Occidental values of their own Western culture. This demarcation between Oriental ecological wisdom and the Occidental stupidity of the West eventually came to frame the deep ecological debate at home and abroad. Sherpa life was to be a model for all Norwegians, and Sherpa-informed Norwegians were to be a subsequent model for the world.

The road trip from Oslo to Varanasi back in 1969, coupled with subsequent mountain climbing in Nepal, left the ecophilosophers with fond memories. For the summer vacation of 1971 Næss and Kvaløy decided to return to Nepal, this time with their fellow climber Faarlund. The journey was to be a two-month-long "pilgrimage" to the remote mountain village of Beding in the Rolwaling valley of Nepal, and a vacation from the "garish, narcotic nightmare" of the European "consumer society."[1] They were following a larger trend of people searching

---

[1] Sigmund Kvaløy, "Likevektssamfunnet: Sherpasamfunnet i Rolwaling," *Aftenposten A-Magasin*, 7–9, 1972, reprinted in Sigmund Kvaløy, *Økokrise, natur og menneske* (Oslo: Samarbeidsgruppa for natur og miljøvern, 1973), 65–88, quotes pp. 65, 86.

Oriental wisdom and alternatives. In the early 1970s thousands of Western hippies went to Katmandu where they had their own "Freak Street" by Durbar Square in which they nurtured unconventional lifestyles and imagined Nepalese ways of living.[2]

The ecophilosophers' financial backing was less exotic, as the journey was paid for by Næss's half-brother, Erling (1901–93), who had become enormously wealthy through industrial whaling in the 1930s and shipping of oil in the 1960s. He took the ecophilosophers along to prove his cultural sincerity for Nepal to Prince Gyanendra, whose personal financial interest he secured by establishing the state-sponsored Royal Nepal Shipping Corporation (in a country without a seacoast). Out of courtesy, they gave the ecophilosophers the necessary travel permissions to visit the closed-for-tourists village of Beding. Naturally, the ecophilosophers kept very quiet about this high-level financial agenda behind their journey. Erling, on the other hand, was open about his business with the corrupt Nepalese, and he amused himself by hiring a helicopter so that he could see with his own eyes what the village of Beding was like, visit his half-brother, and hand out blankets and clothes to the poor.[3] At the time, it should be noted, the environmental impact on climate from all this airborne traveling was hardly known.

The philosophers were not there to seek shipping opportunities, but to climb the mountains of an environment in which they believed people truly lived in harmony with nature. It took, in all, twenty-six Sherpa transporters walking for eight days to make this happen, though they tried to keep their climbing equipment to a minimum. When they arrived they were amazed to find people entirely untouched by Western influences. For two months they lived in a true "steady-state community," Kvaløy observed, with "balance and peace between the people and the nature they depended on."[4] To him the lifestyle of Beding was an antidote to the consumer and ecologically destructive societies of the West. The difference between work and leisure, the unfortunate and the elite, and means and ends were here blurred, as people of Beding only strove for the common good of the village and the environment. It was a "self-supporting society" that "we should envy – especially since we soon will arrive at

---

[2] Torbjørn Ydegaard, *Sherpa – Folket under Everest* (Holte: Skarv, 1988), p. 20.
[3] Erling Dekke Næss, *Autobiography of a Shipping Man* (Colchester, UK: Seatrade Publications, 1977), pp. 252–4. Kvaløy, *Økokrise, natur og menneske*, p. 67.
[4] Kvaløy, *Økokrise, natur og menneske*, pp. 65, 75.

the bitter end of the eco-crisis," Kvaløy argued.[5] Faarlund was equally convinced: "The 110 inhabitants of Beding knew how we should behave in order to prevent the danger of an ecocatastrophe," he claimed.[6] Similarly, Næss later praised the Sherpa community in his Deep Ecology writings as "an extremely nature-friendly non-violent Buddhist culture in an extremely unwelcoming nature."[7] Indeed, in comparison Næss saw Westerners as "worse pests" than the leeches that attacked his own body while he was hiking.[8]

Upon his return to Oslo, Kvaløy concluded that life in Beding was a viable alternative to the industrial society of the European economic growth. In the fall of 1971 he spun into a hectic state of writing, enlarging, and rewriting a previous manuscript about the importance of ecological complexity for social steady-state communities. He now argued that harmonious living depended on being within a community with dense biodiversity.[9] This idea evolved into a larger manuscript in which he argued that such living entailed putting an end to industrial society and turning to agrarian living. His model was the Sherpa, whose "settlement in rhythm with the landscape" conveyed "a lifestyle providing lasting security" for their community through "interaction with nature."[10] Such a "Life Necessities Society" was, in comparison with the standardized "Industrial Growth Society," rich in cultural and ecological complexity and should thus be a model for Norwegian interaction with the environment.[11] The breakdown of ecological complexity caused by the Western industrial world would inevitably lead to an eco-catastrophe, he argued, and it was thus imperative to learn from the good people of Beding: "Sherpa and similar societies should be regarded as a vital source of knowledge to us today."[12]

---

[5] Sigmund Kvaløy, "Rolwaling – et livssamfunn i likevekt," *Mestre fjellet*, 15 (1973), 11–12.
[6] Nils Faarlund, "Hvorfor," *Mestre fjellet*, 13 (1972), 6–7, quote p. 6; "Bidrag til en ekspedisjonssosiologi," *Mestre fjellet*, 13 (1972), 11–14.
[7] Arne Næss, *Økologi, samfunn og livsstil*, 5th ed. (Oslo: Universitetsforlaget, 1976), 309; "Mountains," *The Trumpeter*, 21 (2005), 51–4.
[8] Arne Næss, "Blodigle og menneske," *Mestre fjellet*, 13 (1972), 18.
[9] Sigmund Kvaløy, *Øko-filosofisk fragment: Kompleksitet og komplikasjon* (Oslo: Samarbeidsgruppa for natur og miljøvern, June 1972), 43 pages.
[10] Sigmund Kvaløy, *Økokrise, natur og menneske* (Oslo: Samarbeidsgruppa for natur og miljøvern, 1973), p. 131.
[11] Kvaløy, *Økokrise, natur og menneske*, p. 135.
[12] Sigmund Kvaløy, "Ecophilosophy and ecopolitics: Thinking and acting in response to the threats of ecocatastrophe," *The North American Review*, 259 (Summer 1974), 16–28, quote p. 24.

Faarlund agreed, yet he concluded that one could not expect to re-educate Western grown-ups in the Oriental wisdom. Instead he put his efforts and hopes into educating the very young Norwegians in Sherpa lifestyle, as their "eco-life" was "free-air-life" and a viable alternative to the advancing eco-crisis. Only by learning to live inside nature could one build a "bridge from a human centered (techno-culture) to a human integrated way of understanding nature (eco-culture)," he argued.[13]

Næss was equally convinced about the virtue of Sherpa living. His subsequent lectures about ecology and philosophy, held in the fall of 1971 and spring of 1972, served as evidence of ecological balance not being "an invention of theoreticians, since it has been and to a certain extent still is praxis today in certain societies, as in the Sherpa communities in Nepal."[14] His earlier endorsement of Maoism was now toned down by underlying a revised version of his ecosophy that "Mao has *perhaps* kept a part of the classical Chinese outlook" with respect to humans being fragments in nature.[15] Instead, Næss brought Gandhi's principles of non-violence and his own reading of the Bhagavad-Gita to the core of his ecosophy, arguing the individual self was a fragment within the large Self (with capital S, being the world as a whole). This sense of being a fragment reflected Næss's personal experiences of minuteness when climbing mountains like Tirich Mir, his meeting with Sherpa lifestyle in Beding, as well as the ecologists' research into energy circulation in the Finse region. His ecosophy was, in effect, a philosophy of the Alpine Club with an Oriental touch.

Together Kvaløy, Næss, and Faarlund would recount their experiences in Beding in three articles for the weekend magazine of the largest newspaper in Norway. For most Norwegians this was their first report about life in Nepal, and the articles catalyzed a decade-long longing for Sherpa life, with technical climbers and tourists using their vacations to follow in the footsteps of the ecophilosophers.[16] Yet the lives of the Sherpa did not differ radically from the vanishing class of hardworking fishermen-peasants who once lived as fjord and mountain

---

[13] Nils Faarlund, "Om økoliv," *Mestre fjellet*, 15 (1973), 7–9, quotes pp. 7, 8; "Friluftsliv i barne- og ungdomsskolen," *Vår skole*, 61 (1975), 196–209. Jon Skjeseth, *Mennesket og biosfæren: Biologi for Gymnasets Grunnkurs* (Oslo: Fabritius, 1972).

[14] Arne Næss, *Økologi og filosofi: Et økosofisk arbeidsutkast*, preliminary 3rd ed. (Oslo: Department of Philosophy, 1972), 7.

[15] Næss, *Økologi og filosofi*, 3rd ed., p. 177.

[16] See, for example, Arne Næss Jr., *Drangnag-Ri: Det hellige fjellet* (Oslo: Orion, 1995).

farmers of Norway.[17] What the ecophilosophers' audience saw in their reports from Nepal was thus the superiority of traditional Norwegian mountain and fjord culture, which reemerged in the 1960s in the weekenders' romance with their vacation cottages, many of which were located where there had once been self-sufficient steady-state farming communities. In the following decades Kvaløy would visit Beding no less than twenty-two times, resulting in a long stream of glowing reports about the village's life being in ecological harmony. This he contrasted to the ills of industrial society, represented by the Mardøla hydropower development and the capitalism of the European Community.

THE REFERENDUM ON THE EUROPEAN COMMUNITY

When the ecophilosophers returned to Norway, they immediately became involved in what was perhaps the most divisive political decision of the decade for the nation. Should Norway join the European Community (EC)? The organization was a product of post-war Europe and their aim was to create peace between former enemies using economic integration through a common economic market and a custom union. The philosophers were decidedly against membership because of EC's destruction of nature by the means of capitalism. Upon their return from Nepal they joined a massive political mobilization for a "NO" vote during the year leading up to the scheduled national referendum on September 25, 1972. It became an exacting year, in which almost every publication and appearance addressed the issue. It also created a unified stand in which the many different shades of leftism, counterculture, environmentalism, agrarianism, and also some conservatives would unite in a common call for the rejection of EC membership.

The critiques generally stressed that a membership would undermine national sovereignty, create a greater distance between the people and their political leaders, and, most importantly, undermine Norwegian ownership to natural resources, weaken agriculture, and open up opportunities for callous exploitation of the scenic Norwegian environment by large multinational European companies. The ecophilosophers were also decisively against a membership, and they spent large amounts of time and energy explaining that being outside the European Community was a

---

[17] Sigmund Kvaløy, "Norwegian ecophilosophy and ecopolitics and their influence from Buddhism," in *Buddhist Perspectives on the Ecocrisis*, Klas Sandell (ed.) (Kandy, Sri Lanka: Buddhist Publication Society, 1987), pp. 49–72.

viable alternative path. Indeed, the overwhelming majority of environmentally concerned scholars would lean toward voting against the membership. To them Norway was to be a beacon of green hope, an example of environmentally alternative ways of living that could inspire Europeans into a better lifestyle.

The Co-working Groups for the Protection of Nature and the Environment, hereafter the Deep Ecologists, were prime movers of the debate. They made their case in the booklet *Dette bør du vite of EF* (This you should know about EC, 1972) written by Kvaløy, Erling Amble, Botolv Helland, Karl G. Høyer, Magne Lindholm, Dag Norling, and Arne Vinje. Here they made it clear that the European Community's sole focus on economic growth and industrial development would lead to a global ecological collapse, the depopulation of rural Norway, and an unfortunate centralization of politics. "*Outside* EC Norway will have a greater opportunity to follow an independent and long-term environmental politics by managing our natural resources in harmony with ecological insight," they argued.[18] While a vote in favor of the European Community could only lead to a disastrous future for the environment and Norwegian self-sufficient rural communities. "[T]his industrial-serving mega-society seeks to break apart the established *diversity* of sturdy self-governed and heterogeneously, traditional-colored local communities, – and replace them with a uniform system of government that presupposes uniform social units and a uniform culture: a simplification that increases vulnerability, according to the science of ecology."[19] Selling a remarkable ten thousand copies, the booklet served as the Deep Ecologists' chief unifying text.[20]

The booklet became a sort of manifesto for the Deep Ecologists as they evolved from a small University group to a national organization with branches in various places in Norway that focused on diverse topics, such as petroleum policy, fishery, pollution, ecophilosophy, or local environmental problems. Deep Ecologists were unified into a national organization in 1973, and by 1974 the organization had at least twenty-five active local study groups who arranged a whole range of activities and demonstrations aimed at saving the environment. They would focus on deeper

---

[18] Samarbeidsgruppa for natur og miljøvern (attributed to Erling Amble, Botolv Helland, Karl G. Høyer, Sigmund Kvaløy, Magne Lindholm, Dag Norling, and Arne Vinje), *Dette bør du vite om EF* (Oslo: Pax, 1972), p. 1.

[19] Samarbeidsgruppa, *Dette bør du vite*, p. 91. Tor Bjørklund, *Mot strømmen: Kampen mot EF 1961–1972* (Oslo: Universitetsforlaget, 1982).

[20] Sigmund Kvaløy, "Demokrati," *(snm) nytt*, 7 (Sept. 1976), 7–9.

questions about the nature of the Norwegian society, such as the nature of capitalism, as the underlying cause of environmental problems. The Deep Ecologists were a fairly politically diverse group of environmentalists representing different political and social temperaments. As an alternative to the national anthem they adopted a translation of the American folk-singer Pete Seeger's *My Rainbow Race* (1973), which became the highest-selling single in Norway that year. It became the unifying song of the counterculture generation. Indeed, as late as 2012, forty thousand people gathered for a sing-along of the song in Oslo against terrorism.

According to the Deep Ecologists, the task of pointing out the new environmental direction would require interdisciplinary approaches and research institutions. Unlike the European Community, which based its policies only on the advice of economists, they thought no sole academic discipline should determine the future. A viable path forward would need the analysis of a cluster of disciplines working in close collaboration to address the complexity of ecological crisis and the way out of it. Thus, interdisciplinary environmental research was intrinsically linked with an alternative vision for Norway outside the European Community. In the Cold War divide, it was also important to show that this environmental alternative did not lead to communism.

In the heat of the debate in 1972, the environmental crisis was the cause that united most students against the European Community. Ecological arguments were also the least threatening to leaders of academic communities worried about a leftward drift among the young. At the University of Oslo, for example, the leadership would promote environmental debates as a way of channeling student radicalism toward a productive end. At the end of February 1972 the Academic Collegium approved a symposium under the heading "Humans-Nature-Environment," which became a significant event, at least in terms of attendance. For three days in a row, between four and five hundred students and staff members packed the largest auditorium on campus to listen to lectures given by established and young scholars alike.

The seminar was opened by the University President Johannes Andenæs who in his speech argued that the time was ripe to address environmental issues head-on, within both society and academia. "Research must be put to use" for the environmental cause, he claimed.[21] Ecological ideas were at the heart of the rest of the seminar. The professor

---

[21] Johs. Andenæs quoted in Anonymous, "Naturvern og forskning," *Nytt fra Universitetet i Oslo*, no. 5, 1972, 1–2, UO.

of botany Eilif Dahl gave the keynote lecture on the need to nurture a "global perspective" on ecological issues, followed by a lecture from the biologist Magnar Norderhaug on "Ecology and social development," and the philosopher Hjalmar Hegge on "Historical perspective on human relationships to nature." The next two days followed suit with a similar set of lectures from different disciplines, including papers and presentations by Kvaløy and the professor of law Carl A. Fleicher.[22] The latter created a stir within his own faculty when he blamed the "gray masses of lawyers" and not the law of the nation for a lack of nature protection.[23] With the exception of Andenæs, all these scholars became key agents in Norwegian environmental debate.

The University's Office of Public Affairs used the seminar for all its worth to showcase the University as progressive, but not leftist. It was reported on the front page of two issues of its news bulletin, and the event was, as a consequence, also widely reported in the national press. The symposium was front page news in Norway's leading engineering bulletin, for example, which reminded its readers about the importance of working in balance with nature.[24] The interdisciplinary nature of the seminar gave the University a public face striving for the common good. Kvaløy, who was known for organizing the illegal Mardøla demonstration and subsequent student activities, was, for example, embraced by university administrators. He was not only given speaking time at the seminar, but also an interview presenting him sympathetically in the official news bulletin.[25]

Students were invited to put up a poster exhibition outside the auditorium about ongoing environmental research. The student newspaper followed suit with reports from the seminar and an interview with Kvaløy. Here he called for a massive "scientist boycott" of research supporting the industrial society, and encouraged scientists to get out of their "disciplinary boxes" and engage in interdisciplinary "activist research" to solve environmental problems.[26] The Deep Ecologists at the University were also given due coverage with a lengthy presentation

---

[22] Anonymous, "Menneske – natur – miljø," *Nytt fra Universitetet i Oslo*, no. 3, 1972, 1–3, UO.
[23] Anonymous, "Grå masse av jurister, ikke norsk lov hindrer naturvern," *Aftenposten* Mar. 1, 1972, UO.
[24] Anonymous, "Menneske – natur – miljø," *Ingeniør-nytt*, Mar. 10, 1972, 1, UO.
[25] Anonymous, "Natur- og miljøvern – hva nå?" *Nytt fra Universitetet i Oslo*, no. 5, 1972, 2–3, UO.
[26] Sigmund Kvaløy, "Forskerne ut av sine fagbåser!" *Universitas*, Mar. 14, 1972, UO.

by one of its members.[27] They inspired the newspaper to suggest a "new moral" code for student consumerism:

> Thou shall not build your house on good cultivated soil
> Thou shall not kill vermin with poison
> Thou shall not use paper handkerchiefs
> Thou shall not use paper panties
> Thou shall not buy canned beer
> Thou shall not eat French-fries
> Thou shall not have more than two children[28]

This code, written in the spirit of the Mosaic Law, reflects deep-seated Protestant ethics within Norwegian culture. There is no hint of the author poking fun when it comes to the suggestion of a new ethics for consumption of paper handkerchiefs and popular throwaway panties for females. The code should instead be understood as a sincere suggestion for concrete actions that students could engage in immediately.

The Deep Ecologists fashioned themselves as alternative to the conservative, technocratic, and capitalist European Community, but without leftist answers to the ecological crisis. As a result the university leadership began a process that led to the establishment of *Rådet for natur og miljøfag* (The Council for Nature and Environmental Studies). The process began in the fall of 1971 when the Faculty of Mathematical and Natural Sciences established, in response to student demand, an Environmental Committee to coordinate new research and provide an overview of existing research and teaching on the topic. The Committee was chaired by the chemistry professor Lars Skattebøl who, in November 1971, argued that the faculty should offer a cross-disciplinary master's degree on the topic based on a set of courses in the natural sciences.[29] Skattebøl was not known for being inflamed by environmental concern and his proposal failed to include the social and humanistic sciences. This was particularly upsetting to the ecophilosophers who had initiated most of the environmental debates on campus. Therefore, by January 1972, scholars and students from these parts of the University were starting to pitch in with alternative suggestions for a degree encompassing the humanistic and social fields as well.[30]

---

[27] Bjørn Hersoug, "Politikk og økologi: En ikke-autoritative presentasjon av SNM," *Universitas*, Apr. 7, 1972, UO.
[28] Anonymous, "Ny moral," *Universitas*, Apr. 7, 1972, UO.
[29] Anonymous, "Miljøvern ved Det matematisk-naturvitenskaplige fakultet," *Nytt fra Universitetet i Oslo*, no. 17, Nov. 24, 1971, 7, UO.
[30] Anonymous, "Miljøvern ved Universitetet," *Universitas*, Jan. 18, 1972, UO.

The student activities did not go unnoticed by the university headmastership as they represented an opportunity for the President, Andenæs, to display leadership. Interdisciplinary was another word for inter-faculty activity, which brought the decision-making to the highest level of the University, namely him. The "Humans-Nature-Environment" seminar was one such opportunity for him to show leadership (the opening of the new High Mountain Ecology Research Station at Finse in June the same year was another – as discussed in Chapter 2). Environmental research was daring, radical, and progressive, but not leftist. The university leadership could thus benefit from supporting it as a middle course of the Cold War political divide. The Student Parliament voted against Norwegian European Community membership in April 1972, and their chief reason was the lack of environmental protection within what they saw as a capitalist enterprise geared at callous exploitation of nature.[31] Supporting environmental studies on campus was thus also a way of lending support to the vocal anti-European Community movement on campus. Though the Chancellor showed little academic awareness of environmental questions and problems, many members of the Academic Collegium were genuinely interested.

This, at least, seems to be clear if one is to judge from the conference that the Collegium sponsored at the end of May 1972 on the topic of how to organize the field of environmental studies. It was a by-invitation-only event at the scenic Sole Turisthotel, which included just about thirty students, scholars, and Collegium members in total. At the end the conference recommended establishing a Council for Nature and Environmental Studies, and, even more significantly, considered establishing a required core course in environmental studies at the new institution for *all* students entering the University.[32]

The students must have made an impact at the conference, as the new Council's steering committee initially consisted only of students and recent graduates. They were the undergraduates Anne Bjørnebye and Aanund Hylland, the graduate student of sociology Terje Lind, the recent graduate of chemistry Gunnar Brostigen, and, the most senior scholar and graduate of philosophy, Kvaløy.[33] Though tenured professors were soon

---

[31] Ove Molland, "EEC og miljøvern," *Universitas,* Apr. 7, 1972, 3, UO.
[32] Anonymous, "Undervisning og forskning i natur- og miljøfag ved Universitetet," *Nytt fra Universitetet i Oslo,* no. 10, June 20, 1972, 7–8, UO.
[33] Anonymous, "Rådet for natur- og miljøfag," *Nytt fra Universitetet i Oslo,* no. 11, Sept. 5, 1972, 6, UO.

to enter the Council's steering committee, the initial appointments are surely evidence of the Collegium wanting to involve the young in the decision-making process. It also illustrates the respect Kvaløy enjoyed as an intellectual and social mover of ecological debates at the University and beyond. As will be argued (in Chapter 5), the Council came to establish Environmental Studies as a new field in Norway.

These events should be understood in context of increasingly vocal debates on the upcoming national referendum. It became perhaps the most intense public debate in Norway to date, culminating in a vote against membership in the EC with a 53.5 percent margin. For the Deep Ecologists it felt like everything had turned out for the best. They were excited. The fact that they had won gave them clout and boosted their self-confidence. Instead of joining the capitalist forces, the nation could now devote itself to inspiring Europe and the world by turning itself into a successful test case for alternative ecopolitics and lifestyles. Norway was to lead the way for Europe and the world, they argued, and its ecologically inspired scholars were to be the very vanguard of this alternative nation. Having won, the ecophilosophers began looking for a middle ground in the Cold War divide as an alternative to both capitalist and communist answers to the environmental crisis.

DEEP ECOLOGY IN BUCHAREST

It was in the context of the upcoming referendum on the European Community membership that, at the 3rd World Future Research Conference in Bucharest in early September 1972, Næss introduced a "summary" of the debate with the paper "The Shallow and the Deep Ecology Movement." The conference was organized by the World Futures Studies Federation, initiated by Galtung and his Peace Research Institute in Oslo, which hosted its inaugural conference in 1967. What dominated Future Studies in 1972 was *The Limits to Growth* report for the Club of Rome written by, among others, the twenty-seven-year-old Norwegian solid-state physicist Jørgen Randers (b. 1945).[34] Randers was at the time entirely unknown. It was therefore a shock to Næss and Galtung to see this nobody rise to world fame in the field and especially at a conference they sought to control. Chapter 7 will discuss Randers' contribution at

---

[34] Donella H. Meadows, Dennis L. Meadows, Jørgen Randers, William W. Behrens III, *The Limits to Growth: A Report for the Club of Rome's Project on the Predicament of Mankind* (New York: Signet, 1972).

length. At this stage it should only be noted that the MIT group behind the report was part of a larger trend of environmentalists looking for solutions to ecological problems within established social structures. John McHale, a dominating figure in Future Studies circles, may serve as an example. He argued that the world did not need a social, spiritual, or lifestyle revolution, but instead a technologically driven design revolution.[35] The Romanian scholars made up the majority of the people there, both as presenters and in the audience, and they were vocal supporters of technocratic solutions to social and environmental ills. Licinius Ciplea, for example, gave a paper entitled "The Technological Parameters of Long Range Ecological Politics," in which he argued that better technologies and social management could mobilize enough natural resources for the whole world.[36] At the opening of the Bucharest conference, the technocrats thus had a leading role in setting up questions and formulating answers to the ecological crisis.

For Galtung and Næss, the time was ripe in Bucharest to hit back at what they saw as a "shallow" technocratic analysis of the environmental situation. Galtung spoke first with his paper "*The Limits to Growth* and Class Politics," a head-on attack on the lack of social analysis in the report. It represented an "ideology of the middle class," he argued, that was "politically blind" to the interest of the poor. Indeed, the Club of Rome informed recommendations "was staged by 'The International Union of the World's Middle Class'," and one should therefore "fight these cheap and dangerous solutions" in interest of the workers of the world.[37] Galtung had Marxist sympathies. On the wall behind the stage on which he was speaking was a mural "to the glory of socialist labor," and the lecture was simultaneously translated into key Eastern Bloc languages.[38]

---

[35] John McHale, "Future research: Some integrative and communicative aspects," in Robert Jungk and Johan Galtung (eds.), *Mankind 2000* (Oslo: Universitetsforlaget, 1970), pp. 256–63; *The Future of the Future* (New York: George Baziller, 1969).

[36] Licinius Ciplea, "The technological parameters of long range ecological politics" (abstract), in Helen Seidler and Cristina Krikorian (eds.), *3rd World Future Research Conference: Abstracts* (Bucharest: Centre of Information and Documentation in Social and Political Sciences, 1972), pp. 21–2. Pavel Apostol, "English summary," in *Calitatea vieţii şi explorarea viitorului* (Bucharest: Editura politică, 1975), pp. 258–69.

[37] Johan Galtung, *Økologi og klassepolitik*, Therese Henrichsen (trs.) (Copenhagen: Christian Ejlers' Forlag, 1972), 12, 14, 22. Shorter versions published as "Økologi og klassekamp," *Samtiden*, 82 (1973), 65–83; "*The limits to growth* and class politics," *Journal of Peace Research*, 10, no. 1/2 (1973), 101–14.

[38] Jim Dator, "The WFSF and I," *Futures*, 37 (2005), 371–85, quote p. 373. G. F., "Third World Future Research Conference," *Futures*, 4 (1972), 381–2. Irving H. Buchen, "Futuristic Conference in Romania," *The Futurist*, 7 (Feb. 1973), 31–2. Bart van

4 The Deep Ecologists

His class perspective must thus have been welcome to the chief patron of the Bucharest conference, the Romanian President Nicolae Ceaușescu, who saw class-based Future Studies as an integral part of the "Science of Social Management" on which he based his Marxist regime.[39]

When it was Næss's turn to mount the rostrum in Bucharest, he too took an "anti-class posture," but would otherwise stay away from socialist lingo in presenting "The Shallow and the Deep Ecology Movement." It was immediately understood as an onslaught on the "shallow" technocratic perspective of Randers and the Club of Rome. This "restricted movement which has many friends among the power elite," Næss argued, was in danger of consolidating the debate at the expense of "the deeper movement [which] finds itself in danger of being deceived through smart maneuvers."[40] The fact that there were thus two ecological movements was controversial to Ceaușescu's followers, who could visualize only one movement toward one future. Much of the debate at the conference would center on this point. Næss would, as a consequence, change the title of his paper in the published version from "movement" to "movements" to emphasize the pluralism of possible ecological perspectives, and he borrowed the words "Long Range" from Ciplea to indicate that the future could entail solutions to ecological problems other than Ceaușescu's socialist technocracy.

Strangely, no evidence suggests that the most original aspect of the paper, the eco-centrism, raised any interest in Bucharest. The need to develop a *"relational"* (as opposed to humans being above) nature philosophy, along with *"[b]iospherical egalitarianism,"* social and environmental *"diversity,"* *"[a]nti-class posture,"* campaigns *"against pollution and resource depletion,"* promotion of *"[c]omplexity,"* and *"[l]ocal autonomy and decentralization"* were at the heart of the paper.[41] It reflected the relationship to the environment he had himself seen in

---

Steenbergen, "The first fifteen years: A personal view of the early history of the WFSF," *Futures*, 37 (2005), 355–60.

[39] Nicolae Ceaușescu, "Opening remarks," in "Management Science and Futures Studies in Socialist Romania," *Viitorul Social* (Bucharest: Meridiane Pub. House, 1972), pp. 7–18.

[40] The original lecture has only survived in Romanian as Arne Næss, "Miscarea ecolgică superficială si profundă," in Mihai Botez and Mircea Ioanid (eds.), *Viitorul comun al oamenilor: comunicări prezentate la cea de-a III-a Conferintă mondială de cercetare a viitorului, Bucuresti, septembrie 1972* (Bucharest: Editura politică, 1976), pp. 275–83. Later published as "The shallow and the deep ecology movement," Erling Schøller (trs.), *The Trumpeter*, 24, no. 1 (2008), 59–66.

[41] Arne Næss, "The shallow and the deep, long-range ecology movements: A summary," *Inquiry*, 16 (1973), 95–100, quotes pp. 95–8. Næss's emphasis.

Sherpa culture in the village of Beding, Nepal. Though Næss surely believed in this himself, it is important to note that the aim of his article was to capture the spirit of debates he observed among the Deep Ecologists that surrounded him in Oslo, including the thinking of Kvaløy, their spiritual leader. This perspective emerged from a culture of outdoor lifestyle among Norwegian ecologists, or as Næss put it: "Ecological insight and the lifestyle of the ecological field-worker have *suggested, inspired, and fortified* the perspectives of the deep ecology movement."[42]

Back in Oslo Næss discovered that he had lost his paper, and others would later speculate that it "was confiscated by the Ceaușescu-regime" and that it was probably "preserved somewhere in the archives in Bucharest."[43] As it turns out, neither is the case. Næss must have forgotten that the organizers in Bucharest collected most of the papers from the conference so that they could translate them into Romanian, and the original manuscript is no longer in the Romanian National Archive.[44] Upon returning to Oslo without his manuscript, Næss used his notes to compile an abbreviated version which he published in his own journal *Inquiry* as "The Shallow and the Deep, Long-Range Ecology Movements: A Summary" in 1973.[45] Judging from subsequent citations, it became one of the most famous articles in environmental ethics. In Norway it was received as a concise summary of the opinions held among Deep Ecologists, though they preferred "ecophilosophy," "ecopolitics," or (less often) "ecoreligion" to the term "deep ecology."

MARXIST ATTACK

Ironically, the long-range ecology movement Næss spoke of would fade upon his return to Oslo, as Deep Ecology study groups were taken over by Marxist Leninists. At the University of Oslo Deep Ecology died away as a movement in 1973 after a period of internal cleansings and futile debates about the value of democracy.[46]

---

[42] Næss, "The shallow and the deep," (2008), 65.
[43] Editorial comment, Nina Witoszek and Andrew Brennan (eds.), *Philosophical Dialogues* (New York: Rowman and Littlefield, 1999), 7, note 1.
[44] Marcel Dumitru Ciucă at the Rumanian National Archive to Peder Anker, Nov. 9, 2006, PA.
[45] Næss, "The shallow and the deep," 1973.
[46] Grimeland, *En historie om klatring*, 2004, 122. Jardar Seim, "Miljøvern utan politiske følgjer?" *Syn og segn* 78 (1972), 515–24. Samarbeidsgruppa for natur og miljøvern, *Håndbok i miljøvern: Økopolitisk strategi og taktikk* (Oslo: Cappelen, 1973).

The Deep Ecologists had, up until the election of 1972, collaborated with the Center Party along with various groups on the left and far left side of the Cold War divide. This was a common effort to hinder membership in the European Community. The unity would soon go wrong. After the referendum a vocal group of radical Marxists began telling the ecophilosophers that it was not the European Community's exploitation of nature that was the problem, but instead the capitalist exploitation of the workers of the world.[47] One telling proponent of this line of argument was the German intellectual Hans Magnus Enzensberger, who wrote in 1973 about "the new petit bourgeois" "ecological movement" in Norway and beyond, comments that were taken to heart by Norwegians on the far left.[48]

Among his readers was the Marxist-Leninist student organization Red Frontier, who, according to the student newspaper, "took the piss out" of the short-lived campus environmental organization Green Grass. After a "Green spring there will be a Red Fall" the leftists predicted, hinting at the upcoming national referendum in September 1972.[49] They saw "the fight against the Eco-catastrophe as the bourgeoisie reaction to the capital's dark side," and worried that environmentalism would undermine the true revolutionary spirit of students.[50]

After the referendum in September there was indeed a "Red Fall," as the Marxists-Leninists purged environmental campus organizations as Deep Ecology was seen as reformist and thus not truly revolutionary. The thinking of Kvaløy and his friends was bourgeois, they argued, as he and the Deep Ecology study groups were unable to create a proper mass movement of blue-collar workers. The ecologist Mysterud was the first to notice this leftward turn in the politics of ecology, something he regretted as it undermined the broad science-based environmentalism he sought to mobilize.[51] Thanks to the Marxists, by the end of 1973, the once flourishing Deep Ecology movement faded away along with similar student led environmental campus organizations.

---

[47] Helge Christie, Erling Amble, and Erik Steineger, "To linjer i miljøvern arbeidet," *Miljømagasinet*, 8 (1974), 10–11, 22.
[48] Hans Magnus Enzensberger, "Zur Kritik der Politischen Ökologie," *Kursbuch*, 33 (Oct. 1973), 1–42, translated into Norwegian as "Den politiske økologi – en kritikk," *Vardøger*, 9 (1977), 15–46, quote p. 21.
[49] Anonymous, "Horribelt møte i DNS" and "Grønt Gras og Rød Front," *Universitas*, Apr. 25, 1972, UO.
[50] Anonymous, "Økologidebatten ML-erne aldri forstod," *Universitas*, Apr. 25, 1972, UO.
[51] Ivar Mysterud, "Økopolitikk, biologi og klassekamp," *Norsk natur*, 7 (1971), 123–7. Ivar Mysterud and Iver Mysterud, "Reviving the ghost of broad ecology," *Journal of Social and Evolutionary Systems*, 17 (1994), 167–95.

The Co-working Group's unofficial leader, Kvaløy, was in Nepal in the fall semester of 1973 while these events took place. He was there to do more research on the ecological virtues of the Beding village. Together with a zoologist, a physician, and an ethno-botanist, they sought to find out whether or not "the Sherpa-society in Rolwaling could be understood as a society with a high degree of ecological balance."[52] To Kvaløy this was very much the case. To him it was a steady-state village living in harmony with nature, from which the industrial society was in urgent need to learn. Indeed, "it [was] a society we should envy – especially now [in 1973] when we are about to enter final stages of the eco-crisis."[53] His fellow travelers shared much of Kvaløy's thinking upon departure for Nepal, but at least one of them returned to Oslo as a skeptic. It was not clear to all that the Sherpa's way of naming, organizing, and handling their plants, for example, was that harmonious or ecological, a point the Marxists appreciated.

And Marxists had bigger fish to fry than campus environmentalists. They were well organized and began their subversive attacks on the Deep Ecology organization in earnest in 1974. By the spring of 1978 they had managed to take over the organization, after which they did very little with it. Judging from the meeting records, the debates were so long that most activists would leave from exhaustion.[54] They did little with the organization as their plan was to halt the spread of ecological revisionism and instead mobilize for a Maoist revolution, as they sincerely believed the Chinese offered an ecologically viable regime.[55] It is worth noting that these Marxist initiatives were not just destructive because they inspired environmentalists to establish Chinese-style farming collectives in Norway. Others gave up fighting the Marxists and chose instead to "drop out" completely, living according to Deep Ecology principles in Sherpa-style steady-state agricultural communities in old mountain or fjord farms.[56]

---

[52] Erik Steineger, *Etnobotaniske undersøkelser i et sherpasamfunn i Rolwaling-dalen, Nepal*, MA thesis (Oslo: Matematisk-naturvitenskapelig fakultet, 1977), p. 22.
[53] Sigmund Kvaløy, "Rolwaling – et livssamfunn i likevekt," *Mestre fjellet*, 15 (1973), 11–12, quote p. 12.
[54] Pål Ytreberg, "Diktat fra Høyer, Kvaløy m.fl.," *(snm) nytt*, 5 (May 1976), 9–11. Kvaløy, "Demokrati."
[55] Helge Christie, "Kina," *(snm) nytt*, 9 (Dec. 1976), 22–3. Erling Amble, "Kineserne og økologien," *(snm) nytt*, 7 (Sept. 1977), 20–2. Kjell Gunnar Holm and Knut Sørensen, "Økologi og økopolitikk: Noen trekk ved økobevegelsen i Norge," *Vardøger*, 9 (1977), 47–69.
[56] Stein Jarving, *Grønt liv: Økologisk strategi – populistisk virkelighet: Om jordbrukskollektiv i praksis* (Oslo: Gyldendal, 1974), 17. Anders Lindhjem-Godal, "'Kjernefamilien er en sosial sjukdom': Kollektivliv på Karlsøy i Troms." In Tor Egil Frøland and Trine Rogg Korsvik (eds.), *1968: Opprør og motkultur på norsk* (Oslo: Pax, 2006), pp. 93–118.

Nevertheless, these events came to challenge old friendships, including Johan Galtung's friendship with Kvaløy and Næss. Galtung became a sturdy supporter of Maoist China after a visit in the fall of 1973, claiming that environmentalists had a lot to learn from the country. "The Chinese seemed so happy, so satisfied, so kind," he noted after meeting local peasants.[57] It is worth noting that he, in his library at the International Peace Research Institute in Oslo, had evidence at hand to the contrary, including reports by Amnesty International and others.[58] In any case, back in Oslo, he told environmentalists inspired by "ecological theory" that the Chinese did not "try to have a theoretical superstructure that brings the relationship to nature and the relationship to humans onto the same level."[59] Instead he thought Norwegians should learn from the *"self-reliance"* of decentralized Chinese farming cooperatives.[60] These Chinese community brigades did not depend on a national economic system and dealt with pollution and other environmental issues on a local level, he claimed.

The Marxists used Galtung's argument for all its worth in their ongoing efforts to change the Deep Ecologists. By 1978 the communists had won their battle but lost the war, as Kvaløy, Høyer, Næss, and their many supporters began a new association called *Økopolitisk samarbeidsring* (Ecopolitical Cooperation Ring), which was immune to Marxist attacks. It had no formal structure, and members were recruited, and indeed communicated, only through personal conversations, fax, telephone, or a newsletter (financed by Næss).[61] Within a year it became the intellectual and social backbone of Norwegian environmental debate. Their efforts culminated in the attempt to save the Alta-Kautokeino waterway from hydropower development (Chapter 9). A closer look at their ethical reasoning, academic research, and educational program will be the topic of the next chapter.

---

[57] Anders Magnus and Tor Selstad (interview with Johan Galtung), "Massenes skaperkraft er uendelig," *Miljømagasinet*, 1 (1974), 24–7, quote p. 27.
[58] Amnesty International, *Annual Report 1973–1974* (London: Amnesty International, 1974), 51.
[59] Galtung quoted in Magnus and Selstad, "Massenes skaperkraft er uendelig," p. 24.
[60] Johan Galtung and Fumiko Nishimura, *Kan vi lære av Kineserne?* (Oslo: Gyldendal, 1975), p. 94.
[61] Anonymous, "Økopolitisk samarbeidsring ('Ringen') i stutte ordlag," *Ringen* 1 (1978), 3–5.

5

Environmental Studies

Students of Environmental Studies at the University of Oslo began their semester with a weeklong hike over the scenic Hardangervidda mountain plateau.[1] It was an outdoor experience designed to take the students away from the capitalist and industrial setting of the city and deep into the periphery of a picturesque nature, thus beginning their studies with the right state of mind. Empowered by the mountains, they could enter the valleys of industrialism and shallow ecological thinking with a do-gooding gaze of knowing what's right from wrong. Their guide was the ecophilosopher Nils Faarlund, who told the students that being outside in nature was actually being truly inside. The trip was organized by *Rådet for natur- og miljøfag* ("The Council for Nature and Environmental Studies"), hereafter only Environmental Studies.[2] The institution became the intellectual think tank for the Deep Ecologists who were caught in the middle of the Cold War divide at that time. They were under attack from both Marxists, who saw them as counter-revolutionary, and supporters of the European Community, who thought they were unable to appreciate international cooperation empowered by capitalism. These tensions would energize and radicalize Environmental Studies scholars toward a more ideological vision of a future world in ecological equilibrium. This chapter will review the work of Environmental Studies and, by doing so,

---

[1] Anonymous, "God generalprøve for Miljøfagseminaret," *Nytt fra Universitetet i Oslo*, no. 5 (1975), 2, UO.

[2] Paul Hofseth, *Rådet for natur- og miljøfag: Rapport fra virksomheten 1972–75* (Oslo: Rådet for natur- og miljøfag, 1975); *Rådet for natur- og miljøfag: Rapport fra virksomheten 1972–78* (Oslo: Rådet for natur- og miljøfag, 1978).

discuss how this field established itself in Norway. Despite the Marxist attacks described in the previous chapter, it is important to note that the 1970s was a decade of intellectual confidence among the Deep Ecologists. The fact that the nation had rejected membership of the European Community in September 1972 loomed large in how they came to frame the field. Could Environmental Studies point out an alternative direction for the nation other than communism and consumer capitalism? As the vanguard of social change, the scholars associated with Environmental Studies saw themselves as harboring an environmental vision for Norway that could inspire the world. This was a vision that came to a standstill after the failure to save the Alta-Kautokeino River from hydropower development in 1982. This chapter will revisit that hopeful decade, focusing first on the ethical aspirations, then on the research, and finally on their educational program. As will be apparent, Environmental Studies would in this period grow into the leading institution educating Norwegian politicians, scholars, bureaucrats, and activists in the topic. Indeed, more than 2,000 students would attend their introduction seminar, while a significant number would participate in their re-education program for high-school teachers and college tutors or also take various advance courses.

As discussed in Chapter 3, in June 1972, the Academic Collegium at the University of Oslo had established Environmental Studies as an interdisciplinary institution reporting directly to the University President and not to a particular school, faculty, or department.[3] It was led by key members of the Ecophilosophy Group who began shaping Environmental Studies in the fall of 1972 with the aim of welcoming their first students within a year. Their first employee was Paul Hofseth who as a teaching assistant in philosophy had published a set of exercises in logic for freshmen students, written together with Sigmund Kvaløy and another lecturer in philosophy.[4] As a graduate student of philosophy Hofseth had been an active Deep Ecologist with an interest in pollution. He had been a member of the Ecophilosophy Group since its inception, and, as the administrative leader, he placed ecophilosophy at the core of the Environmental Studies curriculum. The institution had initially only two offices, and based their courses and activities on a series of guest lecturers and

---

[3] Anonymous, "Rådet for natur- og miljøfag," *Nytt fra universitetet i Oslo*, no. 11 (1972), 6, UO. Environmental Studies was led by Anne Bjørnebye, Gunnar Brostigen, Aanund Hylland, Terje Lind, and Sigmund Kvaløy. Anonymous, "Natur og menneske," *Forskningsnytt*, 18, no. 6 (1973), 24.
[4] Paul Hofseth, Ola Hole, and Sigmund Kvaløy, *Logikkoppgaver til Arne Næss: en del elementære logiske emner* (Oslo: Universitetsforlaget, 1968–1973).

seminar leaders from various departments within the University and beyond. This made the tiny institution exciting for the students, but a logistical challenge for Hofseth and his administrative aide, the student of philosophy Arne Vinje (b. 1951). Together they fostered a communal culture of staff, faculty, and students working together, as in having shared lunches, along with parties and even an orchestra. Despite the gravity of the eco-crisis, Environmental Studies was a fun and exciting place to be.

ECOLOGY, COMMUNITY, AND LIFESTYLE

A regular lecturer at Environmental Studies was the philosopher Arne Næss, who, for the rest of his life, would think of it as his academic home. He was welcomed with open arms, and quickly gained the status as their intellectual leader. In that capacity he began formulating an alternative eco-friendly philosophy for the new field. It was a green vision for how Deep Ecologists and Environmental Studies should guide policies and lifestyles away from self-induced ecological destruction.

Anyone seeking Næss's serious attention, however, would not necessarily find him at the University of Oslo, but instead at his beloved mountain cabin Tvergastein, where he spent much of his time philosophizing. Having had a cup of tea with him at his cabin indicated whether a faculty member or student had been willing to, quite literally, walk that extra mile in pursuit of the answers to deeper philosophical questions. Indeed, a visit entailed a four-hour train ride and two-hour hike (each way). Visits were by invitation only, so having been at his cabin became a secret handshake of acceptance by Næss, which provided access to the inner circle of Deep Ecologists. Visiting Næss's Tvergastein was like an initiation reserved for the chosen ones among environmentally inclined scholars, students, and activists. His self-fashioning as a mountain sage became a tool separating friends from foes, the deep from the shallow, as it was hard to gain respect or move forward in the emerging field of Environmental Studies without having taken ecophilosophy seriously and also having been a guest at his cabin. In the process, Tvergastein gained the status as Environmental Studies' mythical locus.

At Tvergastein, at the Hallingskarvet peak, the philosopher laid out what he thought should be the main principles for the Deep Ecologists. Næss named his philosophy "Ecosophy T" to signal that it was his personal view, and he encouraged other environmentalists to formulate their own ecophilosophies A, B, or C, (though few did). The "T" was short for Tvergastein or also *tolkning* (interpretation) as this was important to Næss's early philosophy. The "T" also gave the equation he had used while vacationing at Tirich Mir a decade earlier a new meaning. The $T = G^2/(L_S + Å_s)$ formula stated that T (for *trivsel* – "thriving") or self-realization equaled excitement squared divided by bodily and spiritual pains.[5]

Tvergastein offers an extraordinarily deep panoramic *weltanschauung*. Næss felt small looking out at the overwhelming and vast scenery, an experience that reflects the central distinction in Ecosophy T between the Self (with capital S), representing all beings in the world, and the biotic self (with a lower-case s), representing only the individual.[6] True Self-realization, Næss argued, presupposed the unfolding of the biotic self in harmony with the selfhood of other living beings. Unlike ego-development, self-realization presupposes the unfolding of the true ecological self identifying with the selfhood of others within the Self. There are elements from Benedict de Spinoza's philosophy that appeared in Næss's thinking, such as Spinoza's famous "Whatsoever is, is in God, and without God nothing can be, or be conceived."[7] Næss's philosophy implied an opposition to notions of stewardship of the Earth, because stewardship views the world as a collection of natural resources laid out primarily for human use. In this imagined community, the interests of the majority are constituted by non-human populations, which reflect the fact that Næss spent much of his time alone on the mountain peak. The primacy of wilderness was another important feature of his thinking, along with a celebration of place and belonging, and identification with plants, insects, animals, and indigenous peoples, especially the Sherpa. In short, it was a vision of a future in which the wolf would live with the lamb and the bears with the humans in a mixed community of collective Self-realization.[8] The notion of having a self within a larger Self became important for the Deep Ecological aspiration of being true global citizens within a local community.

Ecosophy T marked a normative mode of theorizing: There is a problem that needs to be solved and therefore a vision of a better order needs

---

[5] Næss, *Opp stupet*, p. 126; *Økologi, samfunn og livsstil*, 5th ed., p. 78.
[6] Næss, *Økologi, samfunn og livsstil*, 5th ed., pp. 264–322.
[7] Benedict de Spinoza, *Ethics*, in *Works of Spinoza*, vol. 1, R. H. M. Elwes (trs.) (New York: Dover Pub., 1955), p. 55 (E1P15). Arne Næss, *Freedom, Emotion and Self-subsistence: The Structure of a Central Part of Spinoza's Ethics* (Oslo: Universitetsforlaget, 1975), 11–30; "Environmental ethics and Spinoza's ethics," *Inquiry* 23 (1980), 313–25.
[8] Arne Næss, "Self-realization in mixed communities of humans, bears, sheep, and wolves," *Inquiry*, 22 (1979), 231–41.

to be promulgated. As Næss saw it "ecosophy" was a normative as opposed to a descriptive "ecophilosophy," though few of his colleagues adopted the distinction. In opposition to the "shallow" approach (concerned primarily with the reduction of environmental damage), he proposed a program of global rescue based on a radical change in the Western world view from hierarchical and anthropocentric to egalitarian and eco-centric. According to Næss, there was an inseparable connection between the human subject as defined in the Western liberal tradition of philosophy and the environmental havoc unleashed by the competitive lifestyle in the industrial society, such as in the European Community. He linked the realization of the liberal private sphere directly with material consumption and to a striving for goods, which prevented the Self-realization of the biosphere. According to Næss, the liberal focus on private self-realization leads to passivity, both with regard to the environment and to the underprivileged: "'Liberalism' [is] a norm for non-intervention when a group or a class bleeds, exploits, domineers or manipulates another group or class – or even threatens to exterminate it. As in a wrestling match with no holds barred, such processes must, according to this liberalism, be left to the *free* interplay of forces – hence the word 'liberal', Latin for 'free'."[9] This rather simplistic Marxist critique was soon transcended into arguments in favor of communitarian lifestyle politics, such as lifestyles predicated on a system of norms outlining the model of a good life in a good biotic community. This community would also include non-human beings, even landscapes and entire ecological systems, as humans to Næss were, like all other living species, just "knots in the biospherical net or field of intrinsic relations."[10] This was a hermeneutically useful image reflecting abstract ecology in which relationships replace individuals. Yet the image of humans as knots in fields of relationships came to haunt Næss's thinking, as the value put on individual life in societies that perceive their members as nodes, units, or tributaries of a larger whole has not been very high, critics would argue (in Chapter 9).

Næss's communitarian thinking holds at its core the importance of identification with everyone and everything, especially the oppressed. "[T]he positive appraisal [of individuality] becomes meaningful only within a value system in which norms for the expression of individuality and for collectivism (in several senses of the word) are allowed to confront

---

[9] Næss, *Økologi, samfunn og livsstil*, 5th ed., p. 320.
[10] Næss, "The Shallow and the Deep" (1973), p. 95.

each other and a ranking of values is suggested."[11] The implication was that the individual character would be seasoned by activism and enriched by diversity within groups with a collectivist ideology. Provided that individual peculiarities are not in conflict with the aims of the group, one may show individuality within a collective. Individuality is essential but only on the condition that one is part of an ecological community. "Distinctive, individual traits ... are enforced and intensified in collectivistic-ideological groups, e.g. in a kibbutz."[12] Diversity should therefore be understood as a biotic diversity and diversity within the Deep Ecology movement, but not necessarily as diversity of opinions and lifestyles within a state. The liberal notion of the self-realization of the private sphere alienates men and women from the entirety of the biosphere. Therefore, attempts to solve environmental problems within the framework of private realization inevitably remain "shallow" solutions. This does not mean, however, that when confronted with individuals obsessed with themselves and material goods, Næss would embark on moralizing reprimands. Næss tended to employ strategies of encouragement, even subtle "bribery," to get the holders of shallow views onto his side. His philosophy was not meant to be an instrument for punishing opponents. It is telling that he in his lectures was fond of quoting this line from Spinoza: "I say it is part of a wise man to refresh and recreate himself with moderate and pleasant food and drink, and also with perfumes, with the soft beauty of growing plants, with dress, with music, with many sports, with theatres, and the like, such as every man may make use of without injury to his neighbor."[13]

Accordingly, at Tvergastein, Næss would enrich himself by studying a minute plant, patch of moss, or beautiful rock, smell and drink a sumptuous herbal tea, and enjoy the physical and emotional pleasure of climbing a mountain. The distinction between deep and shallow ecology reflected whether one was able to absorb and appreciate the joys of the local environment. Indeed, his deep ecological critique of modernity centers around the troubling advancement of a civilization lacking in such appreciations, which in his local context meant more disturbing weekend cottages and new roads, as well as the monstrous hotel below in the Ustaoset valley. Yet Næss did not reflect sufficiently on the irony that even the deep ecologist depended on the icon of

---

[11] Næss, Økologi, samfunn og livsstil, 5th ed., p. 321.
[12] Næss, Økologi, samfunn og livsstil, 5th ed., p. 321.
[13] Spinoza, Ethics, p. 219 (E4P45Sch).

modernity, the train, the very symbol of an advancing civilization, to get back to the University of Oslo.

Næss published his concept of Ecosophy T in what became one of his most celebrated books, namely *Økologi, samfunn og lifsstil* (Ecology, Community, and Lifestyle), which appeared in five different editions. The first three editions entitled *Økologi og filosofi* (Ecology and Philosophy) appeared between 1971 and 1973, and were in the format of intramural manuscripts capturing the collaborative work of the Ecophilosophy Group (see Chapter 3).[14] Here his "ecosophy" of identification and unity with nature would appear in the last chapter, more as an afterthought than as a methodology for the book. This schism would continue in the two subsequent editions with the new title, *Økologi, samfunn og lifsstil*, which appeared in 1974 and 1976, in which Næss would elaborate mostly on ecological perspectives in relation to social sciences.

The book is a tour-de-force, addressing a range of environmental issues discussed in Norway and other parts of the world in the mid-1970s. It includes a chapter about moving from large-scale technology to small "soft" technology for the benefit of local communities. There is a long chapter critiquing capitalist economic growth in which Næss argues for moving toward a zero-growth society in order to protect the environment. An even longer chapter reviews various eco-political and sociological arguments Næss thought favored ecological protection. There is also a short and sharp chapter about philosophy of science where Næss explains why science can't be value neutral with respect to the ways in which it describes nature. And Næss discusses much more, before he finally presents his Ecosophy T at the end. The book is remarkable in that it summarizes and discusses contributions from Norwegian environmentalists and links these to ongoing debates in the larger English-speaking community. He thus offers the reader a more or less complete review, or "cavalcade" according to one reviewer, of the environmental debate as he saw it.[15] The fact that the book was unevenly written gave it a flavor of authenticity and of it coming from a true philosopher.

Ecosophy T was Næss's personal contribution and, as a consequence, had an element of armchair philosophy written at Tvergastein. The rest of the book, however, reflected group work over several years from of the Deep Ecology movements, the Ecophilosophy Group, and debates within

---

[14] Næss, *Økologi og filosofi*, 1–3 ed.
[15] Tor Inge Romøren, "Økologi, samfunn og livsstil" (review), *Norsk filosofisk tidsskrift*, 9, no. 4 (1975), 179–80.

Environmental Studies. Though Næss's name was on the cover, the circle of people around him still felt a sense of ownership over the volume as it captured values and ideas shared among the Deep Ecologists.[16] Næss had a warm and inclusive personality that drew people in to working with him and supporting the book as it evolved. Among activists and scholars the book came to serve as the intellectual focal point and academic framework for future steps. Indeed, the book was one of only three books required on the syllabus for the Environmental Studies introduction course, discussed below. Criticism of the book would therefore come from those who were not involved in either its inception or its legacy.[17]

It was not only as an author but also as an editor that Næss mobilized for the environment. As a founding editor of *Inquiry*, Næss enjoyed respect in the wider academic world for facilitating a well-respected interdisciplinary journal of philosophy and the social sciences. It included early contributions by notable people in philosophy such as Charles Taylor, Donald Davidson, and Jürgen Habermas. Næss would use the journal to promote Deep Ecology, as he did when publishing a "summary" of the movement's philosophy back in 1973 (see Chapter 3). More generally, *Inquiry* would be the launching pad for key early contributions in environmental ethics (John Rodman, Richard Routley (later Sylvan), Genevieve Lloyd), environmental restoration (Robert Elliot), animal liberation and rights (Peter Singer, Colin McGinn, Stephen R. L. Clark, Tom Regan), and environmental history (J. Donald Hughes).[18] The inclusion of articles in *Inquiry* by these important scholars, often at an early stage in their respective academic careers, was done in the spirit of trying to empower the environmental movement around the world.

If Næss was Environmental Studies' chief philosopher, then Kvaløy was their chief ideologist. His manuscript *Øko-filosofisk fragment* (Ecophilosophical fragment) was the second required reading for all its

---

[16] Edvard Barth, "Arne Næss med ny filosofi," *VG*, Nov. 27, 1974, PA.
[17] Dafinn Føllesdal, "Økologi og økonomi" (review), *Kirke og kultur*, 80 (1975), 231–2.
[18] John Rodman, "The liberation of nature?" *Inquiry*, 20 (1977), 83–131. Genevieve Lloyd, "Spinoza's environmental ethics," *Inquiry*, 23 (1980), 293–311. Robert Elliot, "Faking nature," *Inquiry*, 25 (1982), 81–93. Richard Routley, "Alleged problems in attributing beliefs, and intentionality, to animals," *Inquiry*, 24 (1981), 385–417. Peter Singer, "Killing humans and killing animals," *Inquiry*, 22 (1979), 145–56. Colin McGinn, "Evolution, animals, and the basis of morality," *Inquiry*, 22 (1979), 81–99. Stephen R. L. Clark, "The rights of wild things," *Inquiry*, 22 (1979), 171–88. Tom Regan, "An examination and defense of one argument concerning animal rights," *Inquiry*, 22 (1979), 189–219. J. Donald Hughes, "Ecology in ancient Greece," *Inquiry*, 18, no. 2 (1975), 115–25.

students. Just as Næss's book evolved in various editions, Kvaløy's manuscript would also grow over the years with the 4th version from 1973 being the one most widely circulated.[19] To get a copy one had to turn to Vinje, the administrative aide, who printed out the manuscript in its various stages upon request on the Environmental Studies' copy machine. Like nature itself, the book was never finished, but in constant evolution. This gave the reader a sense of being involved in the making of philosophy, in the process of Kvaløy's thinking. And it made him immune to the critic waiting for the final edition to be published so that it could be reviewed and critiqued. Kvaløy, it is worth recalling, was the prime mover behind the Mardøla and Alta demonstrations and the unofficial charismatic leader of the Deep Ecologists. Having a copy of his manuscript signified exclusive membership to an intellectual community.

Despite the ever-changing nature of the manuscript, his ecophilosophy was stable and transparent. At the core was a plea for the survival of the complexity of nature's life force within ecosystems. As he saw it, the nature's complex life force was being destroyed by the industrial society represented by the European Community and the United States. The industrial society model may look "complicated," but it is actually lacking in ecological complexity, he argued. The "complicated" industrial society is one-dimensional and uses standardized movement in mechanical time, while the "complex" ecological society is multi-dimensional, dynamic, and moves in biological time, as in the case of the Beding village in Nepal. In his lectures to a more theoretically oriented audience, he would focus on the difference between complexity and complication, though even highly skilled philosophers would find the distinction bewildering. Surely, there must be complexity in complication and complication in complexity?[20] Indeed, Kvaløy would struggle formulating an ecophilosophy that gained recognition among academics. He was more effective in communicating to environmental activists the difference between the Life Necessities Society and the Industrial Growth Society. Using an overhead projector he would, as an artist, support his view with dramatic drawings of a harmonious and beautiful Life Necessities Society

---

[19] Kvaløy, Øko-filosofisk fragment, 1972–1973, manuscript in different versions evolving from 43 to 173 pages. Last known version published as Mangfold og tid (Trondheim: NTNU Department of Music, 2001).

[20] Witnessed at the Melbu Conference, July 23, 1990, with distinguished thinkers such as Karl-Otto Apel, Matthias Kettener, and Hans Jonas. In Audun Øfsti (ed.), Ecology and Ethics: A Report from the Melbu Conference, 18–23 July 1990 (Trondheim: Nordland Akademi for Kunst og Vitenskap, 1992).

juxtaposed with images of the nightmarish and polluted Industrial Growth Society, asking rhetorically which one people preferred.

Kvaløy's distinction between the Life Necessities Society and the Industrial Growth Society became an effective way of framing the environmental debate among Deep Ecologists. The distinction evoked a Lutheran pietist condition of guilt necessary for offering an ecological awakening and redemption for environmentalists. As a result, scholars within Environmental Studies would typically debate whether or not something supported the Life Necessities Society, whether that was building or not building an electric power station or dam, prospecting or not prospecting for petroleum, supporting a society propelled by economic growth or living in a society with economic equilibrium, etc. These debates were cast in bipolar dichotomies, typical for the Cold War period, and Kvaløy would use his authority to make sure the Deep Ecologists did not drift toward the middle ground, but rather stayed put with their do-gooding gaze in the pursuit of the Life Necessities Society.

THE CASE AGAINST SCIENCE

Scholars lecturing in and students studying Environmental Studies were generally critical of the use (or more often abuse) of science, and would actively pursue interdisciplinary "action research" as an alternative. The uses of science by their conservative, technocratic, or leftist opponents on the political spectrum were often informed by a single discipline, they would argue. They envisioned instead that environmental research would bypass the pitfalls of the Cold War socio-political divide by being interdisciplinary. Science should mirror nature's complexity and scientists should join the effort with their know-how to save the environment through research aimed at solving practical issues. Thus understood, the interdisciplinary action research of Environmental Studies was an effort to find environmentally viable alternatives to the science that supported capitalist or socialist exploitations of nature. Research done without deeper questioning of social and environmental values was, to them, "shallow," hence the importance of distinguishing between deep and shallow ecology. The use of "shallow" scientific research to rationalize and objectify the exploitation of the nation's natural resources, including hydropower developments, was troubling to Environmental Studies scholars.

This sentiment with respect to science was developed in a textbook of philosophy of science published by Næss and his students in 1973. Here they argued that humanity "faces the *ecological* problems science creates" and that it was therefore urgent to find a new way of organizing science.[21] This textbook had a significant distribution as it was used in the mandatory core course in the philosophy of science that *all* students entering the University of Oslo were required to pass. For most students, the book would be their first academic read, creating the initial impression of academic thinking, order, and knowledge. At the end of the term, they had to take rigorous exams on the topic – which a significant number failed – before continuing in more specialized fields. Thus, for example, a student dreaming of becoming a chemist would have to study all "the negative aspects of science" and make sure to remember and stress the importance of "ecologically informed philosophical systems" when answering his or her exam questions.[22]

The authors were not subtle about their philosophy of science views. Indeed, they would warn the incoming new freshmen about all the awful things with which science had provided society in the past, such as weaponry, pollution, and class division. The ecologists were the exception, and ecology was the antidote. Ecologists were the do-gooders and had, as a consequence, Næss argued, a "tremendous and nearly sinister responsibility for our society's future."[23] This was the general sentiment within Environmental Studies, though it is worth noting that not all the ecophilosophers agreed with Næss on the overarching importance of ecology. The graduate student of sociology Sven Erik Skønberg, for example, a longstanding member of the Ecophilosophy Group, sought to downplay the importance of ecology. This field should not be "the new big scientific unifier," he argued, as it could entail a new version of scientistic positivism he could not agree with.[24]

The science of ecology would change in this period, something the scholar-activists associated with Environmental Studies largely failed to notice despite their deep-seated enthusiasm for ecology. When the Norwegian contribution to the International Biological Program faded out in 1974, it marked an end to steady-state ecological research inspired by Eugene and Howard Odum. Some ecologists left the field and became

---

[21] Arne Næss with Per Ariansen, Thomas Krogh, and Hans Eirik Aarek, *Vitenskapsfilosofi: en innføring*, 2nd preliminary ed. (Oslo: Universitetsforlaget, 1973), p. 3.
[22] Næss with Ariansen, Krogh and Aarek, *Vitenskapsfilosofi*, p. 3, 63.
[23] Arne Næss, "Forskerens ansvar i miljøkrisen," *Forskningsnytt*, 17 (1972), 48–51, quote p. 48. Republished in Næss with Ariansen, Krogh and Aarek, *Vitenskapsfilosofi* (1973), pp. 145–52.
[24] Sverre Kværner, "Når vitenskap blir økopolitikk," *Universitas* nr. 6/7, Apr. 26, 1979, 13, UO.

teachers or environmental bureaucrats, while those who remained on campus would turn their focus toward evolutionary ecology and sociobiology. Nevertheless, among the ecophilosophers and the staff at Environmental Studies, steady-state ecology would remain as the all-dominating view of how to understand the natural world and human-nature relationships. The idea of a steady-state society in harmony with steady-state nature would be the norm in Environmental Studies well into the 1990s and beyond. The general anti-science sentiment among the Deep Ecologists may explain why new trends and perspectives in the field of ecology were not adopted or appreciated. The exception was Hofseth, who encouraged empirical environmental research as an antidote to polarized politics.

Næss would spell out his faith in ecology and disillusionment with the other sciences in his talks at Environmental Studies and later in what became one of his most famous lectures, "The Case against Science," given in May 1974 on the occasion of the 50th anniversary of the Catholic University of Nijmegen in the Netherlands. If the Dutch commemorating listeners had expected something cheerful, they must have been disappointed. "My enthusiasm [for] *science in general* is gone," Næss professed.[25] He continued on to say, "In industrial societies science has become gigantic in scope – bureaucratic, impersonal and politically powerful," and scientists failing to take a stand on social and environmental issues were part of this technocratic system.[26] Scientists, as Næss saw it, were unwilling to question authorities, enjoyed undeserved social privileges, were indifferent to non-western societies and rationalities, supported technocracies, and pursued projects that led to environmental degradation. These accusations against the sciences became widely discussed in Norway, and beyond.[27]

One of the debaters was the philosopher of science Paul Feyerabend (1924–94), who had become an acquaintance of Næss after attending a seminar in 1955 at the Ustaoset resort (close to Næss's cabin) at which he "refuted" Næss's *Interpretation and Preciseness* (1953) for its scientism.[28]

---

[25] Arne Næss, "The case against science," in C. I. Dessaur (et al., eds.), *Science between Culture and Counter-Culture* (Nijmegen: Dekker and van de Vegt, 1975), pp. 25–48, quote p. 26, Næss's emphasis.
[26] Næss, "The case against science," p. 27.
[27] Arne Næss, *Anklagene mot vitenskapen* (Oslo: Universitetsforlaget, 1980).
[28] Paul Feyerabend, "Remarks on *Interpretation and Preciseness*" (1955), in Nina Witoszek and Andrew Brennan (eds.), *Philosophical Dialogues: Arne Næss and the Progress of Ecophilosophy* (Lanham: Rowman and Littlefield, 1999), pp. 50–6, quote p. 56. Næss. *Interpretation and Preciseness*.

Næss enjoyed thoughtful criticism of his work, and he would over the years encourage Feyerabend to publish his thinking in the journal *Inquiry*, which Næss edited. The result was, perhaps, Feyerabend's most well-known article, namely "'Science': The myth and its role in society" (1975).[29] Here he spelled out, in no uncertain terms, the anarchist nature of science in which there is no shared or unifying method. To which Næss replied (in the subsequent pages of the same issue) that "science could serve anarchists too" if research was used to benefit the counterculture and the environmental cause.[30]

The problem with Feyerabend's anarchist philosophy and more generally, the counterculture reaction against the scientific community's entanglement with weaponry and industrialism, as Næss saw it, was the all-encompassing dismissal of science without consideration of the few good disciplines in science. In "The Case against Science" Næss argued that certain sciences, particularly ecology, could provide constructive paths for alternative ways of organizing nature and the world. As an example, he pointed to the Deep Ecologists which tended "to give greater priority to action research – relatively short-term, goal-directed, informal investigations directed toward solving practical problems on the way toward a true bio community in ecological equilibrium."[31] These ideals reflected core values within Environmental Studies. Here scholars would aim at action-research that would drive Norway to become an alternative nation in ecological equilibrium:

> A society in ecological equilibrium will probably have to eliminate many privileges. Even at the expense of professional efficiency, students and staff may have to partake in primary production. It is expected that this will also have a beneficial effect upon the prevailing ideology. It may further the basic ecological aim of making life complex rather than complicated, that is, of developing all faculties and opportunities, living in a rich local environment requiring many and varied kind of activity, and on the whole obliterating the strict separation of work and leisure.[32]

Kvaløy and the circle of activists that came to surround him were the philosophical architects of this statement by Næss, and it is telling of the

---

[29] Paul Feyerabend, "'Science:' The myth and its role in society," *Inquiry*, 18 (1975), 167–81.
[30] Arne Næss, "Why not science for anarchists too? A reply to Feyerabend," *Inquiry*, 18 (1975), 183–94. See also, "Paul Feyerabend: A Green Hero?" in G. Munevar (ed.), *Beyond Reason* (Dordrecht: Kluwer, 1991), pp. 403–16.
[31] Næss, "The case against science," p. 46.   [32] Næss, "The case against science," p. 46.

type of thinking and research that took place among scholars associated with Environmental Studies.

Because of their skepticism of science, Environmental Studies scholars tried to avoid traditional academic hierarchies when they pursued research. Research was not done for its own sake, but aimed instead at solving practical environmental problems. Faculty, staff, and students would merge themselves into action research trying to develop environmental approaches or technologies that could help the world. A telling example was the construction of a successful hot-water solar heating unit on the roof of the Department of Biology building.[33] This technology was innovative and received national attention, as well as recognition from the Deep Ecologists.[34] This is worth mentioning, as it indicates that students informed by ecophilosophy did not shy away from addressing "shallow" technological answers to energy questions. Such technologies were not seen as solutions to the ecological crisis, but as integral parts of a larger vision of an alternative nation. In 1977, for example, the students of the Environmental Studies seminar devoted all their combined efforts to study energy, publishing a report on the need to identify, manage, analyze, and explore alternative sources for energy so that Norway could be an alternative ideal for the world to admire.[35] This effort to develop practical solutions as a means for realizing an eco-friendly world was also evident in a new course offered from 1978 which focused on how to save energy in private homes by means of solar heating and other unconventional sources.[36] Staff and students would also do action research on other issues, such as "the ecological crisis in Sahel," arguing that this region of Africa was in urgent need of developmental aid of a kind that did not do environmental harm to the dry semi-desert.[37] Another project was action research addressing why outdoor life values and interests were ignored in the decision-making processes leading to hydropower developments.[38]

---

[33] Rolf Ottesen, "Vellykket solenergiforsøk," *VG*, Sept 22 1975, UO. Anonymous, "Solen – en enorm ressurs: Vellykket forsøk i Norge," *Adresseavisen*, Sept. 23, 1975, UO.
[34] Anonymous, "Miljøteknologiske prosjekt," *(snm)-nytt*, 6 (1977), 22.
[35] Arild Hervik (et al.), *Energianalyser: energiforbruket ved framstilling og distribusjon av matvarer* (Oslo: Rådet for natur og miljøfag, 1977).
[36] Olav Benestad, *Kurs om energi og energisparing* (Oslo: Rådet for natur- og miljøfag, 1978).
[37] Jan Borring and Per Houge, *Den økologiske krisen i Sahel* (Oslo: Rådet for Natur og Miljøfag, 1975).
[38] Ivar Mytting and Rasmus Hansson, *Friluftsliv i konsesjonsbehandling av vassdragssaker* (Oslo: Rådet for natur- og miljøfag, approx.1980).

Hofseth and his colleagues were involved in action-research groups with students addressing questions related to pollution, urban planning, and public transport.[39] Other action researchers found out why hydropower developments and oil drilling were damaging to rural regions. According to Vinje, rural communities should instead help and support the self-sufficient fishermen-peasants.[40] Another Environmental Studies report noted that oil exploration was the chief underlying cause for social unrest and should thus be viewed with suspicion.[41] With major discoveries of oil in the North Sea, scholars at Environmental Studies tried to halt further exploration as they firmly believed petroleum would take Norway away from the eco-political path of showcasing an environmental alternative to the destructive forces of the European Community and capitalism.[42] The same was true for the nation's hydropower-hungry aluminum industry.[43] In the humanities, an action research milestone for Environmental Studies was the first Norwegian environmental encyclopedia being published in 1976.[44]

Ecophilosophical perspectives and ecology were at the heart of all this action research. "Environmental Studies for Ecopaths" (in analogy to sociopaths or psychopaths) was a journalist's telling description of the institution in the fall of 1977. The "hard working" students were in an unusually "stressful environment," he noted.[45] Apparently, none of the students had seen Hofseth, their chief advisor, for months, as he was traveling around the world with the good news about all the action research in Norway.

EDUCATION IN ECOLOGICAL DOGMATISM

Between 1972 and 1975, about fifteen teaching assistants and ten project-based employees had been working within the temporary ad-hoc

---

[39] Anonymous, "NSU Krets, møtereferat," May 22, 1973, ms. 2 pages, PH. Olav Benestad, "Innstilling om nærtrafikken i Oslo-området," Mar. 29 1971, ms. 2 pages, PH.
[40] Arne Vinje, "Distriktsnedbygging eller auka sjølberging?" *Miljømagasinet*, 5 (1973), 32–4; "Norsk økopolitikk: Fram for auka sjølberging," *Miljømagasinet*, 4 (1973), 30–2.
[41] Paul Hofseth and Harald Celius, *Sosiale konsekvenser av oljevirksomhet i Skottland* (Oslo: Rådet for natur og miljøfag, 1975).
[42] Karina Vogt, "Hard kamp om oljeboring nord for 62°," *Universitas* nr. 12/13 1976, 17, UO.
[43] Reidar Eriksen, Per Halvorsen, and Steve I. Johansen, *Aluminiumsindustriens framtid* (Trondheim: Universitetet i Trondheim, 1977).
[44] Ragnar Frislid, Paul Hofseth, and Johan Støyva (eds.), *Miljøleksikon: Økologi, natur- og miljøvern* (Oslo: Stiftelsen NKI, 1976).
[45] Terje Albregtsen, "Rådet for økopate," *Universitas*, 10/11 (1977), 12, UO; "Frå England til Kaukasus," *Universitas*, 10/11 (1977), 15, UO.

Environmental Studies facilities, reflecting a "green wave" of students eager to join the field.[46] By then Environmental Studies was ready to hire staff, create new courses, and begin various environmental research programs.[47] The time was ripe for long-term planning, research applications, and new appointments. The institution would solidify its position within the University with a new ordinance in 1975,[48] and eventually become a permanent institution in 1976.[49]

In the same period Næss noticed that people working at Environmental Studies had begun to harden their positions, and that the debates among the ecophilosophers often lacked the subtleties he had appreciated within the Nature and Humans seminar back in 1970. Næss too would gradually adopt a more dogmatic position. As he told his friend Alfred J. Ayer, the British philosopher and logical positivist, in a radio interview in 1974: "When we believe that we really must do something about some terrible pressing problem, we must somehow narrow down our perspective. [... Students] need rhetoric and dogmatism, I think. Scepticism breeds passivity. I do not feel that way, but the students do."[50] Indeed, ecological rhetoric and dogmatism is an apt description of what the educational program at Environmental Studies came to be.

The educational program at Environmental Studies began with the core course Nature and Humans. It had the same title as the seminar the Ecophilosophy Group organized at the Philosophy Department in 1970 (see Chapter 3). The course should thus be understood as a continuation of the Group's seminar. Hofseth had a warm and inclusive personality and he used the course to bring the Group together again, both socially and intellectually. He invited them, along with other Deep Ecologists, to be guest lecturers and seminar leaders from wherever they were based, most frequently from within the University.[51]

Many students were complaining that the *Examen philosophicum* required core courses for all freshmen students in logic and the history

---

[46] Kjell Jørgensen,"Grønn bølge," *VG*, July 26, 1975, UO.
[47] Anonymous (interview with Paul Hofseth), "Miljøfagsundervisningen ved Universitetet i Oslo," *Nytt fra Universitetet i Oslo*, 13 (1974), 1–2, UO.
[48] Anonymous, "Reglement for Rådet for natur- og miljøfag," *Nytt fra Universitetet i Oslo*, 8 (1975), 4, UO.
[49] Anonymous," Rådet for natur- og miljøfag er blitt permanent," *Nytt fra Universitetet i Oslo*, 6 (1976), 3–4, UO.
[50] Næss quoted in a debate with Alfred J. Ayer in Fons Elders (eds.), *Reflexive Water: The Basic Concerns of Mankind* (London: Souvenir Press, 1974), 26.
[51] Hjalmar Hegge, "Økologi og filosofi," *Forskningsnytt*, 4 (1973), 54–6.

of philosophy were too narrow or irrelevant. Students in the natural sciences were particularly upset. Why should a young freshman dreaming about becoming a geologist study Plato? In 1973, in an attempt to answer these critiques, the exams were modified so that students could choose between different philosophical topics, in addition to courses in logic and the history of philosophy. These were "Primary Sources in Philosophy," "Practical Argumentation," "Contemporary Philosophy," and "Nature and Humans."[52] The last course was geared toward the displeased science students, and Environmental Studies became the institutional home for the course. As it was one of the University's core courses, a steady flow of freshmen arrived at Environmental Studies. To most of them it was their first impression of academic life. Nature and Humans became a popular course and Environmental Studies would soon struggle to find adequate teaching facilities to house all their students.[53] The course grew in size from around 100 students in 1973 to about 300 by 1982. Within that decade more than 2,000 students had received credits from taking the Nature and Humans course.[54]

When Nature and Humans was offered for the first time in the fall of 1973 it received national attention. Months before the semester began, the press wrote about it, and the newspapers continued to cover its content the entire semester.[55] It was the excursions into the forests near Oslo, interdisciplinary lecture series, study groups with only fifteen students, and daring curriculum that raised eyebrows and challenged traditional ideas of education. In particular its ecophilosophical focus received attention as something unique and newsworthy. In the process, the University of Oslo was portrayed, in both liberal and conservative newspapers, as a progressive institution at the forefront of research and pedagogy.

---

[52] Thor Inge Rørvik, *Historien om examen philosophicum 1675–1983* (Oslo: Forum for University History, 1999), note 367, p. 235.
[53] Anonymous, "Miljøfagundervisning ved Universitetet i Oslo," [interview with Paul Hofseth], *Nytt fra Universitetet i Oslo*, 13 (1974), 1–2, UO; "Rådet for natur- og miljøfag er blitt permanent," *Nytt fra Universitetet i Oslo*, 6 (1976), 3–4, UO.
[54] Ola Glesne, "RNM Undervisning," ms. 13 pages, n.d. [early 1990s], PA.
[55] J. B., "Forberedende øko-filosofi," *Adresseavisen*, June 21 1973, UO. John Baardsgaard, "Forbredende økofilosofi," *Morgenbladet*, Aug. 2, 1973, UO. A. M. R., "3700 til Oslo for å immatrikuleres," *Morgenbladet*, Aug. 29, 1973, UO. Anonymous, "Auditorium i Marka," *Aftenposten*, Oct. 1, 1973, UO. Anonymous, "Miljøundervisning for nye studenter," *Aftenposten*, Sept. 27, 1973, UO. Anonymous, "Seminar om natur- og miljøvern," *Hallingdølen*, Nov. 2, 1973, UO.

Hofseth was the prime architect of the Nature and Humans course. The syllabus from the first semester in the fall of 1973 has been lost. Judging from the subsequent catalogue, the lecture list included, besides Kvaløy, Næss, and Faarlund, two philosophers, an agriculturalist and boat builder, a historian of philosophy, and three ecologists. They were all associated with the Ecophilosophy Group, critical of the European Community and hydropower developments, and opponents of the construction of the Mardøla plant. The ideological uniformity of the course is what held its interdisciplinary content together. Hofseth would also include scholars who happened to be in town as visiting lecturers, such as the Swedish biologist and environmentalist Georg Borgström to discuss his book *The Hungry Planet*.[56]

The syllabus consisted of Næss's book and Kvaløy's manuscript, along with the course reader, *Økofilosofisk lesebok* (Ecophilosophical Reader), which was adorned with a drawing by Kvaløy from the Mardøla demonstration and the motto "COMPLEXITY AGAINST COMPLICATION" on the cover (figure 5). As Kvaløy saw it, the "complexity" of the ecological world was resisting the one dimensional "complication" of the industrial world.[57] The drawing shows rows of metal plates being laid upon a pristine landscape with small picturesque farms and the Mardøla Waterfall in the background. In the midst of the drawing one can see the do-gooding environmental activists with their tents trying to halt the advance of industrialism by means of non-violent dialogue and demonstrations.

In the Nature and Humans reader students would study whether or not the ancient Greeks lived in ecological harmony (they did)[58], whether the Scripture conveyed ecological wisdom (it did)[59], and whether "standard

---

[56] Lecturers included the philosophers Jon Wetlesen and Haftor Viestad, the agriculturalist and boat builder Jon Boyer Godal, the historian of philosophy Hjalmar Hegge, and the ecologists Henning Dunker, Magnar Norderhaug, and Ivar Mysterud. George Borgstrøm, *Mat for milliarder* (1962) (Oslo: Gyldendal, 1968).
[57] Sigmund Kvaløy, "Økofilosofi som forståelsesnøkkel," in Paul Hofseth (ed.), *Økofilosofisk lesebok*, vol. 1 (Oslo: Samarbeidsgruppa for natur og miljøvern, 1974), ms. 16 pages. Øystein Nesje, "Økofilosofisk lesebok" (review), *Miljømagasinet*, 6 (1974), 30.
[58] Hans Eirik Aarek, "Gresk naturoppfatning og vitenskap," in Paul Hofseth (ed.), *Økofilosofisk lesebok*, vol. 2. (Oslo: Samarbeidsgruppa for natur og miljøvern, 1974), ms. 20 pages.
[59] Gunnar Breivik, "Læren om Gud og det store huset: (teo-logi og øko-logi)," in Paul Hofseth (ed.), *Økofilosofisk lesebok*, vol. 2. (Oslo: Samarbeidsgruppa for natur og miljøvern, 1974), ms. 17 pages.

FIGURE 5 The front-page of the Ecophilosophical Reader used in the Nature and Humans course. Drawing by Sigmund Kvaløy, 1973.
Courtesy of the University of Oslo Archive

of living" was the same as "quality of life" (it was not)[60], to mention just a few of the topics on the syllabus in addition to other ecophilosophical readings by Kvaløy, Næss, and Peter W. Zapffe. In addition to all the male authors there was also a female anthropologist who upheld the ecological outlook of Fredrik Barth (see Chapter 1).[61] The entire semester was introduced by a lecture on the science of ecology by Ivar Mysterud that captured the basic elements of the Odum brothers' ecosystem methodologies for nature and society.[62] The virtue of outdoor life was at the heart of all the articles, which, according to an external reviewer, were anything but an easy read.[63] The underlying questions in these readings were about how to formulate a good, viable, environmental alternative to the destructive powers of the world, namely the European Community, NATO, the Soviet Union, and the United States. Scholars who supported one of these powers were generally not welcomed as lecturers or as authors for the reader in Environmental Studies.

One such example was the Marxist urban planner Erling Amble, who was not invited to make his case against ecophilosophy and eco-politics in the students' reader. Another was the geologist Ivan Rosenqvist, who was invited to lecture only once or twice and whose many articles were not included in the syllabus. The reason was simple. They represented the Marxist-Leninist line of reasoning that was behind the onslaught on the Deep Ecologists. Yet instead of inviting the Marxists to make their case in the reader or in the classroom, the Nature and Humans course focused on ecophilosophical topics and declined to engage with their critics.

Anfinn Stigen, the classicist, may also serve as an example of a scholar who was not included in Environmental Studies' inner fold. He was an Associate Professor at the Department of Philosophy and was involved in developing and teaching the *Examen philosophicum* curriculum. "There must be an expansion of the humanistic and culture conserving disciplines at the expense of the natural sciences," he argued back in 1971. Ecology

---

[60] Hjalmar Hegge, "Livskvalitet og levestandard," in Paul Hofseth (ed.), *Økofilosofisk lesebok*, vol. 2. (Oslo: Samarbeidsgruppa for natur og miljøvern, 1974), ms. 7 pages.

[61] Ingrid Rudie, "Økologi og kultur," in Paul Hofseth (ed.), *Økofilosofisk lesebok*, vol. 1. (Oslo: Samarbeidsgruppa for natur og miljøvern, 1974), pp. 110–31; *Visible Women in East Coast Malay Society* (Oxford: Oxford University Press, 1994).

[62] Ivar Mysterud, "Noen økologiske grunnbegreper," in Paul Hofseth (ed.), *Økofilosofisk lesebok*, vol. 1. (Oslo: Samarbeidsgruppa for natur og miljøvern, 1974), ms. 48 pages. Eugene P. Odum, *Fundamentals of Ecology*, 3rd ed. (Philadelphia: Saunders Co., 1971). Howard Odum, *Environment, Power and Society* (New York: Wiley, 1971).

[63] Øystein Nesse, "Økofilosofisk lesebok," *Miljømagasinet*, 5 (1974), 31; "Økofilosofisk lesebok," *Miljømagasinet*, 6 (1974), 30.

should be an exception, as this field addressed both natural and human needs. He worried about there being too much biology in ecological research, and therefore thought the philosophers should be in control: "Ecology should be a university discipline, and it is natural that it falls under the field of philosophy."[64] That Stigen thought ecology should be taught as a subfield of philosophy is surely evidence of the importance of ecological thinking at the Department of Philosophy which, in 1971, included the highly visible and vocal Ecophilosophy Group. There were also more pragmatic reasons for Stigen's endorsement of ecology. Perhaps it could be a remedy for displeased natural scientists criticizing the mandatory *Examen philosophicum* courses for paying too much attention to the history of philosophy? To prove his case he set out to write a textbook on the history of human relations to nature that would be used for the new Nature and Humans course at Environmental Studies. The first draft, *Mennesket og naturen* (Humans and Nature, 1973), was inspired in style and content by Clarence Glacken's famous *Traces on the Rhodian Shore* (1967), and sketched out the history of what mostly philosophers had said about human relations to nature since ancient times.[65] As a synopsis of the history of Western intellectual history, it is a remarkable manuscript that easily surpasses similar books in Norwegian at the time. Indeed, within the next decade, Stigen's manuscript evolved into his two-volume masterpiece *Tenkningens historie* (History of Thinking, 1983), a textbook in the history of science and philosophy that over the years has been read by hundreds of thousands of students in Norway preparing for their *Examen philosophicum*.[66]

Despite Stigen's success and importance, his work (in the form of a short article) was on the syllabus for only the first year at Environmental Studies.[67] The reason was quite simple. He was not in the Ecophilosophy Group's inner circle that once took over Næss's Nature and Humans seminar, his lectures and work did not directly address the

---

[64] Karl Gåsvatn (interview with Anfinn Stigen), "Menneskeverd og miljø viktigere enn naturvitenskap," *Vårt land,* May 18, 1971, UO.
[65] Anfinn Stigen, *Mennesket og naturen,* ms. 308 pages, 1973, NB. Clarence J. Glacken, *Traces on the Rhodian Shore: Nature and Culture in Western Thought from Ancient Times to the End of the Eighteenth Century* (Berkeley, CA: University of California Press, 1967).
[66] Anfinn Stigen, *Tenkningens historie,* 2 vol. (Oslo: Gyldendal, 1983).
[67] Anfinn Stigen, "En del hovedpunkter i forelesning 'mennesket og naturen' holdt for examen philosophicum studenter september 1973." In Paul Hofseth (eds.), *Økofilosofisk lesebok,* vol. 2 (Oslo: Samarbeidsgruppa for natur og miljøvern, 1974), ms. 7 pages.

ecological crisis, and he did not deliver a clear ecophilosophical message about the evils of the industrial society and the European Community. Finally, he adopted an anthropocentric understanding of human relations with nature in line with the thinking of the philosopher Immanuel Kant. Thus, he failed to adhere to the social and ideology matrix of Environmental Studies.

A philosopher who did conform was Hjalmar Hegge. With an interest in Johann Wolfgang von Goethe, subjectivism, and the importance of colors to perception, he was a part of the Ecophilosophy Group from its inception. Following German philosopher Jürgen Habermas, he was among one of several thinkers that criticized positivist philosophy and managerial politics based on natural sciences.[68] To him, ecology was a scientific approach to the world that avoided the pitfalls of reductionist mechanical sciences as it (he believed) encompassed secondary sense perceptions such as smell and colors. Unlike atomistic sciences that lead to an unfortunate objectification of humans as manageable individuals in society, ecology offered a unified view of humans as active agents in both nature and society. Hegge set out to show that only an ecologically informed philosophy could offer a viable way out of the environmental crisis.[69] Like Stigen, Hegge also wrote a textbook for the Nature and Humans course. Unlike Stigen's manuscript, it was accepted as a textbook, and the book also became popular with the wider public. *Mennesket og naturen: Naturforståelsen gjennom tidene – med særlig henblikk på vår tids miljøkrise* (Humans and Nature: Understandings of Nature throughout History – With a Special View on the Environmental Crisis of Our Time, 1978), as it was entitled, was a 150-page tour-de-force of Western philosophy of science. He argued that the eco-crisis began with mechanist thinking of the sixteenth-century scientific revolution, and the remedy was a turn toward "soft" technology and human ecology.[70] Hegge felt it important that humans had a unique niche in nature's economy, and he spent quite a lot of time modifying Kvaløy and Næss's philosophies to avoid the pitfalls of biological reductionism. "Social-Darwinism" was not the answer to the eco-crisis, he argued in a critique

---

[68] Hjalmar Hegge, "Jürgen Habermas og erkjennelsesteoriens dilemma," *Norsk filosofisk tidsskrift*, 4 (1969), 133–58; "Theory of Science in the Light of Goethe's Science of Nature," *Inquiry*, 15 (1972), 363–86.
[69] Hjalmar Hegge, "Økologi og filosofi."
[70] Hjalmar Hegge, *Mennesket og naturen: Naturforståelsen gjennom tidene – med særlig henblikk på vår tids miljøkrise* (Oslo: Universitetsforlaget, 1978), 153.

of where the thinking of his colleagues could lead. He instead suggested a "human ecology" inspired by the German Romantics as a remedy.[71]

During the first five years, while ecophilosophers and ecologists dominated the seminar intellectually, students were also exposed to a lecture on natural resource policies.[72] At the time Jørgen Randers, the co-author of *The Limits to Growth* report from 1972, was undoubtedly Norway's most prominent environmental academic, especially with respect to resource policies. Chapter 7 will discuss at length his importance in Norway and beyond. At this stage it's sufficient to note that in the spring of 1974 he was actively seeking a place and an audience for his research in Oslo, as he wanted to return to his hometown after his graduate studies and professorship at MIT. Environmental Studies did not welcome him and instead gave him the cold shoulder, as they deemed him to be a "shallow" technocrat and therefore an opponent of their cause. Scholars lecturing at Environmental Studies were picked chiefly on whether or not they contributed to the Deep Ecological vision for an alternative nation that the world could admire as an example of a possible harmonious global future. As a result, Randers was not on the syllabus for the Nature and Humans course.

In 1979, six years after its inception, the Nature and Humans course was reorganized and the syllabus updated to make room for more social and natural sciences on the syllabus. The reorganization was done by Skønberg, who had taken over as course coordinator. He was an ardent follower of Kvaløy,[73] and he consequently sought to fashion the course so that it would be interdisciplinary but "by no means balanced ... in the sense that all or most views on an issue were being presented," as the main point of the course was to spread and engage with Kvaløy's ecophilosophical perspective.[74] Consequently, the syllabus was still strongly influenced by the past. The article introducing ecology, for example, was informed by the Odum brothers' steady-state nature at a time when most ecologists were debating fresh insights by Edward O. Wilson and

---

[71] Hjalmar Hegge, "Human-økologi eller sosial-darwinisme: Veier og avveier i økofilosofien," *Norsk filosofisk tidsskrift*, 12, no. 1 (1977), 1–24.
[72] Jon Godal, "Litt om Ressurser," in Paul Hofseth (ed.), *Økofilosofisk lesebok*, vol. 1 (Oslo: Samarbeidsgruppa for natur og miljøvern, 1974), ms. 16 pages.
[73] Øystein Nesje and Sven Erik Skønberg, "Økokrisen, Norge, og vi: Intervju med Sigmund Kvaløy," *Miljømagasinet*, 6 (1974), pp. 20–2, 28.
[74] Øystein Nesje and Sven Erik Skønberg, "Forord," in *Natur og menneske: artikkelsamling* (Oslo: Rådet for natur og miljøfag, 1980–82), pp. 1–12, quote p. 6.

Richard Dawkins,[75] and issues related to growth in human populations were supported by well-worn footnotes.[76] Næss – who was hardly known for elegant prose – was taken off the syllabus and replaced with a more accessible text summarizing his views. "On Borneo one can find a thicket primeval forest that not even the sharpest machete can clear. That we do not have in Norway. On the other hand, we have philosophical treatises," Skønberg told his students when he explained the omission.[77]

New on the syllabus was a series of articles focusing on the Global South, which emphasized that students should learn from life in the non-industrial world. The course pushed forward the view that Indigenous people lived in harmony with nature,[78] they could offer an alternative view on the meaning of development,[79] and they had an economy worthy of admiration.[80] These claims were backed up by an account of life in Beding, Nepal, as Kvaløy knew it from his visits with Næss and Faarlund.[81] The turn toward developmental studies sought to help the Global South with ecological insights provided by thinkers from the North and reflected a new interest from students in anthropology.

Throughout the first decade of Environmental Studies, the Nature and Humans course was at its heart both socially and intellectually. It brought the institution together. Environmental Studies was also on a mission to spread the syllabus through their Deep Ecology network by establishing

---

[75] Ola Glesne, "Noen økologiske grunnbegreper," in *Natur og menneske: artikkelsamling* (Oslo: Rådet for natur og miljøfag, [1979]), pp. 13–27. Edward Wilson, *Sociobiology: The New Synthesis* (Cambridge, MA: Harvard University Press, 1975). Richard Dawkins, *The Selfish Gene* (Oxford: Oxford University Press, 1976).
[76] Ann Norderhaug and Magnar Norderhaug, "Norge og overbefolkningen," in *Natur og menneske: artikkelsamling* (Oslo: Rådet for natur og miljøfag, 1979), pp. 156–88.
[77] Skønberg was paraphrasing a well-known aphorism by Darwin P. Erlandsen. Sven Erik Skønberg, "Norsk økofilosofi," in *Natur og menneske: artikkelsamling* (Oslo: Rådet for natur og miljøfag, 1979), pp. 63–81, quote p. 63.
[78] Harald Beyer-Brock, "Den økologiske harmonimodell," in *Natur og menneske: artikkelsamling* (Oslo: Rådet for natur og miljøfag, 1979), pp. 243–8; "Den økologiske 'harmonimodell' sett i lys av jegere og sankere, eller de såkalte naturfolk," *Naturen*, 3 (1977), 99–103.
[79] Erik Nord, "Underutvikling og utvikling," in *Natur og menneske: artikkelsamling* (Oslo: Rådet for natur og miljøfag, 1979), pp. 189–229.
[80] Marshal Sahlins, "Primitiv økonomi," in *Natur og menneske: artikkelsamling* (Oslo: Rådet for natur og miljøfag, 1979), pp. 37–46.
[81] Sigmund Kvaløy, "Økokrise, natur og menneske," in *Natur og menneske: artikkelsamling* (Oslo: Rådet for natur og miljøfag, 1979), pp. 82–119; "Buddisme-økologi. Et tanke slektskap," in *Natur og menneske: artikkelsamling* (Oslo: Rådet for natur og miljøfag, [1979]), p. 249.

similar Nature and Humans courses at other colleges in Norway.[82] In this context, Vinje and Hofseth published an updated reader with a large publishing house in order to reach a national audience.[83] This was done in the spirit of trying to bring about an alternative nation founded on deep ecological values. The idea was to foster a new "counter-expertise" generation of "generalists who could act upon insight and have a critical attitude" to shallow ecological thinking when leaving academia.[84]

In the fall semester of 1974, to answer student demand, Environmental Studies created the *Miljøfagsseminaret* (Environmental Studies Seminar) for those seeking to advance beyond the required Nature and Humans course. It was designed so that students could study environmental issues while, at the same time, working with scholars and staff to do action research aimed at solving actual environmental problems. As a full-time semester seminar (16 credits by today's standard in the USA), it began with the weeklong excursion into scenic nature, giving the students an opportunity to focus their minds on the natural environment.[85] From 1974 to 1982, a total of 176 students took the course. While the ecophilosophers became increasingly dogmatic in the late 1970s, the seminar reflected Hofseth's own move toward more pragmatic, hands-on solutions to the environmental issues. The empirical and practical how-to approach made the candidates attractive for the growing body of administrative positions in the nation's emerging environmental bureaucracy.

Environmental Studies put much effort into building up this educational program in order to satisfy the growing demand in the public sector for people competent in environmental affairs. Their focus was not only on young students, but also on adult education and reeducation.[86] Indeed, between 1977 and 1982 Environmental Studies offered a course

---

[82] Anonymous, "Kurs i miljøkunnskap på Distriktshøskolen," *Lofotposten*, n.d. 1975, UO. Anonymous, "Ny linje med særlig vekt på økologi til høsten," *Sunnmørsposten*, Mar. 19, 1977, UO. Aage Gløen, "Refleksjoner efter kurs i natur- og miljøvernspørsmål i Oppegård," *Østlandets blad*, May 26, 1977, UO.

[83] Paul Hofseth and Arne Vinje (eds.), *Økologi Økofilosofi* (Oslo, Gyldendal, 1975).

[84] Nesje and Skønberg, "Forord," pp. 4, 12.

[85] Anonymous, "God generalprøve for Miljøfagseminaret," *Nytt fra Universitetet i Oslo*, 5, Mar. 18, 1975, 2, UO.

[86] Paul Hofseth, "Voksenopplæring og desentralisert miljøfagundervisning," in Lars Emmelin (ed.), *Miljöverdsutbildning vid universitet och högskoler* (Oslo: Nordisk ministerråd, 1977), pp. 62–70. Per Arild Garnåsjordet, "Forskerutdanning i natur- og miljøfag," in Lars Emmelin (ed.), *Miljöverdsutbildning vid universitet och högskoler* (Oslo: Nordisk ministerråd, 1977), pp. 71–80. Sigmund Lieberg, *Environmental Education in Nordic Compulsory Schools* (Copenhagen: Nordisk ministerråd, 1976).

in environment and nature preservation for college and high-school science teachers that was attended by a total of 266 tutors.[87] Scholars at Environmental Studies also wrote a report on higher education in environmental studies in Norway in which they documented – in no uncertain terms – that work done at Environmental Studies represented the vanguard of environmentalism in Norway.[88]

A missionary undertone or do-gooding gaze on behalf of the environment was a driving force in these writings and courses. The next chapter will discuss this religious aspiration in more detail, arguing that Environmental Studies mobilized a deep seated pietist Norwegian longing for the lost Eden.

---

[87] Ola Glesne, "RNM Undervisning," ms. 13 pages, n.d. [early 1990s], PA.
[88] Trond Knudsen, Karen Johanne Baalsrud, and Paul Hofseth, *Miljøfagundervisning utover videregående skole: en oversikt over undervisningsopplegg og litteratur* (Oslo: Rådet for natur- og miljøfag, 1978).

6

The Call for a New Ecoreligion

Morning has broken like the first morning,
blackbird has spoken like the first bird.
Praise for the singing, praise for the morning,
praise for them springing fresh from the Word!
Norwegian book of hymns, Hymn 801.

"Nature is the true religion for Norwegians. Our gods are named the Mountain, the Plateau, the Ocean."[1] There is some truth to this saying, which has its origin in a comment by the peace researcher Johan Galtung. In Norway it is normal for even devoted Christians to skip Sunday church in favor of a nature walk or cross-country skiing. And when attending church, the faithful often sing hymns filled with nature metaphors. The believer's gaze of knowing the source of goodness may come from the gospel, but it may also come from pristine nature as the nation's spiritual life takes place outdoors in scenic environments rather than inside buildings. The Deep Ecologist Arne Næss was no exception. He looked at the Hallingskarvet Mountain, where his own cabin was located, as a religious force. To him technical "climbing was hailing and pilgrimage" to the mountain, as Hallingskarvet to him had the status of "what one in the mythology calls a god (deva), and fortunately a good one."[2] His longtime

---

[1] Johan Galtung quoted in Niels Chr. Geelmuyden, *Grepet i Ord* (Tjøme: eBokNorden, 2014). Cf. Henrik Ibsen, *Brand*, 1867. Eleanor Farjeon, "Morning has broken," in *Norske salmebok* (Bergen: Eide forlag, 2013), hymn 801, p. 920.

[2] Arne Næss, "Klatrefilosofiske og biografiske betraktninger," *Mestre fjellet*, 17, no. 16 (1975), 17–16.

collaborator Per Ingvar Haukeland articulated a similar sentiment in his book *Himmeljorden* (Heavenly Earth, 2009) framed on his Quaker-inspired beliefs.[3]

How are we to understand this religious point of view? And how did environmentalists engage and utilize religious language and traditions when speaking about the environment? Fortunately, historians of religion have partly answered this question by showing that ecologically informed ethics and politics often invoke the language of religion when making their points. The historian Mark S. Stoll, for example, has shown that the rise of American environmentalism owes a great deal to Christian religious traditions.[4] The case is similar to Norwegian environmentalism, which, according to Tarjei Rønnow, represents a "new pietism" invoking age-old Lutheran values, rituals, and systems of belief when seeking to "save nature."[5] What has yet to be understood are the historical details of how and why environmentalists came to adapt religious language, and how theologians responded. This chapter will review this process in some detail, arguing that the Deep Ecologists were instrumental in giving the Church of Norway the ecological focus it has today.

The Evangelical Lutheran Church of Norway, it is worth noting, is a state church in which roughly eighty percent of Norwegians are registered members. The other twenty percent of people in the country consists mostly of non-believers, and tiny groups of Catholics, Quakers, Jews, Buddhists, Muslims, and Norse pagans. Internationally, the Church receives its chief intellectual support through its membership in the Lutheran World Federation and the World Council of Churches. The King, the Prime Minister, and the majority of the Cabinet Ministers were, as official leaders of the Church, obliged to profess Lutheran faith, making the Church the all-dominating force in Norwegian religious life. It is a fairly democratic institution in which representatives of the parishes, deaneries, and dioceses elect the General Synod, which has the National Council as its executive body. This organizational structure has, as will be apparent, consequences for the way in which ecological

---

[3] Per Ingvar Haukeland, *Himmeljorden: Om det av Gud i Naturen* (Oslo: Kvekerforlaget, 2009).

[4] Mark S. Stoll, *Inherit the Holy Mountain: Religion and the Rise of American Environmentalism* (Oxford: Oxford University Press, 2015).

[5] Tarjei Rønnow, "Takk gode Gud for moder jord, hun gjør oss ett med alt som gror: Religiøsitet og miljøengasjement i Norge," *Norsk antropologisk tidsskrift*, 15 (2004), 18–31; *Saving Nature: Religion as Environmentalism, Environmentalism as Religion* (Münster: LIT Verlag, 2011).

thinking could spread within the Church. How did it respond to the eco-crisis? The attempt to save the Mardøla River from hydropower development in the summer of 1970 was the issue that brought ecological concerns to the public forefront in Norway. How did the Church react to the arguments expressed by vocal Deep Ecologists trying to save the river? These activists began a fierce public debate about nature conservation, focusing on human attitudes to the natural world. As a result, no public institution of moral importance could avoid taking a stand on ecological issues, especially the Church.

The issues at stake were not only about development of rivers, but also about industrialization, human population growth, and pollution. As will be argued, the Deep Ecologists' questioning of economic growth, technocracy, and industrialism appealed to many theologians, who often also sympathized with the Deep Ecologists' endorsement of outdoor life, rural communities, and modest lifestyles. This chapter will review early attempts by theologians and some key lay believers to incorporate ecological perspectives and beliefs into the Church. For them, environmentalism represented an opportunity to revive the Church's pietist Lutheran doctrine among the young and thereby mobilize a new audience. This chapter will first point to the role of religion among ecophilosophers and biologists, as it was within this group that the first Norwegian eco-theological thinking emerged. The subsequent sections will show how the Church responded by endorsing the eco-religious perspective.

DEEP ECOLOGY AND RELIGION

In 1971 Lynn White's article "The Historical Roots of Our Ecologic Crisis" appeared for the first time in Norwegian.[6] In this article the medieval historian accused Judeo-Christian theology of nurturing an exploitative ethic toward the natural world. The anthropocentric domination of nature was at the core of the Bible's message, according to White, as it states that humans were formed in God's image and thus are superior to the rest of the world. The article had originally appeared in *Science* in 1967 and was thus well known among Norwegian ecologists following the international debate. The translation aimed at bringing White's

---

[6] Lynn T. White, "The historical roots of our ecologic crisis," *Science*, 155, no. 3767 (Mar. 10, 1967), 1203–7; translated into Norwegian as "Den økologiske krises historiske røtter," *Naturen*, 95 (1971), 77–92.

critique to a broader Norwegian audience, as it appeared in the popular science journal *Naturen* (Nature).

Most ecologists, environmental activists, and philosophers in Norway were non-believers. It is therefore not surprising that White's article was initially read as a contribution to the argument to weaken the role of religion in society in order to advance the ecological cause. Even though creationism never achieved any real weight in Norway, most scientists saw religion in opposition to science, as faith could not be mixed with ecological facts.[7] There was also a wide mistrust of religion among left-leaning students, activists, and environmentalists who tended to agree with Karl Marx's famous saying that religion "is the opium of the people." Thus, many of the environmentalists would not include religion in their discussions of the eco-crisis, and White's arguments explained why. Instead, people hoped that ecological science in itself could be a substitute giving "aim and meaning" in a secularized world.[8]

Among the philosophically informed ecologists, there was a general uneasiness about this dominating tendency to exclude religious beliefs from the framework of analysis. In 1972, a non-religious graduate student on the International Biological Program at the University of Oslo made a plea to end capitalism and establish a steady-state society based on eco-political principles by emphasizing the importance of moving beyond technological answers to the environmental crisis.[9] This was an issue of nurturing belief in the power of environmental ethics and lifestyles, and increasing faith in the value of a radical moral change in human attitudes toward nature.

As shown in previous chapters, the importance of a moral stand against industrial technocracy was at the core of Deep Ecology. As a consequence, the ecophilosophers would look with hope and admiration upon those with a system of beliefs in tune with their ecological views. They would often make it clear that they were involved in a social movement within which people had different perspectives and reasons for why one should protect the environment. Thus, people with religious beliefs were welcomed to join the group as long as they were credible defenders of nature. Indeed, the difference between being a "deep" and a "shallow" ecologist depended on whether or not one went beyond mere

---

[7] Arne Rønnild, "Gud og naturvitenskapen," *Tidsskrift for teologi og kirke*, 48 (1977), 193–203.
[8] Lyngnes, "Kan biologisk kunnskap gjeve dei unge mål og meining med livet?"
[9] Harald Olsen, "Mot en økopolitisk enhetsfront?" *Kirke og kultur*, 77 (1972), 397–405.

technocratic or economic reasons for sheltering ecological complexity. The environmentalists within Norway's tiny Quaker group were particularly active in engaging with the Deep Ecologists by publishing articles and books on the importance of ecology to Christian spirituality. They also invited Kvaløy, Næss, and several other key members to voice their views in their Quaker journal.[10]

Thus, the ecophilosophers recognized that religion could be a powerful ally for a common cause if its principles and practice showed respect for the environment. Though he wasn't strictly speaking a Deep Ecologist, Johan Galtung's statement at the 3rd World Future Research Conference in Bucharest in 1972 may illustrate this sentiment: "A nature without soul is easy to destroy; a nature with soul is one that invites partnership, respect, equilibrium."[11] Issues related to God and ecology were debated at the Peace Research Institute in Oslo where Galtung was in charge. In 1967 they hosted the first conference for the World Futures Studies Federation, and one of the topics discussed was the separation of humans, God, and nature in Christian thinking that allowed for and encouraged exploitation of the world's material resources.[12] As a remedy, the peace researchers, including Galtung, pointed to the wisdom of Oriental thinking and religion.

There were several reasons behind Galtung and the Deep Ecologists looking toward the Orient for answers. Most generally, this region represented a viable alternative source of inspiration for those who refused to take a side in the Cold War deadlock. Galtung and Næss had (as discussed in Chapter 3) published a couple of books about Gandhi, which pointed toward his non-violent thinking as the key for unlocking tensions between communists and capitalists. In the process they also learned to appreciate Buddhism and the Bhagavad-Gita. This was not only an intellectual issue, as they, along with fellow ecophilosophers, visited India, Nepal, Iran, and Pakistan to draw inspiration from the region. The visit to Nepal and the village of Beding by Kvaløy, Nils Faarlund, and Næss in the summer of 1971 may illustrate this. The nearby mountain Gauri Shankar was considered holy and thus untouchable for the Sherpa living there, an approach to nature the ecophilosophers found impressive.

---

[10] Hans Eirik Aarek, *Kristendom og økologi* (Ås: Kvekerforlaget, 1978). Arne Næss, "Grønn sosialisme," *Kvekeren*, 5 (1972), 71–2. Sigmund Kvaløy, "Trenger mennesket uberørt natur?" *Kvekeren*, 1 (1973), 6–7.

[11] Galtung, "'The limits to growth' and class politics," p. 108.

[12] Guttorm Gjessing, "Ecology and peace research," *Journal of Peace Research*, 4 (1967), 125–39.

6 The Call for a New Ecoreligion

As technical climbers who had traveled to Beding to reach the peak of the mountain, they decided to abandon this aim in respect for Sherpa beliefs. This was a personal sacrifice and a learning experience for all of them as, from then on, they would abandon the view that climbing was about reaching mountain peaks. To Næss the belief in the holiness of the Gauri Shankar would serve as evidence of the power of religion as a source of resistance to the exploitation of nature.[13] Faarlund and Kvaløy would both express similar points of views.[14]

These views raised important questions with respect to religion and science. In February 1972 the ecophilosophers gathered at a small seminar at Tømte Gård, a picturesque botanical Research Station near Oslo, to discuss the issue. The seminar was arranged by David Klein, an ecologist at the University of Alaska who was spending his sabbatical year at the University of Oslo from the fall of 1971 to research reindeer, among other things.[15] Among roughly thirty participants were, aside from Kvaløy and Næss, ecologists such as Ivar Mysterud, Eivind Østbye, and Eigil Reimers (b. 1939).

Næss gave the keynote lecture (which is lost). Judging from Klein's response it is likely that it was about ecology and the Bible, as the section of Næss's "Ecosophy T" that deals with this topic was written in this period. Here White's criticisms of Christian domination of nature served as his point of departure, though Næss would quickly turn to what he saw as a largely forgotten eco-friendly outlook on the Bible. Inspired by the studies of John N. Black and Clarence Glacken, among others, he pointed out that one could not judge the environmental friendliness of a person based on whether or not he or she believed in the Bible.[16] Næss was not a believer himself, but saw Christians as potential allies for the emerging Deep Ecology movement. There was plenty of support for an ecological sensitivity in the Bible, he argued, and quoted several passages from both the Old and the New Testament to support his view.

---

[13] Arne Næss, "Skytsgudinnen Gauri Shankar: Appell om fredning," *Mestre fjellet*, 13 (1972), 15.
[14] Nils Faarlund, "Glimt fra klatringen på eggen," *Mestre fjellet*, 13 (1972), 9–10. Sigmund Kvaløy Setreng, "Tseringma-hymnen og det hellige fjell Tseringma," in Sven Erik Skønberg (ed.), *Grønn pepper i turbinene* (Oslo: Universitetsforlaget, 1985), pp. 81–4.
[15] Eigil Reimers, David R. Klein, and Rolf Sørumgård, "Calving time, growth rate, and body size of Norwegian reindeer on different ranges," *Arctic and Alpine Research*, 15 (1983), 107–18.
[16] Næss, *Økologi og filosofi*, 3rd ed., 160–8. John N. Black, *The Dominion of Man: The Search for Ecological Responsibility* (Edinburgh: Edinburgh University Press, 1970). Glacken, *Traces on the Rhodian Shore*, 1967.

Næss was not the only one at Tømte who saw religion as a source of insight for understanding the deeper meaning of ecology. Most active was Kvaløy who upon his return from his travels to Nepal became deeply fascinated by Buddhism and began in earnest to study the Bhagavad-Gita. It was especially the Tantric idea of a spiritual dimension to the web of life which fascinated Kvaløy, as it revealed "mother earth's treasures" and allowed an animistic view of nature's ecology.[17] This was not only of academic importance to Kvaløy, as in this period he also began to practice Buddhism. Indeed, he would draw elaborate pictures depicting monks in Beding, meditating on the holiness of the mountain Gauri Shankar that, in his words, depicted a "reunion with the One that flows through the entire nature."[18] As a charismatic leader of the ecophilosophy group, the Deep Ecology movement, and the Mardøla demonstrations, he was most definitely an authority among both students and nature protectors. That Buddhism could offer a way forward in understanding nature's rhythms and life on Earth raised interest and eyebrows among the concerned environmentalists.

At the Tømte seminar there were thus three competing answers to the question of the role of religion in environmentalism in response to White's criticisms of Christian domination of nature. The ecologists, including Mysterud and Østbye, thought the ecological debate would be better off if one stuck to ethical issues and kept religion out of the picture. Næss, on the other hand, thought that potential allies for the Deep Ecology movement could be gained by mobilizing a more humble human caretaker role from the Bible, while Kvaløy abandoned the Christian heritage altogether in favor of Buddhism.

Coming from the University of Alaska, Klein found ecophilosophy to be a new intellectual territory. On the one hand, he was fascinated and flattered by the philosophers taking an interest in his lectures on wildlife ecology and management as well as his collaborative research on wild reindeer with Reimers. On the other hand, he saw a flight from reason in religious adaptations of ecology. At Tømte he asked the audience:

---

[17] Sigmund Kvaløy, "Mother Earth's treasures and their revealers," in Padma Tshewang, Phuntsok Tashi, Chris Butters, and Sigmund Sætreng (eds.), *The Treasure Revealers of Bhutan* (Kathmandu: Bibliothecha Himalayica, 1995), pp. 139–58; "Norwegian Ecophilosophy and Ecopolitics and their Influence from Buddhism."

[18] Sigmund Kvaløy, "Gjenforeningen med det Ene som gjennomstrømmer all natur" (drawing). In Gunnar Breivik and Haakon Løymo (eds.), *Friluftsliv fra Fridtjof Nansen til våre dager* (Oslo: Universitetsforlaget, 1978), p. 193.

What form will this new ecophilosophy take? Will it supplant, alter or be absorbed into existing religious theology and become the new ecoreligion that offers the salvation of mankind as a substitute for salvation of the individual; or will it be merely another parameter of human understanding, outside of religion, scientifically based, but recognized for its importance to the future of human society.[19]

Klein was in favor of the last option. To him this was an issue of intellectual hierarchy: science and not religion should be at the core of knowledge. Yet he recognized that the "mass media capitalizing on the public interest in ecology, plus the inexactness of ecology as a science," made his field vulnerable to absorption into existing cultural conceptions and religions.[20] When Klein wrote his paper ecology was much in the news, both in Norway and in the USA, and the research field's lack of precision was also widely recognized among biologists. What worried Klein was the bending of ecological research in support of what could easily end up as authoritarian religious dogma. "[T]he current ecological movement [is] strongly infused with a 'religious' emotionalism and a revival of vitalism in attitudes toward nature," he claimed.[21] Moreover:

[S]ome philosophers and ecologist-conservationists have ... become spokesmen for the developing ecoreligion. They argue that the survival of the human species in the face of an impending "eco-crisis" is dependent upon the widespread adoption of a religious humility toward nature. They admittedly are searching for a "panacea for the masses" on the premise that the end (in this case the survival of mankind) justifies the means. Their motivations therefore, while sincere, are pragmatic rather than epistemological.[22]

Næss was the chief target of this criticism as he valued a potential ecoreligion on pragmatic grounds. Klein would have none of it. He also warned against developing a new ecoreligion on epistemological grounds, as Kvaløy suggested. Klein believed that it could easily, like all religions, develop into an "emotional self-righteousness" ideology that would justify and encourage irrational or destructive acts "in the name of piety."[23] Therefore, the idea of fundamentalism developing in the name of the

---

[19] David R. Klein, "The Emerging Ecophilosophy," unpublished, Feb. 1972, typescript 7 pages, quote p. 1, PA. I am grateful to Klein for making the manuscript available. David R. Klein, *The Making of an Ecologist*, Karen Brewster (ed.) (Fairbanks, Alaska: University of Alaska Press, 2019), 437–56.
[20] Klein, "The Emerging Ecophilosophy," p. 1.
[21] Klein, "The Emerging Ecophilosophy," p. 2.
[22] Klein, "The Emerging Ecophilosophy," pp. 3–4.
[23] Klein, "The Emerging Ecophilosophy," p. 4.

environment and environmental good was the issue at stake here. As Klein said, "One wonders how many Giordano Brunos might be at least figuratively burned at the stake in the name of an ecoreligion."[24]

Instead of an ecoreligion, Klein argued, the philosophers should formulate a new eco-ethics or philosophy with a scientific foundation. Mysterud and Østbye agreed, and they had an impact. Næss, for example, thought Klein's "warning against ecoreligion" was "very relevant!"[25] Two years later he would recall the paper saying that "Klein may be right in his fear that the ecological movement, as any other, will foster some sectarianism and thereby intolerance, arrogance, verbal rituals instead of debate, [and] sentimentality instead of spontaneity." Yet he could not agree with Klein that an ecophilosophy or ecoreligion firmly based on non-violence "would lead to persecution of the ecosophic 'infidel'."[26]

The ecophilosophers at the Tømte seminar would, in effect, take Klein's warnings to heart, as their subsequent writings would focus on philosophical and not theological arguments. This was not a hard choice for Næss, who wrote about theology for the sole purpose of broadening his audience, while in public appearances Kvaløy would focus on environmental issues and less on his Buddhist beliefs. Yet the inclusive mood of thinking with respect to ethics, beliefs, and religion by ecophilosophers and some ecologists sent important signals to the Christian community. "Ecosophy is a kind of philosophy and not religion," Næss pointed out. "Yet it can easily be given a religious meaning."[27] What that "meaning" entailed would soon be explained by lay churchgoers and an emerging group of eco-theologians.

ECOLOGICAL DEBATE WITHIN THE CHURCH

The Christian community was not indifferent to the ongoing environmental debate, the Mardøla demonstrations, White's criticisms, or the ecophilosophical activities. Though it is unfeasible to locate all responses, the following passages indicate that reactions from churchgoers varied from flat-out rejection of the relevance of environmentalism to faith, to deep-felt sympathy toward the cause.

---

[24] Klein, "The Emerging Ecophilosophy," p. 5.
[25] Næss, *Økologi og filosofi*, 3rd ed., p. 214.
[26] Næss, *Økologi, samfunn og livsstil*, 4th ed., p. 211.
[27] Næss, *Økologi, samfunn og livsstil*, 5th ed., p. 278. Milada Blekastad, "Poesi og økologi – to sider av same sak?" *Forskningsnytt*, 19, no. 5 (1974), 19–23.

6 The Call for a New Ecoreligion

Among those rejecting environmentalism altogether were both conservative and left-leaning theologians. The way to God, according to conservative theologians, was through prayer, reading of the Scripture, and participation in Church rituals. The fact that population growth was an underlying cause for environmental problems also seemed to contradict the key call in the Bible to "[b]e fruitful, and multiply, and replenish the earth, and subdue it."[28] The radicals, on the other hand, were worried that nature protection could take attention away from helping the poor. "There is no road from the [natural] world to God," a socialist student of theology argued in 1970. "To arrive at faith in God by studying nature, speculating about the path of the stars or sitting by the Vøringsfossen [waterfall], is according the Christian thinking not only a completely absurd thought, it is also a sin that lead humans away from their original destiny," namely faith in Christ and care for fellow human beings.[29] Vøringsfossen, it is worth noting, was a prime tourist destination in the scenic Norwegian fjords threatened by hydropower development, and it had been the object of romantic longing for at least a century. The idea that admiring the splendor of the waterfall had nothing to do with religion was particularly upsetting to environmentalists who desperately needed support in their (ultimately) failed attempt to save it from destruction.

The orthodox standpoint of both conservative and leftist theologians with respect to nature protection would gradually change. After all, old school churchgoers were also nature goers devoted to outdoor life, an activity that for some represented "a partial return to the state of nature" when humans "went naked in the Garden of Eden, and lived directly from nature's gifts."[30] A growing group of radicals within the Church were also turning their attention to nature protection, as an environmental socialist observed in 1971.[31] The non-violent demonstration to protect the Mardøla River in the summer of 1970, fronted by the ecophilosophers, was admired in a theological journal.[32] One of the key activists at Mardøla would in the same journal argue that the demonstration was signaling "one of the most exciting watersheds in Western history"

---

[28] The Bible, Genesis 1, 28. Jakob Try, "Befolkningsproblem, matvaresituasjon og kortsynthet," *Kirke og kultur,* 73 (1968), 326–38.
[29] Trond Skard Dokka quoted in Pål Repstad (ed.), *Kirken og samfunnet* (Stavanger: Nomi Forlag, 1970), p. 106.
[30] Borchgrevink, "Naturfølelse og naturvern," pp. 360–1.
[31] Bjørn Unneberg, *Grønn sosialisme for utkantproletarer* (Oslo: Cultura Forlag, 1971), p. 41.
[32] Berit G. Holm, "Ikkevold – teori og praksis," *Kirke og kultur,* 76 (1971), 411–29.

between "the literal interpretation of the Jewish command about conquering the earth" and a new "understanding of values" and "protection of life" in nature. "The issue at stake," the activist claimed, was to be found "in the realm of ethics and religion."[33] The Mardøla experience had given him a feeling of being part of the "the wheel of life" or "the brotherhood with our fellow earth" which meant that "we must give up increasing our [material] wealth" and halter the population growth.[34] A similar sentiment was expressed by Ole Jensen (1937), a lecturer in philosophy of religion at the University of Århus, Denmark, who visited the University of Oslo in September 1971 with the paper, "Pollution is Blasphemy." "We have caught the wrath of the Gods, as we have replaced gratitude with usurpation and exploitation, as we continuously exceed our limits [to growth]."[35] Following White, he argued that unchecked economic growth was an act of hubris, "a gigantic suicidal foolishness," caused by Western Christendom.[36] As a remedy Jensen pointed to the value of Indigenous religions and Indian mysticism.[37]

Rolf Edberg (1912–97) was one of those who managed to turn Christians on both sides of the Cold War divide toward the environmental cause. He was the Swedish ambassador to Norway who, through a series of books, questioned the technological understanding of the human condition.[38] As early as 1966, he published a book on the importance of taking better care of the Earth, and a series of popular books on ecology with religious undertones hit the bookstores in the subsequent decade in Norwegian, Swedish, and English.[39] They were inspired by the ecophilosophy of Kvaløy

---

[33] Jon Godal, "Mardøla-aksjonen og norske bønders vandring til Kongen i København," *Kirke og kultur*, 76 (1971), 494–8, quotes pp. 496, 497.

[34] Jon Godal, "Om hardingfele og naturvern," *Kirke og kultur*, 77 (1972), 406–8, quote p. 408.

[35] Ole Jensen, "Teologisk argumentasjon for tesen: Forurensning er blasfemi," *Kirke og kultur*, 77 (1972), 385–96, quote p. 387.

[36] Jensen, "Teologisk argumentasjon," p. 386.

[37] Ole Jensen, *I vækstens vold: økologi og religion* (Copenhagen: Fremda, 1976). Henning Nørhøj, *Moder jord: om kristendom og økologi* (Copenhagen: Nyt Nordisk forlag, 1977).

[38] Rolf Edberg, "Jordens resurser och den tekniska människan," *Kirke og kultur*, 72 (1967), 195–211; *Et støvgrann som glimter: Ødelegger vi mulighetene for fortsatt liv på jorden?* Hans Heiberg (trs.) (Oslo: Aschehoug, 1967). Juel Stubberud, "Rolf Edberg og Norge," in *Rolf heter jag* (Karlsatd: Föreningen för Värmlandslitteratur, 2000), pp. 119–26.

[39] Rolf Edberg, *Spillran av ett moln: Anteckningar i färdaboken* (Stockholm, Norstedt, 1966); *Vid trädets fot: Lekmannafunderingar mot höstlig bakgrund* (Stockholm, Norstedt, 1971); *Brev till Columbus* (Stockholm: Norstedt, 1974); *The Dream of Kilimanjaro* (New York: Pantheon Books, 1976); *Tomorrow Will Be Too Late: Dialogue on the Threshold of the Third Millennium* (Moscow: Progress Publishers, 1989).

6 The Call for a New Ecoreligion

and Næss, though Edberg could, in the capacity of being an ambassador, not publicly endorse their radicalism. Instead he raised environmental concerns in a non-inflammatory manner, and he mobilized passages from the Bible about humility toward the Creation to make his points.[40]

The young feminist Dagny Kaul was another – in comparison to Edberg – more radical churchgoer using ecophilosophy in her theological thinking. Instead of mobilizing distinctions such as "deep" versus "shallow" or "ecological" versus "technocratic" in dividing friends from foes, Kaul introduced in 1973 (for the first time in Norwegian) the distinction of "biocentric" versus "anthropocentric" in talking about understandings of nature. She was inspired by the Presbyterian minister from Minnesota Frederic Elder, who discussed this demarcation at length, first in his MA thesis from Harvard Divinity School completed in 1968 and later in subsequent articles and books.[41] Using Elder as a point of departure, Kaul argued that anthropocentrism was identical with the exploitative Christian attitude White described, while biocentrism entailed a numinous experience of nature as the Lord's Creation. Seeing nature as a whole through the science of ecology entailed for her not only a deep respect for all living creatures' inherent value, but also an opportunity for renewal of theological ontology that could unite humans with the natural world.[42] This ontological project was taken quite seriously in alternative Christian circles, such as the Rudolf Steiner School,[43] and became the center of focus again much later on when Kaul became the first eco-feminist in Norway.[44] At the Norwegian Parliament the representative for The Christian Democratic Party Toralf Westermoen argued that "ecophilosophy was almost like a religion," a fact that was both problematic and inspiring perspective for people of faith.[45]

---

[40] Åsmund Bjørnstad, "Økologi, etikk og religion – ein samtale med Rolf Edbergs forfatterskap," *Kirke og kultur,* 88 (1975), 206–15.

[41] Frederick Elder, "Two modern doctrines of nature," in Donald R. Cutler (ed.), *The World Year Book of Religion: The Religious Situation,* vol. 2 (London: Evans Brothers, 1969), pp. 367–94; *Prophecy Concerning Man and Environment,* MA thesis (Cambridge, MA: Harvard Divinity School, 1968); *Crisis in Eden: A Religious Study of Man and Environment* (Nashville: Abingdon Press, 1970).

[42] Dagny Kaul, "Dilemmaet i moderne naturoppfatning," *Norsk teologisk tidsskrift,* 74 (1973), 163–81.

[43] Svein Aage Christoffersen, "Biologi og kristendom" (review), *Norsk teologisk tidsskrift,* 74 (1973), 182. Johannes Hemleben, *Biologi og kristendom* (Copenhagen: Borgens forlag, 1972).

[44] Dagny Kaul, "Ecofeminism in the Nordic Countries," *Journal of the European Society of Women in Theological Research,* 2 (1994), 102–9.

[45] Toralf Westermoen in *Forhandlinger i Stortinget* 538 (May 13, 1975), 4172.

These different opinions about the importance of ecophilosophy and environmentalism to Christians were signs of a more fundamental change within the Church. To understand how these came about, one has to take a short detour abroad, to Geneva in May 1971, to a key meeting of a study group within the ecumenical World Council of Churches, whose conclusions became important to the Norwegian scene – events that will be discussed in Chapter 7.

The meeting was about how churches were to respond to the growing environmental movement. It resulted in the statement, "The Global Environment, Responsible Choice, and Social Justice," which was approved by the Council's Executive Committee and submitted to the United Nations Conference on the Human Environment in Stockholm, which met in June 1972. The document was the main contribution from the world's Lutheran communities to the Conference and it aimed at stimulating a religiously informed environmental debate. It stated that "the world around us ... has value in itself" and called for better "stewardship for the Creator" through "a responsible global environmental policy."[46] Most importantly, the statement encouraged the world's Christians to engage in the environmental movement. The World Student Christian Federation, for example, invited Thomas Sieger Derr, a professor at Smith College in the United States, to expand on the issue, and the result was the widely read *Ecology and Human Liberation* (1973).[47] In his review of various Christian responses to the environmental crisis, Derr argued that humans were the guardians of a nature that should not be exploited but cherished as a divine creation. There was a need to limit population growth, he recognized, but in a cautious way and not at the expense of people's natural birthright.

Per Voksø (1923–2002), who had participated at various Council meetings as early as 1948, followed the activities of the World Council closely. As a lay churchgoer in 1970 he was democratically elected as the leader of the National Council of the Church of Norway, with the power to oversee all its activities. Inspired by the conclusions of the World Council's study group and Derr's book, he saw that the environmental movement raised vital topics for all Christians. "We have been given an

---

[46] Executive Committee of the World Council of Churches, "The Global Environment, Responsible Choice and Social Justice," *The Ecumenical Review*, 23 (1971), 438–42, quote p. 438.
[47] Thomas Sieger Derr, *Ecology and Human Liberation: A Theological Critique of the Use and Abuse of Our Birthright* (Geneva: World Council of Churches, 1973).

6 The Call for a New Ecoreligion

Earth to manage, we are not allowed to destroy it," he claimed.[48] He asked the Council's Research Department, along with the Council for Church Collaboration and the Church Academy, to organize a conference on the topic, and this took place at the end of September 1973. This top-down institutional effort to address environmentalism represented a turning point in the history of eco-theology in Norway, as ecology from then on would gradually move from the periphery to the center stage of Church debate. Though the individual papers at the conference did not represent the views of the Church, the conference sent a clear message from the Church's executive body about the need to address environmentalism.

The conference began with papers by scholars from outside the Church who, in effect, were invited to set the agenda. The ecologist Oddvar Skre, for example, presented his latest research on acid rain, and concluded that "the ideology of economic growth should be replaced by a society in ecological equilibrium"[49] Likewise, Olsen suggested an "eco-political minimum program" for the Church based on ecological equilibrium principles.[50] Others pointed to the international legal and political ramifications of the eco-crisis.[51]

The theologians responded with papers about the culture of materialism in an industrialized society and the need to respect the integrity of the Lord's Creation. Within The Norwegian School of Theology, for example, the opponents of capitalism favored greater social responsibility among Christians, especially toward the poor. Environmental problems were the result of private ownership and exploitation of land by people who did not recognize that humans had nature on loan, one of them argued, as eco-centered faith was not the way forward. "Don't let the Church's preachers become [natural] resource and environmental

---

[48] Per Voksø, "Innledning," in Per Voksø (eds.), *Mennesket og miljøet* (Oslo: Kirkerådets utvalg for forsking og utredning, Luther forlag, 1975), pp. 7–10, quote p. 7.

[49] Oddvar Skre, "Mennesket og naturmiljøet: Ressursfordeling og ressursbehov i dag og i morgen," in Per Voksø (ed.), *Mennesket og miljøet* (Oslo: Kirkerådets utvalg for forsking og utredning, Luther forlag, 1975), pp. 11–35, quote p. 29.

[50] Harald Olsen, "Utkast til et økopolitisk program," in Per Voksø (ed.), *Mennesket og miljøet* (Oslo: Kirkerådets utvalg for forsking og utredning, Luther forlag, 1975), pp. 78–96, quote p. 78.

[51] Erik Nord, "Økokrisens internasjonale perspektiver," in Per Voksø (ed.), *Mennesket og miljøet* (Oslo: Kirkerådets utvalg for forsking og utredning, Luther forlag, 1975), pp. 50–5. Kjell Skjelsbæk, "Økokrisen som en utfordring til velferdssamfunnets ideologi og struktur," in Per Voksø (ed.), *Mennesket og miljøet* (Oslo: Kirkerådets utvalg for forsking og utredning, Luther forlag, 1975), pp. 56–70.

parsons!" he warned the Council, it would only lead to a "re-mystification of nature which is in dispute with the biblical doctrine of Creation."[52] The leading lay-Christian intellectual raised similar concerns in a "eco-political" plea for human managerial responsibility for an "Earth belonging to the Lord."[53] A lecturer in history of religion at the University of Bergen, Gaute Gunleiksrud (1936–2008), took a stand against White's thesis. Since one could not blame theology for the abuse of nature, he argued, the solution to the eco-crisis should consequently not come from the Church: "The belief that the Kingdom of God has become near through Christ is something totally different than working to protect and improve the old world ... One could benefit from being careful with placing ecology and Christian belief together."[54] Nevertheless, Gunleiksrud thought the Church should embrace environmentalism on pragmatic grounds. That ecophilosophers publicly embraced "ecological models in pantheistic (especially Indian) religiosity [and] myths about Mother Earth" was of concern in an increasingly secularized society, and the Church should "in this situation of urgency" be willing "to talk about God when we normally would talk about humans and their ethical responsibility" toward the Creation.[55]

These comments illustrate a dilemma: the belief in salvation and the coming of Christ had nothing to do with the environmental state of the material world. Yet the pietist Church had always been critical of the consumerism of industrial society. Caring for the earth as God's Creation could, perhaps, curb materialism and prepare the soul. Besides, it was clear to all by 1973 that environmentalism was a major moral force within society, especially among the young. The Church would have to respond by emphasizing human managerial responsibility. This, at least, was the argument of Jens Gabriel Hauge (1927–2005), who was a professor of biochemistry at the Norwegian Veterinary School and leader of the Council's Research Department. We must be "society's watchdog,"

---

[52] Torleiv Austad, "Kirkens medansvar for den rådende sosiale praksis," in Per Voksø (ed.), *Mennesket og miljøet* (Oslo: Kirkerådets utvalg for forsking og utredning, Luther forlag, 1975), pp. 36–49, quotes pp. 43, 47.
[53] Jens Wisløff, "Utkast til et økopolitisk program," in Per Voksø (ed.), *Mennesket og miljøet* (Oslo: Kirkerådets utvalg for forsking og utredning, Luther forlag, 1975), pp. 71–7, quote p. 75.
[54] Gaute Gunleiksrud, "Kristne perspektiver på økologi: om skapertro, menneskesyn og forvalteransvar," in Per Voksø (ed.), *Mennesket og miljøet* (Oslo: Kirkerådets utvalg for forsking og utredning, Luther forlag, 1975), pp. 97–111, quote p. 98.
[55] Gunleiksrud, "Kristne perspektiver på økologi," p. 101.

he argued, and make sure "political decisions are made according to the Bible's managerial thinking."[56]

ECORELIGION ON THE SYLLABUS

In the winter of 1974 an article about the emerging new ecoreligion appeared on the syllabus for a mandatory core *Examen philosophicum* course at the University of Oslo. It was written by Gunnar Breivik (b. 1943), a keen follower of the ecophilosophical debate. It is worth discussing this item in some detail as it indicates an important shift from intramural theological debate to a more missionary trend on the behalf of ecoreligion toward students.

Breivik was the son of Birgir Breivik (1912–96), who was a major mover within *leksmannsbevegelsen* (the lay-pietist movement). The members of the *leksmannsbevegelsen* constituted some of the most committed members of the Church. Birgir Breivik was an elected member of the Norwegian Parliament (1965–70) as a politician of The Christian Democratic Party, and the Assistant General Secretary (1965–70) and then General Secretary (1970–82) for the Norwegian Lutheran Mission. The lay-pietist movement he represented had its stronghold among peasants and fishermen on the western coast of Norway where the Breivik family was from, a place where Lutheran faith went hand in hand with community activism, and there was much skepticism toward centralized politics, alcohol, and materialism.[57]

Gunnar Breivik followed the path of his father in describing himself as a "new-pietist" from the lay church movement, which had "conversion and mission" at its core.[58] He graduated from The Norwegian School of Theology in 1969 with philosophy as an intermediate subject. The chief aim of the School of Theology, it is worth noting, was to educate vicars to go on to work in local parishes around Norway. It was privately funded and known to take a more conservative stand on religious issues in comparison to the more research-oriented Faculty of Theology at the

---

[56] Jens Gabriel Hauge, "Kirkens engasjement i økokrisen: Oljeuttalelsen som vedlegg," in Per Voksø (ed.), *Mennesket og miljøet* (Oslo: Kirkerådets utvalg for forsking og utredning, Luther forlag, 1975), pp. 113–20, quote p. 116.
[57] Geir Gundersen, "Lekmannsrørsla og klassekampen," *Ung teologi*, 5 (1971), 47–61.
[58] Gunnar Breivik, "Teologi og politikk," in Pål Repstad (ed.), *Kirken og samfunnet* (Stavanger: Nomi Forlag, 1970), pp. 108–20, quote p. 112; "Biografiske opplysninger," in Vegard Fusche Moe and Sigmund Loland (eds.), *I bevegelse: et festskrift til Gunnar Breivik på hans 60-årsdag* (Oslo: Gyldendal, 2003), 231–40.

University of Oslo. The School did not, for example, have the right to issue a Doctoral degree, but used an exchange program to pass especially talented students to its counterpart, the Faculty of Protestant Theology at the University of Tübingen in Germany.

Breivik was one of the scholarship recipients who thus came to study at Tübingen for the academic year of 1970–71. He earned the grant by submitting three articles on Martin Heidegger, theology, and politics respectively, which must have impressed the grant committee. Among the students at the competing Faculty of Theology there was, at the time, a vocal group of radical students questioning whether or not a political revolution in God's name was justified in view of the ongoing Vietnam War, poverty, and other social injustices.[59] Breivik attacked them head-on: "God's kingdom *breaks in*, it cannot be established by people through political and social revolution and upheaval."[60] What worried him was the uncritical theological adaptation of the social and political sciences. "Society and politics are situated in the periphery," Breivik argued, while "prophetic-critical character" of Christendom was at the center of belief.[61] He saw in Heidegger's philosophy a potential to reengage a unified and consistent theology that harkened back to the unity and purity of its Medieval and scriptural origins. "Perhaps after a while we will be in a position to practice theology within a larger dimension and thus the history will open up for us," he envisioned.[62] It was this longing for theological unity that later reemerged in Breivik's eco-theological writings about pre-industrial Christianity and the purity of nature as a source of religious reflection.

After Breivik's graduate studies in Tübingen had ended in 1971 (without a degree), he enrolled at the Norwegian School of Sport Sciences where Faarlund taught his ecophilosophy of outdoor life class. Breivik must have been taken in by ecophilosophy and the environmental movement, as he would eventually abandon the idea of becoming a vicar in favor of a life more oriented to the outdoors. Outdoor life represented the way forward for a new society reconciled with nature. "Outdoor life is politics today," he would say, as it was on issues related to this lifestyle

---

[59] Andreas Skartvet (ed.), *Revolusjon i Guds namn?* (Oslo: Samlaget, 1968). Nils Johan Lavik and Jardar Seim (eds.), *Deilig er jorden? Ti innlegg om demokrati, revolusjon og kristendom* (Oslo: Pax, 1969).
[60] Breivik, "Teologi og politikk," p. 110.
[61] Breivik, "Teologi og politikk," pp. 113, 120.
[62] Gunnar Breivik, "Om teologiens opprinnelse," *Norsk teologisk tidsskrift*, 71 (1970), 176–91, quote p. 190; "Heidegger og teologien," *Ung teologi*, 3 (1970), 81–92.

and its "fights for nature" that principles of ecology would be truly realized.[63] At the School he took an intermediate degree in 1973, after which Breivik worked as a high school teacher in Oslo while finishing up his Master of Arts thesis in 1975.[64]

The debates around ecoreligion were largely an internal affair among theologians until the winter of 1974. A 1973 reform of the University of Oslo's core courses *Examen philosophicum* added an essay by Breivik into the syllabus so that it became mandatory reading for a substantial number of students. It was for the Nature and Humans course discussed in Chapter 5, which contained a series of articles by other key academic environmentalists from Norway. This was the first time that not only ecoreligion but also ecophilosophical issues in general became the topic of tricky exam questions that students had to answer in order to continue their studies in any field at the University of Oslo.

A head-on attack on Protestant theology for its exclusion of nature was at the core of Breivik's article. "Nature as a category does not exist" in the theological disciplines, he argued.[65] Christian ethics was only concerned with humans and society, he claimed, and if nature appeared in moral discussions it was only as a resource for human welfare. Based on this criticism, which echoed White's paper, Breivik launched his own alternative ecological interpretation of Genesis with a focus on humans as gardeners of God's Creation. To Breivik "eco-philosophy, eco-life, eco-politics" signified a radical turn toward trying to serve nature "in His honor" as Adam and Eve once did as gardeners in Paradise.[66] It is naive to expect a return to Paradise by our own will: "Yet it is not naivety trying to adapt the basic attitude of the gardener. It is not naivety to begin to *collaborate with nature*, built on the insights of the ecological laws. It is not naivety to try to restrict the Earth's population. It is we who began the fight *against* nature. It is we that have to change."[67] Breivik pointed to a series of passages from the Bible, including words of wisdom from the Psalms to support his claims. The Bible said that humans should "replenish the earth, and subdue it: and have dominion over the fish of the sea,

---

[63] Gunnar Breivik, "Friluftsliv: en vei til et nytt samfunn," *Mestre fjellet*, 6 (1973), 23, 39.
[64] Gunnar Breivik, *Idrettens filosofi*, MA thesis (Oslo: The Norwegian School of Sport Sciences, 1975).
[65] Breivik, "Læren om Gud og det store huset," p. 1. Breivik argued against views held by Peter Wilhelm Bøckman, *Liv, fellesskap, tjeneste: en kristen etikk* (Oslo: Universitetsforlaget, 1970), and Per Øverland, *Kristen etikk* (Oslo: Lunde, 1970).
[66] Breivik, "Læren om Gud og det store huset," p. 6.
[67] Breivik, "Læren om Gud og det store huset," p. 13.

and over the fowl of the air, and over every living thing that moveth upon the earth."[68] Yet Breivik argued that this should be read with a focus on passages which emphasized human humility toward Creation: "When I consider thy heavens, the work of thy fingers, the moon and the stars, which thou hast ordained; What is man, that thou art mindful of him? and the son of man, that thou visitest him?"[69] Thus, the article was an exegesis of quotes from the Bible, which could support humility toward nature and an ethics of gardening God's estate in His honor. What students reading the article were meant to conclude was that the current industrial exploitation of Creation was not in honor of God, and that true Christians therefore had to change their lifestyle so that the original ecological harmony of nature could be restored. Those who did not get the point would risk failing their exams and, as a consequence, have to leave campus.

Breivik's article and its status on the syllabus of the University core course did not please conservative theologians. The chief among them was Inge Lønning (1938–2013). He was a graduate student enrolled at the Department of Theology when Breivik was studying at The School of Theology, who went on to become a professor of theology at the University of Oslo in 1971, and subsequently the chief editor of the leading journal *Kirke og kultur* (Church and Culture). He was also an active member of the Conservative Party and brother of the Bishop of Borg (a key diocese that surrounds Oslo). Should "theology be the maid of ecosophy?" he wondered, noting that "the tendency to offer the service of theology within the ecophilosophical discipline [was] advancing rapidly."[70] Lønning could accept Næss's "arbitrary" use of the Bible to "support an ecophilosophical/political program" as he was not religious. Breivik, on the other hand, was "a theologian by profession" and his article was "partly official," as it was the only theological text on the entire *Examen philosophicum* syllabus.[71] His article was thus, in effect, the first meeting that potential students would have with the discipline of theology, though freshmen with a religious bent could opt out of the "Nature and Humans" seminar and replace it with one of the other courses. Lønning believed that, by arguing that nature as a category was excluded, Breivik gave "a grossly misleading picture of the

---

[68] The Bible, Genesis 1, 28.   [69] The Bible, Psalm 8, 3–4.
[70] Inge Lønning, "Teologien som økofilosofiens tjenestepike?" *Kirke og kultur*, 80 (1975), 237–8, quote p. 237.
[71] Lønning, "Teologien som økofilosofiens tjenestepike?" p. 237.

history of theology," and that Breivik had projected his "social gospel" of saving the environment onto the "natural gospel" of the Bible. The article was "not acceptable" as a foundation on which students were supposed to build their academic career, Lønning argued "with a heavy underlining."[72]

The criticism would not stop Breivik, who, during this time, abandoned his theological career in favor of his studies with Faarlund at the School of Sport Sciences. In his entry for the second edition of the "Nature and Humans" reader, he maintained his eco-religious views. "The lifestyle today of the industrial human being is not in God's honor," he argued, setting his hopes on any religion that recognized "equality in the biosphere."[73]

Putting ecoreligion on the syllabus and thus in the minds of young students became an important task for Breivik in the subsequent years. The message that high school students were to learn, for example, was that there were two conflicting Christian models on how to deal with nature: one emphasizing a human right for exploitation of an obedient nature, and another with equality and equilibrium within the environment as the focal point. The first model had led to the eco-crisis, while the second promised a way out of it. He quoted the Book of Ecclesiastes as evidence for the claim that humans did not have a higher moral status than other species: "For that which befalleth the sons of men befalleth beasts; even one thing befalleth them: as the one dieth, so dieth the other; yea, they have all one breath; so that a man hath no preeminence above a beast." The guiding principle Christian students were to draw from his analysis was "solidarity within the biosphere, management in honor of God."[74] As Breivik saw it, cleaning up pollution was a penitential exercise for human sins toward Him and His Creation, and consequently an important task for young Christians.

THE GREENING OF THE CHURCH

The debate about ecoreligion would cause tension as well as optimism among believers with respect to a renewal of the Church. The idea that

---

[72] Lønning, "Teologien som økofilosofiens tjenestepike?" p. 238.
[73] Gunnar Breivik, "Religion, livsform og natur," in Paul Hofseth and Arne Vinje (eds.), Økologi: Økofilosofi (Oslo: Gyldendal, 1975), 82–95, quotes pp. 85, 90.
[74] The Bible, Ecclesiastes 3, 19. Gunnar Breivik, "Forurensning og naturvern," in Lars Østnor (ed.), Nestekjærlighet i samfunnet: Sosialetisk spørsmål i kristent lys (Oslo: Luther Forlag, 1975), pp. 120–32, quotes pp. 130, 131.

human population growth was one of the prime reasons for the eco-crisis represented a challenge to members of the Church who saw the birth of a human being to be something positive.[75] Another problem was that the high moral ground of the environmentalists made others look dissolute, as the lifestyle demands for right ecological living were high and the questioning of industrialized society was radical. It was not easy, even for the devoted, to live according to eco-religious and philosophical principles. These issues and other similar issues threatened to push different types of environmental believers apart:

> Some believe that the time is ripe to move from words to action and find a way of life that is more in agreement with Christian belief. Others can't break out and must find content with small steps. Still others must stay within the old structure as they have necessary political work to do. The situation is too critical for letting these groups be played up against each other. The body of Christ is one, but has many parts.[76]

This call for unity and respect for each other, made by Gunleiksrud in 1975, may serve as evidence of a Church divided on how to incorporate ecological perspectives into a theological framework.

These tensions would persist for years, though subsequent events indicate that the Church as a whole gradually moved toward eco-theology. A sign of this shift came in 1978 when the Council of the Church of Norway's Research Department arranged another conference to address the ecological crisis. At the time a major new hydropower development on the Alta-Kautokeino River was in the news, and environmentalism was on the political agenda, especially on the left side of the Cold War political divide. The Church sought to nurture support from both sides. For the 1978 meeting, the eco-crisis represented an opportunity to be radical and progressive within acceptable socio-political borders.

The event was organized by a Christian biologist, who argued that Christians should take a stand against economic growth and also promote "changes in basic attitudes" to nature.[77] It was important for the

---

[75] Jens Gabriel Hauge, "Kirkens Verdensråd og befolkningsproblemene," *Kirke og kultur*, 80 (1975), 76–85. Ola Rokkones, "Behovet for en norsk befolkningspolitikk," *Kirke og kultur*, 80 (1975), 92–101. Erling Berge, "Befolkning og befolkningspolitikk," *Kirke og kultur*, 80 (1975), 102–10.

[76] Gaute Gunleiksrud, "Om å være kristen i et i-land i en u- og øko-tid," *Kirke og kultur*, 80 (1975), 193–205, quote p. 205.

[77] Harald Olsen, "Forord," in Harald Olsen (ed.), *Mot et samfunn i likevekt: fra de nordiske kirkers arbeid med ressurs- og miljøspørsmål* (Oslo: Land og Kirke, 1978), pp. 7–9, quote p. 8.

6 The Call for a New Ecoreligion

Church to expose "idols of the syndrome of growth and false paradise," another conference participant argued.[78] Environmentalism framed as protection of Creation could offer a way out of materialism for congregations. The Church should take its share of the blame for the "Babylon" of capitalism and exploitation of nature of modern society, and work to nurture an ecological way of thinking.[79] These and similar statements were radical, even revolutionary, but not socialist. If anything, they represented traditional lay-pietism in new environmental clothing.

At the heart of the discussion was a paper by Breivik, which may have been his first appearance within a sanctioned research conference by the Church. Since 1975 he had been the first professor of outdoor-life at the Norwegian School of Sport Sciences, where he taught the art of "free-air life," a discipline based on the teachings of Faarlund, Kvaløy, and Næss.[80] At the conference he began with a head-on attack on Lutheran ecclesia: it had been "sleeping and a hanger-on, as e.g. in Germany during the last war," with respect to exploitation of nature.[81] As a remedy he rehearsed his earlier argument about managing the Earth in honor of God as gardeners of his Creation. What was new was Breivik's emphasis on the necessity of an eco-centric ethic, and he suggested several reinterpretations of key scriptural passages to make his case: "In the beginning God created the heaven and the earth," said the Bible, which for Breivik meant that "[e]very species and the whole nature have value in themselves. They are thus not only valuable as food or tools for humans. Nature has inherent value."[82] If the Earth were created by God, then He is its owner, Breivik argued, and humans should consider themselves as guests who are visiting Him and as living on land that is not theirs. The debated passage in Genesis where God tells humans to "[b]e fruitful, and multiply, and replenish the earth, and subdue it," was, according to Breivik, not God giving humans carte blanche to exploit nature, but instead, a call to "fill in an assigned 'ecological space'."[83] He also reminded the audience that

---

[78] Jonas O. Jonson, "Skapelsen: Frelsens sakrament," in Harald Olsen (ed.), *Mot et samfunn i likevekt* (Oslo: Land og Kirke, 1978), pp. 124–37, quote p. 135.

[79] Gaute Gunleiksrud, "Vektsamfunnets krise og kirkens evangelium," in Harald Olsen (eds.), *Mot et samfunn i likevekt* (Oslo: Land og Kirke, 1978), pp. 138–54, quote p. 140.

[80] Gunnar Breivik, *Friluftsliv: noen filosofiske og pedagogiske aspekter* (Oslo: Norges Idrettshøgskole, 1979). Gunnar Breivik and Haakon Løymo (eds.), *Friluftsliv fra Fridtjof Nansen til våre dager* (Oslo: Universitetsforlaget, 1978).

[81] Gunnar Breivik, "Likevektssamfunnet – et teologisk vurdering," in *Mot et samfunn i likevekt*, Harald Olsen (ed.) (Oslo: Land og Kirke, 1978), pp. 108–23, quote p. 108.

[82] The Bible, Genesis 1, 1. Breivik, "Likevektssamfunnet," p. 120.

[83] The Bible, Genesis 1, 28. Breivik, "Likevektssamfunnet," p. 120.

trying "to imitate [the life of] Christ implied a simple life in frugality," which was incompatible with the consumerism of modern society.[84]

Breivik made an impact. The conclusion of the conference was inspired directly by his statements and came in the form of an "ecclesiastical plan of action" to mobilize the Bishops through the Church National Council to further research, organize, and implement an eco-ethic within the entire Church.[85] The first step was to assign the anthology from the conference as a textbook. It was used well into the early 1980s by the chief organizer of non-academic religious training, the Norwegian Council for Christian Studies, who provided funding for any study group willing to read and discuss the anthology.

Young students of theology would not uncritically adopt the ecoreligion of Breivik and his ecophilosophical partisans. Yet their challenges led to new readings of the Scripture that emphasized human modesty and respect for Creation.[86] Breivik himself would also stress that the inherent value of nature and its species were upheld by God, and that humans were housekeepers in nature's household manifesting His goodness.[87] As one young scholar put it: "[t]hat Nature has value independently of humans does not mean that it is holy."[88] Thus, ecoreligion did not imply any pantheism or worship of nature itself. It implied instead a religiously informed ecological housekeeping on God's behalf, and since God's demands were omnipresent, young intellectual theologians consequently began addressing practical issues such as the use of energy to heat churches and clerical offices.[89]

---

[84] Breivik, "Likevektssamfunnet," p. 122.
[85] Svein Takle, "Momenter for et kirkelig handlingsprogram," in Harald Olsen (ed.), *Mot et samfunn i likevekt* (Oslo: Land og Kirke, 1978), pp. 155–63.
[86] Roar Strømme, *Økologi og teologi: tankar om ei kristen naturforståing innfor den økologiske krisa*, MA thesis (Oslo: Menighetsfakultetet, 1978); "Teologien i møte med øko-krisa," *Ung teologi*, 12 (1979), 1–11. Olav Øygard, *Preken i møte med den økologiske krise*, MA thesis (Oslo: Menighetsfakultetet, 1981). Magne Fitjar, *Økologi og verdi hos Arne Næss og Ole Jensen: semesteroppgave i miljøfag* (Bergen: Department of Geography, 1983). Jan-Olav Henriksen, *Mennesket og naturen: etiske og religionsfilosofiske perspektiver på naturen og økokrisen* (Oslo: Menighetsfakultetet, 1991).
[87] Gunnar Breivik, "Kristen tro og natur-forståelse," *Kirke og kultur*, 84 (1979), 345–52. Trond Berg Eriksen, "Naturen som appellinstans," *Kirke og kultur*, 79 (1974), 293–6.
[88] Per Tangaard, *Energi over alle grenser: kristent livssyn og forvaltning av ressurser* (Oslo: Credo, 1983), 14.
[89] Knut Hofstad, "Energibruk – et etisk problem?" *Kirke og kultur*, 83 (1978), 297–300. Inger Heiberg, "Energibruk – et etisk problem?" *Kirke og kultur*, 83 (1978), 445. Roar Mjelva, "Termodynamikkens 2. hovedsetning som etisk motivasjon," *Kirke og kultur*, 83 (1978), 445–6.

6 The Call for a New Ecoreligion 141

To mobilize the young, scholars interested in ecoreligion tried to change both the high school syllabi for both science and religious studies. All high school students in Norway had to take exams in Christianity in addition to biology and other sciences. The fact that non-believers, Jews, and an increasing population of Muslim immigrants had to study Christianity (often taught by practicing Christians) was a topic of heated public debate. The attempt to include ecoreligion in the curriculum should be understood in this context, as a way of addressing pressing moral issues relevant to all peoples of the world. The biology syllabus was also under public scrutiny in the early 1980s for failing to address topics of current interest, such as genetics and environmentalism. The attempt to move ecoreligion into the biology curriculum should also be understood in this context, as a response to science teachers explaining human social behavior and environmental concerns in reductionist language.[90] Hauge thought religion should be introduced in the teaching of evolution as this was a sign of God's creativity in action that would mobilize students' respect.[91] To this argument theologians replied that God was the Creator of the world's ecology, and that students should learn to take better care of it.[92] Though the ecologists did not generally agree with the Christian gospel, Breivik believed it was important to nurture a reciprocal relationship between science and Christianity classes.[93] One should fill schoolbooks about science and religion with the new ecological reading of the Bible, he argued.[94]

The call for a new eco-theology in Norway began in the early 1970s with students calling for the inclusion of concern for nature in religious

---

[90] Lars Viggo Berntsen, "Menneskesynet i biologilærebøker i skolen," in Peder Borgen (ed.), *Mennesket og naturen i kristendom og naturvitenskap* (Trondheim: Tapir, 1980), pp. 58–104.

[91] Jens Gabriel Hauge, "Mennesket og naturen fra naturvitenskaplig syn," in *Mennesket og naturen i kristendom og naturvitenskap* (Trondheim: Tapir, 1980), pp. 9–28.

[92] Dagfinn Rian, "Mennesket og naturen i det Gamle Testamentet," in *Mennesket og naturen i kristendom og naturvitenskap* (Trondheim: Tapir, 1980), pp. 29–42. Peder Borgen, "Helbredelsesundere i det Nye Testemente: Noen synspunkter," in *Mennesket og naturen i kristendom og naturvitenskap* (Trondheim: Tapir, 1980), pp. 43–64. Peter Wilhelm Bøckman, "Synet på mennesket og naturen i kristen systematikk," in *Mennesket og naturen i kristendom og naturvitenskap* (Trondheim: Tapir, 1980), pp. 65–84. Peder Borgen (ed), *Miljøkrise og verdivalg: miljøkrisen i kristent perspektiv og som utfordring i samfunn og skole* (Trondheim: Tapir, 1991).

[93] Gunnar Breivik, "Menneskets plass og funksjon i naturen i følge kristendommen og den økologiske tenkning: en sammenlignende og kritisk analyse," in *Mennesket og naturen i kristendom og naturvitenskap* (Trondheim: Tapir, 1980), pp. 105–27.

[94] Gunnar Breivik, "Teologi og økologi," *Prismet*, 31 (1980), 4–7.

debate, and ended a decade later with an equally forceful plea for telling students about ecoreligion in religious as well as science textbooks. The ecological debate promised not only a renewal of Lutheran pietism and therefore of the Church, but also a renewed focus on caring for the Creation. The next chapter will continue discussing how religion also came to frame the thinking of those who were antagonistic to Deep Ecology. It is a story of how a Norwegian environmentalist came to bring ecological concerns and the quest for sustainability abroad to the World Council of Churches.

7

The Sustainable Society

"[T]he doing of science is a much, much more personal, social, and subjective process than we have even dared to imagine in our wildest dreams."[1] This is a daring comment, especially on the front-page of a MIT thesis by an author famous for his use of objectifying computers.[2] Yet it was the quote that Jørgen Randers (b. 1945), one of the co-authors of the 1972 *The Limits to Growth* report, chose as his motto. This chapter will untangle some of the subjective processes Randers used throughout his research and uncover his do-gooding gaze or how he came "to realize the wonders of religious belief" through this process.[3]

It is worth reviewing his work in some detail as it is important to understand key concepts and terms leading up to the 1987 *Our Common Future* report from the World Commission on Environment and Development, which was chaired by the Norwegian politician Gro Harlem Brundtland. Central to this history is the phrase the "sustainable society," which Randers coined in 1974. I will argue that in creating his vision for a viable environmental future, he sought to open a new, endless frontier for science with the larger goal of mobilizing a defence of nature. His chief patrons came from within Lutheran communities, and it is their

---

[1] Ian I. Mitroff, "The myth of objectivity or why science needs a new psychology of science," *Management Science*, 18, no. 10 (June 1972), 613–18, quote p. 615. Quoted in Jørgen Randers, *Conceptualizing Dynamic Models of Social Systems: Lessons from a Study of Social Change*, PhD thesis (Cambridge, MA: A. P. Sloan School of Management, MIT, 1973), p. 5.

[2] Lorraine Daston and Peter Galison, *Objectivity* (New York: Zone Books, 2007), pp. 309–61.

[3] Randers, *Conceptualizing*, p. 4.

shared ecumenical hope that came to frame the early understandings of sustainability. The word "sustainable," it is worth mentioning, has been in use among economists for at least the last 250 years, specifically as a way to describe economic policies that can be sustained over a long period. Historians of ideas have made considerable efforts to trace the concept back to Enlightenment scholars and beyond.[4] These efforts have been helpful in tracing the idea of sustainability up to recent affairs, but have been unsuccessful in describing how sustainability relates to events in Norway and Lutheran theology.

The proximity of science to religion is a contested terrain, especially among biologists worried about creationism as an alternative explanation for evolution.[5] It is therefore worth noting that neither Randers nor the Church leaders discussed in this chapter thought that religion should intervene in scientific affairs. Instead, they believed Christian faith could offer hope and motivation for taking action on behalf of the environment, the poor, and future generations of people. Religion could thus offer a set of "valence values," to borrow Matthew Stanley's term, which would guide scientific research in the direction of a sustainable society on Earth.[6]

THE LIMITS TO GROWTH REPORT

To understand Randers' participation in Church debates about sustainability, it is necessary to conduct a short review of his background leading up to *The Limits to Growth* report of 1972. He was the son of Gunnar Randers (1914–92), the Director of the Institute of Energy Technology at Kjeller, near Oslo. Gunnar was a student of, and later assistant to, the astrophysicist Svein Rosseland (1894–1995). Rosseland, among other things, was in charge of the "Oslo Analyzer."[7] This computer, which operated between 1938 and 1954, was at its time one of the

---

[4] Lukas Vischer, "Climate change, sustainability and Christian witness," *Ecumenical Review*, 49 (1997), 142–61. Simon Dresner, *The Principles of Sustainability* (London: Earthscan, 2002), pp. 9–59. Ulrich Grober, *Sustainability: A Cultural History* (Cambridge: UIT Cambridge, 2012), pp. 155–86. Jeremy L. Caradonna, *Sutainability: A History* (Oxford: Oxford University Press, 2014). Paul Warde, *The Invention of Sustainability: Nature and Destiny, c. 1500–1870* (Cambridge: Cambridge University Press, 2018).

[5] See, for example, Richard Dawkins, *The God Delusion* (London: Black Swan, 2006).

[6] Matthew Stanley, *Practical Mystic: Religion, Science, and A. S. Eddington* (Chicago: Chicago University Press, 2007), pp. 239–45.

[7] Per A. Holst, "Svein Rosseland and the Oslo Analyzer," *IEEE Annals of the History of Computing*, 18, no. 4 (1996), 16–26. Thue and Helsvik, *1946–1975 Den store transformasjonen*, pp. 77–113.

world's largest differential analyzers, originally developed by Vannevar Bush at the Massachusetts Institute of Technology (MIT). Rosseland visited MIT and corresponded with Bush about its importance, and it came to invigorate the work of astrophysicists at the University of Oslo which, thanks to the Oslo Analyzer, was at the forefront of the field. Thus, early on, the values that computer engineering had for scientific research were impressed on the young Jørgen.

His father was also very much a proponent of Bush's famous *Science: The Endless Frontier* report to President Franklin D. Roosevelt of 1945. Here Bush famously stated that "Scientific progress is one essential key to our security as a nation, to our better health, to more jobs, to a higher standard of living, and to our cultural progress" – an idea about the role of science and the "pioneer spirit" of scientists that came to dominate such thinking in the United States for decades.[8] Randers, the elder, followed this example in Norway with high profile promotion and advocacy of technological and scientific research as a key to Norwegian prosperity. It was the nuclear sciences and power that were to propel the country, he stated, in a series of popular books on the topic.[9] As Director at Kjeller from 1948 to 1968 he was known not only for his progressive view on nuclear science, but also as a member of the Labor Party who staunchly defended Norwegian membership of NATO and the European Community (EC), including Euratom.[10] All this gave him an important public persona and made him vulnerable for attack, especially from people on the left side of the Cold War divide, who were skeptical of NATO and the nuclear industry's entanglements with weaponry.

The young Jørgen Randers would follow in his father's footsteps in believing in the importance of science and computers. He also began his academic life by studying physics and received a master's thesis at Kjeller in 1969 on the topic of solid-state physics on the scattering of inelastic neutrons.[11] Yet there were also important differences between them.

---

[8] Vannevar Bush, *Science the Endless Frontier: A Report to the President*, July 1945 (Washington: National Science Foundation, reprint 1960), p. 2.
[9] Gunnar Randers, *Atomkraften: verdens håp eller undergang* (Oslo: Cappelen, 1946); *Atomer og sunn fornuft* (Oslo: Aschehoug, 1950); *Atomenergi som industriell kraftkilde* (Kjeller: Institutt for Atomenergi, 1953).
[10] Gunnar Randers, "Norges stilling til Euratom," *Teknisk ukeblad*, 109 (1962), 773. Olav Njølstad, *Strålende forskning: Institutt for Energiteknikk 1948–1998* (Oslo: Tano Aschehoug, 1999), p. 155.
[11] Jørgen Randers, *En undersøkelse av spinnsystemet i α-Fe$_2$O$_3$ ved uelastisk neutronspredning*, MA thesis (Kjeller: Institutt for Atomenergi, 1969).

He would, for example, distance himself from his father's vocal support of nuclear power, and would not engage in raging debates on Norwegian membership in the EC, which culminated in a national referendum in September 1972. He was listed in 1967 as a member of the Conservative Student Union and he did his mandatory military service. Yet there is no evidence of him being passionate about these conservative commitments. With respect to his father's linear view of ongoing scientific progress inspired by Bush's *Endless Frontier*, the young Randers would agree on the importance of science for society but would, as will be apparent, differ with Bush on the "pioneer spirit" of natural scientists.

Debates about scientific and social progress in Norway were shaped and molded by the nation's natural resource policies. To some, such as Professor of Geology Ivan Rosenqvist, there were more than plenty. The mountainous country had high waterfalls that should be turned into hydropower, he argued, and newly discovered oil and gas fields in the North Sea indicated a plentitude of new riches to be tapped into. Others, like Gunnar Randers, thought nuclear energy was necessary to secure further economic growth and the prosperity of the welfare state. Yet another group, represented by the increasingly vocal Deep Ecologists, argued that the exploitation of natural resources made possible by scientists did not lead to social progress at all, but instead to an ecological disaster. These debates were quite intense. Indeed, forty years later, Randers still has vivid memories of family dinners in which his father would voice his frustrations about Rosenqvist or some other antagonist. Thus, questions related to scientific progress and natural resources were the chief academic themes he knew (besides computers and counting neutrons) before he entered MIT as a PhD student in 1970 with a grant from The Norway-America Association.

At MIT he was supposed to continue with his physics studies, though he had "serious agony" about it as he would rather "pursue a topic that engaged more directly with society and its problems."[12] He first began to study macromolecules, but abandoned it after hearing Jay W. Forrester presenting on the concept of urban dynamics modeling at an open seminar.[13] He consequently enrolled at MIT's Sloan School of Management

---

[12] Haakon Olsen, "Fysikermøtet i Bergen 16–18 juni 1971: System dynamics" (review of a lecture by Randers), *Fra fysikkens verden*, 33, no. 4 (1971), 69–72, quote p. 69.

[13] Jørgen Randers, "From limits to growth to sustainable development *or* SD (sustainable development) in a SD (system dynamics) perspective," *Systems Dynamics Review*, 16, no. 3 (2000), 213–24, p. 213.

to work with a team of researchers and students under the guidance of Forrester. This was a radical shift of field, as the School was a hot-bed for business leaders by virtue of its focus on managerial sciences and entrepreneurship.

Forrester believed his students should stake out alternative paths for a world that was not progressing at all. The physical "[s]cience is no longer a frontier," he would tell his students at MIT as, to him, the processes of discovery in natural sciences were an organized normality. Instead he argued that "the next frontier for human endeavor will be to pioneer a better understanding of the nature of our social systems."[14] This attempt to shift Bush's focus on natural sciences toward a new frontier for managerial sciences became important to Randers, who from now on came to place system dynamics at the very edge of human exploration. What looked like an end to technocratic optimism to his father was to Randers a new beginning for the managerial sciences.[15] This sense of pushing forward the frontier of research would later become evident in Randers' thinking about the importance of managerial leadership in the development of a sustainable society. Indeed, as will be argued (in Chapter 9), Norway as a country was to be the pioneer, showcasing environmental leadership to the world.

At the Sloan School, Forrester placed Randers in the project team developing his *World Dynamics* (1971) study into a formed report for the Club of Rome. It was a medium-sized research project with a total budget of 200,000 dollars. The Director of this team of seventeen researchers and graduate students was Dennis L. Meadows, who made Donella H. Meadows responsible for a subgroup looking into population dynamics. William W. Behrens was in charge of another subgroup researching resource questions, while Randers was leading a subgroup working on the role of pollution. They began investigating the dynamics of solid waste within nature and society, a topic that was inspired by Rachel Carson's *Silent Spring* (1962) argument about the circulation of DDT within a closed ecosystem.[16] Randers was not in charge of

---

[14] Jay W. Forrester, *World Dynamics* (Cambridge: Wright-Allen Press, 1971), p. 127.
[15] Gunnar Randers, *Lysår* (Oslo: Gyldendal, 1975), pp. 295–301.
[16] Jørgen Randers, "System simulation to test environmental policy: DDT," *International Journal of Environmental Studies*, 4, no. 1 (1972), 51–61; "DDT movement in the global environment," in Dennis L. Meadows and Donella H. Meadows (eds.), *Toward Global Equilibrium* (Cambridge, MA: Wright-Allen Press, 1973), pp. 49–83. Jørgen Randers and Dennis L. Meadows, "The dynamics of solid waste," *Technology Review*, 75 (Mar./Apr. 1972), 20–32; "The dynamics of solid waste," in Dennis L. Meadows and Donella

formulating the methodology and overall approach of the MIT project, though it is safe to say that he had a significant impact on the content, especially in creating the "World 3" computer model. Indeed, he was listed as third author (among the four group leaders) when *The Limits to Growth: A Report for the Club of Rome's Project on the Predicament of Mankind* was released in 1972.[17]

This report and its aftermath has been the topic of several historical studies, and thus there is no need to go into depth about it here.[18] Briefly, *The Limits to Growth* sought to understand the world as a global system, specifically focusing on the way in which population, industrial output, food production, non-renewable resource availability, and the level of pollution interact. They reached the dramatic conclusion that growth in human population and material production could not continue indefinitely due to the finite nature of the world's resources. It became perhaps one of the most debated environmental reports of modern times, thanks in part to the public relations firm that handled the book, Calvin Kyle Associates, which used clever marketing to push sales. To make sure it got attention, it was published simultaneously in half a dozen languages and sent for free to 1,200 selected world leaders.[19] As a result, over the years the report sold a total of nine million copies. The report and the PR stunt were financed by the industrialist Aurelio Peccei and the Volkswagen Foundation, funds which made sure the report dominated environmental debate after its release in March. The reverberations of the report continued through the United Nations Conference on the Human Environment in Stockholm in June 1972, and beyond.[20]

H. Meadows (eds.), *Toward Global Equilibrium* (Cambridge, MA: Wright-Allen Press, 1973), pp. 165–211.

[17] Meadows (et al.), *The Limits to Growth*.

[18] Paul Sabin, *The Bet: Paul Ehrlich, Julian Simon, and Our Gamble over Earth's Future* (New Haven: Yale University Press, 2013), pp. 80–93. Matthew Connelly, *Fatal Misconception: The Struggle to Control World Population* (Cambridge, MA: Harvard University Press, 2008), pp. 340–1. Paul N. Edwards, "The world in a machine: Origins and impacts of early computerized global systems," in Agatha C. Hughes and Thomas P. Hughes (eds.), *Systems, Experts, and Computers* (Cambridge, MA: The MIT Press, 2000), pp. 221–54. Charles T. Rubin, *The Green Crusade: Rethinking the Roots of Environmentalism* (New York: The Free Press, 1994), pp. 130–73. Paul Neurath, *From Malthus to the Club of Rome and Back: Problems of Limits to Growth, Population Control, and Migrations* (London: Sharpe, 1994).

[19] Robert Gillette, "The limits to growth: Hard sell for a computer view of doomsday," *Science*, 175, no. 4026 (Mar. 10, 1972), 1088–1092.

[20] Wade Rowland, *The Plot to Save the World: The Life and Times of the Stockholm Conference on the Human Environment* (Toronto: Clarke, Irwin, 1973), pp. 9–25.

7 The Sustainable Society

Though *Limits to Growth* predicted limits to natural resources, it did not predict limits to existing political systems. The MIT group was, in this respect, part of a larger trend of environmentalists looking for solutions to ecological problems within established social structures. Most prominent among them was the designer Richard Buckminster Fuller, whose widely read *Operating Manual for Spaceship Earth* (1969) did more than merely hint at an engineering and managerial answer to the ecological crisis.[21]

It is hard to find the word "sustainable" in systems dynamics literature from this period. When in use, the MIT group used it descriptively as a synonym for equilibrium. Forrester, for example, used the word "sustainable" at least once in his *World Dynamics* (1971) to describe an economic system in equilibrium.[22] To him it was a technical expression. The word seems to have appeared only once in *Limits to Growth* when they stated that: "We are searching for a model output that represents a world system that is: 1. *sustainable* without sudden and uncontrolled collapse; and 2. capable of satisfying the basic material requirements of all of its people."[23] Randers himself used the word similarly once in his thesis proposal from 1972 in describing the need to move the world "in a new and sustainable direction," which meant in the direction of equilibrium (as opposed to the direction of inevitable collapse).[24] This would change between 1972 and 1974, as sustainability gradually evolved from a rarely used descriptive word into a larger normative vision for a viable environmental future. As will be apparent, Randers played a central role in this process.

THE CALL FOR A GOLDEN AGE IN EQUILIBRIUM

In June 1971, well before the publication of *Limits to Growth*, Randers gave a lecture on "The Carrying Capacity of our Global Environment – A Look at the Ethical Alternatives" for a Working Committee on Church

---

United Nations, *Report of the United Nations Conference on the Human Environment* (New York: United Nations, 1973). Arne Semb-Johansson, "Stockholm-konferansen kan få stor betydning," *Forskningsnytt*, 17 (1972), 7–10, Meadows (et al.), *The Limits to Growth*, p. 11. Ugo Bardi, *The Limits to Growth Revisited* (New York: Springer, 2011), pp. 5–13.

[21] Richard Buckminster Fuller, *Operating Manual for Spaceship Earth* (Edwardsville: Southern Illinois University Press, 1969). Peder Anker, "Buckminster Fuller as Captain of Spaceship Earth," *Minerva*, 45 (2007), 417–34.

[22] Forrester, *World Dynamics*, 1971, 12.

[23] Meadows (et al.), *Limits to Growth*, 1972, 158.

[24] Jørgen Randers, "The Diffusion of New Ideas and Values – A Dynamic Model of the General Process: A Proposal to the National Council of Churches," June 30, 1972, 10 pages, D-1889, p. 1, SD.

and Society within the ecumenical World Council of Churches (WCC). The event took place in Nemi, a suburb of Rome, Italy, and was designed to address the role of science in the search for "Quality of Life." It was a high-power meeting with notable intellectuals, such as Margaret Mead and Theodore Roszak, in which the Church sought to find its voice in the growing countercultural and environmental debate. Randers was invited through the Club of Rome to present the ongoing research at MIT. In the words of one participant, he was "a talented youthful MIT student," who suggested "that we all mark time" in a common effort to reach ecological equilibrium.[25]

In the early 1970s human ecologists and sociologists explored social and natural conditions for raising "the quality of life" of people. The main finding of this research was that merely economic and material parameters did not measure social improvements, and that one also had to take into account social interactions and environmental conditions in order to determine the "quality" of social life.[26] The main target of this research was the assumption often held by social economists and politicians alike that economic activity (as expressed, say, in GDP per person) was an adequate standard on which to measure the wellbeing of a nation. Others were perhaps equally important, such as spiritual, social, cultural, and ecological parameters. This quality-of-life research found its chief audience within the World Future Society, which was an organization that sought to open up a multitude of alternative visions for the world's future aside from the dominating capitalist and socialist dogmas of the Cold War.

The Nemi meeting was part of a five-year ecumenical inquiry sponsored by WCC that began in 1969 called "The Future of Man and Society." The meeting was called as a response to the founding of the World Futures Studies Federation, which was initiated by Johan Galtung and his Peace Research Institute in Oslo with a conference in 1967. Yet scholars active in the Church inquiry hardly became active in Future Studies circles, as their research paths took a life of their own with publications in their new journal *Anticipation: Christian Thought in Future Perspective* (1970–83). They met for the first time in Geneva in

---

[25] Benjamin C. W. Nwosu, "Quality of life on the technological options: The African perspective," *Anticipation*, 17 (May 1974), 31–5, quote p. 33.

[26] Sylivan J. Kaplan and Evelyn Kivy-Rosenberg (eds.), *Ecology and the Quality of Life* (Springfield, IL: Charles C. Thomas, 1973). Norman C. Dalkey with Daniel L. Rourke, Ralph Lewis and David Snyder, *Studies in the Quality of Life* (Lexington, MA: Lexington Books, 1972).

1970 under the banner "Technology, Faith and the Future of Man." The published papers from the conference would "catalogue the negative effects of modern technology," question the almighty power of technology, call for a renewed dialogue between scientists and theologians, and stress the importance of maintaining faith in God in times of crisis.[27] Worries about the ecological state of the world factored most heavily in their work, though they also addressed human population growth, the possibility of manipulating biological genes, the industrialization and urbanization of societies, and the importance of keeping computers at arm's length. At the core was the importance of upholding the future role of Christianity in a changing world.

It was this group of about thirty scientists and theologians that Randers met in Nemi when he presented his "Carrying Capacity" paper. It was an important lecture for him. It was one of his first public appearances, and when it appeared in print, in the theological journal *Anticipation*, it became his first publication. However, he did not bring good news for the Christian thinkers. He began by reminding them of the famous line from the Bible: "For which of you, intending to build a tower, sitteth not down first, and counteth the cost, whether he have sufficient to finish it?"[28] It was meant as an allegory for the importance of using long-term cost analysis to find solutions for an Earth in deep trouble. In summarizing the major findings of the forthcoming report to the Club of Rome, Randers told the Church leaders that "our globe is finite" and that it is suffering from "desperate land shortage," "heat increase," and the inability to absorb pollution.[29] The exponential growth in use of finite natural resources, he argued, would "inevitably lead us to some sort of collapse" unless people began taking into account long-term needs including the needs "of those who will live on the planet 100 years from now."[30] It was the concern for the next generations that moved Randers to engage Christians, as he thought people of faith could move politics in a more responsible direction. "Probably only religion has the moral force to bring such a change" in long-term objectives by bringing to an end the politics of growth, he argued.[31] It was with the help of religion that one could

---

[27] Samuel L. Parmar, "Forward," in David M. Gill (ed.), *From Here to Where? Technology, Faith and the Future of Man* (Geneva: World Council of Churches, 1970), pp. 5–8, quote p. 5.
[28] The Bible, Luke 14, 28. Jørgen Randers, "The carrying capacity of our global environment – A look at the ethical alternatives," *Anticipation*, 8 (1971), 2–11, quote p. 2.
[29] Randers, "Carrying capacity," 1971, 2, 3, 4.
[30] Randers, "Carrying capacity," 1971, 7, 9.   [31] Randers, "Carrying capacity," 1971, 9.

hope to "transfer into an equilibrium state" or "*The Golden Age,*" which will "put the human race into harmony with the world's ecosystem," increase "the quality of life for the individual," and lead to "profound flowering of the arts."[32] "[T]he churches have always been a leader," Randers concluded in his plea to the World Council, and therefore they should lead the way in the necessary transition "from growth to equilibrium."[33]

Randers appealed to deep-seated Christian beliefs and traditions. In the wake of Lynn White's article "The Historical Roots of Our Ecologic Crisis" (1967), in which the medieval historian accused Judeo-Christian theology of nurturing an exploitative ethic toward the natural world, there was a longing for medieval times among Christian environmentalists. Randers appealed to this wish to again see the Church as the leading moral and political force in society. More importantly, the "Golden Age" in Christian thinking is synonymous with the lost Eden that one day will reemerge as the Kingdom of God with the reign of Christ. In this future Golden Age humans will live in harmony with the earth and each other, there will be peace between animals ("the lion will eat straw like the ox"), and there will be no need for agricultural exploitation of nature.[34]

The paper generated debate among the Nemi participants around the idea of moral conflict between present and future generations of human beings. The gist of Randers' lecture, one participant later recalled, was that "only religion appears to afford the necessary moral strength to effect any change on behalf of those yet unborn."[35] The Christian Gospel of hope for a "Golden Age" could thus infuse the environmental debate with the power of faith in the future. Randers' paper was republished in several versions and became, in the subsequent years, a standard reference in steady-state economics and environmental studies.[36]

---

[32] Randers, "Carrying capacity," 1971, 10, 11. Randers' emphasis (subtitle).
[33] Randers, "Carrying capacity," 1971, 11.
[34] The Bible, Isaiah 65, 25. White, "The historical roots of our ecologic crisis."
[35] Martti Lindqvist, *Economic Growth and the Quality of Life: An Analysis of the Debate within the World Council of Churches 1966–1974* (Helsinki: The Finnish Society for Missiology and Ecumenics, 1975), 95.
[36] Randers, "Carrying capacity," 1971, reappeared in many different versions, such as Jørgen Randers with Donella Meadows, "The carrying capacity of the globe," *Sloan Management Review*, 13, no. 2 (1972), 11–27; "The carrying capacity of our global environment: A look at the ethical alternatives," in Herman E. Daly (ed.), *Toward a Steady State Economy* (San Francisco: Freeman, 1973), pp. 283–306.

LEADING THE SUSTAINABLE EFFORT

The spring semester of 1972 was hectic and exciting for Randers, with the publication of *Limits to Growth* in March and the subsequent debate around it. As a co-author of the book, he emerged in the public realm as an important figure in the international environmental debate. Yet he was still a graduate student, and it was time for him to settle on a thesis topic. He chose to address one key criticism of the report: that humankind did not face a predicament, as the problems described in *Limits to Growth* would catalyze radical changes in human behavior that would solve the problems laid out and thus prove the predictions in the report wrong. In other words, he wanted to investigate how the power of new ideas could generate social change.

His plan reflected a widespread belief, both in the popular and academic culture of the early 1970s, that society lay on the cusp of revolutionary changes. A typical example may be Alvin Toffler's widely read *Future Shock* (1970), which held that the world was about to change radically due to a series of new technologies and social practices.[37] This sense of radical transformation was particularly intense among religious leaders, who with admiration or dismay saw numerous new congregations arise. The phenomenon was scrutinized in church circles, as in the project "Insearch: The Future of Religion in America" led by John E. Biersdorf, a clergyman who headed the National Council of Churches of Christ's Department of the Ministry in the USA.[38]

In the spring of 1972 Randers explored the feasibility of studying such radical value changes by using system dynamics methodology, and he contacted the Planning and Research Department of the National Council in New York to find financial and intellectual patronage. The Council, it is worth noting, was the leading non-orthodox ecumenical association. It acted as an umbrella organization for churches with a liberal theological outlook, and it was a stern supporter of civil rights activism and a host of social welfare programs.[39] Thus, its leaders not only observed but also actively promoted the need to radically redefine Christian values and

---

[37] Alvin Toffler, *Future Shock* (New York: Random House, 1970). Tord Høivik (eds.), *År 2000* (Oslo: Pax, 1969).
[38] John E. Biersdorf, *Elements of Research Design for a Study of Value Change in Religion in American Society* (New York: Working Paper from the National Council of Churches, 1972).
[39] Henry J. Pratt, *The Liberalization of American Protestantism* (Detroit: Wayne State University Press, 1972). James F. Findlay, *Church People in the Struggle: The National*

teachings. The same was true for their work on environmental issues. As Randers put it in his PhD thesis, they held that "large scale change in social attitudes and values [...] is desirable to insure a sustainable global society in earth's finite environment."[40]

In June 1972 Randers submitted a research proposal to these "moral leaders," as he called them. He wrote that he could offer them "a dynamic model" of "the diffusion of new ideas and values" in human populations of relevance to their church planning.[41] His study could also offer a manual on "how to succeed in quickly diffusing the new values and gaining their acceptance by many people in a relatively short time" so that human activity would move with speed "in a new and sustainable direction."[42] By using the modeling programs of the System Dynamics Group, Randers suggested developing "a simulation game to be played" by the Church leaders so that they could predict value changes in society and thus in their congregations.[43]

The Council was excited about Randers' ideas. As he presented his proposal to them during the time when the *Limits to Growth* report still dominated most environmental debates, it was fairly easy to explain his needs to grant committees. The Council provided him with enough funding for a salary, secretarial and editorial support, social benefits, computer and material expenses, as well as a generous travel budget. Additional grants from the Minna-James-Heineman Foundation and the Zaffaroni Foundation gave him even better financial flexibility. Perhaps equally important was the intellectual support from Biersdorf and Neil Douglas from the Council, both of whom Randers would later thank in his thesis acknowledgments for opening him up to the wonders of religious beliefs.[44] Whenever issues went beyond his advisor Jay W. Forrester's domain, Randers would call upon Biersdorf or Douglas. He was also close to Poikail George and Frank White, both of whom also worked for the Council. In addition Everett Perry, who was on the Board

---

Council of Churches and the Black Freedom Movement, 1950–1970 (New York: Oxford University Press, 1993).

[40] Randers, *Conceptualizing*, 1973, p. 65.
[41] Randers, "The Diffusion of New Ideas and Values," ms. 1972, 1, SD.
[42] Randers, "The Diffusion of New Ideas and Values," ms. 1972, 3, 1, SD.
[43] Randers, "The Diffusion of New Ideas and Values," ms. 1972, 8, SD.
[44] Randers, *Conceptualizing*, 1973, p. 4, 69 (note 1). Jørgen Randers, "Behavior Change Induced by Diffusion of New Ideas – A Dynamic Model of the General Process: A Proposal to the National Council of Churches," Sept. 25, 1972, 5 pages, D-1890, budget on p. 5, SD.

of the National Mission for the United Presbyterian Church, and Herbert Dordick, the Director of Telecommunications at New York City Government, provided external expertise. Dordick, the only exception to this high-power theological support group, was at the time exploring how ideas spread in urban environments though new telecommunications devices, ideas which he much later summarized in his widely read *The Information Society* (1993).[45]

As "leaders of movements," the advisory group at the National Council in New York became Randers' intended audience (as he describes in his final thesis proposal from November 1972).[46] Social movements were to him "myth-making groups trying to impart a sense of increased power and meaning to their members."[47] What the leaders were to get from Randers' work was a model capable of predicting the lifecycle of their respective movements by punching data into a model and running it on a computer.[48] Biersdorf had the relevant data through his "Insearch" project, and the only thing missing was a model capable of making predictions about how these movements would develop on a timeline. In effect, Randers sought to understand the trends of human belief systems as an extension of human use or abuse of natural resources.

The underlying issue was the problem of solving the environmental problems in time, or before the collapse predicted in *Limits to Growth*. There was a "mismatch," Meadows and Randers argued in an article from the period, "between the time-span of environmental problems and the time-horizons of institutions designed to deal with those problems."[49] They were pessimistic about the capability to solve the problems in time unless "a specific commitment is made to the future" with a planning horizon of fifty years or so.[50] They argued that if the environmental movement organizes itself so that they have the time-horizon of other political institutions, they "cannot be expected to succeed in stopping

---

[45] Herbert S. Dordick and Jack Lyle, *Access by Local Political Candidates to Cable Television: A Report of an Experiment* (Santa Monica, CA: Rand, 1971). Herbert S. Dordick and Georgette Wang, *The Information Society: A Retrospective View* (Newberry Park: Sage Publications, 1993).
[46] Jørgen Randers, "The Lifecycle of a Movement: Outline of a Research Project," Nov. 1972, 35 pages, D-1891, frontpage, SD.
[47] Randers, "The Lifecycle of a Movement," ms. 1972, 1, SD.
[48] Randers, "The Lifecycle of a Movement," ms. 1972, 1, 6, SD.
[49] Dennis L. Meadows and Jørgen Randers, "Adding the time dimension to environmental policy." *International Organization*, 26, no. 2 (1972), 213–33, quote p. 214.
[50] Meadows and Randers, "Adding the time dimension," p. 232.

environmental deterioration."[51] What worried Randers was "the slowness in large social systems" as it takes a long time to get environmentally positive results due to social changes.[52] The churches, on the other hand, worked with a more viable timeline.

The thesis topic also reflected a sense of being at the center of a growing environmental movement, as, from March 1972 until he settled in Oslo in 1974, Randers constantly traveled and debated *Limits to Growth*. In his diary from January 1973, for example, he notes that he "lectured all over the US[A]" about the report, and voices frustration over not finding time to work on his new project.[53] His top-down managerial approach to movements and social change was definitely not done from an ivory tower, but instead reflected a sense of being right in the midst of a social upheaval. Indeed, the authors of *Limits of Growth* were themselves prime movers of the environmental debate. It is thus tempting to read Randers' thesis as a personal attempt to come to terms with his sudden status as a leader of a movement. His success raised the question of what it would take to sustain the debate.

A key term that became important in the initial model building was "the sustainable effort," which was defined as the "total amount of resources" a movement could expend in trying to achieve its goal.[54] This term differs from the descriptive way the word "sustainable" was used by other scholars working with Forrester. As Randers indicated (in Figure 6.), the "sustainable effort" of a social movement included allocation of efforts to increase its relevance, visibility, income, services, etc. in order to gain momentum for the cause. Sustainability thus understood was a way of describing the survival capacity of a movement based on measuring its "efforts."

The sustainable efforts made by an organization or social movement would enhance the quality of its member experience and thus produce more members, some of whom would become active participants in providing more sustainable efforts which would lead to more members, etc. This feedback loop served as the basis for what became Randers' model of the lifecycle of movements. The dynamic of a lifecycle could be positive by generating new members or negative, depending on the capability of maintaining the "sustainable effort." What determined the

---

[51] Meadows and Randers, "Adding the time dimension," p. 232.
[52] Jørgen Randers (interview), *Aftenposten*, 11. Nov. 1972, PA.
[53] Randers, *Conceptualizing*, p. 112.
[54] Randers, "The Lifecycle of a Movement," ms. 1972, 17, SD.

7 The Sustainable Society

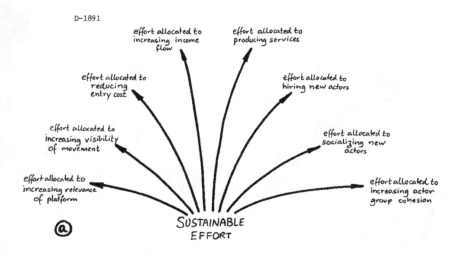

FIGURE 6 Sustainable effort as Jørgen Randers saw it in the manuscript "The Lifecycle of a Movement" from November 1972.
Courtesy of Jørgen Randers

process was both the quality of member experience and actor experience, as shown in the loops of Figure 7.

These somewhat simplistic models would grow in complexity the following year as Randers' work matured into his dissertation entitled *Conceptualizing Dynamic Models of Social Systems: Lessons from a Study of Social Change*.[55] There is not much on religion in these pages. Rather, Randers focused on the general dynamics of social movements as a consequence of introducing an idea into society. The overall perspective of the thesis was very much a top-down approach that provided tools for leaders of movements – a type of reasoning that was typical within the Sloan School of Management.

What is notable about this is that progressive Church leaders at a time of religious upheaval would look to Randers and his ideas about social movements in order to make sense of the dynamics of their organizations. He provided them with managerial tools inspired by natural resource management to understand and deal with their respective congregations

---

[55] Randers, *Conceptualizing*.; "The Dynamic Interaction Between an Action Group and Society: A PhD Dissertation Proposal," Apr. 1, 1973, 48 pages, D-1892, SD.

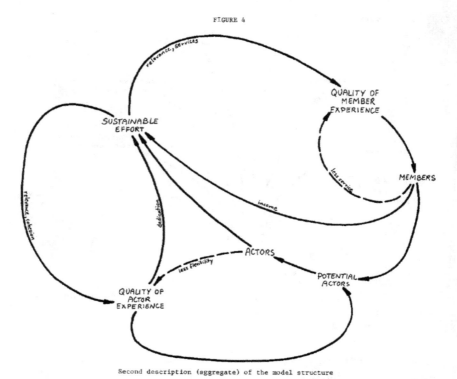

FIGURE 7 The lifecycle of a social movement as Jørgen Randers saw it in November 1972.
Courtesy of Jørgen Randers

at times when the member base was fluctuating greatly. For example, Randers' work was "received with great interest" by representatives of the Jesus Movement and Pentecostals, among others, at the second conference on the Relevance of Organized Religion in January 1973.[56] In the process, Church leaders learned about the importance of leading a "sustainable effort" in order to reach the Golden Age of sustainable equilibrium. As will be argued (in Chapter 9), this corresponded with "sustainable development" toward "sustainability" as defined by the World Commission for Development and Environment in 1987. Meanwhile, Randers finished his thesis in September 1973, and was subsequently promoted to Assistant Professor in management at MIT.

[56] Randers, *Conceptualizing*, p. 112.

THE SUSTAINABLE SOCIETY IN BUCHAREST

In the meantime the World Council of Churches continued with their "Science and Technology for Human Development" inquiries, with new meetings and a string of publications. The highlight was, perhaps, the participation of Church leaders in the 1972 United Nations Conference on the Human Environment in Stockholm, Sweden. The implications of the *Limits to Growth* report continued to dominate these debates, which focused on the need to develop relevant technologies for a more modest society respecting God's Creation. Key publications in 1973 included Thomas S. Derr's *Ecology and Human Liberation* and the Council's *Genetics and the Quality of Life* report, which addressed the possibility of manipulating the human biological makeup to improve the quality of life.[57] These books and articles came in response to the Nemi meeting back in 1971, and tried to find a new relationship between humans and nature, population policy, and better quality of life for people of faith. Interestingly, one of the debaters was Ernst F. Schumacher, who launched his "Small is Beautiful" argument in this religious context.[58]

These debates came to a climax with the World Council of Churches' conference "Science and Technology for Human Development: The Ambiguous Future and the Christian Hope," which took place in Bucharest at the end of June 1974. The United Nations had designated 1974 as the World Population Year and a major conference about it was set to take place, also in Bucharest, a month later. A chief purpose of the Church leaders was to prepare well for this meeting. Because the human world population was expected to raise from about four billion in 1973 to well over six billion by the end of the millennium, this raised key theological questions with respect to family planning, social justice, and human values. *Limits to Growth* would frame much of the debates, according to the editor of WCC's intramural journal *Study Encounter,* who in 1973 noted that the Council "found itself having to sort out the crucial issues in the public debate raging around the Club of Rome's report."[59]

---

[57] Martti Lindqvist, *The Biological Manipulation of Man and the Quality of Life* (Helsinki: Research Institute of Lutheran Church, 1972). Anonymous, *Genetics and the Quality of Life: Report of a Consultation Church and Society, June 1973* (Geneva: Christian Medical Commission, 1974).

[58] Ernst F. Schumacher, "Small is beautiful," *Study Encounter* 9, no. 4 (1973), 13–16. Special issues of *The Ecumenical Review* 26, no. 1 (1974); *Study Encounter* 10, no. 1–4 (1974); *Anticipation* 17–19 (1974).

[59] Editorial comment, *Study Encounter* 9, no. 4 (1973), p. 13.

At the conference a gathering of about 120 "Christian laymen from many branches of science and technology and public life" addressed the ways in which people of faith should respond to the consequences of economic growth, technological developments, and population growth.[60] Environmental degradation and human poverty were the two main problems, the invitation to the conference stated, and the participants were asked to discuss if "the instrumentalities of scientific rationality ... threaten the right relation between man and nature," and where to draw the "distinction between what is needed and what is superfluous."[61] Though the conference was to address more-mainstream theological questions, such as the unity of the gospel and the meaning of confession, environmental and developmental issues took center stage. The "Selected Preparatory Papers" published in *Anticipation* a month before the event focused on the pitfalls of economic growth, the ethics of natural resource use, the lack of quality of life in both rich and poor nations, and the role of religion in society.[62]

In the early 1970s, Bucharest was a contested territory in a world dominated by the Cold War divide. Nicolae Ceaușescu had been the Secretary General of the Communist Party since 1965 and Romania's President since 1968. Though he shared communist interests with his Soviet neighbor and other East Bloc countries, he condemned the Soviet invasion of Czechoslovakia in 1968 and refused to send military troops. This made him into a darling of the West, despite his reputation as a brutal dictator who used the secret police to establish a system of fear by rounding up and imprisoning dissidents.[63] Foreigners traveling to Romania, however, hardly noticed this fear, as the government carefully orchestrated their visit so that they would leave with the best possible impression of the country. Norwegians were not immune to all the friendliness if one is to judge from Randers' lack of criticism of Ceaușescu's government. The same goes for the Christian professor of

---

[60] Paul Abrecht, "Science and technology for human development – The ambiguous future and the Christian hope," *Study Encounter*, 10 (1974), 1–2.
[61] Anonymous, "Fifth Assembly: Notes for sections," *Study Encounter*, 10, no. 1 (1974), 1–16, quote p. 16.
[62] World Council of Churches, "Selected preparatory papers," *Anticipation* 17 (May 1974), 1–61.
[63] Julian Hale, *Ceaușescu's Romania: A Political Documentary* (London: George G. Harrap, 1971). Amnesty International, *Annual Report 1972–1973* (London: Amnesty International, 1973), p. 67; *Annual Report 1973–1974* (London: Amnesty International, 1974), p. 64.

biochemistry at the University of Oslo, Jens Gabriel Hauge, who also attended the conference.[64]

The local protégé who defended Ceaușescu was Mircea Malitza. He was a professor of mathematics at the University of Bucharest who served as Deputy Minister of Foreign Affairs (1962–70), Minister of Education (1970–72), and Minister and Counselor of the President (from 1972). Thus he was in the inner circle of Ceaușescu's dictatorship. Besides mathematical work, he published on the history of diplomacy and the politics of negotiations, and as an affiliate and later honorary member of the Club of Rome he would co-author its report *No Limits to Learning* (1979).[65] To the WCC delegates he would rage about the pitfalls of "consumer society" where "individual consumers" were merely following "logic of profit" and were unable to care for the poor.[66] As an alternative he quoted Ceaușescu's speech on "sustained industrialization" aiming at "raising ... the living standards" of Romanian people and the workers of the world without lapsing into materialistic consumerism.[67] Though Malitza was a keynote speaker on the first day of the conference, he did not dominate it. Indeed, the participants were concerned about the social situation of Christians in a communist country, as the services and biblical meditations organized in collaboration with the Romanian Orthodox Patriarchate were overly well attended.

The conference began with a paper by Lynn White, in which he repeated his accusation that Christian human-centered theology was the underlying cause for the ecological crisis, and that one should embrace Franciscan perspectives as a remedy.[68] Another key plenary presentation was given by Kenneth Boulding, Samuel L. Parmar, and George Borgström on shared moral and social challenges in view of the *Limits to Growth* report.[69] These presentations situated the debate between the

---

[64] Jens Gabriel Hauge, *Gud og naturen: Om vitenskap og kristen tro* (Oslo: Genesis forlag, 1999).
[65] James W. Botkin, Mahdi Elmandjra, and Mircea Malitza, *No Limits to Learning: Bridging the Human Gap: A Report to the Club of Rome* (Oxford: Pergamon Press, 1979).
[66] Mircea Malitza, "Technological development and the future of Man in a socialist society," *Anticipation*, 18 (1974), 23–5, quote p. 25.
[67] Nicolae Ceaușescu quoted in Malitza, "Technological development," p. 24.
[68] White, "The historical roots," 1967; "Theology and the future of compassion" (unpublished) short résumé in Paul Abrecht, "An ecumenical vision of the future," *Anticipation*, 18 (1974), 3–6.
[69] Samuel L. Parmar, "Ethical Guidelines and Social Options after the Limits to Growth Debate," *Anticipation*, 18 (1974), 20–2. George Borgström, "World food scarcity and

call from White and an emerging group of eco-theologians to show more respect and care for the Creation, and on the opposite side, the focus from the admirers of the Club of Rome report on the gloomy end of natural resources and economic growth.

After these keynote lectures, a set of working groups were organized to generate a report in the form of "A New Ecumenical Vision of the Future" that could provide religious communities with a framework for approaching developmental and environmental problems with Christian hope.[70] Charles Birch, a professor of biology at the University of Sydney, chaired the working group which Randers attended. Originally trained at Oxford University, Birch was a widely respected geneticist and population ecologist who also believed in God's existence. He believed that constructive dialogue between science and religion was possible if scientists provided facts that religious leaders could use to stake out a vision for the future. In his memoirs Birch recalls how, in the workshop, he pushed for a discussion of the future based on the warnings in *Limits to Growth* with respect to the world's finite resources, pollution from industries, damaging effects of economic growth, and the importance of living within the Earth's limits. Yet he got nowhere as the delegates from the Global South world were hostile: "Don't talk to us about limits to growth, they said, when what we need is to grow as the rich countries have grown."[71] The phrase "ecologically sustainable society" entered the discussion at this point:

> At a coffee break Jorgen Randers said to me: "We have to find some phrase other than limits to growth that is positive in its impact. Limits has a negative connotation. Other suggestions such as a stationary state, an equilibrium society and a steady state society are too static." Then he suggested: "What about the ecologically sustainable society?" meaning the society that could persist indefinitely into the future because it sustained the ecological base on which society is utterly dependent.[72]

Randers had been backpacking for the previous three months, and he also had an annoying itch on his arm. It was a personal relief for him that the phrase was immediately adopted by the working group so that the discussion could move on and focus on its requirements.

---

the struggle for human survival," *Anticipation*, 18 (1974), 17–19. I have been unable to locate Kenneth Boulding's paper.
[70] World Council of Churches, "Science and technology for human development: The ambiguous future and the Christian hope: Report," *Anticipation*, 19 (1974), 1–43.
[71] Charles Birch, *Regaining Compassion for Humanity and Nature* (Kensington: New South Wales University Press, 1993), p. 114.
[72] Birch, *Regaining Compassion*, p. 114.

At the plenary meeting of the Conference *"Sustainable Society"* was accepted as the key concept necessary for envisioning an ecumenical vision of the future, despite criticisms of it being "a too static and mechanistic approach" from African, Asian, and Latin American delegates.[73] The "sense of an ending" to a materialistic lifestyle on Earth signaled to the majority of the Conference participants the beginning of a "new historical situation," with a promise of a return to the Christian "tradition of asceticism" and a renewed faith in the Gospel's promise of "the new creation of Christ."[74] The resurrection of Christ entailed a sustainable and just society for all, and thus an ecumenical vision for the future all Christians should strive for. At the core of the conference report was a guide to how the Christian community should address secular questions about the role of science and technology for human development. Aiming at "a robust sustainable society" was the answer, as it was a state in which (1) there was "social stability" and equitable distribution of opportunities, (2) production of food within the "capacity of the ecosystem," (3) use of non-renewable resources which did not exceed "the increase in resources made available through technological innovation," and (4) a level of human activity which did not suffer from "natural variation in global climate."[75] "In essence, the sustainable society will be one with a stable population and with a fixed material wealth per person, a society actively pursuing quality of life in basically non-material dimensions such as leisure, service, arts, education, and sport."[76] The secular language of this description is misleading, as there is ample evidence elsewhere in the report that their hope for a sustainable society had a Christian bearing. "Hope for the future is a gift of grace," the Conference typically stated, "and the struggles for the new future a result of a faith that transcends all historical prospects."[77] The sustainable society should thus be understood within the context of the Gospel of hope: "We [Christians] look ... for a new life and new age in the future, in ourselves as new creatures, in society as the New Jerusalem, and in history as the promised Kingdom ... The future is a realm of hope and not of despair for those who know God. It is toward this eschatological goal that the creative and 'luring' work of God is directed."[78] The hope for a

---

[73] Abrecht, "An ecumenical vision," p. 4. Abrecht's emphasis.
[74] World Council Report, "Science and technology," p. 5.
[75] World Council Report, "Science and technology," p. 12.
[76] World Council Report, "Science and technology," p. 12.
[77] World Council Report, "Science and technology," p. 33.
[78] World Council Report, "Science and technology," p. 34.

sustainable society expressed by Conference participants was thus a secular articulation of the Christian longing for the Promised Land, the New Jerusalem.

The Council was unsuccessful in bringing this message to the United Nations World Population Conference the next month, as there are no references to sustainability or theological issues in their reports.[79] The initial reactions from some Christian participants reflecting back on these events were also skeptical. A French delegate noted, for example, that environmental issues would help to recruit the young for the Churches: "Ecology is a fashion. Thanks to ecology, a youthful vigor and freshness has been restored to ethical reflection" he stated in a paper marked by a cynical sarcastic subtext.[80] Another participant thought that the "ecological approach" of the sustainable society was "markedly futuristic" in not addressing the Cold War divide and that it thus failed in providing a strategy for "political action" for the Christian community.[81] Despite such reactions, most Conference participants thought "sustainability" was a productive concept around which the Christians could engage the secular society with a renewed hope for the Creation.[82] Kenneth Boulding, for example, was an active Quaker and returned to the USA arguing that the "sustainable society" expression he had picked up at the Conference signaled hope for the future.[83] Soon theologians were busy probing the meaning of sustainability from a Christian perspective, as in Robert Stivers' *The Sustainable Society* (1976).[84] With the help of Randers as a consultant, the concept was eventually incorporated in

---

[79] World Population Conference, *The Population Debate: Dimensions and Perspectives: Papers of the World Population Conference, Bucharest, 1974*, 2 vol. (New York: United Nations, 1975). Lars Levi and Lars Andersson, *Population, Environment and Quality of Life: A Contribution to the United Nations World Population Conference* (Stockholm: Allmänna Förlaget, 1974).

[80] André Dumas, "The ecological crisis and the doctrine of creation," *The Ecumenical Review*, 27 (1975), 24–35, quotes pp. 24, 34.

[81] Lindqvist, *Economic Growth*, 1975, 98.

[82] World Council of Churches Central Committee and David E. Johnson (eds.), *Uppsala to Nairobi, 1968–1975: Report of the Central Committee to the Fifth Assembly of the World Council of Churches* (New York: Friendship Press, 1975), pp. 109–16. Paul Bock, *In Search of a Responsible World Society: The Social Teachings of the World Council of Churches* (Philadelphia: Westminster Press, 1974).

[83] Kenneth Boulding quoted in Cliff Smith, "Economist urges tax boost," *Medina County Gazette*, Aug. 28, 1974, 18.

[84] Robert Stivers, *The Sustainable Society: Ethics and Economic Growth* (Philadelphia: Westminster Press, 1976). John B. Cobb, *Sustainability: Economics, Ecology, and Justice* (New York: Orbis Books, 1992), pp. 45–8.

1979 into the World Council of Churches' seven year program: "The Search for a Just, Participatory and Sustainable Society."[85]

THE LIMITS TO GROWTH IN NORWAY

When Jørgen Randers left for MIT in 1970 he was entirely unknown to Norwegians, besides a handful of people who might have heard of his MA thesis from 1969 about the scattering of neutrons.[86] It was therefore a shock to the Norwegian environmentalists to see this twenty-seven-year-old nobody rise to world fame as a co-author of *Limits to Growth*. The sudden distinction of a graduate student was looked upon with suspicion. Yet the Norwegian tall poppy syndrome (Law of Jante) was not the chief reason environmental scholars were skeptical. It was the managerial reform program of the report that upset those who sought radical environmental answers to the question of what to do with Norway's natural resources.

Limits to Growth was immediately translated into Norwegian with the new subtitle "MIT's research report on the world's continuing growth." On the back cover was a quote from the world's first Minister of the Environment, Olav Gjærevoll, who proclaimed that "this book will have a vehement significance for our way of thinking and our course of action."[87] He served as Minister between May and September 1972, after which he, along with the entire cabinet, resigned. They had suffered a humiliating defeat in the national referendum on Norwegian membership of the European Community (EC). Most environmentalists looked with suspicion at Gjærevoll's support of the EC, as generally they were vividly against Norwegian membership. As discussed in previous chapters, both ecologists and ecophilosophers were on a national campaign against what they regarded as a capitalist international organization at the root cause of environmental degradation. It is thus unlikely that potential readers glancing at the Norwegian edition of *Limits to Growth* in bookstores

---

[85] World Council of Churches Central Committee, "Report of the Advisory Committee on 'The search for a just, participatory and sustainable society'," in Koson Srisang (ed.), *Perspectives on Political Ethics: An Ecumenical Enquiry* (Geneva: WCC, 1979), pp. 174–93, Randers is listed as consultant on p. 175.

[86] Randers, *En undersøkelse av spinnsystemet*, 1969; *Conceptualizing Dynamic Models*, pp. 107–20.

[87] Olav Gjærevoll quoted on the back cover of Donella H. Meadows, Dennis L. Meadows, Jørgen Randers, and William W. Behrens III, *Hvor går grensen? MITs forskningsrapport om verdens fortsatte vekst*, Leif Bakke (trs.) (Oslo: Cappelen, 1972).

found Gjærevoll's favorable blurb encouraging. Instead, his statement placed the book firmly within a set of literature addressing the need to reform the Labor Party, debates most radical environmentalists refused to engage in. To make matters worse, the name Randers in Norway was associated with the nuclear advocate and chief NATO bureaucrat Gunnar Randers. Being his son was certainly not an asset for Jørgen in the environmental debate, as they could be confused. An eco-Marxist reaction to *Limits to Growth* from a philosophy student, for example, approached writings from the younger Randers with much suspicion as he assumed that the connection meant NATO was behind it.[88]

Yet it was the managerial ethos and lack of social-class analysis in *Limits to Growth* that Norwegian environmentalists would find most troublesome. Most prominent among them was the futurist and sociologist Johan Galtung, who (as discussed in Chapter 4) launched a most sour critique at the World Future Research Conference in Bucharest in early September 1972, labeling the report as a product of an "ideology of the middle class." The philosopher Arne Næss was there as well with his onslaught on the "shallow" technocratic perspective of *Limits to Growth* and the environmental approach of the Club of Rome. It was the lack of philosophical analysis of and commitment to broader social and environmental issues that upset Næss: "The shallow ecology movement has just two objectives: Combating pollution and combating the depletion of natural resources. The objectives are isolated from the broader problems concerning ways of life, economic systems, power structures, and the differences between and inside nations."[89] As Næss saw it, Randers and the system dynamics method he represented were unable to address the underlying "deep" issues that caused the environmental crisis at home.

Both Galtung and Næss elevated their own thinking by drawing up a distinction between their own respectively "radical" and "deep" points of view versus Randers' "middle class" and "shallow" ecology. Their arguments had a lasting effect on the reception of *Limits to Growth* in Norway, and on Randers' ability to find an immediate audience at home among environmental scholar-activists. He was living in Boston between 1970 and 1974 and, as he only visited Norway for short periods, he could not follow up the local reception of the report. As major movers of academic debate in Norway, Galtung and Næss thus managed to marginalize Randers by bumping up their own thinking at his expense. They

---

[88] Gunnar Skirbekk, *Økologi og politikk* (Bergen: Universitetet i Bergen, 1972), 44, note 3.
[89] Næss, "The shallow and the deep," 1972, 59–60.

were effective, as there are hardly any debates or comments in Norwegian peace research and ecophilosophical literature regarding *Limits to Growth* in the years following its release. This is quite remarkable, given the intense international debate of a book with a Norwegian co-author. It was not until the fifth edition of his deep ecology book from 1976 that Næss would offer a somewhat balanced evaluation of *Limits to Growth*, still quoting at length from Galtung's onslaught from 1972.[90] At that time Randers was, as will be apparent, a local force to be reckoned with as Director of the Resource Policy Group in Oslo. Indeed, throughout his life he was invited only two or three times to give a lecture at the University of Oslo, which would inevitably turn into verbal assaults thanks to Galtung, Næss, and their supporters.

One of the few documented public exchanges in which Randers engaged the Deep Ecologists was arranged by the *Forbrukerrådet* (Consumer's Council), a public institution devoted to consumer interests in Oslo. It was the Council's attempt to address environmental issues on their terms. Judging from the published version of the debate, it seems clear that Randers and the Deep Ecologists imagined different societies altogether. The ecologist Eilif Dahl was his chief opponent, arguing that a program of consumer indoctrination in the spirit of Mao was necessary to halt population growth and turn society toward ecological equilibrium.[91] Randers was, in comparison, more optimistic on behalf of the consumers' ability to foster change: "Many have labeled us doomsday prophets. But ... we see a new order of society that will improve the quality of life for many people over a long period ... [As] super technocrats we have arrived at the same conclusion as the hippies and others who believe that the most important thing in life is to have contact with people, experience things, not produce or work your head off, but have a rich life."[92] To Dahl this line of argument was surely evidence of "shallow" thinking. Relaxation was not the answer to the problem of economic growth and it was not what the environmental movement needed most, he argued. Most worrying, though, was Randers' lack of political commitment to an altogether different way of organizing the world.

That Randers thought halting economic growth was a lifestyle and not a political issue is evident in another public appearance of this

---

[90] Næss, *Økologi, samfunn og livsstil*, 5th ed., pp. 216–23.
[91] Tryggen Larsen, "En samtale om verden: Vi står overfor bestemte begrensninger med store konsekvenser," *Forbrukerrapporten*, 10 (1972), 4–10.
[92] Randers quoted in Larsen, "En samtale om verden," p. 10.

period. It was in front of a friendly audience at the Norwegian Physics Society. Here he told them that addressing limits to growth in practical terms meant using "time on music, painting art, writing books, or – theoretical physics!"[93]

While being criticized by Deep Ecologists for his alleged "middle class" perspective and "shallow" technocratic approach to environmental issues, Randers was also confronted by scholars who dismissed future studies altogether. One critique stated, for example, that future studies had an "imperialistic tendency" in trying to make the common future the object of a narrow managerial discipline.[94] Others did not believe in any limits to growth. A book reviewer in one of Norway's largest newspapers thought Randers was simply irrational.[95] One of the most articulated versions of this criticism came from a group of researchers at the University of Sussex who published a lengthy critique in 1973. In it the authors argued, among other things, that if one ran the mathematical model used in *Limits to Growth* in reverse on known historical data, the model would not match the actual historical development. Thus, one should be highly skeptical of the model's ability to predict the future.

In Oslo, the professor of geology Ivan Rosenqvist received the Sussex report with open arms, and used it to attack Randers as a "doomster" whose success relied on "a psychological factor" in people's curiosity in bad news.[96] Arguments that Rosenqvist had previously used against the energy pessimism of the elder Randers in the 1950s would now reemerge in sweeping attacks on his son. Rosenqvist was not impressed by his use of "modern computers and intense propaganda" in the *Limits to Growth* report and stated, "a political view will not be more objective by running it through a computer."[97] The "ongoing ecological debate" about "renewable and non-renewable resources" was problematic to him since the nature of resources was poorly understood by ecologists

---

[93] Randers quoted in Olsen, "Fysikermøtet i Bergen," p. 71.
[94] Tord Høivik, "Framtidsforsking – et urovekkende fenomen?" *Forskningsnytt*, 18, no. 6 (1973), 21–4, quote p. 21.
[95] Per Andersen, "Gjetning og virkelighet" (review), *VG* Dec. 12, 1972, 3, PA.
[96] Ivan Th. Rosenqvist, "Verdifullt korrketiv til dommedagsprofetiene" (review), *Forskningsnytt*, 19 (1974), 35. H. S. D. Cole, Christopher Freeman, Marie Jahoda and K. L. R. Pavitt, *Thinking about the Future: A Critique of The Limits to Growth* (London: Sussex University Press, 1973). Robert McCutcheon, *Limits of a Modern World: A Study of the "Limits to Growth" Debate* (London: Butterworths, 1979).
[97] Ivan Th. Rosenqvist, "Har vi nok ressurser?" in Mauritz Sundt Mortensen (ed.), *I forskningens lys* (Oslo: NAVF, 1974), pp. 343–58, quotes pp. 345, 346.

and system dynamics theoreticians alike.[98] There were plenty of natural resources and no limits to growth, Rosenqvist argued, even with radical population growth.

A letter to the editor in support of Randers from the physiologist Anton Hauge was a rare exception to all the criticisms he received in Oslo.[99] Indeed, forty years later Randers would still shiver from the attacks he experienced from established professors such as Rosenqvist, Galtung, and Næss when he presented *Limits to Growth* at the University of Oslo. They took the moral high ground against the young scholar and deemed him unworthy of any significant attention.

THE RESOURCE POLICY GROUP

In 1974 Randers returned to Oslo after what must have been four remarkable years as a graduate student and subsequently a professor at MIT. Intellectually, it had been a productive period where he had produced an impressive list of publications, while socially the Sloan School of Management had propelled him into the very core of international environmental debate. Yet despite all his intellectual and social credit abroad, Oslo scholars and environmentalists did not welcome him with open arms and he was quickly marginalized as a thinker not worth listening to. Nor did he receive attention from the theologians. As shown in Chapter 6, only a few of them took an interest in environmental issues and, when doing so, they would focus narrowly on Norwegian debates and the circle of ecophilosophers surrounding Næss.

As a result Randers would turn to the only group who had shown genuine interest in his work, namely Labor Party intellectuals. He consequently became a member of the Party. Chief among them was Labor Party Minister of Industry Finn Lied. Lied was a personal friend of Randers' father, Gunnar Randers, and a fellow member of the Party, as well as the Chair of the Board of the state's chief oil company, Statoil ("state oil"), the Research Director of the Norwegian Defense Research Establishment, and Chair of the Board of the Norwegian Technical Research Council (NTNF), to mention just a few of his numerous public responsibilities. In the wake of the oil crisis in 1973, during which Norwegians were not allowed to drive their cars on the weekend or fill up their cars with gas after 7 p.m., the Parliament asked Lied to write a

---

[98] Rosenqvist, "Har vi nok ressurser?" p. 344.
[99] Anton Hauge, "Dommedagsprofetiene," *Forskningsnytt*, 19, no. 5 (1974), 31.

white paper on the apparent limits of natural resources. The result was a report stressing the need to explore more natural resources while also investigating the nation's resource economy. *Limits to Growth* as well as the competing Sussex report, would frame much of this discussion, giving both environmentalists and resource optimists something to bite on.[100] Among the debaters was the newly appointed Minister of the Environment Gro Harlem Brundtland (1939), who, from the rostrum of the Parliament, talked about the "finite limits to growth in the use of energy in the world" and the need to determine the nation's natural resource policy on solid research.[101]

Randers arrived in Oslo in the midst of these debates with barely enough financial backing to start his own Resource Policy Group through the Norwegian, Swedish, and Danish technical research councils. Randers' dream was to create "an institute for policy analysis that could provide relative neutral descriptions of what the effects of different policies would be."[102] But the research councils did not allow for much free contemplation about global resource issues. Instead the Group was asked to do industrial branch analysis, for example, for the Scandinavian pulp and paper industry, which resulted in a string of dry reports. Apparently, the foresters were down-to-earth clients with limited interest in highbrow visions for the future. Then again, the concluding report was not very encouraging, declaring "the Scandinavian forest industry viewed as a whole will not be able to increase its wood consumption significantly during the next thirty years."[103]

These forestry reports did not hinder Randers from addressing more principal issues, as he did in *The Quest for a Sustainable Society* (1975). This is most likely the first time the word "sustainable" appeared in the title of a publication dealing with environmental issues. Here Randers would reiterate and elaborate on the World Council of Churches' principles for sustainability, saying that "one of the major goals of the

---

[100] Finn Lied (et al.), *Norges ressurssituasjon i global sammenheng*, NOU 1974: 55 (Oslo: Universitetsforlaget, 1974).

[101] Gro Harlem Brundtland "Energiforsyning i Norge i framtida," in *Stortingsforhandlinger 1974/1975*, May 13, 1975, p. 4163. Yngve Nilsen, *En felles plattform? Norsk oljeindustri og klimadebatten i Norge fram til 1998* (Oslo: TIK Senter, 2001), pp. 37–65.

[102] Randers quoted in Mariken Vaa, "Samtaler i samtiden: Mellom olje og sol" (interview), *Samtiden*, 89 (1980), 9–13, quote p. 9. Besides Lie, key supporters of Randers were Rolf Marstrander and Bertil Agdur.

[103] Lennart Stenberg, *Longterm Development in the Scandinavian Forest Sector: A Study of Transition Problems using the System Dynamics Approach*, GRS-88 (Oslo: Gruppen for Ressursstudier, 1977), p. 5.

7 The Sustainable Society

sustainable society is to deliver to the next generation a carrying capacity better than the one inherited from the past."[104] The report was supposed to appear in the Council's anthology *Life within Limits*, which never materialized. Instead it came to serve as the programmatic statement for the Resource Policy Group. What was needed, Randers argued, was a "Movement towards the Sustainable Society ... while maintaining an acceptable level of welfare in the process." As will be shown (in Chapter 9), this gradualist approach to environmental change would be important for the way in which sustainable development eventually became defined by the World Commission on Environment and Development in 1987.

By 1975, the sustainable society was not only a synonym for a state in equilibrium (as expressed in *The Limits to Growth* and Forrester's *World Model*). The phrase also entailed making a "sustainable effort" and showing leadership in maintaining the environmental movement (as outlined in Randers' PhD thesis of 1973). Moreover, it meant focusing on quality of life and taking a stand against the materialism of consumer society. Also, the sustainable society was at the time discussed almost exclusively in intellectual circles connected to the World Council of Churches. In these groups it represented an ecumenical faith in the coming of the environmental harmony of the Golden Age.

Randers would soon translate this broad thinking about sustainability into a program for Norwegian foreign policy which, he argued, should focus on improving quality of life, rather than on material welfare for people around the world. In practical terms, that meant "a less open economy" in the world, self-sufficient nations, and keeping Norway outside the European Community.[105] In terms of national policy, Randers argued that Norwegian politicians should try to halt economic growth and prepare for a sustainable society that could inspire and be a model for the rest of the world. The question was "How to Stop Industrial Growth with Minimal Pain?"[106] He argued that, in order to do that, one should undermine the chief motivating force behind economic growth, namely incentive-based salaries, and instead give everyone an equal and unchangeable "citizen salary" paid for by the state. A "reduction in the

---

[104] Jørgen Randers, *The Quest for a Sustainable Society*, GRS-9 (Oslo: Gruppen for Ressursstudier, 1975), p. 7.
[105] Jørgen Randers, *En ramme for norsk utenrikspolitikk*, GRS-56 (Oslo: Gruppen for Ressursstudier, 1975), p. 7.
[106] Jørgen Randers, "How to stop industrial growth with minimal pain?" *Technological Forecasting and Social Change*, 11, no. 4 (1978), 371–82.

working hours and longer vacations" would also be helpful in generating more jobs while at the same time damping economic growth.[107] This attempt to "revolt from the middle ground" was met with a lukewarm response from all parties involved in the Cold War deadlock.[108]

At the same time Brundtland became Minister of the Environment. She was mildly suspicious about such proposals, but would not keep them at arm's length. As a politician, she recognized the need for renewal within the Labor Party in order to make it relevant to younger demographics, and she was genuinely interested in new ideas and perspectives. The same was true for Lied who wrote a report for the Resource Policy Group emphasizing the value of systems dynamics to the *"broad policy analysis and long term planning"* for the Party he represented.[109] This was his opening address to The Fifth International System Dynamics Conference, which Randers arranged in August 1976 at the Geilo ski-resort. Here the growing community of system dynamics scholars from all over the world met to discuss methodological issues and examine questions such as how to choose a problem, what to include in a model, the amount of details, and how to make it relevant to the right audience.

The Conference has in retrospect been celebrated as a turning point in system dynamics methodology and was of key importance for the formation of the System Dynamics Society. *Elements of the System Dynamics Method* (1980), the conference anthology Randers edited, was the chief methodological reference tool among members of this Society for at least a decade.[110] Yet the Conference and the anthology were hardly noticed among Norwegian scholars. It is equally telling that Randers became a formal member of the Club of Rome in 1977, but was never acknowledged with a membership in the Norwegian Academy of Science and

---

[107] Jan-Evert Nilsson and Jørgen Randers, *Den unødvendige arbeidsløsheten*, GRS-217 (Oslo: Gruppen for Ressursstudier, 1979), p. 16.
[108] Jørgen Randers, "Utopier og lønnssystem," *Samtiden*, 87 (1978), 349–51. Inspired by Niels Meyer, Helveg Petersen, and Villy Sørensen, *Oprør fra midten* (Copenhagen: Gyldendal, 1978).
[109] Finn Lied, *Social Difficulties versus Social Problems*, GRS-76 (Oslo: Gruppen for Ressursstudier, 1976), p. 6. Lied's emphasis.
[110] Jørgen Randers and Leif K. Ervik (eds.), *The System Dynamics Method: Proceedings of the 5. International Systems Dynamics Conference* (Oslo: Gruppen for Ressursstudier, 1976). David Andersen (et al.), "How the System Dynamics Society came to be: A collective memoir," *System Dynamics Review*, 23, no. 2/3 (2007), 219–27. Jørgen Randers (ed.), *Elements of the System Dynamics Method* (Cambridge, MA: MIT Press, 1980); "The 1976 International Conference on System Dynamics," unpublished, Jan., 2007, 2 pages, SD.

Letters. Somehow, he was never able to shake off Galtung, Næss, and Rosenqvist's portrait of him as a "shallow" intellectual.

In 1981 Randers threw in the towel. The late 1970s was a period of economic depression in Norway, in which environmental activists became increasingly radical. When he was asked by the students of the Norwegian School of Management to become a candidate for the School's President, he accepted and won the election. "The world is moving towards a resource crisis," he told a student newspaper, "yet I have resigned in the fight for limiting economic growth, as I realize that 99 percent of Norwegians still wants growth in material consumption."[111] Following the liberalist economic thinking of his new patron, he began endorsing political efforts that would spur economic growth and renewal.[112] In his new role as President he tried to spur green business initiatives that aimed to make money using environmentally friendly production methods. More recently he emerged as a key authority in the nation's climate debate, favoring economic incentives to reduce greenhouse gas emissions, and as the Deputy Director General of WWF International in Geneva.

---

[111] Anonymous, "Ressursprofeten som ble rektor: Randers den resignerte," *Universitas* no. 5, Mar. 22, 1983, PA.

[112] Jørgen Randers, "Industripolitikk i Norge," *Kontrast*, 18 (1982), 44–9.

8

The Acid Rain Debate

On December 23, 1969, the Phillips Petroleum Company announced that they had found oil in the North Sea. After many empty wells, the Ekofisk oilfield was the first major find in the Norwegian oil sector. "A sense of sheik well-being spread around" in the new "oil nation," a journalist noted, as the oilfield was estimated to be among the twenty largest in the world.[1] It was a "fairy-tale" that came true setting the nation in a Klondike black gold rush.[2] Indeed, Ekofisk and subsequent discoveries of oil and gas would forever change the nation's industries and finances. Norway would, over the next half a century, be propeled into being one of the richest countries in the world.

Only months before Phillips' announcement about the oilfield, the press wrote for the first time about climate change. It came in an article published in one of the country's largest newspapers. It claimed that industrial smoke would cause a "hothouse effect" and result in a colder overall climate for the world due to suspended dust in the atmosphere keeping the sunshine out.[3] By 1971 the same paper reported that the hothouse effect would instead cause global warming due to carbon dioxide emissions from petroleum. It was said this "may cause the polar ice to melt, the ocean to rise above its shores, cities and large territories of land to be submerged under water, [and] humans to be displaced to the mountains."[4]

---

[1] Kjell Stahl Johannsessen, "Oljesommer," in Odd Harbek (eds.), *Nordsjøoljen: Ny norsk naturressurs* (Oslo: Minerva Forlag, 1970), pp. 7–17, quote p. 7. Phillipsgruppen, *Ekofisk: olje fra Nordsjøen* (Oslo: Phillipsgruppen, ca. 1973).
[2] Odd Karsten Tveit, *Nordsjøoljen* (Oslo: Grøndahl, 1973), p. 1.
[3] Asbjørn Barlup, "Mere støv i luften – kaldere klima," *VG*, Nov. 14, 1969, PA.
[4] Anonymous, "Og havet vil stige," *VG*, March 27, 1971, PA.

8 The Acid Rain Debate

Global warming was at the time, as Spencer R. Weart has shown, a topic of intramural scientific discussion which had barely reached the larger public.[5] It is therefore not surprising that the journalists first reported cooling instead of warming. What is notable is that these reports emerged in the context of questioning industrial growth, dependence on petroleum, and the problem of airborne pollution. Yet climate change as a topic would stay on the margin of Norwegian environmental and scientific debate until the late 1980s. If addressed at all, it was in context of debating other types of air pollution, such as emissions of sulfur dioxide, which causes acid rain.

The booming petroleum industry was the result of *kraftsosialisme* (power-socialism) of the Labor Party along with capitalist friendly policies of the conservatives. Since the end of the war both groups had argued that extracting as much natural resources as possible would propel the nation into prosperity. Such thinking would be questioned by a growing group of young moderate Labor Party environmentalists along with more radical ecophilosophers in the 1970s. What was the environmental and social impact of petroleum, they asked. By examining the work and thinking of the geologists, this chapter will review the environmental policy dimensions of the petroleum industry as seen from the vantage point of the power-socialists. A 1970 application by the Norwegian electric company Hafslund to build an oil-burning power plant at Slagentangen will serve as a focal point of this chapter.[6] At Slagentangen the Esso Company (now Exxon) already operated the first gasoline refinery in Norway. The plant was opened in 1960 with much fanfare by representatives of the Labor Party eager to showcase how power-socialism would modernize the country. The importance of the refinery grew with the Ekofisk discovery, and the building of a power plant meant for its supporters that the oil from Ekofisk would be used in Norway and not exported. It was also located at the heart of the beautiful Oslo fjord

---

[5] Spencer R. Weart, *The Discovery of Global Warming* (Cambridge, MA: Harvard University Press, 2003). James Rodger Fleming, *The Callendar Effect* (Boston: American Meteorological Society, 2007).

[6] Øyvind Nøttestad, *SFT: Fra forkynner til forvalter* (Oslo: SFT, 1994), pp. 14–53. Bjarne Sivertsen, *Beregning av midlere belastning gjennom lengere tid som resultat av utslippene fra varmekraftverk på Slagentangen* (Kjeller: Norsk Institutt for Luftforskning, May 1971). The petroleum plant had in 1976 a permit to pollute 550 kg/hour pure sulphur into the air. Rune Frank Andersen and Tom-Olaf Norheim Kjær, *Esso-Raffineriene ved Slagentangen og Valløy og deres betydning for Tønsberg-distriktet* (Bergen: Norges Handelshøyskole, 1976), p. 19.

and surrounded by vacation cottages whose owners had previously raised serious resistance to Esso's refinery. The potential plant angered the ecologists who pointed out that it would generate airborne acid rain damaging to the environment. The question of how to deal with acid rain turned into a formative environmental debate as the underlying question addressed the future of power-socialism and the industrialization of Norway. Whether or not to grant Hafslund the permit became an issue, based on the political and social views of the observers, concerning which rationality and whose knowledge one should trust in when visioning the best future for the nation and the world.

POWER-SOCIALISM AND THE SOCIAL FUNCTION OF SCIENCE

In 1966 the professor of geology at the University of Oslo Ivan Th. Rosenqvist (1916–94) blamed environmentalists for undermining the industrialization of Norway. Their warnings against degradation of the natural environment, hazards of industrial pollution, and exhaustion of natural resources were to him a secular adaptation of the "doomsday" predictions in the Revelations of St. John. In making his case he pointed out "the effect of carbon dioxide which creates a hothouse window ... causes the temperature to rise." There was no reason to fear this effect, he argued. Instead, one should welcome global warming as an increase in temperatures "in the Nordic countries will hardly be unpleasant."[7] This may be the first time anyone addressed the issue of climate change in Norwegian, and so it's notable that Rosenqvist did so in a defense of industrial growth and the use of natural resources for the common good.

His argument belongs in a long tradition of Norwegian geologists defending the extraction of natural resources. Reaching back to the silver mines of Kongsberg, which at their peak in 1770s had over 4,000 employees and supplied over ten percent of the Danish-Norwegian union's gross national product, the geologists have been on the side of industrialism. Norwegian geologists have, since Kongsberg, seen their research as the very key for the wealth of the nation. Indeed, finding and analyzing natural resources have been to them the equivalent of doing something meaningful and good for Norway and, ultimately, the world. In the 1950s and 60s the Department of Geology at the University of Oslo was a particularly exciting place for such thinking, boosted by new

---

[7] Ivan Th. Rosenqvist, "Jordens undergang," *Kirke og kultur*, 71 (1966), 468–79, quotes pp. 469, 475, 476.

8 The Acid Rain Debate

instruments, research money, and a new building finished in 1958. The faculty took great pride in the field's history, in which the polar explorer and humanist Fridtjof Nansen (1861–1930) and the nation builder Waldemar Chr. Brøgger (1851–1940) loomed large.[8] They belong within a tradition of exploration aimed at annexation of land and use of natural resources for the benefit of the nation. An example may be the geologist and polar explorer Adolf Hoel (1879–1964), who was appointed President of the University by occupying Nazi authorities, a legacy of the Department rarely mentioned by its faculty.[9] Indeed, few geologists would question the political heritage of their discipline, but instead adopt and continue its imperial tradition of supporting annexation and exploitation of natural resources for the benefit of the nation.

In the 1960s this tradition among the geologists would take a decidedly leftist turn, expressed in the doctrine of power-socialism. Those on the far left, including Rosenqvist, believed that scientific planning of energy production was the way forward. It was an argument echoing Vladimir Lenin's famous reduction of socialism to "Soviet power plus electrification of the whole country."[10] According to this view, the future welfare of the working class depended on the production of electricity distributed by a Communist Party and guided by the scientific elite. One who offered intellectual guidance was the British crystallographer John D. Bernal (1901–71) who became a member of the Norwegian Academy of Science and Letters in 1966 and was invited to Oslo to give the prestigious Hassel Lecture in 1967 (though he was unable to come for health reasons).[11] Bernal believed science should benefit the whole society, as he famously argued in *The Social Function of Science* (1939). "It is in geology and mineralogy that we meet with the most clear connections with economic realities in the location and working of mineral resources. A really adequate teaching of geology implies not only some of this technical knowledge but the economic and political knowledge necessary to

---

[8] Geir Hestmark, *Vitenskap og nasjon – Waldemar Christopher Brøgger 1851–1905* (Oslo, Aschehoug, 1999). See also Einar-Arne Drivenes and Harald Dag Jølle (eds.), *Norsk polarhistorie*, vol. 2. (Oslo: Gyldendal, 2004).
[9] Aadne Ore and Ove Arbo Høeg, "Universitetets geologiske institusjoner," in *Universitetet i Oslo: 1911–1961*, vol. 1 (Oslo: Universitetsforlaget, 1961), pp. 561–91. Svein B. Manum, "Institutt for Geologi og geologibygningen 1958–1993," *Institutt for Geologi: Rapport*, 65 (1993), 1–6.
[10] Vladimir Lenin, *Collected Works*, vol. 31 (1920) (Moscow: Progress Publishers, 1966), p. 516.
[11] Otto Bastiansen, "Forord." In John D. Bernal, *Vitenskapens historie* (Oslo: Pax, 1978), pp. 11–12.

complete it."[12] Thus, it was the responsibility of a scientist to make sure research not only was made available but was also used for the benefit of all. After the war he emerged a prominent follower of Joseph Stalin. Inspired by the Soviet leader, Bernal argued that scientists could only improve life in society if they were liberated from destructive capitalism. The social function of science was to better society and the living conditions for the workers of the world, and the means to achieve this was centralized socialist planning in a communist state.

Rosenqvist was the leading figure in the University of Oslo's Department of Geology and a key follower of both Stalin and Bernal. At the lunch table he would sit at its head, with the rest of the geologists organized around the table according to rank and goodwill. Though not everyone complied, this is a telling image of how he fashioned himself, namely as a leader of a cadre of science comrades on a power-socialist mission. This political agenda framed Rosenqvist's scientific work from his early days as a student. His chief topic, radiological research of clay,[13] was of key importance in the communist material understanding of the origin of life in the primeval soup. Two leading figures were the Soviet biochemist Alexander Oparin and the British geneticist John B. S. Haldane, who both pointed to the role of clay in understanding life's origin. This was brought to the forefront of the debate in a 1947 lecture by Bernal, in which he argued that clay minerals may have had a catalytic role in the process leading to the origin of life.[14] Oparin, Haldane, and Bernal were all prime movers of a debate on the importance of social planning of scientific research in the interest of the world's needy, and Rosenqvist followed suit.[15]

[12] John D. Bernal, *The Social Function of Science* (1939) (London: Routledge, 1946), p. 255.
[13] Ivan Th. Rosenqvist, "Om leires kvikkagtighet," *Særtrykk av meddelelser fra vegdirektøren*, 799 (1946), 5–12; "Om leires plastisitet," *Særtrykk av meddelelser fra vegdirektøren*, 799 (1946), 12–16; "Om de Norske kvikkleirers egenskaper og mineralogiske sammensetning," *Teknisk ukeblad*, 93 (Okt. 1946), 571–6.
[14] John B. S. Haldane, "The origin of life," *The Rationalist Annual*, 1929, 3–10. Alexander I. Oparin, *The Origin of Life* (New York: Macmillan, 1938). John. D. Bernal, "The physical basis of life," *The Proceedings of the Physical Society*, 62, no. 10 (1949), 597–618. Cyril Ponnamperuma, Akira Shimoyama, and Elaine Friebele, "Clay and the origin of life," *Origins of Life and Evolution of Biospheres*, 12 (1982), 9–40. J. Maynard Smith and E. Szathmáry, *The Origins of Life: From the Birth of Life to the Origin of Language* (Oxford: Oxford University Press, 1999).
[15] Gary Werskey, *The Visible College: A Collective Biography of British Scientists and Socialists of the 1930s* (London: Free Association Books, 1988). Vidar Enebakk, "The three Merton theses," *Journal of Classical Sociology*, 7 (2007), 221–38.

Whether or not clay research could prove anything about the origin of life, it was surely helpful in understanding sedimentology, a field intrinsically linked with finding and producing petroleum. In 1963 Norway proclaimed sovereignty of its continental shelf.[16] This annexation was widely supported among geologists who thought of this "new 'wet' Norway" as an integral part of the nation, as it consisted of Norwegian glacial sediments. They believed this "new territory" should reach as far north as to include the continental shelf of Spitsbergen, a daring argument since the status of the archipelago and its surroundings was disputed.[17] Exactly where the shelf ended and the deep ocean began was contested, in part due to the Norwegian Trench. It is a very deep water trench just off the coast of the southern part of the country, after which there is a shallow ocean plateau between Norway and neighboring Denmark, Netherland, and Britain. And it was under this shallow plateau where the petroleum was located. It was thus crucial for Norwegian interests to argue that the nation's continental shelf extended beyond the Trench, and that's where the discipline of sedimentology proved helpful. When the sovereignty was initially claimed, the Norwegian geologists knew well that there could be rich petroleum fields beyond the Trench, and they therefore argued that the Trench was irrelevant to determine the continental shelf's extent as the Norwegian landmass continued under it.[18] The geologist Thomas Barth, for example, was one stern supporter of this seabed annexation, even if he was unsure about its scientific value. He pointed to the importance of researching the geological formation of the deep seas, as they were in "legal vacuum" with respect to their potential natural resources and thus up for grab.[19]

Even though the geologists were firm supporters of Norwegian seabed annexations, they were initially kept at a distance when it came to research and exploration of the annexed continental shelf. Instead, this was done by non-Norwegian, private companies who were given exclusive exploration rights by Norwegian authorities sanctioned by the Labor Party. The thinking behind this policy was that it would be too large of an

---

[16] Leif T. Løddesøl, "Norske regler om oljeutvinning," *Lov og rett*, (1965), 154–60.
[17] Lidvin M. Osland, "Olje- og oljegeologi," in Odd Harbek (ed.), *Nordsjøoljen: Ny norsk naturressurs* (Oslo: Minerva Forlag, 1970), pp. 18–31, quote p. 31.
[18] Christoffer Oftedahl, "Gode muligheter for olje- eller gassfunn på kontinentalsokkelen," *Forskningsnytt*, 4 (1965), 56–7.
[19] Thomas Fredrik Weiby Barth, "Innledning" and "Geologiske randbemerkninger," in Jens Evensen, *Muligheter og rettigheter på havbunnen: Dyphavet – et nytt ekspansjonsfelt?* (Oslo: Elingaard Forlag, 1970), pp. 9–11, 47–52.

enterprise in terms of exploration costs and financial risk for a small nation to undertake, so it would be better if it was done by larger foreign companies with the proper experience.[20] Thus, even gravimetric and magnetic surveys of the seas came under strict government control, and no scientist or company was allowed to research anything but designated areas.[21] It is telling that in 1972 one had to turn to the Ministry of Commerce to learn about subsea sedimentology of the North Sea.[22] Thus, the scientific knowledge and expertise were behind closed doors in out-of-state companies. As a consequence Norwegian geologists did not play a role in early company histories,[23] or in the political and social analyses of oil of the early 1970s.[24]

This centralized political planning of science was in line with Rosenqvist's views, but he did not agree with the outsourcing of research and exploration to foreign special interest groups and companies. He was dismayed by the exclusion of Norwegian geologists and what he saw as a capitalist assault on natural resources in the North Sea. "Wherever the corpse is, there the vultures will gather," he would say to his students, quoting the Bible.[25] It was nevertheless important to educate Norwegian students in sedimentology so that they, at a later stage, could help their land in securing the country's petroleum. Rosenqvist would tell blue-collar members of the labor union Iron and Metal in Oslo about the importance of keeping international capitalism away from "our resources" in the North Sea. The oil and gas should, in addition to furthering hydropower developments, secure the welfare state as well as

[20] Statens Oljeråd, *Innstilling nr. 6 fra Statens Oljeråd om endringer i Kgl. Res. av 9 april 1965 om utforskning og utnyttelse av undersjøiske petroliumsforekomster* (Oslo: Statens Oljeråd, May 5, 1972).

[21] Jens Evensen, *Oversikt over Oljepolitiske Spørsmål: bl.a. på bakgrunn av utenlandsk oljelovgivning og utenlandsk konsesjonspolitikk* (Oslo: Industridepartementet, 1971), pp. 13–14.

[22] Fredrik Hagemann, "Muligheter for å finne olje på den norske kontinentalsokkel," in Mimi Lønnum (ed.), *Norsk oljepolitikk* (Oslo: Elingaard forlag, 1972), pp. 11–33.

[23] Bjørn Vidar Lerøen, *From Groningen to Troll: Norske Shell – 25 years on the Norwegian Continental Shelf* (Oslo: Norske Shell, 1990). Bjørn Vidar Lerøen, *Troll over Troubled Water* (Oslo: Statoil, 2003). Anonymous, *Oljen og vi* (Oslo: Norske Esso, 1973), pp. 15–20.

[24] Peter R. Odell, *Olje og makt* (Oslo: Gyldendal, 1972). Øystein Noreng, "Norwegian oil industry on the continental shelf – social impact, possibilities, problems and policies," in Maurice Scarlett (ed.), *Consequences of Offshore Oil and Gas* (St. John's: Memorial University of Newfoundland, 1977), pp. 59–84; *The Oil Industry and the Government Strategy in the North Sea* (Boulder, CO: Croom Helm, 1980).

[25] Ivan Th. Rosenqvist, "Universitetet og kontinentalsokkelen," *Nytt fra Universitetet i Oslo*, no. 17 (1974), 1–4, 4, UO. The Bible, Matthew 24, 28.

industrial jobs on Norwegian soil. In the chief communist newspaper he would typically raise the question: "Who should actually have rights of disposal over the oil deposits – society or the oil companies!"[26]

Rosenqvist took pride in having predicted the booming petroleum industry in his 1967 vision of "The World in Year 2000."[27] This guessing was well informed, as he and his fellow geologists had marveled at private exploration of various companies of the annexed continental shelf. The fact that the geologists were left in the dark was a source of frustration, but it also allowed space for imagination on how this research should be organized as soon as they got access. Following the argument in Bernal's *The Social Function of Science*, Rosenqvist argued that scientific research should be the object of social planning. The best way to secure scientific relevance for the nation was to reorganize the university system analogous to the way in which Norway organized health, fire, and road services. These were public hierarchical institutions led by state departments and controlled by the Parliament. In 1966 Rosenqvist proposed a new "University of Norway," organized along the same principles, to secure a "unity" of knowledge and power. "I do not think that the self-government of universities is appropriate for our modern society," he claimed.[28] He imagined instead a politically centralized university in which scientists would be given overreaching social tasks without having to worry about funding or satisfying short-term political goals. It was a radical program meant to liberate scientists and the university from special interest groups, political factions, and capitalist forces. At the same time it was supposed to allow long-term planning and steering of scientific activities so that research would benefit the welfare and prosperity of the nation and ultimately the workers of the world. To him, giving Hafslund a permit to build their plant at Slagentangen was a matter of course, as the plant would generate electricity and thus prosperity for the nation.

While Rosenqvist was pondering these ideas, the University of Oslo grew into a large campus both in the number of students and in financial and material resources. In this process geology failed to grow at the same speed as other departments, and by the early 1970s it became a relatively

[26] Ivan Th. Rosenqvist, "Skal internasjonal kapital bestemme over våre ressurser?" *Friheten*, 6 (1973), 7.
[27] Ivan Th. Rosenqvist, "Verden i år 2000," Lecture at NRK Radio, fall 1967, *Forskningsnytt*, 13, no. 1 (1968), 13–15.
[28] Anonymous (interview) with Ivan Th. Rosenqvist, "Radikal professor," *Arbeiderbladet* Oct. 29, 1966, 11–12, RA.

marginal field in comparison to, in particular, biology and ecology. This had consequences in the intramural politics of the University. Rosenqvist felt that geologists were losing ground. He wrote several editorials in the official Labor Party newspaper about the problem, arguing that the university was about to become "a rubber-stamping tea-party," writing charged quasi-scientific reports for political interest groups. He argued that the leadership nurtured a culture in which "the strong are oppressing the weak" research fields.[29] And since it is "the one who is paying the orchestra who decides the music," Rosenqvist feared that special interest groups within the government could steer research results and financially favor fields with the most students.[30]

THE POWER-SOCIALISM OF THE LABOR PARTY

Rosenqvist's criticisms were directed at the ruling Labor Party, and centered around the importance of defending the nation's intellectual and natural resources against special interest groups, military industry, and capitalism. It was an attempt to turn leftward the rebuilding effort led by the Labor Party that – with the exception of a month's interlude in 1963 – was in power from 1945 to 1965. In this period there was a broad consensus about the need to exploit natural resources such as minerals, plants, and fish for future prosperity, though there was disagreement about which resources the nation could and should focus on. The doctrine of power-socialism would also dominate within the Labor Party in holding that electric power was the key in securing equal material welfare and social opportunities for all.

Yet, unlike the communists, the Labor Party believed that a mixed economy of planning and marked liberalism would secure electric power and the material welfare for all. Mixed economy entailed membership in the European Community (EC), which was met by head-on resistance from the far left, who viewed the EC as capitalist forces incapable of uniting the workers of the world. These two factions of Norwegian power-socialism – the socialist planners and the mixed economists – should be understood in view of a struggle to construct a modern nation within the context of the European Community, NATO, and Cold War tensions. Yet, for all their differences, both power-socialist planners and mixed economists supported Hafslund's application.

[29] Ivan Th. Rosenqvist, "Skinndemorati?" *Arbeiderbladet*, Jan. 16, 1970, RA.
[30] Ivan Th. Rosenqvist, "Universitetets dilemma," *Arbeiderbladet*, Mar. 13, 1970, RA.

8 The Acid Rain Debate

One key issue among the power-socialists was nuclear energy. With the introduction of atomic weaponry in 1945, nuclear energy was widely seen as important to Norway's future, and the Labor Party thus voted in favor of building a nuclear test reactor. In this process, Norway's nuclear physicists became, to Rosenqvist, a prime example of how intellectual soberness could be corrupted by a selfish drive for research money made available by special interests groups, military industry, and industrial capitalism. Chief among them was Jørgen Randers' father Gunnar who worked in close collaboration with the Norwegian Defense Research Establishment on building a nuclear test reactor. Rosenqvist fought against this decision, arguing, in Norway's leading engineering journal, that the nation's lack of natural uranium and plentitude of alternative energy resources did not justify spending money on the project.[31] Radioactive pollution was not the issue, he claimed, and promised, if necessary, to sit on top of the test reactor dressed only in his underwear in order to protest the project.[32] What worried him was that the "nuclear prophets" would move Norway towards NATO and the capitalism of the European Community.[33] A Euratom membership would draw Norway further away from the communist path. He was not alone, as the fight against Norwegian membership in the EC was one of the few topics on which the country's communists could all agree.[34] Randers and the nuclear physicists at Kjeller, on the other hand, were eager supporters of Euratom, and they did not take Rosenqvist's critique lightly. Their reaction came in the form of "some of the most forbidding attacks" Rosenqvist would ever experience.[35]

The alternative to nuclear energy, according to Rosenqvist, was to utilize other energy resources as in the case of the proposal for a Slagentangen plant. He went public with a series of popular articles on this issue, arguing that the earth had more than enough natural resources for everyone.[36] It was misleading to count only known natural resources, as the nuclear lobbyist did, when predicting the future. One also had to

---

[31] Ivan Th. Rosenqvist, "Norges stilling til Euratom," *Teknisk ukeblad*, 109, no. 29 (1962), 1–3. Randers, "Norges stilling til Euratom." Njølstad, *Strålende forskning*, p. 155.
[32] Odd Letnes, "Virkeligheten som simuleringspill," *Apollon*, 1 (1999), 9–11.
[33] Anonymous (interview) with Ivan Th. Rosenqvist, "Radikal professor," *Arbeiderbladet* Oct. 29, 1966, 11–12, RA.
[34] Gunhild Lurås, *Kamerater? Striden i Norges Kommunistiske Parti 1963–1967*, MA thesis (Oslo: University of Oslo, 2002), pp. 58–61.
[35] Ivan Th. Rosenqvist, "Norges stilling til Euratom," *Teknisk ukeblad*, 118, no. 8 (1971), 18.
[36] Ivan Th. Rosenqvist, "Jordens energireserver i geokjemisk lys," *Teknisk ukeblad*, 109 (1962), 1077–80.

take into account all the unknown resources geologists would discover in the future. This optimism was tempered by the policies of the Labor Party. Thanks to their support of the EC and NATO, Rosenqvist thought "that our time, with all its progress, was a reactionary epoch, in which independent intellectual activity has a difficult time, while full and half fascist organizations and publications have a distribution that one would deny possible only a few years ago."[37] He was most worried about the renewed German domination in Europe and the Cold War hostility to socialism that appeared fascist to him. "You have a hard time ahead of you," he told festive students in his graduation speech at their last day at the University of Oslo in 1962.[38]

As it turned out, the students did rather well, thanks to economic growth propelled by massive hydropower developments built on Norway's high mountains and numerous waterfalls. With the discovery of petroleum, things would look even better. By the mid-1970s it was clear to all that the petroleum was to radically change Norway financially, technically, and environmentally. A sense of worldly power came to politicians and diplomats who began pondering how Norway, as a self-sufficient oil nation, could be a peacemaker on the international scene, especially after the Arab oil boycott of 1973.[39] With that also came worries about the lack of Norwegian petrochemical and geological expertise,[40] and a general need to educate Norwegians about the oil.[41] The result was a new parliamentary bill of 1974, which put greater emphasis on the importance of building up national oil industries, companies, know-how, and science.[42] It was thus not until the late 1970s that Norwegian geologists would take part in exploring the North Sea.[43]

---

[37] Ivan Th. Rosenqvist, "Kandidatfesten 1962," 4 pages, RA; "Realister ut i arbeidslivet," *Husbjørnen*, 13, no. 2 (1963), 4–5, RA.

[38] Ivan Th. Rosenqvist, "Kandidatfesten 1962," 4 pages, RA.

[39] John C. Ausland, *Norway, Oil, and Foreign Policy* (Colorado: Westview Press, 1979). Odd Karsten Tveit, *Vår olje og vår kraft* (Oslo: Grøndahl, 1973). Tor Dagfinn Veen, *Oljen i Nordsjøen* (Stavanger: Rogalandsbanken, 1973).

[40] Nils Bøckman, *Olje: hovedbegrepene i petroleumsteknologien: kortfattet oversikt over norsk oljepolitikk* (Oslo: Hartmark, 1972).

[41] Axel Schou, *Olje: Oljegeografi i motoralderen* (Oslo: Aschehoug, 1965). Terje Jacobsen (ed.), *Olje: fra kilde til forbruker* (Oslo: Schibsteds Forlag, 1973).

[42] Anonymous, *Petroleumsvirksomhetens plass i det norske samfunn*, St. meld. no. 25. (1973–74), adopted Feb. 14, 1974.

[43] Ole-Jacob Kvinnsland, "The Norwegian experience," in Maurice Scarlett (ed.), *Consequences of Offshore Oil and Gas* (St. John's: Memorial University of Newfoundland, 1977), pp. 85–105. Stig S. Kvendseth, *Giant Discovery: A History of Ekofisk through the first 20 years* (Stavanger: Phillips, 1988), pp. 19–32.

Indeed, the discovery of petroleum would change the life and work of many Norwegian geologists. A telling image of this shift can be found in the textbook *Oljen og det norske samfunn* (The Oil and the Norwegian Society, 1976), which portrayed the polar explorer and geologist Fridtjof Nansen as a oil-sheik on a money bill.[44] With an oil platform substituted for the Royal Norwegian Lion, the bill was to indicate that the nation by 1983 would turn into a sheikdom led by the geologists and engineers.

THE CASE AGAINST ENVIRONMENTALISM

The power-socialists – communists as well as mixed economists – were the key target of the eco-populists, ecologists, and deep ecologists such as the ecologist Ivar Mysterud, and the ecophilosophers Sigmund Kvaløy and Arne Næss (discussed in previous chapters). They were all opposed to the petroleum industry and the Slagentangen plant proposal, as it would enforce uncontrollable economic growth and exploitation of natural resources. Instead they thought one should plan for a "steady-state" economy, which mirrored the steady-state balance of the economy of nature that they knew from the science of ecology.[45] To them the oil and gas discoveries were not good news. The coming of large international companies like Esso and Phillips raised questions. Could Norway "survive as a socialist colored lamb in a world of capitalist wolves?"[46] The discoveries in the North Sea meant choosing between two different natural resources, oil or fish, as oil spills and chemical fallout eventually would ruin the ocean's fish stock.[47] They were also dismayed when the oil industry used the famous Earth-rise image from the moon to illustrate that oil too was an integral part of the Earth's environmental "life cycle."[48] What the petroleum-driven industrial modernization would mean to the fisherman-peasant culture of coastal Norway was also worrisome.[49] Many feminists agreed and questioned

---

[44] Knut Bryn (et al.), *Oljen og det norske samfunn* (Oslo: Tanum, 1976), p. 110.
[45] Mysterud and Norderhaug, "Koblingen mellom økologi og politikk." Kvaløy, "Økologi – vannkraft – samfunn."
[46] Atle Seierstad, *Norge og oljen* (Oslo: Pax, 1970), p. 7.
[47] Thorvaldur Arnason, *Olje eller fisk? En vurdering av forurensningsfaren som mulig konflikt mellom oljeaktiviteten og fiskeriene på vår kontinentalsokkel* (Trondheim: Kommit, 1973).
[48] Elf Norge, *Om olje* (Stavanger: Elf Aquitaine A/S, 1976), p. 9.
[49] Finn Mørch Andersen (et al.), *Om olje, vett og vern* (Trondehim: NTH, 1974). Kari Bruun Wyller and Thomas Chr. Wyller (eds.), *Norsk oljepolitikk* (Oslo: Gyldendal, 1975).

whether or not women should "wriggle with" the oil industry, and they were critical to "the economic growth philosophy" and the lack of "life quality" and "balance with nature" of the whole petroleum business.[50]

Such ecologically informed populism and philosophizing was, to the power-socialists, a failed type of radicalism that would not lead to a classless society. They came into fashion, Rosenqvist claimed, in the fall of 1968 when "the ripples from the student protests out in the world reached the Norwegian coast."[51] Studying at the University of Oslo was free of charge. And students occupying the Department of Philosophy, where the ecophilosopher Arne Næss worked, were upset about a reform suggestion, which, in effect, would mean that students had to end their years in higher education within a reasonable time frame. To the young, the reforms meant abandoning the Humboldtian idea of academic liberty with an efficiency model they associated with a capitalist mood of reasoning. Rosenqvist favored the reformers, as he "had difficulties understanding that one advanced the transition to socialism or in other ways reduced the gap between industrialized and developing countries by being opposed to improving the efficiency."[52] For his support, Rosenqvist became an outcast among a new generation of radicals demanding the liberty to determine the speed and content of their own education at no individual cost – instead, relying on governmental support. Among those opposed to the reforms were the ecophilosophers, who believed that academic efficiency upheld a culture of economic growth that would lead to the eco-crisis. As an alternative they promoted academic self-sufficiency. Rosenqvist would have none of it. This "zero-growth society," he responded, will "hardly be accepted by either the underdeveloped or the wealthy nations" and more research should thus focus on finding and developing more resources as there were more than plenty of them.[53] To the ecologists' concern about exhausting natural resources, Rosenqvist argued that more of them would become available for exploration as their value increased. It was a question of digging deeper for minerals, drilling further down for oil and gas, using more fertilizers to generate food, or, in other ways, trusting the intellectual abilities and ingenuity of future

---

[50] Brita Brandtzæg (et al.), *Vil vi sprelle med? En bok om kvinner og olje* (Oslo: Pax, 1975), pp. 32, 108. Similarly in Vesla Vetlesen, *Kvinner i olje-Norge* (Oslo: Folkets brevskole, 1975).
[51] Ivan Th. Rosenqvist, "Reaksjonær radikalisme?" ms. 2 pages, RA. Christiansen and Vold, *Kampen om universitetet*.
[52] Ivan Th. Rosenqvist, "Reaksjonær radikalisme?" ms. 2 pages, RA.
[53] Rosenqvist, "Har vi nok ressurser?" p. 358.

engineers and scientists.[54] Resources were not limited like bread "from which our generation cuts a thick slice," but, instead, were available in variable plentitude within different layers of the Earth's crust.[55] "We have to continue on the path of the working class and produce our away out of poverty, as the working class has done, for one, in the Soviet Union," Rosenqvist argued. He had no sympathy for academic "well-fed zero-growth philosophers," pessimists, and other "romantics."[56] Moreover, keeping untouched ecosystems off limits to developers to promote outdoor leisure activities was a bourgeois upper-class activity. "The leggings-gang," Rosenqvist noted, in a condescending reference to outdoor footwear, did not actually walk in untouched nature, and they had no respect for the poor. "The entire human existence is based on an unending and winning struggle against nature," he argued, and "[i]t is unfair that we shall take the side of an 'untouched' nature while people are starving."[57] The ecologists and environmentalists undermined the policy of exploitation of natural resources to the benefit of the needy. "The environmental problems are cosmetic in a global perspective in comparison to war, starvation and analphabetism," he would tell the Deep Ecologists.[58] They understood nature not as a resource for work but in terms of outdoor recreation and vacationing. "Humans exist only because it has emerged victorious from the fight against nature," he would hold against them. "It is only rich and egotistical people that can avoid producing goods the poor need in order to have a more pleasant vacation."[59]

The environmentalists did not take Rosenqvist's criticisms lightly. "Place Rosenqvist in the pillory!" said Bredo Berntsen, who thought he was "reactionary and backward-looking" by not supporting "eco-political social steering" of the nation.[60] They accused Rosenqvist of lacking

---

[54] Ivan R. Rosenqvist, "Tanker over verdens råstoffreserver og Norge," *Forskningsnytt*, 12 (1967), 8–12; "Verdens råstoffer og Norge," *Aftenposten*, Aug. 4, 1967, RA.

[55] Ivan Th. Rosenqvist, "Energi og andre ressurser," *Årbok 1976* (Trondheim: Norges Teknisk Vitenskapsakademi, 1976), 1–12, quote p. 2.

[56] Ivan Th. Rosenqvist in interview with Kåre Andre Nilsen, "Jorden har ressurser til fortsatt vekst," *Friheten*, Oct. 1974, 7–12; "Verdens mineralressurser er enorme," *Teknisk ukeblad*, 122, no. 43 (Oct. 1975), 18–19; "World energy resources," in M. W. Thring and R. J. Crookes (eds.), *Energy and Humanity* (Stevenage: Peter Peregrinus, 1974), pp. 8–18.

[57] Ivan Th. Rosenqvist, "Seierrik kamp mot naturen om vi skal kunne overleve," *Arbeiderbladet*, Sept. 30, 1974, RA.

[58] Ivan Th. Rosenqvist, "Den store miljøbløffen," *Vegviseren*, 16 (1989), 8–9.

[59] Ivan Th. Rosenqvist, "Energi og solidaritet," *Arbeiderbladet*, Jan. 2, 1979, 5, RA.

[60] Bredo Berntsen, "Sett Rosenqvist i gapestokken!" *Orientering* 11 (1974), 10.

ecological knowledge and ignoring the damages of economic growth.[61] "We who call ourselves socialists must not support the diehard view that the world's natural resources are endless," one critic claimed.[62] Yet another thought Rosenqvist's "number magic" in support of industrial growth was at the very heart of the environmental problem.[63] His arguments made him into an anti-environmentalist in the eyes of his opponents. Yet he claimed he cared for nature and that his scientific work was in the world's best interest. To him the ecological debate was an issue of which rationality and whose knowledge one should trust in efforts to protect nature.

Despite his disagreements with the ecologists and ecophilosophers, it is important to note that the entire radical left, including Rosenqvist, were united in their efforts to stop Norwegian membership of the European Community. When a national referendum was held to decide the matter in September 1972, they all joined hands in united opposition. And they won. Whether or not Norway should join Euratom became an issue, with Rosenqvist arguing against it.[64] Rosenqvist believed natural gas, for a nation with ample amount of this resource, was a viable alternative to nuclear power,[65] an industry intrinsically linked to weaponry and NATO.[66]

LABOR PARTY ENVIRONMENTALISM

The power-socialist doctrine dominated the Labor Party until they lost power to a constellation of conservative parties in 1965. In 1971 they returned to power, eager to show that the Party could and would renew

[61] Odd Rune Austgulen (et al.), *Ressurser, befolkning: en kommentar til NOU 1974, no. 55* (Bergen: Norges handelshøyskole, 1975). Knut Breirem, *Norges ressurssituasjon i global sammenheng: utdrag og kommentarer til NOU 1974:55* (Ås: Norsk Institutt for Næringsmiddelforskning, 1974). Harald Myrås (et al.), *Kritiske og supplerende kommentarer til NOU 1974:55* (Trondheim: Komiteen for miljøvern, 1975).
[62] Nils Ottesen, "Håpløshetens evangelium," *Orientering*, 11 (1974), 10.
[63] Jan Borring, "En tallmagiker refser romantikerne," *Orientering*, 11 (1974), 10.
[64] Rosenqvist, "Norges stilling til Euratom," 1971, 18.
[65] Ivan Th. Rosenqvist, "Kraftverk basert på naturgass," *Teknisk ukeblad*, 119, no. 24 (1972), 19; "Hvorfor bokføre gasskraft, vasskraft og uran etter ulike prinsipper," *Teknisk ukeblad*, 119, no. 48 (1972), 31; "Vasskraft, naturvern og varmekraft," *Syn og segn*, 79 (1973), 110–12; "Norge og 'energikrisen'," *Morgenbladet*, Sept. 19, 1973, RA.
[66] Rosenqvist was a co-author of Folkebevegelsen mot Norsk medlemskap i Fellesmarkedet, *Folkebevegelsens melding om Norges forhold til De Europeiske Felleskap (EF)* (Oslo: Folkebevegelsen mot Norsk medlemskap i Fellesmarkedet, 1972), pp. 66–78. Ivan Th. Rosenqvist, "Atomenergi, atomkapprustning og keiserens nye klær," *Samtiden*, 81, no. 3 (1972), 129–34.

itself ideologically. An emerging group of environmentalists within the Labor Party questioned the power-socialism doctrine and shared the ecological concerns of the ecophilosophers and the eco-populists. Yet they did not believe in a revolutionary break with capitalism or in being outside of the European Community. They questioned economic growth, which they believed came at too high a social and environmental cost, but they did not question the political order of society. Instead they looked for solutions to ecological problems within established social structures and through international cooperation. One key mover was Eilif Dahl, the professor of botany who was the first to introduce ecology as a research topic in 1963 (see chapter 2). Throughout the 1960s he addressed environmental problems head-on, from within, as an active member in the Labor Party. Dahl's wartime resistance as a XU spy, work at the Army Headquarters in London, and active service as a longtime member of the Party gave him political clout among the old-guard.

When Hafslund applied for a permit to build an oil burning power plant at Slagentangen, Dahl saw it as an opportunity to question the Labor Party's power-socialism doctrine. He wrote a consulting report together with the ecologist Oddvar Skre on behalf of the Council of Smoke Injury, a forerunner of what later became the Norwegian Pollution Council Authority. The high symbolic value of the plant raised the stake in what was an exceedingly critical report from an environmental point of view. The report was based on a previous report also written by Dahl and Skre on behalf of the Nordic Research Council, Nordforsk, which was founded in 1971 to coordinate research for the Nordic Council of Ministers. They were busy at the time preparing for the United Nations Conference on the Human Environment that was to take place in Stockholm in June 1972.[67] Since the late 1960s there had been a growing concern in Sweden about the effect of airborne industrial pollution from Europe on their forest industry, a topic they sought to bring to international attention at the conference.[68] At the heart of the Swedish agenda was not only raising international awareness about airborne pollution but also

---

[67] Rowland, *The Plot to Save the World*. Karl F. Kaltenborn, "Miljøvern – globale løsninger for globale problemer," *Teknisk ukeblad*, 119, no. 28 (1972), 4. United Nations, *Report of the United Nations*.

[68] Svante Oden, *Aspects of the Atmospheric Corrosion Climate* (Stockholm: IVA's Korrosionsnämnd, 1965); "Regionala aspekter på miljöstörningar," *Vann*, 4, no. 3 (1969), 93–112. Ministry of Foreign Affairs and Ministry of Agriculture, *Air Pollution across National Boundaries: The Impact on the Environment of Sulfur in Air and Precipitation: Sweden's Case Study for the United Nations Conference on the Human Environment*

presenting analytical tools that could solve the environmental crisis. One such tool was socio-economics, an academic field with strong intellectual ties to the mixed-economy approach within both the Swedish and the Norwegian Labor Parties. In an attempt to mobilize allies, the Swedes would thus commission a report from Norwegian scholars who shared their point of view.

In the Slagentangen report Dahl and Skre argued that one had to scrutinize the potential power plant from the point of view of a socio-economic cost–benefit analysis before giving any building permits.[69] The main cost, they argued, was a growth reduction in surrounding forests caused by emissions of sulfuric acid damaging the soil nutrients. In addition, acid pollution would cause other socio-economic expenses such as corrosion of paint and damage to fish populations. Elsewhere Skre put the political aim of the report in clear terms: "We have to slacken the pace of growth of material welfare so that the balance of nature shall be established again."[70] The report was quite speculative in providing an exact calculation of expenses. The ecologists thus became an easy target when an abbreviated version of the report appeared in *Teknisk ukeblad* (Technical Weekly), which was a widely read journal among engineers and scientists alike. The critics labeled Dahl as an "alarmist" and "køpenickiade" (ludicrous swindler) playing with facts to advance his cause.[71]

Teknisk ukeblad had, through 1971, run a series of favorable articles about the environmental cause, addressing the role of science and the need to take action.[72] Technocratic solutions to pollution dominated the

---

(Stockholm: Bocktrykeriet, 1971). Eilif Dahl, "Omkring nedbørens forsuring og plantenes næringstilgang," *Vann*, 4, no. 3 (1969), 120–3.

[69] Eilif Dahl and Oddvar Skre, *En undersøkelse av virkningen av sur nedbør på produktiviteten i landbruket* (Stockholm: Nordforsk, Miljøvårdssekretariatet, 1971); *En vurdering av mulige eller sannsynlige skader for landbruket ved utslipp av røyk fra et planlagt varmekraftverk på Slagentangen* (Oslo: Røykskaderådet, 1971). Inspired by Erik Dahmén, *Set pris på miljøet* (Oslo: Det Norske Samlaget, 1970). Eilif Dahl, "Kostnader ved utslipp av svoveldioksyder i atmosfæren," *Teknisk ukeblad*, 118, no. 50 (1971), M1–2.

[70] Oddvar Skre, *Sur nedbør: Årsaker og verknader* (Oslo: Norges Naturvernforbund, 1972), 48.

[71] Aksel Lydersen, "Kostnader ved utslipp av svoveloksyder i atmosfæren," *Teknisk ukeblad*, 119, no. 9 (1972), 19. Nils Andreas Sørensen, "Kostnader ved utslipp av svoveloksyder i atmosfæren," *Teknisk ukeblad*, 119, no. 16 (1972), 46.

[72] Helmer Dahl, "Forurensning, forskere og politikere," *Teknisk ukeblad*, 118, no. 9 (1971), 22–5. J. A. Andersen, "Våre jordressurser: Dagens vekstkurve tilsier termisk ubalanse om 50 år," *Teknisk ukeblad*, 118, no. 36 (1971), 15–18, 23. Anonymous, "Alle prater naturvern … Disse gjør noe," *Teknisk ukeblad*, 118, no. 40 (1971), 17–18. Anders Omholt, "Naturessursene i samfunnspolitisk perspektiv," *Teknisk ukeblad*, 119, no. 20 (1972), 15–16, 32.

articles, in which one recurrent theme was the value of gas above oil, nuclear, and hydropower plants. After all, burning gas would only emit risk-free carbon dioxide.[73] One key mover was Gudmund Harlem (1917–88) who had served as Minister of Public Health and Defense during two Labor Party governments and, at the time, was the Chairman of the Board of the Norwegian Technical and Scientific Research Council (NTNF). In the process he had turned into a Labor Party environmentalist, arguing that one should research problems related to emissions of sulfuric acid and search for new environmental technologies.[74] With political support from Harlem, Dahl published a defense with some confidence that research funds were on their way.[75] Indeed, two weeks after Dahl was labeled a "ludicrous swindler," Nordforsk announced a major science program, which aimed at understanding long-range transport of air pollutions, including acid rain.[76]

Supporters of an oil plant at Slagentangen would hit back, as a gas plant was not an option at this location.[77] The question of acid rain was an onslaught on power-socialism in their eyes. Rosenqvist was among them. He arrested Dahl on a key scientific technicality, namely the acid buffer capacity of calcium in soil and clay.[78] This was not the first time Dahl and Rosenqvist had disagreed. In the early 1960s they had engaged in an exchange about how to proceed in locating areas that were ice-free in Scandinavia during the glacial period. Such areas were vital in understanding the origin and history of regional plants and animals. In a sharp criticism of Rosenqvist, Dahl argued that such areas did once exist along the northern coast, by pointing to levels of geological disintegration in

---

[73] Nils Kvåle, "Flytende naturgass – vårt fremtidige drivstoff?" *Teknisk ukeblad*, 118, no. 7 (1971), 19–22. Arthur Landberg, "Naturgasskraftverk – alternativ til olje/atomkraftverk?" *Teknisk ukeblad*, 118, no. 25 (1971), 28, 32; "Naturgasskraftverk i elektrisitetsforsyningen," *Teknisk ukeblad*, 119, no. 1 (1972), 11, 15; "Naturgasskraft i et optimalt sammensatt kraftsystem." *Teknisk ukeblad*, 119, no. 13 (1972), 4–5.
[74] Anonymous, "Forurensningene kan bringes under rimelig kontroll," *Teknisk ukeblad*, 119, no. 18 (1972), 3–4.
[75] Eilif Dahl, "Kostnader ved utslipp av svoveloksyder i atmosfæren" *Teknisk ukeblad*, 119, no.22 (1972), 3–5. Egil Aune, "Sur nedbørs følger for skogbruket," *Teknisk ukeblad*, 119, no. 24 (1972), 29–30.
[76] Brynjulf Ottar," "OECD/Nordforsk-projektet tar sikte på å klarlegge spredningsmønster for sur nedbør i Europa," *Teknisk ukeblad*, 119, no. 24 (1972), 15–16.
[77] Arthur Landberg, "Kraftverk basert på naturgass," *Teknisk ukeblad*, 119, no. 25 (1972), 27–8. Aksel and Dagfin Lydersen, "Kostnader ved utslipp av svovel i atmosfæren," *Teknisk ukeblad*, 119, no. 25 (1972), 27.
[78] Ingebrigt Jenssen and Ivan Th. Rosenqvist, "Kalsiumutvasking og syrenedfall," *Teknisk ukeblad*, 119, no. 25 (1972), 27.

sediments and clay.[79] Rosenqvist replied that he found it hard to believe that ecologists had much to offer clay studies, and that Dahl had failed to understand an important indicator of disintegration, namely alkaline absorption in different sections of clay.[80] It was the same issue of the soil and clay chemistry that reappeared when Dahl wrote about the damaging effect of acid rain on forest growth.[81] Despite Rosenqvist's criticism, Dahl's views prevailed, as Hafslund never got the permit needed to build the proposed plant.

Rosenqvist's criticism was based on one of Norway's largest post-war research projects in geology, namely the so-called Numedal-project, which started in 1966 and continued through the early 1970s. The aim of the project was to understand the nature of the sediments in the North Sea basin, by studying their origins in the Norwegian mountains, which were once carved out by glaciers. The continuous movements of sediments by water were at the heart of the project, which followed geological particles from the Hardangervidda mountain plateau through the river of the Numedal Valley and the coastal city of Larvik to the seabed. The team was led by Rosenqvist, and they began by analyzing the chemical components of rainfall to understand the weathering process in the high mountains. The team members followed the water and sediments all the way down to the oil platforms at the North Sea from which they got deep sea samples.[82] This was as close as the geologists could get to the oil without violating research restrictions. Rosenqvist had, in the Numedal project, followed the changing chemical nature of water, and could not see the effect of acid rain on soil.[83]

---

[79] Eilif Dahl, "Refugieproblemet og de kvartærgeologiske metodene," *Svensk naturvitenskap*, 14 (1961), 81–96.

[80] Ivan Th. Rosenqvist, "Refugieproblemet og de kvartærgeologiske metodene," *Norsk Geologisk Tidsskrift*, 41 (1961), 319–21. Eilif Dahl, "Bemerkninger om refugieproblemet og de kvartærgeologiske metodene," *Norsk Geologisk Tidsskrift*, 43 (1963), 260–5. Ivan Th. Rosenqvist, "Svar til Eilif Dahl," *Norsk Geologisk Tidsskrift*, 43 (1963), 266.

[81] Ivan Th. Rosenqvist, "Refugieproblemet og de kvartærgeologiske metodene," *Norsk Geologisk Tidsskrift*, 41 (1961), 319–21. Eilif Dahl, "Bemerkninger om refugieproblemet og de kvartærgeologiske metodene," *Norsk Geologisk Tidsskrift*, 43 (1963), 260–5. Ivan Th. Rosenqvist, "Svar til Eilif Dahl," *Norsk Geologisk Tidsskrift*, 43 (1963), 266.

[82] Ivan Th. Rosenqvist, *Numedalsprosjektet – en tverr-geovitenskapelig undersøkelse*, preliminary report, 2 Oct. (Oslo: Department of Geology, Univeristy of Oslo, 1970); "Origin and mineralogy glacial and interglacial clays of southern Norway," *Clays and Clay Minerals*, 23 (1972), 153–9; "Sub-Moraine Deposits in Numedal," *Bulletin of the Geological Institutions of the University of Uppsala*, 5 (1973), 7–12.

[83] Ivan Th. Rosenqvist, "Refugieproblemet og de kvartærgeologiske metodene," *Norsk Geologisk Tidsskrift*, 41 (1961), 319–21. Eilif Dahl, "Bemerkninger om refugieproblemet

Yet Rosenqvist's scientific disagreements with Dahl were not at the heart of the issue, as he would agree with Dahl, in an intramural publication, that acid rain under certain conditions could have damaging consequences on fish populations.[84] What troubled Rosenqvist was instead the damaging effect ecological argumentation could have on power-plant building and thus on the future welfare of the nation. Rosenqvist was irritated by the way in which Dahl and his fellow Labor Party environmentalists would undermine a united scientific effort to help the nation and, ultimately, the workers of the world out of poverty. The solidarity between scientists and the needy made "in many ways the scientific worker into a proletarian," he believed.[85] The unity of knowledge and science policy that Rosenqvist imagined to be present in the "University of Norway" ideals required "a common defense against the abuse of scientific results" from special interest groups such as the environmentalists. It was therefore most unfortunate that "some groups of researchers within biology and the environmental sciences would stand up against others within chemistry and technology."[86] Worse, instead of contributing to the welfare of the nation, Dahl and his ecology colleagues would "just walk around and shake their heads when DDT is proven to exist in penguin fat in the Antarctic."[87]

The underlying agenda behind this skirmish between Dahl and Rosenqvist was the establishment of the world's first Ministry of the Environment by the Labor Party environmentalists.[88] The new Prime Minister Trygve Bratteli agreed that a new Ministry would appeal to young voters concerned about hydropower developments, as in the case of the Mardøla demonstrations that took place in the summer of 1970 (see chapter 3). Perhaps such a Ministry could answer increasingly vocal criticisms from young ecophilosophers and also address the environmental activists' concerns about pollution and the exhaustion of natural

---

og de kvartærgeologiske metodene," *Norsk Geologisk Tidsskrift*, 43 (1963), 260–5. Ivan Th. Rosenqvist, "Svar til Eilif Dahl," *Norsk Geologisk Tidsskrift*, 43 (1963), 266.

[84] Inge Bryhni and Ivan Th. Rosenqvist, "De geologiske vitenskaper og menneskene," in Ivan Th. Rosenqvist (ed.), *Geologien og mennesket* (Oslo: Gyldendal, 1973), pp. 9–21, p. 17.

[85] Ivan Th. Rosenqvist, "Avskjedsord til realkandidatene," *Nytt fra Universitetet i Oslo*, no. 13 (1972), 3–4, 3, UO.

[86] Ivan Th. Rosenqvist, "Avskjedsord til realkandidatene," (1972), 4, RA.

[87] Ivan Th. Rosenqvist, "Avskjedsord til realkandidatene," (1972), 4, RA; "Cand.real. festen våren 1972" ms. 5 pages, RA.

[88] Per M. Jørgensen (eds.), *Botanikkens historie i Norge* (Oslo: Fagbokforlaget, 2007), p. 324. Olav Gjærevoll, *Mine memoarer* (Trondheim: Arbeiderbevegelsens historielag, 1998).

resources? Bratteli appointed Dahl's close friend and fellow botanist, Olav Gjærevoll (1916–94), as the first Cabinet Minister of the Ministry in May 1972. Gjærevoll was deeply impressed by the *The Limits to Growth* report issued in March of the same year, for which he wrote a sympathetic blurb, and he supported its Norwegian co-author Jørgen Randers (discussed in Chapter 7). As a former President of the Council of Environmental Protection, Gjærevoll was a stern proponent of national parks.[89] He would bring the concerns expressed in *The Limits to Growth* and Dahl's ecological perspectives to the core of the new Ministry through various informal working groups. The Ministry would, for example, have its own "Chief Ecologist" empowered to oversee and approve all its policies, a job given to the ecologist Rolf Vik from 1972 to 1974. Vik and his fellow Labor Party environmentalists within the Ministry would, in subsequent years, establish their own ecologically informed solutions to a whole set of issues, national as well as international.

In the eyes of Rosenqvist, the new Ministry and the Labor Party environmentalists were collaborators with the special interest groups who were undermining the modernization of Norway. Worries about degradation of the natural environment, pollution, population growth, and abuse of natural resources were unfounded, he argued. And their neo-Malthusian thinking sounded to him like doomsday predictions.[90] The world was not over-populated, there were plenty of natural resources, he claimed, even with radical population growth. And there was no danger of global self-poisoning from the greenhouse effect. He would typically defend power-socialism under the heading: "Brain Power or Hydro-Power?" Hydropower was a necessity for social welfare, he argued, as the alternative was the less desirable nuclear energy. In response to Labor Party environmentalists, he argued that, in the future, Norway could replace its energy consuming aluminum industry with an "intellectual industry" powered by its water resources.[91] Thus, there were no natural limits to growth. On the contrary, "the Norwegian resource situation [was] the best in the world."[92]

---

[89] Olav Gjærevoll, *Naturvern i Norge* (Oslo: Hygea, 1967).
[90] Ivan Th. Rosenqvist, "Verdifullt korrektiv til dommedagsprofetiene," *Forskningsnytt*, 19 (1974), 35.
[91] Ivan Th. Rosenqvist, "Vett eller vasskraft?" *Syn og segn*, 62, no. 9 (1966), 1–5; "Muligheter for kjemisk intelligensindustri i Norge," *Tidskrift for kjemi, bergvesen og metallurgi*, 8/9 (1967), 142–6.
[92] Lied (et al.), *Norges ressurssituasjon*, p. 201.

THE ACID RAIN DEBATE

At the end of September 1972 the Labor Party suffered a humiliating political defeat with the country voting against membership of the European Community in the national referendum. As a result, Bratteli, along with his entire cabinet, resigned, and they were subsequently replaced with a conservative government. A year later, however, Bratteli and the Labor Party returned to power, which the Labor Party would keep until 1981. Among Party environmentalists was Gro Harlem Brundtland (b. 1939), who served as Minister of the Environment from 1974 to 1979.

Brundtland took her medical exams at the University of Oslo in 1963, and followed up with a Master of Public Health from Harvard University in 1965. She became active within the Labor Party through her job as Consultant Physician at the Oslo Board of Health from 1968 to 1974. She was known there for fighting for women's abortion rights, a struggle that was particularly intense in debates leading up to the Norwegian Law of Self-Determination of 1975. Brundtland was in the midst of these events, which led her to view scientists and experts with some skepticism. In the abortion debate, she noted, "experts" were presenting a "mixture of facts and personal beliefs" in a way that "abused – knowingly or unknowingly – their expert or scientific role in a political context."[93] It was as a young feminist that she was chosen to become Cabinet Minister of the Environment. Her experience as a physician and supporter of abortion rights came to frame the way in which she engaged with natural scientists on environmental issues. "Politics is like preventive health care," she would say.[94] In the process she transferred decision-making about a patient's body to the body politic. She was able to read complicated scientific papers, despite having been unable to finish her doctoral dissertation with only one coauthored study (in the history of science of medical records).[95] She took interest in research about sexual behavior among young people, which, in her opinion, documented women's need for self-determination with respect to abortion. She had faith in the idea that the

---

[93] Gro Harlem Brundtland, "Forskning, forvaltning og politikk," *Ting*, 2 (1977), 24–31, quote p. 28. Ellen Schrumpf, *Abortsakens historie* (Oslo: Tiden, 1984).
[94] Brundtland quoted in Steinar Hansson and Ingolf Håkon Teigene, *Makt og mannefall: Historien om Gro Harlem Brundtland* (Oslo: Cappelen, 1992), p. 38.
[95] Gro Harlem Brundtland and Lars Walløe, "Menarcheal age in Norway in the 19th century: A re-evaluation of historical sources," *Annals of Human Biology*, 3 (1976), 363–74. Gro Harlem Brundtland and Knut Liestøl, "Seasonal variations in menarche in Oslo," *Annals of Human Biology*, 9 (1982), 35–43.

right knowledge would lead to the right action. This, at least, was the gist in a paper she gave to members of the Norwegian Association of Researchers in 1977. She recognized that different scientific "specialists" could have competing explanations of reality, and it was therefore of key importance to find scientific "generalists" with the ability to "translate" and "mediate" clusters of relevant facts to the politicians.[96] Addressing the problem of "which expert one should listen to" was a matter of willingness to base decisions upon scientific uncertainty, which was normal in the medical treatment of patients.[97] It was based on this argument of risk that she would argue that the environmental effect of resource exhaustion and pollution entailed limits to economic growth.[98]

When Brundtland became Minister of the Environment in 1974, she inherited the research program "Acid Precipitation: Effects on Forest and Fish" (SNSF), which was financed mostly by the Ministry, but also had support from Harlem (her father) at the Norwegian Technical and Scientific Research Council and the Labor Party's Minister of Agriculture, Thorstein Treholt, who had mobilized the Norwegian Agricultural Science Foundation for the project. Dahl had also pushed for the program so that it could vindicate him from the accusation made in *Teknisk ukeblad* that he was an academic "ludicrous swindler." More generally, the program was meant to showcase that the Labor Party took environmental questions seriously, and that it was possible through international and (especially) European cooperation to find technical and political solutions to these problems.

Between 1972 and 1976 the Acid Precipitation Program carried out large-scale scientific investigations into the possible effects of acid rain on forests and fish.[99] The research has been reviewed in a first-rate study by the historian of science Rachel E. Rothschild. She documents how Brundtland, through the program and with the help of the Norwegian atmospheric chemist Brynjulf Ottar, mapped acid precipitation in both East and West European countries, thanks to an extensive scientific

---

[96] Brundtland," Forskning, forvaltning og politikk," p. 25.
[97] Brundtland," Forskning, forvaltning og politikk," p. 29.
[98] Gro Harlem Brundtland, "Energiforsyning i Norge i framtida," in *Stortingsforhandlinger 1974/1975*, May 13, 1975, p. 4163. Yngve Nilsen, *En felles plattform? Norsk oljeindustri og klimadebatten i Norge fram til 1998* (Oslo: TIK Senter, 2001), pp. 37–65.
[99] Ivan Th. Rosenqvist, "Refugieproblemet og de kvartærgeologiske metodene," *Norsk Geologisk Tidsskrift*, 41 (1961), 319–21. Eilif Dahl, "Bemerkninger om refugieproblemet og de kvartærgeologiske metodene," *Norsk Geologisk Tidsskrift*, 43 (1963), 260–5. Ivan Th. Rosenqvist, "Svar til Eilif Dahl," *Norsk Geologisk Tidsskrift*, 43 (1963), 266.

research network.[100] The program not only documented the problem of acid rain, but also showed the importance of Norwegian collaboration across the Iron Curtain with Eastern Bloc countries, as well as with the European Community. The program tapped into a deeper tradition of multinational thinking in Europe about the scale of climate research.[101] To Brundtland it was paramount to showcase that the EC cared about and could take action with respect to environmental issues, thus undermining the arguments against the EC from the vocal Deep Ecologists. The program resulted in a European monitoring program of acid rain, which laid the groundwork for finding a solution to the problem through the vehicle of European environmental diplomacy. Some critics, especially the British, argued that there was a need for more knowledge to take political action and some of the scientists involved in the program were perhaps more concerned with providing scientific advice than facts.[102] The Ministry of the Environment had apparently decided in advance that acid rain was a problem, and that the task of the scientists was to verify this conclusion.[103] Dahl remained aloof, and would later claim that he had nothing to do with the results of the Acid Precipitation Program, which documented the damaging effects of acid rain, particularly on Norwegian fish populations in rivers and mountain lakes.[104]

When the results of the Acid Precipitation program were first presented in a seminar in the fall of 1976, Rosenqvist reiterated his earlier criticisms of Dahl on the chemical dynamics of rain on soil and clay. He must have been blunt, if one is to judge from reports from journalists who covered

---

[100] Rachel E. Rothschild, *Poisonous Skies: Acid Rain and the Globalization of Pollution* (Chicago: University of Chicago Press, 2019), 56–7.
[101] Deborah R. Coen, *Climate in Motion: Science, Empire, and the Problem of Scale* (Chicago: University of Chicago Press, 2018).
[102] Nils Roll-Hansen, *Ideological Obstacles to Scientific Advice in Politics? The Case of 'Forest Rain' from 'Acid Rain'* (Oslo: Makt og demokratiutredningen, 2002); "Science, politics, and the mass media: On biased communication of environmental issues," *Science, Technology and Human Values*, 19 (1994), 324–41; *Sur nedbør – et storprosjekt i norsk miljøforskning* (Oslo; NAVF, 1986); Nils Roll-Hansen and Geir Hestmark, *Miljøforskning mellom vitenskap og politikk* (Oslo: NAVF, 1990).
[103] Ministry of the Environment, *Sur nedbør og dens virkninger i Norge* (Oslo: Miljøverndepartementet, July 1974); *Internasjonale tiltak for bekjempelse av sur nedbør* (Oslo: Miljøverndepartementet, Sept. 1974).
[104] Eilif Dahl, *Sur nedbør og skog – tilbakeblikk og perspektiver*, ms. 21 pages, 1985, 7, LS. Gunnar Abrahamsen and Finn H. Brække (eds. et al.), *Impact of Acid Precipitation on Forest and Freshwater Ecosystems in Norway: Summary Report on the Research Results from Phase 1 (1972–1975) of the SNSF-Project* (Oslo: Sur nedbørs virkning på skog og fisk, 1976).

the meeting.[105] The prime reason for acidity in water causing fish death was not acid rain but the changing environmental history of the land, Rosenqvist argued. According to Marxist theory, slavery, feudalism, capitalism, and the classless society were all stages of a necessary biological process, which in its last material manifestation, would appear as a conflict between humans and nature. Following this narrative, Rosenqvist understood changes in the fauna and flora of Norway in light of different usages of the land by hunter-gatherer, agricultural, and industrial societies. This perspective harkened back to Rosenqvist's debates with Dahl in the early 1960s about reading the environmental history of landscapes in the alkalinity of clay sections. "In the early stone age," Rosenqvist explained, "the entire Southern part of Norway up to the timberline [was] covered with forests," and there were hardly any populations of fish in lakes or rivers.[106] With the coming of the agricultural age, peasants would, through nomadic alpine dairy, cultivate grass, fish, and livestock, a process which created a more alkaline soil. The shift towards industrial farming and vacant alpine pastures changed much of the landscape back to forests again, he argued, a process which "within a few decades radically changed the chemical buffer level of the fluvial basin."[107] As a result, the rivers and lakes of Norway were much more vulnerable to acid rain from Europe, and one should consequently blame the changing Norwegian agricultural policy, and not oil-burning Europeans, for the problems. Rosenqvist would not keep his views to himself. Instead he reached out to British scientists with his arguments and even appeared in a British documentary on the topic.[108]

---

[105] Anonymous, "Bombe fra geologi-professor: Nedbøren avgjør ikke surhet i vassdragene," *Aftenposten*, Nov. 26, 1976, 1, RA. Anonymous, "Sur nedbør-forskere skeptiske til prof. Rosenqvists teorier," *Aftenposten*, Nov. 27, 1976, 4, RA. Anonymous, "Professor Rosenqvist: Negative kommentarer skyldes misforståelser," *Aftenposten*, Nov. 27, 1976, 4, RA. Anonymous, "Faglig isolasjon fare for forskere," *Aftenposten*, Nov. 27, 1976, 4, RA. Helge Røed," Oppsiktsvekkende fra professor Rosenqvist: Det er ikke nedbøren som forsurer våre elver og vann," *Arbeiderbladet*, Nov. 26, 1976, 1, 7, RA. Anonymous, "Statssekretær i MD: Rosenqvists teori ikke ny," *Aftenposten*, Nov. 27, 1976, 1, 4, RA. Bo Lilledal Andersen,"Forskning om sur nedbør: Viktige forhold ikke undersøkt!" *Nationen*, Nov. 27, 1976, 1, RA. Rothschild, *Poisonous Skies*, 74–7.
[106] Ivan Th. Rosenqvist, *Et bidrag til analyse av geologiske materialers bufferegenskaper mot sterke syrer i nedbørsvann* (Oslo: NAVF, 1976), 115–16, quote p. 115.
[107] Ivan Th. Rosenqvist, *Sur jord surt vann* (Oslo: Ingeniørforlaget, 1977), 99–103, quote p. 101.
[108] Anonymous, "Norway is angry about film on acid rain," *New Scientist*, 1418 (Oct. 31, 1985), 13. I am grateful to Rachel Rothschild for this reference.

The public criticism and alternative explanation of the widespread fish death came as a surprise to Brundtland, who, in early April 1977, labeled Rosenqvist a "køpenickiade" at a press conference.[109] In Norwegian this is a somewhat archaic Germanic word used very rarely, as it left bewildered journalists scrambling through dictionaries trying to find out what it meant. In translation, it essentially means "ludicrous swindler." It was also the same word used against Dahl in the acid rain exchange in *Teknisk ukeblad* five years earlier. Brundtland may have picked it up through that previous usage and decided to return the insult against Dahl's chief opponent. In any case, with such a claim coming from a Minister against a well-respected scientist, acid rain became a media circus with numerous articles covering the evolving debate.[110] Some were concerned about the damaging effect that Rosenqvist's argument had on ongoing international negotiations aiming to reduce sulfuric acid emissions. To others it was a question of defending the freedom of science against politically charged contract research.[111] At the University, witty students nicknamed him "Ivan pH Rosenqvist" and "Ivan the Terrible" while others fashioned him after the uncompromising heroic priest in Henrik Ibsen's *Brand*. It is telling that a gossip magazine arranged, "This week's most exciting meeting," between Rosenqvist and Brundtland, in which they would have to make their case in plain language.

---

[109] Arne Sellæg, "Professorrapport blir kalt 'tull': Kritkk mot sur nedbør-forskning tilbakevises," *Dagbladet*, Apr. 13, 1977, RA. Gro Harlem Brundtland, *Mitt liv 1939–1986* (Oslo: Gyldendal, 1997), 175.

[110] Anonymous, "Sur nedbør-debatt kan gi nye krav," *Aftenposten*, Nov. 30, 1976, 1, RA. Anonymous, "Fortsatt innsats nødvendig for å finne virkningene av sur nedbør," *Aftenposten*, Nov. 30, 1976, last page, RA. Anonymous, "Nye synspunkter på forsuringen av våre vassdrag," *Nytt fra Universitetet i Oslo*, Nov. 30, 1976, 1–2, UO. Anonymous, "Rosenqvists bidrag viktig," *Aftenposten*, Dec. 1, 1976, 1, 4, RA. Anonymous, "Sur nedbør-forskere avviser Rosenqvist," *Arbeiderbladet*, Dec. 1, 1976, 7, RA. Bo Lilledal Andersen, "Kjemi-geolog bak omstridt rapport om sur nedbør," *Nationen*, Dec. 4, 1976, 9, RA. John S. Gray, "Rosenqvist-rapporten: En fundamentalt riktig hypotese," *Aftenposten*, Dec. 6, 1976, 2, RA. Per Jørgensen, Harald Bergseth, Johannes Kjensmo, Eigil Hesstvedt, "Riktig å påpeke mangler ved SNSF-prosjektet," *Aftenposten*, Mar. 31, 1977, RA. Gunnar Magnus, "Gro H.B. Min sti er ren," *Aftenposten*, Nov. 11, 1977, 1, RA.

[111] Forskerforbundet, "Styrepapirer 1977," Archive of the Norwegian Association of Researchers, page 5–6. Yngve Nilsen, *En sterk stilling? Norsk Forskerforbunds historie 1955–2005* (Oslo: Vigmostad, 2005), pp. 93–4. Arne Semb-Johansson, *Noen mimringer fra min tid som generalsekretær i Det Norske Videnskaps-Akademi*, unpublished 1985, Archive of The Norwegian Academy of Science and Letters, pp. 27–8. Kim Gunnar Helsvig, *Elitisme på Norsk: Det Norske Videnskaps-Akademi 1945–2007* (Oslo: Novus forlag, 2007), p. 160.

"It was beautiful music to the ears of all those who would not accept that we had an international [environmental] problem," Brundtland later claimed.[112] In her opinion, Rosenqvist's work undermined efforts to halt the European industrial pollution of sulfuric acid, which ended up as acid rain in her native Norway. In the subsequent debate Brundtland argued that Rosenqvist missed the point. What concerned her was not the history or exact cause of acidification of water, but what she, as an environmental politician, could do about the problem. She sought scientific facts that could help her in taking the right political action. "Is Norway exposed to pollution, transported from far away, that is of a degree and kind that we could do something about it?" was her key question.[113] The clay and soil chemical factors Rosenqvist pointed to were irrelevant to her, not because they were untrue, but because she, as an environmental politician, could not do anything about them. She accused Rosenqvist of confusing public opinion with a narrow set of facts, which did not take into account a broader ecological perspective or political realities with respect to how his science could be used by the polluters. Rosenqvist, on the other hand, was well aware of the political implications. He talked with Brundtland not only as a scientist, but also as a "worker on the left side of the labor movement."[114] To him, the political issue at stake was Norway's future use of its natural resources, which meant building oil-plants that would generate inexpensive electricity for the needy.

To summarize, Rosenqvist followed the doctrine of power-socialism that both Soviet communists, which he identified with, and the first postwar generation of Labor Party members adopted as a means for modernizing the nation through industrialization. This doctrine was challenged in the mid-1960s by radical agrarian eco-populists seeking a revolutionary break with industrial society and also by moderate environmentalists within the second generation of Labor Party members, who advanced their cause through existing political structures. Rosenqvist targeted environmentalists and ecologists as opponents of industrialization and resource exploration: "We need energy to develop. I have no faith in the blissful Nepalise society in equilibrium that Arne Næss tells us about."[115] These

---

[112] Brundtland, *Mitt liv 1939–1986*, p. 173. On Rosenqvist as an "anti-environmentalist" see John Hille, *Miljøtrusler for døve ører* (Oslo: Fremtiden i våre henders forskningsinstitutt, 2001). Erling Dokk Holm, "Rosenqvist saken," *F.eks*, 3 (1994), 22, 24.
[113] Anonymous, "Ukens mest spennende møte," *Nå* 13 (April 1977), 2–5, 4, RA.
[114] Anonymous, "Ukens mest spennende møte," p. 5.
[115] Ivan Rosenqvist quoted in Bjørn Talén, "Suksess for 'sosialisme på norsk'," *VG*, April 21, 1980, 4, RA.

8 The Acid Rain Debate

FIGURE 8 The Minister of the Environment, Gro Harlem Bruntland, answering the world press about the major "Bravo" oil spill in the North Sea, 1977.
Photo: NTB. Courtesy of Scanpix

debates became an issue of which field of science and whose knowledge one should trust in determining the right policy. In the process both sides of the debate (represented by Rosenqvist and Dahl) were labeled scientific "swindlers" by their opponents. Rosenqvist's chief target, however, was Dahl's patron, the Ministry of the Environment, which was controlled by the environmental reformers within the Labor Party. His scientific disagreements with Brundtland should thus be understood as part of his defense of his belief in industrialism and power to the proletarians.

In the midst of these debates the chief pipeline in an oil platform called "Bravo" exploded, causing a major oil spill that lasted for a week from the end of April until the beginning of May, 1977. This put Brundtland under an unwanted spotlight with national and international media covering the evolving disaster on an hourly basis (Figure 8). Her capacity as a Minister of the Environment was put to the test. And judging from her later political career she handled it well. The immediate political effect, however, was an energized environmental movement questioning Brundtland and the industrialization of Norway. All of which will be the topic of the next chapter.

9

Our Common Future

"A bang, I see a flash of light before I get hit in the air. So this is what's at the end of life, I think, imagining myself being thrown into the air, how long I don't know. Lying in the snow waiting for everything to end."[1] The Sámi civil rights leader Niillas A. Somby survived, but lost his arm in his failed attempt to blow up the bridge leading to the construction site of the Alta-Kautokeino river power plant. It was March 1982 and the Supreme Court had just ruled that the development of the waterway was lawful. Both events were front-page news in all major newspapers. After being told he faced at least a decade in prison, Somby fled with his family to First Nations people in Canada, who helped them to hide and escape extradition to Norway. In hindsight, the explosion at the bridge was an act of desperation, reflecting the breaking point of the bitterest Sámi civil rights and environmental conflicts in the nation's history.

Somby was recovering in the hospital when Gro Harlem Brundtland, the Labor Party leader behind the decision to build the hydropower plant, was asked to chair the World Commission on Environment and Development. Wisely, she kept quiet about the invite as the timing was not right for the announcement of her as the United Nations' voice for environmentalism and the interests of the Global South, including the rights of Indigenous people. Ten years later, in June 1992, Brundtland led a delegation of Norwegian environmental politicians to promote sustainable development at the Earth Summit in Rio de Janeiro (formally known

---

[1] Niillas A. Somby, "Et lysglimt," in Sven Erik Skønberg (ed.), *Grønn pepper i turbinene* (Oslo: Universitetsforlaget, 1985), pp. 112–22, quote p. 112. Robert Paine, *Dam a River, Damn a People?* (Copenhagen: IWGIA, 1992).

as the UN Conference of Environment and Development). This chapter will discuss this decade and the ways in which Brundtland appropriated the Alta experience as Chair of the Commission. During the decade leading up to the Earth Summit in Rio, the Deep Ecologists became increasingly fundamentalist and politically irrelevant in Norway, while they also had their first international breakthrough in North America, thanks to the environmental organization Earth First! Yet the end of the Cold War in 1989, I argue, would lead to a shift away from Deep Ecological to global climatological perspectives. Propelled by the sentiment that capitalism had won over communism, Brundtland and her delegation to the Earth Summit would frame the solution to climate change in cost–benefit terms, rather than in socialist terms.[2]

THE ALTA DEMONSTRATIONS

In the late 1970s the Ecopolitical Cooperation Ring, the political arm of the Deep Ecologists, began organizing what became the most dramatic civil disobedience demonstration in post-war Norwegian history. In comparison, the events became as dramatic and poignant as the recent Dacota Access Pipeline protests at the Standing Rock Indian Reservation in the USA. There is not enough space here to review the remarkable effort to save the Alta-Kautokeino waterway in the north of Norway from hydropower development. Fortunately, historians have already documented the remarkable events.[3] Shortly, after an application process that began in 1968, the Norwegian Parliament voted in 1978 in favor of the project, thanks to support from the Labor Party government with Gro Harlem Brundtland as Minister of Environmental Affairs. Key members of the Cooperation Ring were furious. "IS IT TIME FOR ANOTHER MARDØLA DEMONSTRATION?" they challenged.[4]

The issue at stake was not only saving a truly pristine environment, but also protecting the civil rights of the Indigenous Sámi population who

---

[2] Kristin Asdal, *Politikkens natur – naturens politikk* (Oslo: Universitetsforlaget, 2011), pp. 173–210.
[3] Ron Eyerman, "Intellectuals and Popular Movements: The Alta confrontation in Norway," *Praxis International*, 3 (1983), 185–98. Lars Martin Hjorthol, *Alta: Kraftkampen som utfordret statens makt* (Oslo: Gyldendal, 2006). Yngve Nilsen, "Ideologi eller kompleksitet? Motstand mot vannkraftutbygging i Norge i 1970-årene," *Historisk tidsskrift*, 87 (2008), 61–84. Jansen, *Makt og miljø*.
[4] Jan-Erik Kofoed, "Nok ein sigar for kraftfantastane?" *(snm) nytt* 1 (Jan. 1978), 3. Per Annar Holm, "Sårene som aldri gror," *VG*, July 26, 1980, 46, RA.

lived and worked in the Alta-Kautokeino canyon. The Sámi reminded the ecophilosophers of the Sherpa culture in Nepal they knew and idolized. The environmental future of the nation hung on this debate: should one build the hydropower project that would generate electricity for a consumer-capitalist society or should the river be preserved as an integral part of a steady-state society in harmony with nature? The events in Alta also became important in sending a message to the rest of the world, especially to the European Community, that it was possible to maintain and develop an ecological society free from the pitfalls of industrialism.

Though many people took on leadership roles in making the Alta demonstrations happen, Somby and Kvaløy became chief ideological spokespeople, respectively, on Sámi civil rights and environmental issues. Kvaløy had huge credibility among Deep Ecologists as the chief organizer of the earlier Mardøla demonstrations, along with his resistance to membership in the European Community. Hydropower or no hydropower, membership or no membership were the debates that divided friends from foes in Kvaløy's world. Cast in a bipolar Cold War culture, his ecophilosophy came to reflect this either/or dichotomy. As a leading charismatic figure among the Deep Ecologists, Kvaløy framed the environmental debates throughout the 1970s in terms of what was either deep or shallow thinking. His ecophilosophy would boil down to a simple message: Do you support the "Industrial Growth Society" or the "Life Necessities Society"?[5] The Life Necessities Society was modeled on the lives of the Sherpa in the village of Beding in Nepal and also on the lives of the Sámi, while the Industrial Growth Society was the equivalent of membership in the European Community. The lack of philosophical subtleties in Kvaløy's ecophilosophy was not a problem for the many demonstrators at Alta for whom the issue boiled down to whether or not they would build a hydropower dam there. Kvaløy coined their chief slogan: "La elva leve!" (Let the river live!), reflecting his ecophilosophy of letting the life force in nature flow (Figure 9).

By the summer of 1979, demonstrators were in place blocking the road to the Alta-Kautokeino dam construction site, which they did until the fall of 1981 when the largest police operation in the nation's history removed strictly non-violent but very determined demonstrators. For more than two years these events would occupy the country's environmental and social debate, often as front-page news. The debates were no less intense

---

[5] Kvaløy, "Ecophilosophy and ecopolitics," p. 16.

FIGURE 9 Demonstrators blocking the road to the Alta hydropower construction site. The writing on the rocks reads "LA ELVA LEVE" (Let the river live). September 1979.
Photo: Erik Thorberg. Courtesy of NTB Scanpix

at the universities as professors, as well as students, would leave their offices and classes to join the protestors.[6] Indeed, some classes were either suspended or ran at a minimum with substitution classes in ecophilosophy and ecology held instead on-site in Alta.[7] Yet, for all their efforts, the police operations put an effective end to the demonstrations. Frustrated with the situation, Kvaløy and a limited group within the Cooperation Ring contemplated sabotaging the construction as an alternative to protesting in order to halt the dam construction.[8] In February 1982 the Supreme Court ruled that the project for developing hydropower in the Alta-Kautokeino waterway was lawful, and the environmentalists gave up their cause, with the exception of Somby and two of his friends, who, in a last attempt to stop the dam, tried to blow up the bridge leading to the site. The Sámi and Deep Ecologists had lost, and Brundtland bore the

---

[6] Lennart Hovland, "Skal statsansatte få fri til Alta-aksjoner?" *Morgenbladet*, Jan. 8, 1981, 9, RA.
[7] Ottar Grepstad, "Folkeuniversitet i fjellet," *Universitas* 11 (Sept. 17, 1979), 11, UO.
[8] Jan Borring (interview with Sigmund Kvaløy), "På tide med aksjoner mot demninger og maskiner," *Miljømagasinet*, 2 (1981), 4–5, 36.

majority of the blame for the disaster. As Minister for the Environment between 1974 and 1979 and subsequently Prime Minister from February to October 1981, she had wholeheartedly defended developing the waterway in the very heart of Sámi land.

THE END OF DEEP ECOLOGY IN NORWAY

The defeat in Alta meant an end to Deep Ecology as a movement and intellectual endeavor in Norway. The failure to stop the hydro-dam construction caused much soul searching and bitterness among the Deep Ecologists.[9] Their vision for an alternative ecological steady-state nation had been held together by an ideological uniformity against industrial society, the European Community, and hydropower projects. When this shared vision for an alternative nation began to crack with the defeat in Alta, their arguments began to lose their relevance, students lost interest, and long loyal supporters began drifting away. This reflected a national trend. While twenty-five percent of Norwegian voters in 1977 had environmental issues as their top priority, the number had dropped to five percent by 1985.[10] As one Deep Ecologist noted about the early 1980s: "With the oil-age and the 'YAP-period' (Young Aspiring Professional) in Norway ... the bottom fell out of the Norwegian commitment to nature-friendly lifestyles."[11] At the institutional home of Deep Ecology, Environmental Studies at the University of Oslo, the students began voting with their feet as the numbers taking their courses would gradually drop. Those who stayed were advised not to seek a career as action researchers or ecologists, but instead find positions within the growing environmental bureaucracy.[12] When some students instead got research jobs in private biotechnology firms, a scholar at Environmental Studies asked: "Are the biologists selling their soul?"[13] His answer was yes. Among the Deep Ecologists there was time for self-examination. Had

---

[9] Kjell Haagensen and Atle Midttun (eds.), *Kraftutbygging, konflikt og aksjoner* (Oslo: Universitetsforlaget, 1984). Bernt Hagtvet (ed.), *Den vanskelige ulydigheten* (Oslo: Pax, 1981).

[10] Bernt Aardal, "Nordmenns holdninger til miljøvern," in Bjørn Alstad (ed.), *Norske meninger 1946–93* (Oslo: Sigma, 1993), pp. 583–620, 584.

[11] Børge Dahle, *Prosjektbeskrivelse: Gleden ved å leve naturvennlig: Stetind arnestedet for sammenføyningen av filosofi og økologi*, Archive of Tyssfjord Municipality, 2009, typecript 19 pages, quote p. 19.

[12] Paul Hofseth, "Biologer i forvaltninger," *Bio*, 1/2 (1984), 5–11.

[13] Hermod Haug, "Bioteknologi – selger biologene sjela si?" *Bio*, 2 (1987), 4–5.

they in the midst of their efforts to save the environment forgotten to enjoy nature?[14]

Some Deep Ecologists ended up drifting towards a less radical and more pragmatist position. At Environmental Studies there were seven full-time and ten to fifteen part-time employees, of which only their new leader, Ola Glesne, was tenured.[15] To keep the institution going under budget constraints, they established *Stiftelsen miljøforskning* (The Environmental Research Foundation) to avoid university bureaucratic red tape when accepting public and private research funds. They were following a general entrepreneurial trend in academia that enabled financial flexibility and at the same time established client relationships in research. The Foundation thus had the positive effect of keeping staff occupied with new projects and opportunities, while at the same time it drew attention away from the larger vision for an alternative nation. A report about the environmental virtue of flea markets for the Ministry of the Environment describing them as an "amusing trade in which everyone earns and nobody gets cheated," may serve as an example.[16]

For key Deep Ecologists the soul searching led to a hardening of their thinking, and the group's core became increasingly fundamentalist. In the early 1980s Kvaløy inherited the farm Setreng at Singsås in Budalen, in South Trønderlag, from his uncle.[17] It is a charming old-fashioned farm that is steeped in history. He moved there and changed his name to Kvaløy Setreng to reflect a sense of the farm now being part of him. Anyone who wanted serious attention from the ecophilosopher would have to reeducate themselves and thereby forge a closer relationship with nature by working with him on the farm, if only for a couple of hours. Haymaking was a favorite. Eager to practice what he taught, Kvaløy Setreng made his farm into a Life Necessities Society showcase, complete with a tiny Buddhist temple a la Beding in Nepal. When staying in Oslo he lived in an apartment facing Bygdøy Allé, which at the time was one of the city's worst streets in terms of pollution and heavy traffic. The contrast between the organic and industrial life could not have been starker and more personal. From his farm he would send

---

[14] Ola Glesne and Rasmus Hansson (interview with Nils Faarlund), "Har miljørørsla glemt naturen?" *Miljømagasinet*, 7 (1983), 4–5.
[15] T.M.S., "Rådet for natur- og miljøfag," *Nytt fra Universitetet i Oslo*, Nov. 8, 1987, 19, UO.
[16] Jon Gulowsen (et al.), *Loppemarked: Humørfylt handel hvor alle tjener og ingen blir snytt* (Oslo: Stiftelsen miljøforskning, 1985).
[17] Jon Solem, "Naturverner for vår tid?" *Harvest* (blog, Sept. 21, 2014).

a steady stream of warnings, to whoever would listen, about the immediate collapse of the industrial society. "[M]any will starve to death and kill each other," he said in an interview with a magazine devoted to young environmentalists. Indeed, after the ecological collapse "a billion people will starve to death, and we will be forced to farm [potatoes] in Siberia."[18] He also began substituting the Industrial Growth Society in his English lectures with "Advanced, Competitive, Industrial, Domination" using the acronym ACID.[19] His point was to focus on the destructive power of industrial society, which, like acid, would penetrate and destroy the organic Life Necessities Society.

To Kvaløy Setreng's dismay, the village of Beding in Nepal, which had served as an idealized model in the 1970s for the future, changed – and not for the better. The power of ACID had arrived there in the form of tourism, roads, sanitation, and communication, all of which gradually brought Beding out of its harmonious state of ecological self-sufficiency. Disappointed, he turned his attention instead to Bhutan, at the time, an absolute monarchy largely closed to the rest of the world. To him, it was the world's last bastion of ecological self-sufficiency in danger of being encroached upon by the ACID of the industrial world. Indeed, for the last part of his life Kvaløy Setreng would be a personal advisor to the young King of Bhutan, Jigme Khesar Namgyel Wangchuck, on how to make sure the country remained a true Life Necessities Society by promoting happiness in harmony with nature instead of capitalist consumption. In the role as the King's advisor, Kvaløy Setreng would late in life find himself in heated debates about why people would flee from Bhutan due to the country's human rights violations.[20]

Kvaløy Setreng's former teacher and fellow Deep Ecologist, Arne Næss, shared his admiration for life in Bhutan. In the late 1980s the country would for him also replace Nepal as the ideal state from which the world had to learn. For example, the country made sure its citizens would not drift into shallow ecological values after traveling abroad. Næss noted: "[In Bhutan] any students who go abroad for higher education must, immediately upon their return, spend six months travelling through the countryside for a *re-education* on the actual

---

[18] Sigmund Kvaløy Setreng, "Å dyrke tobakken sjøl," *Natur og Samfunn*, 4/5 (1990), 12. Similarly in Sætra, *Jamvektssamfunnet er ikkje noko urtete-selskap*.
[19] Sigmund Kvaløy Setreng, "Gaia versus Servoglobe,"in Roy Bhaskar (et al. eds.), *Ecophilosophy in a World Crisis* (London: Routledge, 2012), pp. 99–114.
[20] Sigmund Kvaløy Setreng, "Kampen om Bhutan," *Dagbladet*, March 18, 2008, NB. Richard Skretteberg, "Shangri-la, Shangri-lei," *Dagbladet*, Feb. 21, 2008, NB.

conditions and values of the people of their own country."[21] Assuming that the students in question had learned what Næss termed a shallow ecological point of view, it meant that Bhutan used the power of the state rightfully in ordering their "re-education" after being contaminated by foreign universities. And Bhutan was not known for having a strong record when it came to human rights when forcing students to be reeducated in rural values.

Kvaløy Setreng was in favor of such reeducation policies as this reflected how he welcomed visitors at his farm, while Næss at heart was no such fundamentalist. Instead, Næss played with ideas, as his musings on Bhutan illustrate. The problem was that such ideas, whether or not they were to be taken entirely seriously, did not fascinate the young. The times were changing, and both ecophilosophers had lost touch with their followers, which dwindled in numbers. High-power introduction courses and textbooks in environmental ethics and ecology would not change this general trend.[22] Norway's demographic was also shifting with the arrival of more immigrants. For Nina Witoszek, a refugee arriving in Norway after escaping communist Poland due to her translation of George Orwell's *Animal Farm* and other underground publishing activities, Deep Ecology looked like an authoritarian peasant's philosophy in its lack of appreciation of high-culture.[23] At the University of Trondheim and the University of Bergen, attempts were made to answer such criticisms and renew the ecophilosophical project by merging it with Karl-Otto Apel's transcendental pragmatics.[24] While at the University of Oslo the last Deep Ecologists would seek refuge in the Department of Philosophy engaging in acute debates about the difference between "inherent" and "intrinsic" value in nature.[25] As important as such philosophizing may be, this

---

[21] Arne Næss, *Ecology, Community and Lifestyle: Outline of an Ecosophy*, David Rothenberg (trs.) (Cambridge: Cambridge University Press, 1989), 101. Næss's emphasis.

[22] Per Ariansen, *Miljøfilosofi: En innføring* (Oslo: Universitetsforlaget, 1992). Arne Semb-Johansson, Jon Lund Hansen and Ivar Mysterud, *Bred Økologi: En tverrfaglig utfordring* (Oslo: Cappelen, 1993).

[23] Nina Witoszek, "Marx, Næss, og Gaia: Hva skal vi gjøre med kulturen?" *Kontrast*, 122, no. 3/4 (1990), 4–10.

[24] Audun Øfsti (ed.), *Ecology and Ethics: A Report from the Melbu Conference, 18–23 July 1990* (Trondheim: Nordland Akademi for Kunst og Vitenskap, 1992). Gunnar Skirbekk, *Eco-Philosophical Manuscripts* (Bergen: Ariadne, 1992).

[25] Jon Wetlesen, "Value in nature: Intrinsic or inherent?" in Nina Witoszek and Andrew Brennan (eds.), *Philosophical Dialogues: Arne Næss and the Progress of Ecophilosophy* (Boston: Rowman and Littlefield, 1999), pp. 405–17. This article was written in the late 1980s/early 1990s.

thinking did not energize young environmentalists. As Næss later admitted, in Norway, Deep Ecology became "too narrow – [a] kind of sect."[26]

DEEP ECOLOGY GOES GLOBAL

While Deep Ecology dwindled away as an intellectual movement in Norway, Næss enjoyed an intellectual breakthrough internationally. The initial sign of this recognition came in an article by the American sociologist Bill Devall (1938–2009) entitled "The Deep Ecology Movement" (1980). It took Næss's "Summary" from 1973 of his talk in Bucharest as a point of departure (see Chapter 4). In the same vein as Næss and additionally inspired by the historian of ecology Donald Worster, Devall would divide friends from foes by pointing to the legacy of "deep" thinkers, such as Aldo Leopold, Ernst F. Schumacher, George Sessions, Paul Shepard, and Gary Snyder, as opposed to "shallow" managerial ecology.[27] His article might have suffered the fate of most academic writings if it had not been for Dave Foreman who took Devall and Næss's thinking to heart when he, in 1980, founded Earth First! The organization's core principles stated: "Wilderness has a right to exist for its own sake. All life forms, from virus to the great whales, have an inherent and equal right to existence. Humankind is no greater than any other form of life and has no legitimate claim to dominate Earth."[28] These principles became the backbone of a hard-hitting undercover organization that got much attention due to their military-styled radicalism and "ecotage" (as in "sabotage"). Devall and Sessions became the organization's philosophers through the book *Deep Ecology: Living as if Nature Mattered* (1985). It not only endorses Earth First! but also lists the organization's addresses around the world as places to go for readers interested in joining "deep ecology action groups."[29] In the volume Næss is portrayed as Earth First!'s intellectual harbinger, and his Ecosophy

---

[26] Arne Næss, "The shallow and the deep, long-range ecology movements: A summary," in Nina Witoszek and Andrew Brennan (eds.), *Philosophical Dialogues: Arne Næss and the Progress of Ecophilosophy* (Boston: Rowman and Littlefield, 1999), pp. 3–7, note p. 7.

[27] Bill Devall, "The Deep Ecology Movement," *Natural Resources Journal*, 20 (1980), 299–322. Donald Worster, *Nature's Economy: The Roots of Ecology* (San Francisco: Sierra Club Books, 1977).

[28] Dave Foreman, *Earth First Statement of Principles* (ms. Sept. 1980). Republished online at the Environment and Society Portal, Multimedia Library.

[29] Bill Devall and George Sessions, *Deep Ecology: Living as If Nature Mattered* (Salt Lake City: Gibbs Smith, 1985), pp. 257–8. Michael Tobias (eds.), *Deep Ecology* (San Marcos, CA: Avant Books, 1984).

T appears in its first English translation as an appendix at the end of the volume. This was all exciting for Næss, who had found a new audience willing to engage him. Indeed, inspired by these events, Alan R. Drengson started *Trumpeter: Journal of Ecosophy* (1983), a Canadian journal devoted to environmental philosophy in the spirit of Næss. At the time, there was only a limited amount of related material by Næss available in English. As a result, Næss began giving guest appearances in North America and published a string of articles on the topic for his new audience. The most important one was, perhaps, "Deep Ecology and Ultimate Premises" (1988), which laid out the core of his thinking. This included the widely distributed "A Platform for Deep Ecology," which reflected and emulated Foreman's "Statement of Principles" for Earth First!. Næss's platform was published in *The Ecologist,* which portrayed him as "the father of the Deep Ecology movement."[30]

All the attention brought a series of mostly North American environmental philosophers to visit Næss at Environmental Studies in Oslo. Two of them included Peter Reed and David Rothenberg, who, in 1984, had just finished their undergraduate degrees, Rothenberg at Harvard University and Reed at Bowdoin College. Together with Esben Leifsen, they reestablished the Ecophilosophy Group, which had not been active for years. With self-designed stationary, they invited new recruits and reenergized former members. Næss was thrilled, and invited them along for philosophizing while mountaineering, climbing, skiing, and visiting Tvergastein. The result was a well-argued paper by Reed published after his unfortunate death (from an avalanche in Jotunheimen in 1987), and an equally elegant paper by Rothenberg suggesting a platform for Deep Ecology.[31] They both learned Norwegian in the process and set forth translating the reader for the Nature and Humans course, including Peter W. Zapffe's poetic "Last Messiah" (1933), all of which appeared in English as *Wisdom in the Open Air: The Norwegian Roots of Deep Ecology* (1993).[32] While in Norway, Rothenberg also began translating Næss's *Økologi, Samfunn and Livsstil* (Ecology, Community and Lifestyle, 1976), turning Næss's dense idioms into elegant prose. When it

---

[30] Arne Næss, "Deep ecology and ultimate premises," *The Ecologist,* 18, no. 4/5 (1988), 128–31. Edward Goldsmith's editorial description, p. 117.
[31] Peter Reed, "Man apart: An alternative to the self-realization approach, *Environmental Ethics,* 11 (1989), 53–69. David Rothenberg, "A platform of deep ecology," *The Environmentalist,* 7 (1987), 185–90.
[32] David Rothenberg and Peter Reed (trs.) (eds.), *Wisdom of the Open Air: The Norwegian Roots of Deep Ecology* (Minneapolis: University of Minnesota Press, 1992).

appeared in 1989, it was an updated and revised volume relevant to the English-speaking audience and environmental affairs of the 1980s. Rothenberg also published a book-length interview with Næss, which is arguably the best introduction to his thinking.[33]

As Earth First! grew in its radicalism in the 1980s, it came to erode the pluralism and non-violence prized by its parent philosophy. Earth First! took as its mission to defend the Earth from industrial society. It employed methods described in the group's manual, *Ecodefence* (1985), which explains how to destroy defaulters' bulldozers, puncture their car tyres, hack into the databases of their companies, return their executives' pollution to their own gardens, and use a sling to break the windows of people with environmentally destructive lifestyles.[34] Although professing pluralism and non-violence, the organization was run like a guerrilla group ready to destroy in order to prevent destruction. They were concerned about people, but the Earth came first. Some of Foreman's followers became non-compromising ideologists using the Deep Ecology literature to promote ideas that were foreign to Næss. They concluded, for example, that draconian birth-control measures were necessary, and spoke of AIDS as a self-protective reaction of Earth against an overpopulated humanity.[35] They were not alone in these views. The founder of the Gaia theory, James Lovelock, who began engaging the Deep Ecologists in the early 1990s, wrote that humans were "like a disease" threatening to kill Gaia.[36] Soon Deep Ecologists found themselves in debates on whether mass starvation in Ethiopia was a good thing.[37]

The direct association with Earth First! and their green rage made Næss and the Deep Ecologists vulnerable for criticism. After all, members of Earth First! were not inconsistent with his ecophilosophy in their

---

[33] David Rothenberg, *Arne Næss: Gjør det vondt å tenke?* (Oslo: Grøndahl, 1992); *Is It Painful to Think?*
[34] Dave Foreman and Bill Heywood (eds.), *Ecodefence: A Field Guide to Monkeywrenching* (Tucson, AZ: Ned Ludd Book, 1985).
[35] Miss Ann Trophy (attributed to Christopher Manes) "Population and AIDS," *Earth First!* May 1, 1987, 32. Daniel Conner, "Is AIDS the answer to and environmentalist's prayer?" *Earth First!* Dec. 22, 1987, 14–16. Christopher Manes, *Green Rage: Radical Environmentalism and the Unmaking of Civilization* (Boston: Little, Brown and Comp., 1990). Martha F. Lee, *Earth First! Environmental Apocalypse* (New York: Syracuse University Press, 1995).
[36] James Lovelock, *Gaia: The Practical Science of Planetary Medicine* (London: Gaia Books Limited, 1991), pp. 153–5.
[37] Sale Kirkpatrick, "The cutting edge: Deep ecology and its critics," *The Nation*, 246, no. 19 (May 1988), 670–4.

radical approach to society and in arguing that AIDS and starvation could provide a long-term solution for the Earth.[38] The fact that most of the Deep Ecologists were men and that Earth First! had a military macho culture was questioned by an emerging group of eco-feminists. Perhaps the feminists were "deeper than deep ecology" with their gender-based social analysis?[39] Indeed, *How Deep Is Deep Ecology?* wondered another critic in a booklet from 1989, which questioned whether Næss had thought deeply enough about the structure of capitalism and possible Malthusian implications of this philosophy.[40] Næss also had to answer to a "third-world critique" of his ecophilosophy, despite his own self-understanding of being a stern supporter of the Global South.[41] Perhaps most damaging was the anarchist and social political theorist Murray Bookchin, who had a significant following within the US counterculture and beyond. He thought Foreman and the Deep Ecologists advanced "a 'black hole' of half-digested, ill-formed, and half-baked ideas ... a bottomless pit in which vague notions and moods of all kinds can be sucked into the depths of an ideological toxic dump."[42]

As if the criticism from the feminists and social anarchists was not enough, in the mid-1980s, the animal liberation and rights activists also began questioning the Deep Ecologists. The specific issue at stake was Norwegian whaling. The dominating view in Norway was that whaling was an issue of resource management. Jørgen Randers, for example, argued in 1975 that, in order for the hunting "to be sustainable, one will have to keep the catch of whales below a certain annual quota securing their multiplication."[43] Ten years later, the ecologist Arne Semb-Johansson and the physiologist Lars Walløe reiterated the argument, adding that there was a need for "a vigorous programme of research and monitoring."[44]

---

[38] Peder Anker and Nina Witoszek, "The dream of the biocentric community and the structure of utopias," *Worldviews*, 2 (1998), 239–56.
[39] Ariel Kay Salleh, "Deeper than deep ecology: The eco-feminist connection," *Environmental Ethics*, 6, no. 4 (1984), 340–5. Kaul, "Ecofeminism in the Nordic countries."
[40] George Bradford, *How Deep Is Deep Ecology* (Hadley: Themes Change, 1989).
[41] Ramachandra Guha, "Radical American environmentalism and wilderness preservation: A Third World critique," *Environmental Ethics*, 11 (1989), 73–83.
[42] Murray Bookchin, "Social ecology versus deep ecology," *Green Perspectives*, 4/5 (1987), 1–23, quote p. 4.
[43] Randers, *A Quest for Sustainable Society*, p. 1.
[44] Roy M. Anderson, Raymond J. H. Beverton, Arne Semb-Johansson, and Lars Walløe, *The State of the Northeast Atlantic Minke Whale Stock: Report of the Group of Scientists Appointed by the Norwegian Government to Review the Basis for Norway's Harvesting of Minke Whales* (Ås: Økoforsk, 1987), p. 78.

The Deep Ecologists, including Næss, had largely stayed away from the issue as whales were hunted by the rural fishermen-peasants they adored (see Chapter 1). Besides, they were, at heart, mountain climbers with a focus on the high altitude and not so much on what was going on in the ocean. Progressive young radicals were also generally in favor of whalers as they belonged to the idealized group of fishermen-peasants (see Chapter 1). Typically, when students in the early 1990s were served whale meat in the university cantina in Oslo, they would queue up in long lines for a plate in a show of support for whalers whose hunting the international environmentalists had tried to stop. It is telling that when the esteemed American environmental ethicist J. Baird Callicott visited Oslo in 1993 to lay out his well-thought-out criticisms of Norwegian whaling, he had to endure sitting next to an arrogant student of philosophy eating whale meat at a restaurant after his lecture.[45]

International environmentalists were enraged by Norwegian hunting of minke whales in view of the nation's grave history of hunting whales to the brink of extinction, and they began organizing boycotts of the nation's seafood and tourism industry.[46] Greenpeace tried to stop commercial whaling, and the famed ocean activist Paul Watson and his Sea Shepherd organization went as far as to try to sink the whaling boat *Nybræna* in 1992. It was international news, and, according to a *New York Times* article, not of the type the "Green Queen" Prime Minister Brundtland preferred. "It's a completely illogical, irrational wrongly-based campaign" against Norway, she argued, as "sustainable development" to her meant managing resources based on science, not emotions.[47] Most Norwegians would side with Brundtland who, in 1993, registered an objection with the International Whaling Commission's ban on commercial whaling. The common sentiment in Norway was that killing minke whales was similar to that of butchering cows. It was a non-issue as long as the hunt was painless and minke whales were not endangered. Yet it was perfectly

---

[45] J. Baird Callicott, paper at The Ethics Seminar, University of Oslo, Oct. 8, 1993. Published as "Whaling in Sand County: A dialectical hunt for land-ethical answers to questions about the morality of Norwegian minke-whale catching," *Colorado Journal of International Environmental Law and Policy*, 8 (1997), 1–30. I was the student dining with Callicott.

[46] Eugene Linden, "Sharpening the Harpoons" and "Sustainable Follies," *Time*, May 24, 1993, 56–7. D. Graham Burnett, *The Sounding of the Whale: Science and Cetaceans in the Twentieth Century* (Chicago: University of Chicago Press, 2012).

[47] Gro Harlem Brundtland quoted in John Darnton, "Norwegians claim their whaling rights," *New York Times*, Aug. 7 1993, 1.

unclear how painful the hunt actually was to the whales, and even the closest associates of Brundtland had to admit scientific uncertainty with respect to estimations of whale populations,[48] with the joke being that it was like counting Russian submarines. Gradually, as a consequence of these debates, Næss would formulate an opinion against whale hunting, though he would endorse it if it could be proven to be healthy for the ecosystem (i.e. for reducing an overpopulation of whales).[49] These arguments focused on ecology and not the rights or welfare of individual whales. And this distinction was exactly what international animal rights and liberation activists found most troubling. Though whale defenders were unable to halt Norwegian hunting, they did manage to question the Deep Ecologists' self-confidence of being the world's environmental pioneers.

The situation was similar with respect to the yearly slaughtering of harp seal pups which was hardly questioned by the Norwegians discussed in this book, despite head-on resistance from Greenpeace and other international environmental organizations.[50] The Deep Ecologists would, in comparison, be more favorable to the protection of endangered animals such as wolves, beers, wolverines, and lynx, all of which rural farmers in Norway hunt with joy and determination to protect their oversized population of sheep. And these hunts were generally sanctioned and even financially supported by County or State environmental agencies. Næss and the ecologist Ivar Mysterud would defend both wolves and sheep in an article from 1987 in which they argued that both animals possessed intrinsic value as members of a "mixed community."[51] They described the wolves in accordance with the Norwegian political ideal, namely as good social democrats within an ecocentric commune and that they should therefore be protected. Instead of a class/gender power struggle, they postulated a symbiosis of humans, animals, and plants – all of them guaranteed the right to self-realization. The ecocentric community was to be rational and yet compassionate, individualistic and yet

---

[48] Lars Walløe, "Whale numbers in dispute," *Nature*, 362 (April 1, 1993), 389.
[49] Arne Næss, "Om høsting av hval," *Natur og Miljø Bullettin*, July 27, 1992.
[50] Frank Zelko, "Blood on the ice: The Greenpeace campaign against the harp seal slaughter," in Marco Armiero and Lise Sedrez (eds.), *A History of Environmentalism: Local Struggles, Global Histories* (London: Bloomsbury, 2014), pp. 107–27.
[51] Arne Næss and Ivar Mysterud, "Philosophy of wolf policies I: General principles and preliminary exploration of selected norms," *Conservation Biology*, 1, no. 1 (May 1987), 22–34. Næss, "Self-realization in mixed communities of humans, bears, sheep, and wolves."

ecological, creative and yet self-limiting. In effect, they proposed a utopian dream of Biblical proportions (in which "the wolf and the lamb shall graze together"[52]) that overrode the individual rights and welfare of both animals, along with the interest of the rural farmers they idealized.

Næss enjoyed thoughtful criticism, and when he was attacked numerous scholars would rush to the defense of both him and Deep Ecology more generally. They argued that it was not a fundamentalist platform, but instead a respectable philosophy asking deeper questions about our relationship with the environment.[53] The Schumacher College founded in 1990 in the UK, for example, adopted Deep Ecology as its core message, along with the Gaia teachings of Lovelock. Yet the damage was done. The Deep Ecologists were somehow unable to shake off the image of them as raging Earth First!ers roaming the wilderness and carrying out ecotage. As Næss later confessed: "Dave Foreman had been a disaster for Deep Ecology."[54]

OUR COMMON FUTURE

If the Deep Ecologists were struggling after the Alta conflict, Gro Harlem Brundtland, the leader of the Labor Party, did not feel much better about how she had handled her decision. Indeed, many years later, she would look back at the events in Alta with regrets. By 1982 she had effectively won the battle, but had lost the larger war with the Sámi and the Deep Ecologists as she had lost face and credibility as defender of Indigenous rights and the environment. The Bravo oil spill of 1977 would still haunt her, as would the long vicious debate on how to handle acid rain (Chapter 8). The new conservative government that replaced her in the fall of 1981 would gleefully acknowledge the importance of national parks and point to the failures of callous technocratic planners and power-socialists within the Labor Party. She did not take these criticisms lightly.

---

[52] The Bible, Isaiah 65, 25.
[53] Warwick Fox, *Toward a Transpersonal Ecology; Developing new Foundations for Environmentalism* (Boston: Shambhala, 1990). Lawrence E. Johnson, *A Morally Deep World; An Essay on Moral Significance and Environmental Ethics* (Cambridge: Cambridge University Press, 1991). Bolof Stridbeck, *Ekosofi och etik* (Göteborg: Bokskogen, 1994). Alan R. Drengson, *The Practice of Technology: Exploring Technology, Ecophilosophy, and Spiritual Disciplines for Vital Links* (New York: State University of New York Press, 1995).
[54] Personal conversation with Arne Næss, Aug. 20, 1998, quoted with permission. Arne Næss, "Letter to Dave Foreman, 23 June 1988," in Nina Witoszek and Andrew Brennan (eds.), *Philosophical Dialogues* (New York: Rowman and Littlefield, 1999), pp. 227–31.

The opportunity to recast herself as an environmentalist and champion of Indigenous rights came when Brundtland was asked to chair the World Commission on Environment and Development in March 1982. She was told by the Director of the United Nations Environment Programme that she was selected because she was the only person who had been both a Minister of the Environment and a Prime Minister.[55] In Oslo, she mustered a group of experts to whom she could turn for advice on how best to chair the Commission. The group included obvious choices like her former PhD advisor Walløe, the former Minister of Industry, Finn Lied, and the Labor Party's former Deputy Director of the Planning Department in the Ministry of Finance and Professor of Law, Hans Christian Bugge. The long-time member of the Labor Party and ecologist Eilif Dahl (discussed in Chapter 2) was also on the list. More surprising was the choice of Paul Hofseth, the former leader of Environmental Studies who had been a stern opponent of the Alta power plant.[56] A conciliatory move by Brundtland, perhaps, or also a sign that the Deep Ecologist' pragmatist leaning had taken hold.

There is no need to review the history of the Brundtland Commission here, as a recent thorough historical study has covered much of the material.[57] What is significant is that by the 1980s the vision for a "sustainable society" (as described in Chapter 7) began to have a life of its own outside Church circles. One early secular approach was the anthology *The Sustainable Society: Implications for Limited Growth* (1977), which does not refer to religious issues.[58] Lester Brown, the director of the Worldwatch Institute in Washington, introduced "the sustainable society" to a larger audience in 1981.[59] Around the same

---

[55] Gro Harlem Brundtland, *Madam Prime Minister: A Life in Power and Politics* (New York: Farrar, Straus and Giroux, 2002), pp. 191–231.

[56] Gro Harlem Brundtland to Paul Hofseth, March 20, 1985, and June 10, 1986, PH.

[57] Iris Borowy, *Defining Sustainable Development for Our Common Future: A History of the World Commission on Environment and Development (Brundtland Commission)* (London: Routledge, 2014).

[58] Dennis Pirages (ed.), *The Sustainable Society: Implications for Limited Growth* (New York: Praeger, 1977). James C. Coomer (ed.), *Quest for a Sustainable Society* (New York: Pergamon, 1979). Robert D. Holsworth, *Public Interest Liberalism and the Crisis of Affluence: Reflections on Nader, Environmentalism, and the Politics of a Sustainable Society* (Boston: G. K. Hall, 1980).

[59] Lester R. Brown, *Building a Sustainable Society* (New York: Norton, 1981). The term was in intramural use within the institute, as in Erik Eckholm, *The Dispossessed of the Earth: Land Reform and Sustainable Development* (Washington: Worldwatch Institute Report 30, 1979). Lester R. Brown and Pamela Shaw, *Six Steps to a Sustainable Society* (Washington: Worldwatch Institute Report 48, 1982).

time, biologists began using the word "sustainability" as a descriptive term for factual processes in nature.[60] Reports by Brundtland's patron, the United Nations Environment Programme, also used "sustainable development" as the guiding principle for nature conservation and environmental development in Africa in the early 1980s.[61] What is notable in these secular adaptations is that the longing for the Promised Land of harmonious sustainability as a resurrection of the lost Eden, *remained*. What Brundtland did when she made her opening speech for the Commission in Geneva in 1984 was to simply reinvigorate the terminology when arguing that "[p]olicy paths to sustainable development" were "a central concern."[62] Humanity has to "meet ... the needs of the present without compromising the ability of future generations to meet their own needs," as the World Commission would eventually come to define sustainable development in its final report.[63]

Interestingly, in the same opening speech, Brundtland brought global warming to the forefront of the Commission. "Climatic changes induced by rising levels of carbon dioxide" could cause "massive economic and social consequences," she argued.[64] The issue came to Brundtland and the World Commission's attention in May 1984 through one of the World Resource Institute's meetings, which provided a paper for policymaking on changing environmental conditions in the atmosphere, such as the depletion of the ozone layer, greater formations of acid rain, and accumulation of carbon dioxide.[65] As shown in Chapter 8, acid rain and

---

[60] Richard Carpenter (ed.), *Assessing Tropical Forest Lands: Their Suitability for Sustainable Uses* (Dublin: Tycooly International, 1981). Dietrich Knorr (ed.), *Sustainable Food Systems* (Chichester, UK: Ellis Horwood, 1983).

[61] International Union for Conservation of Nature and Natural Resources, the United Nations Environmental Programme, and World Wildlife Fund, *World Conservation Strategy: Living Resource Conservation for Sustainable Development* (New York: IUCN-UNEP-WWF, 1980). United Nations Environmental Programme, *Environment and Development in Africa* (New York: UNEP, 1981).

[62] Gro Harlem Brundtland, "Statement," Opening Session of the Inaugural Meeting of the World Commission on Environment and Development, Geneva, Oct. 1–3, 1984, vol. 39, doc. 3, WC.

[63] World Commission on Environment and Development, *Our Common Future* (Oxford: Oxford University Press, 1987), p. 8.

[64] Brundtland, "Statement," 1984.

[65] Stephen H. Schneider and Starley L. Thompson, "Future changes in the atmosphere," in Robert Repetto (ed.), *The Global Possible: Resources, Development, and the New Century* (New Haven: Yale University Press 1985), pp. 397–430. Bert Bolin (et al.), *The Greenhouse Effect: Climatic Change and Ecosystems* (Chichester: John Wiley, 1986); *A History of the Science and Politics of Climate Change* (Cambridge: Cambridge University Press, 2007), pp. 33–78.

atmospheric politics were familiar terrain for Brundtland, which she preferred discussing to the environment on the ground. Addressing acid rain had served her as a way of forging cooperation in Europe. "International Pact Sought on Acid Rain" was the headline in a newspaper announcing the creation of the "Brundtland Commission" in 1984, in which Brundtland told the press that the European agreement on acid rain "could become the basis for a global agreement" on also other climatic issues.[66] The branding of the Commission with her name was a way of building on her legacy of acid rain diplomacy. Perhaps the problem of climate change in a similar way as acid rain could facilitate world cooperation through the United Nations? Her attention to the issue of climatic change was reinforced through a written submission to the Commission's public hearing in Ottawa in 1986 by the climatologist Kenneth Hare of Trinity College, Canada.[67] What caught Brundtland's interest were not only the catastrophic consequences of climate change; ecological doom was old news to her, as Deep Ecologists for a decade had provided her with a stream of reports on the proximity of a civilizational collapse. Though she was genuinely concerned about ecological issues, the possibility of moving the environmental debate into the scientific domain of climatology was intriguing. Climate studies, it is worth noting, has deep traditions in Norway reaching back to the work of Vilhelm Bjerknes (1862–1951) and the Bergen School of Meteorology, which modernized the science of atmospheric weather and geophysics by the means of mathematical modeling and data analysis.[68] Norway also has a tradition of researching subjects relevant to understand climate change, such as glaciology, the movement of polar ice, and the storage of carbon dioxide in the ocean.[69] There was thus a scientific community in Norway ready to address global warming. Even more importantly, the politics of the atmosphere evoked a political regime that spoke to the patron of the Commission, the United Nations. In the narration of a global future in

---

[66] Pat Orvis, "International pact sought on acid rain," *Winnipeg Free Press*, Mar. 14, 1984, p. 27.
[67] Fredrick Kenneth Hare, "Mandate for Change: The Relevance of Climate," Ottawa, May 26–27, 1986, WC.
[68] Robert Marc Friedman, *Appropriating the Weather: Vilhelm Bjerknes and the Construction of a Modern Meteorology* (Ithaca: Cornell University Press, 1989). Yngve Nilsen and Magnus Vollset, *Vinden dreier: meteorologiens historie i Norge* (Oslo: Scandinavian Academic Press, 2016).
[69] Magnus Vollset, Rune Hornnes, and Gunnar Ellingsen, *Calculating the World: The History of Geophysics as Seen from Bergen* (Oslo: Fagbokforlaget, 2018), pp. 310–17.

the Commission's report, Cheryl Lousley notes, "imagine a world as if outside colonial histories and postcolonial contexts" and socio-political realities on the ground.[70] The problem of global warming had the potential of uniting the world through the United Nations, and the Commission's final report, *Our Common Future* (1987), would thus spell out the dangers of climate change as one of the world's chief environmental challenges.[71] And as a consequence, Brundtland and the Commission would initiate a process that led to the formation of the Intergovernmental Panel on Climate Change in 1988, chaired by the Swedish professor in metrology Bert Bolin (1925–2007).

THE WORLD'S "PIONEER COUNTRY"

Brundtland received a half-hearted applause when she presented *Our Common Future* at home in 1987. The bitterness from Alta was still lingering among environmentalists during her second term as Prime Minister (1986–89). The rights and interests of Indigenous peoples had been mentioned several times in the World Commission's report, and she would follow this up by establishing The Sámi Parliament of Norway for internal self-rule in 1989. Nevertheless, the fact that she would enjoy fame as an environmentalist abroad was understood among the Deep Ecologists as ironic, at best. They did not recognize her, in the words of international press, as a "Norse Goddess" who had successfully "managed to combine feminism and environmental concerns" at home.[72] And when she presented the report at Harvard University with the lecture "The Politics of Oil: A View from Norway," in which she called for "a more equitable distribution of wealth" in the world, it was to the Deep Ecologists just plain political hypocrisy.[73] The initial reactions to *Our Common Future* among ecophilosophers were therefore to ignore

---

[70] Cheryl Lousley, "Narrating a Global Future: Our common future and the public hearings of the World Commission on Environment and Development," in Elizabeth DeLoughrey, Jill Didur, and Anthony Carrigan (eds.), *Global Ecologies and the Environmental Humanities: Postcolonial Approaches* (New York: Routledge, 2015), pp. 245–67.
[71] World Commission, *Our Common Future*, pp. 12, 33–6, 45, 128, 147–50, 242, 245.
[72] Francis X. Clines, "Oslo Journal: New Age of Norse Goddess?" *The New York Times*, Jan. 6, 1987, A4. Kay Longcope, "Norway's Prime Minister of Equality Gro Harlem Brundtland lets her voice be heard," *Boston Globe*, Sept. 22, 1987, p. 69.
[73] Gro Harlem Brundtland, "The politics of oil: A view from Norway," *Energy Policy*, April 1988, 102–9, quote p. 109. Given as the A. J. Meyer Memorial Lecture in International Energy Policy at the John F. Kennedy School of Government at Harvard University, Sept. 21, 1987.

Brundtland and assume that she had not been involved in the formulation of the report or in the writing of her Harvard lecture. Kvaløy Setreng, for example, did not mention her in his review of it, in which he argued that *Our Common Future* supported his own theories about the inevitable ecological collapse of the industrial world.[74] Similarly with Næss, who argued that "sustainability" was another word for ecological self-sufficiency he professed.[75] Brundtland, however, made it perfectly clear in the media that she, as Prime Minister, stood by the report, though few environmentalists took her seriously.

A top priority for Brundtland was to issue a white paper which would flatten criticisms at home that the Labor Party did not care about environmental issues. When the paper was sent for Parliamentary approval, Brundtland, as Prime Minster, put her full force behind it, determined to silence opponents and put both herself and the Labor Party on the environmental offensive. As was the tradition with Parliamentary papers, *Miljø og utvikling* (Environment and Development, 1989), as the white paper was entitled, had an anonymous author, though it was largely written by Hofseth and the biologist Peter Johan Schei under the guidance of the Ministry of the Environment.[76] At the core of the paper was a vision of Norway as *"en pådriver"* ("a driving force") and *"et foregangsland"* ("a pioneer country") for environmental change.[77] Norway was to show the world the path towards a sustainable society, a vision harboring back to Environmental Studies' ecophilosophical idea of Norway being an alternative nation for the world to admire (see Chapter 5). The thought of Norway being a "pioneer country" also reflected the missionary longing that echoed the religious meaning of sustainability once provided by the World Council of Churches (see Chapter 7). Indeed, Brundtland would describe the ethos of the sustainability as "a religious belief."[78] The white paper addressed a host of issues related to *Our Common Future*, such as the importance of protecting biodiversity, public transportation, financial support of developing countries, minimizing acid rain, ending

---

[74] Sigmund Kvaløy Setreng, "*Vår felles framtid* – symptom på katastrofe?" *Nytt fra Universitetet i Oslo*, Nov. 8, 1987, 16–19, UO.

[75] Arne Næss, "Bærekraftig utvikling: En begrepsavklaring," *U-Nytt*, 3 (1990), 8–9.

[76] Paul Hofseth to the author, May 19, 2010, PA.

[77] Ministry of the Environment, *Miljø og utvikling: Norges oppfølging av Verdenskommisjonens rapport*, St. meld. no. 46 (1988–1989) (Oslo: Government Printing, 1989), p. 8, my emphasis.

[78] Gro Harlem Brundtland, "The test of our civilization" (interview), *New Perspectives Quarterly*, 6 (1989), 4–7, quote p. 6.

ozone layer depletion, and protecting the oceans. It also promised to reorganize and strengthen Norway's environmental agencies and, perhaps most exciting for the academic community, to increase research funds. Yet climatic change was at the forefront of *Miljø og utvikling*, labeled as "perhaps the most pressing environmental issue for the 1990s." And Brundtland was determined to do something about it. She asked the Parliament to approve a policy that would "reduce the CO_2 emissions so that they will be stabilized in the 1990s and in year 2000 at the latest." Thereafter, the goal stated, the emissions were to "subside."[79]

The opposition naturally ridiculed the ambition as unnecessary and not founded on scientific facts, with the most vicious attacks coming from Ivan Rosenqvist, whom Brundtland, in 1977, had labeled a "ludicrous swindler" due to his views on the effects of acid rain (see Chapter 8). In 1989 he was shocked by the "ignorance, bluff, and partly dishonest use of data" among climatologists.[80] The underlying issue to him was not poor research, but how climate policies could undermine the industrialization of the nation and the production of petroleum. Rosenqvist had a captivating personality and a significant following. In his footsteps a series of prominent Norwegian scientists argued that anthropogenic climate change was a hoax.[81] This included a stinging critique of global warming research by the Nobel laureate in physics, Ivar Giæver,[82] as well as a plea for more "sobering talk" among climatologists from the same scientists who, back in 1972, had labeled acid rain researchers as "swindlers."[83]

To counter such claims, Brundtland initiated research programs and two new centers: the Centre for Development and the Environment

---

[79] Ministry of the Environment, *Miljø og utvikling*, p. 10.
[80] Rosenqvist, "Den store miljøbløffen." For a parallel history of climate skepticism on the political right, see Naomi Oreskes and Erik M. Conway, *Merchants of Doubt* (New York: Bloomsbury, 2010).
[81] Tom V. Segalstad, "Klimatrusel og dommedagsprofetier," *Aftenposten*, Sept. 5, 1989, RA. Asmunn Moene, "Klimaet sørger naturen selv for," *Aftenposten*, Nov. 11, 1989, 3, RA. Kjetil Haarstad, "Ingen dramatisk drivhuseffekt," *Teknisk ukeblad*, 136, no. 10 (March 9, 1989), 24. Ivar Aanderaa, "Trenger vi mer CO_2?" *Aftenposten*, July 26, 1991, 3, RA. Karl Graf, "Solen bestemmer klimaet," *Teknisk ukeblad*, 138, no. 29 (Aug. 22, 1991), 12–13. Richard H. Westergaard, "Feil front i miljøkampen," *Aftenposten*, June 12, 1992, RA. Zbigniew Jaworowski, Tom V. Segalstad, and N. Ono, "Do glaciers tell a true atmospheric CO_2 story?" *The Science of the Total Environment*, 114 (1992), 227–84. Z. Jaworowski, Tom Segalstad, and V Hisdal, *Atmospheric CO_2 and Global Warming: A Critical Review*, 2nd ed. (Oslo: Norsk Polarinsitutt, 1992).
[82] Knut Dybdahl "Lite imponerende" (interview with Ivar Giæver), *Teknisk ukeblad*, 140, no. 45 (Dec. 9, 1993), 16.
[83] Aksel Lydersen, "Luftforurensninger og edrulig tale," *Afteposten*, June 26, 1989, 5, RA.

(SUM), and a Center for International Climate Environmental Research, Oslo (CICERO). The task of these centers was to provide science to the politicians. They were to research how to realize the idea of "sustainable development" in Norway and beyond, and provide a path for how the nation could become the world's "pioneer country" in this regard. Though officially independent, Labor Party environmental politics would in subtle and not-so-subtle ways frame research agendas at both centers. A portrait of Brundtland hung prominently in the meeting area of SUM (and is indeed still hanging at its Director's office), for example, and the hands-on Chairman of its Board, Bugge, was one of her acolytes. Not only had he been one of her advisors for the World Commission, but, back in 1977, he was one of the principal authors of the Norwegian Official Report that vindicated Brundtland of any responsibility for the Bravo oil spill.[84]

The Centre for Development and the Environment was not created from scratch, but instead absorbed Environmental Studies, which had been the bulwark of Deep Ecology scholar-activism since 1972 (see Chapter 5). As longtime opponents of Brundtland and her environmental policies, its researchers found this reorganization challenging. Soon tensions and disagreements emerged with respect to action research and the role of ecology in envisioning a sustainable future. Should the Center question the deeper foundations of society or simply (as Brundtland thought) generate ecological facts to be used at the political table? Unable to find a clear answer, environmental research at SUM became gradually marginalized by its Chairman. It is telling that when Reed and Rothenberg's translation of the Nature and Humans Course Reader appeared in English in 1993, it was taken off the syllabus in Oslo. Instead of capitalizing on its growing international fame as the intellectual home of Deep Ecology, the Center that absorbed Environmental Studies sought to reinvent itself by focusing on developmental studies of the Global South. During this period, an aging Næss was the only scholar from Environmental Studies who stayed put in his office. To new scholars moving in, he was a charming emblem of the past with a ring of fame surrounding him, suitable for generating funds and public attention.

---

[84] Willy Andersen, Hans Christian Bugge, Dag Meier-Hansen, Oscar Wergeland Branck, and Ståle Eskeland, *Bravoutblåsningen: Aksjonsledelsens rapport*, NOU 57 (Oslo: Universitetsforlaget, 1977).

At the Center for International Climate Environmental Research the story was different.[85] Its first Chairman was Henrik Ager-Hanssen. He had served as Vice Chief Executive (and briefly as Acting Chief Executive) of the all-dominating, state-owned Norwegian oil company Statoil ("state oil") for twenty-four years, and had just stepped down to be the company's chief advisor on corporate greening. His role was to make sure that climate research at CICERO would not question or undermine Norway's booming petroleum industry. Their first Director, Ted Hanisch, was a keen supporter of Brundtland, serving as her Parliamentary Secretary from 1986 to 1989. This close link to the Labor Party and Statoil was not accidental. The aim for CICERO was to envision a way forward where the ambitious Norwegian climate politics could exist in harmony with oil and gas exploitation. Typically, Hanisch would, in one of his first public appearances as CICERO's Director, ridicule Næss and the Deep Ecologists for academic elitism and lack of understanding of the needs of ordinary people, all while avoiding a discussion on whether or not Norway would have to bring production of petroleum to a close due to climate change.[86]

While these new research centers were in the process of establishing themselves, other large research programs began investigating climate change.[87] The Norwegian Research Council for Sciences and the Humanities (NAVF) and the European Science Foundation (ESF) arranged a large conference to kick start such research in Europe. It happened in the Norwegian city of Bergen in 1990 in the context of the Regional Conference addressing the World Commission's *Our Common Future*. Most of Europe's environmental ministers attended the meeting to prepare for the forthcoming 1992 Earth Summit in Rio de Janeiro. Perhaps Europe's environmental leaders could agree on a research path for climate change similar to the Acid Precipitation Program of the 1970s? Creating a coalition of European environmental ministers for sustainability was Brundtland's ambition.[88] Politically, the conference was a disaster, as activists blocked the buses carrying the ministers on their way to the hotel.

---

[85] Anonymous, *CICERO senter for klimaforskning: en evaluering* (Oslo: Norges forskningsråd, 2000).
[86] Ted Hanisch, "Økokrise – fra viten til handling," in Svein Gjerdåker, Lars Gule, and Bernt Hagtvet (eds.), *Den uoverstigelige grense* (Oslo: Cappelen, 1991), pp. 165–73.
[87] Geir O. Braathen *Sluttrapport fra forskningsprogram om klima- og ozon spørsmål 1989–1998* (Oslo: Norwegian Institute for Air Research, 2000).
[88] Gro Harlem Brundtland, "Også rapporter kan være bærekraftige," *U-nytt*, 3 (1990), 30–1.

Ironically, the buses were supposed to showcase the excellent public transportation. The ministers were stuck for more than an hour, while the activists shouted "Bergen meeting talking and eating!," after which the ministers had to run the gauntlet of activists in order to get to their meeting rooms. (The police did not intervene as they were settling scores with local politicians who had accused them of being too violent in an unrelated case.)

Among the 138 scientists attending the conference it was paramount to show that they were not only "talking and eating" but actually contributing. The result was a thick anthology, produced with great speed, in which climatic change was at the forefront. It included conclusions and recommendations for politicians preparing for Rio de Janiero, stating that climate change was real, and that the way forward was in the domain of international law, as well as "cost effective" financial initiatives designed to curb emissions of greenhouse gases.[89]

A SUSTAINABLE CLIMATE

All this was happening while Brundtland's government was in opposition for about a year. The Labor Party would, however, regain power in the fall of 1990. For her third term as Prime Minister (1990–96), she appointed Thorbjørn Berntsen (b. 1935) as the new Minister of the Environment. Known by friends and foes as "The Slugger," he was a man of action, and a clear sign that Brundtland was determined to reach her ambitious goal of making Norway into a pioneer country for the world by stabilizing the country's climate emissions by the millennium. Yet the prospect of curbing the emissions that had looked reasonable in 1989 looked overambitious by 1990. What had changed was the gradual realization that emission reduction was not possible while Norway's oil and gas production was, at the same time, dramatically increasing. How could one increase petroleum production and spur economic growth while at the same time reducing the emissions? Or, in the language of *Our Common Future*, how could one meet "the needs of the present without compromising the ability of future generations?"

Brundtland appointed the leader of the Labor Party's youth wing Jens Stoltenberg (b. 1959) to be the State Secretary at the Ministry of the

---

[89] Anonymous, "Executive summary," in Jostein Mykletun (ed.), *Sustainable Development, Science Policy: The Conference Report* (Oslo: Norwegian Research Council for Science and the Humanities, 1990), pp. 5–16, quote p. 9.

Environment, and "The Slugger" delegated this difficult question to him. At the time, he was thirty-one years old and working for Statistics Norway. He had, back in 1985, completed his *candidatus oeconomices* degree which was specially designed for talented students of macroeconomics. What made the degree stand out was that its students could focus on economics for five years. The Department of Economics, it is worth noting, was the very jewel of the University of Oslo, having produced two former Nobel laureates and with an intense research tradition. It is a department from which historically most of Norway's leading economic bureaucrats had emerged.

Despite their talents, the economists had, since the 1970s, hardly been a productive force with respect to environmental issues. With the Deep Ecologists framing the debate, economists were asked whether or not it was possible to put a monetary value on wilderness (it was not!), and how one could envision an alternative, non-growth, ecologically informed economy.[90] These were large questions, to which the economists provided few answers. Instead, economists tended to reduce environmental issues to the monetary value of natural resources.[91] Things were now changing with the end of the Cold War in 1989 and the general sentiment that capitalism had won over communism. Moreover, there was more of a tradition of mathematical modeling in climate research than in the life sciences, which may also, perhaps, explain why the economists rose to the podium with mathematical solutions to climate change. In any case, Stoltenberg saw in climatic change an opportunity to engage the macroeconomic tradition of the Labor Party with respect to environmental affairs.

Historically, the Department of Economics at the University of Oslo had been filled with dedicated leftists, with John Maynard Keynes as their protagonist and Milton Friedman as their antagonist. Stoltenberg was no exception to this trend. His degree thesis *Makroøkonomisk planlegging under usikkerhet* (Macroeconomic planning under uncertainty, 1985) was about developing an optimal plan for the nation's future oil revenue. Today the thesis is widely accepted as the very architecture of what became the Government Pension Fund of Norway (known as the "oil fund"), which by 2011 evolved into the largest sovereign wealth fund in the world, owning 1.3 percent of the world's

---

[90] Næss, *Økologi, safmunn og livsstil*, pp. 116–75.
[91] Kristin Asdal, *Knappe ressurser? Økonomenes grep om miljøfeltet* (Oslo: Universitetsforlaget, 1998).

traded stocks and shares in addition to large portfolios of fixed-income investments and real estate.[92]

In 1990, Stoltenberg knew what was worth knowing about the past, present, and future of Norway's petroleum economy, and he was a keen proponent of exponential growth of its industry. He was also an outdoor enthusiast (an ardent hiker and cross-country skier), and he did not take environmental issues and climatic change lightly.[93] How could one nurture Norway's oil and gas exploitation while at the same time curbing the world's greenhouse gas emissions? Stoltenberg would bring the question to his former student friends and professors at the Department of Economics, while also including Hanisch and his colleagues from CICERO. Reflecting the end of the Cold War, a growing body of literature on environmental cost–benefit economics had emerged.[94] Drawing on the cost–benefit literature and inspired by the US emissions trading system for sulphur dioxide quotas, they came to the conclusion that the most cost-effective way of reducing greenhouse gases without having to curb oil production would be to introduce a similar system for Europe, and perhaps the entire world. With plenty of money from the oil, Norway could then buy such quotas and reach its millennium goal.

There was only one problem: One would first have to establish an emissions market supported by an international regime. Thanks to the remarkable political petroleum history by Gisle Andersen, Erik Martiniussen, Yngve Nilsen, and Anne Karin Sæther, there is now a viable account of what happened next.[95] In the years leading up to the Rio meeting, Norway engaged in an intense diplomatic campaign led by Stoltenberg's father, Thorvald Stoltenberg, who was Brundtland's Minister of Foreign Affairs. In keeping with the division of labor between scientists and politicians (suggested by Brundtland), the actual traveling

---

[92] Maria Reinertsen, "Oljefondets utspring," *Morgenbladet*, May 22, 2009, RA. Jens Stoltenberg, *Makroøkonomisk planlegging under usikkerhet – en empirisk analyse* (Oslo: Statistics Norway, 1985). Maria Reinertsen, *Ligningen for lykke* (Oslo: Cappelen, 2010), pp. 110–24.

[93] Kjetil B. Alstadheim, *Klimaparadokset: Jens Stoltenberg om vår tids største utfordring* (Oslo: Aschehoug, 2010), pp. 8, 13. Thor Viksveen, *Jens Stoltenberg: Et portrett* (Oslo: Pax, 2011), pp. 243–56.

[94] Samuel Randalls, "Optimal climate change: Economics and climate science policy histories (from heuristic to normative)," *Osiris*, 26 (2011), 224–42.

[95] Nilsen, *En felles plattform*. Erik Martiniussen, *Drivhuseffekten: Klimapolitikken som forsvant* (Oslo: Manifest, 2013). Anne Karin Sæther, *De beste intensjoner: Oljelandet i klimakampen* (Oslo: Cappelen, 2017). Gisle Andersen, *Parlamentets natur: Utviklingen av norsk miljø- og petroliumspolitikk* (Oslo: Universitetsforlaget, 2017).

was done by professional diplomats, mostly his Deputy Secretary Kåre Bryn assisted by Harald Dovland and Jostein Leiro. They were met with much resistance in European countries who argued that Norway should perhaps curb its own emissions instead of buying the achievement of others. The reception was not much better in newly industrialized countries such as India, Thailand, and Malaysia. When Brundtland traveled to Rio de Janeiro with her delegation to promote the idea, she too failed to convince the world about the virtue of carbon emissions trading. What was achieved was a Framework Convention on Climate Change that established a diplomatic way forward toward a 1997 meeting in Kyoto. The world's delegates at the Earth Summit had widely diverse opinions about how to achieve sustainable development, and agreed, consequently, on a Convention on Biological Diversity.

Back in Oslo they realized that they would have to muster support from the Global South. Without these votes they would have no chance at getting acceptance for emission trading in the upcoming meeting in Kyoto. The following year Norwegian diplomats consequently spent time trying to convince the leaders of the world's poorest nations about the value of carbon emissions trading. What they put forward was a system where a rich country would introduce a carbon-clean development initiative in a poor country and get credit for that in their carbon account at home. For example, if Norway installed solar cells in sunny Burkina Faso, they could get carbon emissions credit for the project in Norway. To prove their sincerity, Norway actually did install solar cells in Burkina Faso. Between 1992 and 1997 Norway undertook numerous projects like these, mostly in the Global South, mustering support for what would be called Clean Development Mechanism or CDM.

CDMs would mean business in Norway, as one of the nation's more obscure industries is certifications provided by Det Norske Veritas (DNV), which is one of the three largest classification companies in the world (the others being Lloyd's Register and the American Bureau of Shipping). With more than 10,000 employees, DNV is a voice to be reckoned with in a small nation. For them, the verification of emissions cuts, carbon equivalents, and the Clean Development Mechanisms paved the way for their employees to engage in environmentalism. Every CDM project would have to be researched and certified, and doing so meant corporate greening of a business closely associated with shipping and petroleum industries. Stoltenberg visited the DNV headquarters and promised jobs, and appeared in their intramural news bulletin. He would later take pride in having helped DNV to become the largest CDM certifier in the world, with about half of the global market certified through DNV. Though never a highly profitable business, DNV was a leader of such certifications until 2014 when the market for CDMs collapsed.[96]

By 1997, Norway had secured a majority vote from the Global South with the help of CDM test projects, and Norwegian diplomats were confident when they arrived in Kyoto. In United Nations international agreements every vote is equal, whether you represent the United States or Antigua, Belize, and Guyana (the last three being allies of Norway). As a result, in Kyoto, countries committed to reducing greenhouse gas emissions. They could do so in different ways: at home, by trading carbon dioxide equivalent quotas, and by buying clean development mechanism certificates. Soon, the European Union established a market for emissions trading, and the certification industry began issuing purchasable CDMs based on projects mostly located in Asia and the Global South. As a significant buyer in these new markets, Norway could comply with the Kyoto protocols. Over the years, the purchasing of emission quotas and development certificates came at a significant financial cost.[97] Yet to understand this endeavor only in terms of economic efficiency would be to miss the point, as there is a long tradition for paying indulgences in a nation dominated by Christian moral codes. What was most important to the Labor Party environmentalists was to showcase Norway as a virtuous "pioneer country" to its own citizens and the world. Promoting "sustainable development" was, as this book has shown, a secular expression for a religious call to prepare the ground for the Promised Land. And it was all paid for by the very cause of climatic change – petroleum.

---

[96] Alstadheim, *Klimaparadokset*, p. 207. DNV-GL, "DNV GL is ceasing to provide validation and verification services for CDM" (company announcement), Feb. 14, 2014, dnvgl.com. Gard Paulsen (et al.), *Building Trust: The History of DNV, 1864–2014* (Oslo: Dinamo Forlag, 2014), pp. 263–4. I am grateful to Gard Paulson and John Peter Collett for comments.

[97] Håken Torfinn Karlsen, *The Cost of Participating in the Greenhouse Gas Emission Permit Marked* (Oslo: Statistics Norway, 2014).

The Alternative Nation

"It is in the wilderness that the line must be drawn; there we must begin to build a wall of silence around those values in nature that die when they are taken by force, and that unfold their deepest wonders only in the still hour of prayer."[1] The philosopher Petter W. Zapffe's words, written after having climbed the steep Stetind Mountain in 1937, would ring true to the Deep Ecologists discussed in this book. Indeed, many of them would conduct a yearly pilgrimage to Stetind in the north of Norway to honor Zapffe with an outdoor seminar on how to stop the troubling eco-crisis.

This book has discussed the ways in which nature in the periphery – both the metaphorical and real Stetind – became a moral and political place of resistance to environmental ruin. The Norwegian culture of outdoor life, literally "free-air-life," in remote areas framed what was considered good and morally superior. To do what is good presupposes knowledge about what is right, and what was deemed right was a life situated remotely, as in the mountains, among rural fishermen-peasants, or in a bucolic village in Nepal. The power of the periphery in these places lay in scholar-activists seeing them as sites of self-sufficient ecological harmony, and thus they were viewed as having a moral quality that could offer emancipation and redemption to the environmental offender who lived in the polluted center. At the local level, the ills took place in the neighboring factory town or city, especially Oslo, while at the global level the remote and pristine Norway became the solution for a world in crisis. It was a bi-polar mode of argumentation typical for the Cold War, which

---

[1] Petter W. Zapffe, "Stetind" (1937), in *Essays og epistler*, pp. 56–61, quote p. 56. Translated and quoted in Reed and Rothenberg (eds. trs.), *Wisdom in the Open Air*, p. 37.

challenged participants in ecological debates to take a definitive either/or stand, such as either building or not building a hydropower dam or endorsing either a "deep" or "shallow" ecological point of view.

The Stetind Mountain was one of many examples of the power of the periphery. The ocean explorer Thor Heyerdahl found his environmental "paradise" (his word) on the Pacific island of Fatu-Hiva, where he pursued an idealized Stone Age type of living with his wife. Their life on the island became his personal Archimedean point from which he could evaluate the environmental ills of the world. A similar experience occurred with the archeologist and explorer Helge Ingstad, who, in his books and lectures about living with First Nations people in Canada, portrayed a nobler way of existing with nature than that of urbanized Western lifestyles. Such romanticisms were foreign to the anthropologist Fredric Barth, who introduced methodological ecology to Norway in the 1950s for the purpose of studying people living in the periphery. Yet Barth's students used his methodology to generate studies that idealized Norwegian rural fishermen-peasants while denigrating urban life in the city. The imagined or real fishermen-peasants were ecologically self-sufficient and they were viewed as admirable in comparison to those who faced the ills of industrialization. Being able to grasp both the remote and the near allowed a worldly ecological reasoning, as in the case of Heyerdahl's promotion of the United Nations or Barth's universalization of his studies of the people of Swat in North Pakistan.

The simple life in the imagined, physical, or historical remote space evokes a deep-seated Norwegian cultural trope, namely the allure of a life lost. "Soon Norway will not have any farmers and fishermen left," the biologist Dag Hessen notes, "yet we are still a land of farmers and fishermen."[2] The worldwide bestselling fishermen's tale, *Shark Drunk* (2017), about catching large sharks in the pristine Norwegian arctic archipelago of Vesterålen, captures the allure of remote and pristine places well.[3] The Austrian logician Ludwig Wittgenstein's remote cottage deep in the Norwegian fjords has captivated the nation's philosophers as the most appropriate site for true thinking, philosophical pilgrimage, and inauguration, culminating with its restoration in 2019. Less highbrow but equally telling is that the quaint art of chopping, stacking, and drying of firewood can capture the imagination of the nation, with a book on the topic selling a

---

[2] Dag Hessen, *Landskap i endring* (Oslo: Pax, 2016), p. 7.
[3] Morten A. Strøksnes, *Shark Drunk: The Art of Catching a Large Shark from a Tiny Rubber Dinghy in a Big Ocean* (New York: Knopf, 2017).

remarkable half a million copies along with a highly popular six hour "slow TV" show on how to maintain a crackling fireplace.[4] Another best-selling example is a novel by Roy Jacobsen, *The Invisible* (2013), which tells the story about the lives of self-sufficient fishermen-peasants on a remote coastal island in the 1920s.[5] It taps into deep-seated ideas of Norwegian heritage and longings for a simpler time that has been lost. Historically, the powers of such peripheries have spurred archconservative imaginations, as in the case of Knut Hamsun's *Growth of the Soil* (1917), or left-leaning dreams of ecological self-sufficiency, as in the case of the scholar-activists discussed in this book. In both instances, the imagined or real life in the periphery has represented what is good and thus what people living in the center should admire and strive for.

Accordingly, the High Mountain Ecology Research Station at the remote mountains of Finse was where ecology, as a biological field in Norway, was formed. The Station was located in the periphery, at the heart of outdoor mountaineering. Ecological sciences in Norway grew out of a culture in which nature was understood not as a place of work, but as a place for outdoor vacationing and recreation. The ecologists understood the landscape to be in ecological balance, and juxtaposed it with the unbalanced industrialized environments down in the valleys or in the cities. What one should strive for, they argued, was a steady-state nation which the world could admire, inspired specifically by the steady-state ecology of Finse and the nearby Hardangervidda. The Station became one of the largest ecological research stations in Europe and the chief Norwegian contribution to the International Biological Program. The 1962 translation of Rachel Carson's *Silent Spring* propelled the program forward, which was active between 1964 and 1974 and financially supported over 200 graduate students and scholars.

The philosophers were impressed with the ecologists and they began formulating their own ecophilosophies inspired by the ecologists' work. At the very peak of the Hallingskarvet Mountain, next to Finse, the philosopher Arne Næss built a cottage and a shed for technical climbing and thinking. Here he and his mountaineering friends formulated a philosophy of respect for nature from which people in the industrial lowlands should hear. At the University of Oslo they created The Ecophilosophy Group, chaired by a charismatic philosopher Sigmund Kvaløy. The Group came to

---

[4] NRK/Netflix, *National Firewood Night*, 2013. Lars Mytting, *Norwegian Wood: Chopping, Stacking, and Drying Wood the Scandinavian Way* (New York: Abrams Image, 2015).
[5] Roy Jacobsen, *The Invisible* (London: MacLehose, 2017).

frame environmental debate in binary terms: either you supported the Life Necessities Society or you supported the Industrial Growth Society. The former was inspired by the traditional Norwegian rural life of fishermen-peasants in the periphery which was viewed as worth striving for, while the latter was the society most people were actually living in but should abandon. His arguments evoked a Lutheran pietist condition of guilt necessary for offering an ecological awakening and redemption for the environmental activist. The ecophilosophers' most formative experience and initiation was their attempt in 1970 to save the Mardøla waterfall from hydro-development through civil disobedience, an experience that led to the formation of the Deep Ecology movement.

The Sherpa community in the remote village of Beding in Nepal became the prime model for the ecophilosophers, who saw their lifestyle as being in true harmony with nature. The Sherpa became the Oriental oracles of ecological wisdom worth admiring, in contrast to the Occidental horror and futility of the Western industrial society. As a consequence, Sherpa life was to be a model for all Norwegians, and, in turn, the Sherpa-informed Norwegians were to be a model for Europe and the world. If Norway could return to the country's traditional fisherman-peasant culture it could eventually become more like the society of the Sherpa and thus serve as an alternative nation from which the rest of world could learn. It was a radical vision of the nation evolving into an ecological self-sufficient lodestar for the world instead of joining the industrial and economic growth-driven European Community. The Deep Ecology movement adopted this vision and progressively evolved into a fairly large organization of hundreds of devoted vocal scholar-activists. They knew right from wrong, and used every opportunity to argue that the ecological steady-state society they envisioned was not an herbal-tea party, but a revolutionary break with industrial growth.

The focus of ecologists, as well as mountain-climbing ecophilosophers, on the periphery of the high altitude may explain why protecting the oceans was not at the forefront of Norwegian nature conservation, despite the country having the world's second longest coastline (with Canada having the longest). The lack of questioning of whaling surely puzzled foreign activists, while the harvesting of seaweed may serve as an example of an issue nearly everyone ignored.[6] Though there was some serious

---

[6] Sophia Efstathiou and Bjørn K. Myskja, "Appreciation through use: How industrial technology articulates an ecology of values around Norwegian seaweed," *Philosophy and Technology* (2018), 1–20.

questioning in the 1970s of the petroleum industry's activities in the North Sea, the environmental health of the ocean, dumping of waste, salmon aquaculture, butchering of harp seal pups, or the interests of whales hardly rose to the forefront of the debate.

Tellingly, the Deep Ecology scholars who established Environmental Studies as a discipline in Norway sent students who needed to develop the right ecological state of mind to the scenic Hardangervidda mountain plateau near Finse for a mandatory course trip. The field of Environmental Studies had an interdisciplinary focus held together by an ecophilosophical vision for students trained and fluent in ecological self-sufficiency. Environmental Studies became an influential hotbed for ecologically informed scholarship advising both Norway and the world on what to do about the ecological crisis and how to fundamentally rethink the human relationship to the natural world. It was perhaps the first academic institution in Europe on the topic, and they attracted scholars and students concerned about the globalization of pollution, the damaging aspects of industrialization, callous technocratic positivist research, human population growth, and the need to ground environmentalism in ecological principles. Their questioning of economic growth, technocracy, and industrialism was informed by the ideas of populist agrarian socialism, which placed greater value on rural communities and traditional lifestyles.

The spiritual life of Norwegians often takes place outdoors in scenic environments rather than inside churches or buildings, and ecologically informed scholars thus came to use religious language and traditions when thinking about the environment. The Deep Ecologists were appealing to deep-seated pietist Christian traditions in Norway, and the all-dominating Evangelical Lutheran Church of Norway responded favorably to their call to save nature. Deep Ecology represented to them a new pietism invoking age-old Lutheran values and systems of belief. The result was an overall greening of church life and attempts to drive the Lutheran Church in a more eco-religious direction. In subsequent events, secular Norwegian economic policies of purchasing carbon emissions quota and clean development mechanisms came to reflect Christian codes of paying indulgences.

One of the main targets of the Deep Ecologists was the "shallow" Norwegian co-author of *The Limits to Growth* (1972), Jørgen Randers, who at the time was a graduate student at the Sloan School of Management at the Massachusetts Institute of Technology. His PhD was financed by the ecumenical movement, and he therefore included religious leaders as advisors for his PhD. Randers coined the phrase "the ecologically sustainable society" to describe an environmental-friendly life within environmental limits, and church leaders began using the phrase in their outreach to non-believers as a secular expression of their longing for a Golden Age. Sustainability as understood by theologians within the World Council of Churches captured the Biblical promise of the second coming of Eden. Randers was sympathetic to this interpretation, and upon returning to Oslo in 1974, advocated for sustainable development as a gradualist (as opposed to revolutionist) path to the ecological self-sufficient society the Deep Ecologists envisioned. He would struggle to find a platform for such thinking in Norway, with the exception of environmentally concerned members within the Labor Party seeking a gradualist approach to ecological debates.

One of them was Gro Harlem Brundtland, who, in her capacity as Minister of the Environment between 1974 and 1979, faced environmental activists and Deep Ecologists in various debates. As a medical doctor, she took a strictly anthropocentric stand against those claiming to speak on behalf of nature, arguing that only human bureaucratic rules should be heeded. Yet she also represented the younger generation of Labor Party members who were eager to rethink the Party's policies and traditions, especially with respect to environmental issues and the use of natural resources. She resisted the polarization of ecological debate and sought a middle-ground approach to environmental affairs. And, unlike the Deep Ecologists, she insisted on a genuine engagement between Norway and the European Community in order to solve environmental issues. Her test case was international diplomatic and scientific cooperation to address the problem of acid rain.

The discovery of petroleum in the North Sea in 1969 would, in the decades that followed, gradually transform Norway into a nation financially dependent on oil and gas. This sparked debates about how best to manage these natural resources and use the new wealth. The geologists took the lead, and chief among them was Ivan Th. Rosenqvist. In contrast to Randers, he was optimistic with respect to the quantity of natural resources and on the importance of economic growth. As a representative of the radical left, he thought using petroleum would be to the benefit of the workers of the world. Environmental problems, such as acid rain, were to him minor issues in comparison to the importance of lifting people out of poverty. He would hold on to these anti-environmentalist opinions to the very end, even when mounting evidence necessitated revising his stance on acid rain and climate change. He became a thorn in the side of not only radical Deep Ecologists, but also Brundtland during her attempts to negotiate international solutions to the problem of acid rain.

In 1982, the Deep Ecologists gave up trying to halt the construction of the Alta-Kautokeino River power plant in the midst of Sámi territory, ending the bitterest environmental and civil rights conflict in the nation's history. This also meant an end to Deep Ecology as a political movement in Norway. Paradoxically, they had their international breakthrough during this period, thanks to the US-based radical environmental organization Earth First! The tensions and conflicts between the more fundamentalist Deep Ecologists and the moderate reformers within the Labor Party fizzled out with the moderates having claimed the victory. The activists and the Sámi had failed to save the Alta River, but they forced Brundtland to take Indigenous civil rights and environmental issues more seriously, something that she did as Chair for the World Commission on Environment and Development. In the Commission's report, *Our Common Future* (1987), the sustainable society Randers had imagined became a vision everyone should strive for, while "sustainable development" was the path worth struggling for in order to achieve that distant goal. In effect, the Commission adopted the language that the World Council of Churches had developed back in the 1970s in order to disperse a secular expression of the Christian gospel about preparing for the resurrection of Eden. Sustainable development was, in effect, a gradualist approach to reach the self-sufficient ecological harmony that the Deep Ecologists envisioned and longed for. The periphery – the life at Finse and that of the Sherpa – had become the model and the revelation the entire world should strive for when seeking "sustainable development" that would ultimately lead to the sustainable society.

The *Our Common Future* report also turned the environmental debate in Norway away from ecology toward climate change and climatology. Building on her experience in atmospheric pollution diplomacy with respect to acid rain in Europe, Brundtland mobilized the United Nations to address climatic change at the Earth Summit in Rio de Janeiro, in 1992, by establishing the Framework Convention on Climate Change. At home, as the country's Prime Minister, she envisioned Norway as "a driving force" and a "pioneer country" for sustainable development in the world. Norway was to show the world the path toward a sustainable society by addressing climate change head-on. In the aftermath of the Cold War, propelled forward by the sentiment that capitalism had won over communism, Brundtland and her delegation to the Earth Summit framed the solution to climate change in cost–benefit terms. Her advisor, the economist Jens

Stoltenberg, sought to implement her vision by advocating for the climate economics of carbon emissions trading at the Kyoto conference in 1997 and later as the United Nations Special Envoy on Climate Change.

Both Brundtland and Stoltenberg had, in effect, adopted the Deep Ecologists' plea from the 1970s for making Norway into an environmentally friendly alternative nation for the world to admire. The concept of being an environmental "pioneer country" was an integral part of the government's general foreign policy of turning Norway into a "humanitarian superpower" and thus mobilizing Norway as a strong player for the good in a troubled world.[7] Norway's "pioneer" environmental policy would put the country on the diplomatic scene by empowering its politicians to take the lead in international negotiations and portraying the country as the world's environmental leader.

The do-gooding environmental gaze on the world did not necessarily lead to sound environmental policies at home. A leading Norwegian environmental ethicist rightly notes that "there is very little to be proud about" with respect to environmental protection in Norway.[8] The high ideals of sustainability may, at best, have captured the longings of the nation, though the ideals would not easily transfer into practical politics or behavior of everyday life. The pushback from the powers of the center was also significant, as in the case of Rosenqvist and his followers who argued against environmental protection and thought of climate change as a scientific hoax. This book should not be taken as evidence to gloss over the fact that Norwegian anti-environmentalism has been significant: the hunting of whales, harp seal pups, wolves, beers, wolverines, and lynx, the dumping of toxic mining waste in the fjords, the overfishing, the pollution from salmon aquaculture, the use of snowmobiles, the industrial farming, the hydropower dams, the commercialization of nature reserves, and, more recently, the building of windmills and electric transmission grids in pristine nature. Not to mention the day-to-day politic of pumping as much petroleum as possible up from the ocean floor despite knowing that this would contribute to environmental ills and climatic change. Given the long list of grievances, it is not surprising that the next generation of ecophilosophers is equally as upset about current environmental affairs as those discussed in this book.[9]

---

[7] Tvedt, *Det internasjonale gjennombruddet* (Oslo: Dreyer, 2017).
[8] Arne Johan Vetlesen, *The Denial of Nature: Environmental Philosophy in the Era of Global Capitalism* (London: Taylor and Francis, 2015), p. x.
[9] Trond Gansmo Jacobsen, *Økofilosofi* (Oslo: Fagbokforlaget, 2007).

With respect to international policies, the do-gooding gaze did not necessarily mean that Norway treated the world outside its borders with environmental respect. In the shadow of sustainability diplomacy, the political and financial interests of the nation would take the lead. In Antarctica, Norway has portrayed itself as a champion of good environmental stewardship, yet these conservation efforts reflected the very moral limits to Norwegian territorial claims.[10] The state's petroleum company, Statoil, recently changed its name to Equinor to signal a shift in a greener direction, sold its holdings in the polluting Canadian tar sands, and began investing in offshore wind power. These initiatives have taken the center stage in the company's self-fashioning, while Equinor has, at the same time, increased its petroleum production, thanks to oilfields in Algeria, Angola, Azerbaijan, Brazil, Canada, Nigeria, and more, not to mention the company's drilling in the vulnerable Barents Sea in the Arctic. The investments in sustainability look shallow, for example, to the many foreign environmentalists protesting Equinor's deep-sea drilling plans in the Great Australian Bight. What did generate debate at home was the major pollution disaster in 2018 caused by Norsk Hydro's alumina refinery in Brazil, of which the Norwegian State owns roughly one third. The recent public outcry came despite the fact that the Norwegian aluminum industry has been the cause of dire environmental and social tragedies in the Amazonas reaching back to 1970s.[11] The sentiment of Norwegians as being the world's environmental do-gooders has allowed its many companies and ventures abroad to operate largely out of sight.

Indeed, the self-fashioning as the world's green do-gooders has hindered a reality check with respect to discussing the nation's international environmental endeavors. To follow the money of a rich nation on an environmental mission of bettering the world may not lead to the green results imagined, as in the case of the large funds used to purchase Clean Development Mechanism certificates.[12] And it is hard to find critical literature about the international investments of the nation's prime owner of "green" hydroelectric power, Statkraft ("state power"). Their various developments in the pristine wilderness of countries like Nepal, India, Brazil, Chile, and Peru have hardly been questioned in Norway.

---

[10] Alejandra Mancilla, "The moral limits of territorial claims in Antarctica," *Ethics and International Affairs*, 32, no. 3 (2018), 339–60.

[11] Dan Børge Akerø, *Norge i Brasil: Militærdiktatur, folkemord og norsk aluminium* (Oslo: Aschehoug, 1979).

[12] Martiniussen, *Drivhuseffekten: Klimapolitikken som forsvant*.

The point is not to insinuate that some dark troubling untold stories are hidden here, but instead to note that the Norwegian self-understanding of being environmentally good to the world hinders critical investigations into what is actually going on. Norway's $2.6 billion contribution to the International Climate and Forest Initiative to save the world's tropical rainforests may serve as an exception that proves the rule. In a rare move by the Office of the Auditor General, the initiative was evaluated as being largely ineffective and unsatisfactory due to corruption and fraud.[13] Yet the fact that good intentions don't always lead to good results hardly upset Norwegian environmentalists, as the power of the periphery is a system of belief.

While Norwegians imagined their country as a microcosm setting the environmental standards for the world, it was the high ideals of mountains and the imagined life of self-sufficient fishermen-peasants that would set the standard at home. The power of this periphery was largely a social construction of science-activists living in the urban center. As Kari Marie Norgaard has shown, the actual life of those living in the small-town Norwegian countryside is far from ecologically self-sufficient with people living in denial about climate change.[14] Yet a constant stream of feel-good sentiments in their direction is coming from urban environmentalists with a longing for the periphery. Vacationing in mountain and fjord cottages is still a key component of Norwegian social life, with people, in effect, living a dual life in the nation's periphery and center, which causes tensions with respect to social identity, taxation, and democratic participation.[15] It is this particular tension that this book has investigated, showing the ways in which both imagined and real life in the periphery would shape environmental policies in the center.

Today, activists reminiscent of the scholar-activists discussed in this book make up the small Green Party in Norway. In Oslo they are in a power-broker position and have managed to enforce an environmental regime that is not symbolic, leading up to the city being awarded the European Green Capital of 2019. They aim at turning Oslo, by 2030, into the first carbon-neutral city in the world. By speaking truth to power,

---

[13] The Norwegian Parliament allocated during the period 2008–2017 a total of NOK 23.5 billion to the initiative. Riksrevisjonen, *The Office of the Auditor General of Norway's Investigation of Norway's International Climate and Forest Initiative* (Bergen: Fagbokforlaget, 2019), 7–8.
[14] Kari Marie Norgaard, *Living in Denial: Climate Change, Emotions and Everyday Life* (Cambridge, MA: MIT Press, 2011).
[15] Olav Norheim, "Det gløymde folket," *Syn og segn*, 123:3 (2017), 47–53.

Green Party leaders have made it clear that they "don't want to support a government that continues to explore new oil. That would be hypocrisy."[16] Standing up in this way to the nation's powerful petroleum lobby has led the Parliament to decide that the massive Government Pension Fund of Norway should divest from fossil fuels and invest more in renewable energy. This decision was picked up by major news outlets and environmental NGOs around the world. "Huge huge huge win" for the divest movement, the founder of 350.org, Bill McKibben, tweeted to a largely American audience fed up with President Donald Trump's environmental policies.[17] As it turns out, the fine print of the Norwegian divestment plan was murky. Yet in the divided climate politics of the USA, which are framed by binaries similar to those of the Cold War, it was a beacon of good news and an example to admire for Green New Deal advocates. Using its position as the European Green Capital and representing an example to follow for fossil fuel divesting, Norwegian politicians tapped into a tradition, described in this book, of seeking to shine as the world's green do-gooders. The power of the periphery is what allowed Norway to emerge as an environmental pioneer for the world.

[16] Lan Marie Nguyen Berg, Deputy Mayor of Transport and Environment in Oslo, quoted in Jonathan Watts, "Norway's push for Arctic oil and gas threatens Paris climate goals," *The Guardian*, Aug. 10. 2017.
[17] Bill McKibben, *Twitter* @billmckibben, Mar. 8, 2019.

Bibliography

All translations, unless otherwise noted, are by the author.

MANUSCRIPT COLLECTIONS

AN   Arne Næss Archive, Centre for Development and the Environment, University of Oslo.
HH   Hjalmar Hegge's Press Clip Archive, held at PA.
LS   Norwegian University of Life Sciences Library Archive, Ås.
NB   The National Library of Norway. (Nationalbiblioteket, Oslo.)
PA   Author's Personal Archive.
PH   Paul Hofseth's Personal Archive.
RA   The National Archives of Norway. (Riksarkivet, Oslo.)
SD   System Dynamics Group Literature Collection, MIT.
UO   University of Oslo's Press Clip Archive.
WC   World Commission on Environment and Development Archive, IDRC Digital Library.

Aardal, Bernt, "Nordmenns holdninger til miljøvern," in Bjørn Alstad (ed.), *Norske meninger 1946–93* (Oslo: Sigma, 1993), pp. 583–620.
Aarek, Hans Eirik, "Gresk naturoppfatning og vitenskap," in Paul Hofseth (ed.), *Økofilosofisk lesebok*, vol. 2. (Oslo: Samarbeidsgruppa for natur og miljøvern, 1974), ms. 20 pages.
   Kristendom og økologi (Ås: Kvekerforlaget, 1978).
Abrahamsen, Gunnar, Finn H. Brække, et al. (eds.), *Impact of Acid Precipitation on Forest and Freshwater Ecosystems in Norway: Summary Report on the Research Results from Phase 1 (1972–1975) of the SNSF-Project* (Oslo: Sur nedbørs virkning på skog og fisk, 1976).
Abrecht, Paul, "An ecumenical vision of the future," *Anticipation*, 18 (1974), 3–6.

"Science and technology for human development – The ambiguous future and the Christian hope," *Study Encounter*, 10 (1974), 1–2.
Akerø, Dan Børge, *Norge i Brasil: Militærdiktatur, folkemord og norsk aluminium* (Oslo: Aschehoug, 1979).
Allee, Warder C., Alfred E. Emerson, Orlando Park, Thomas Park, and Karl P. Schmidt, *Principles of Animal Ecology* (Philadelphia: W. B. Saunders Co., 1949).
Alnæs, Finn, *Svart snø eller samvern: Dokumentarbok fra en brytningstid* (Oslo: Aschehoug, 1976).
Alstadheim, Kjetil B., *Klimaparadokset: Jens Stoltenberg om vår tids største utfordring* (Oslo: Aschehoug, 2010).
Amble, Erling, *Avfallsbehandling og planlegging* (Oslo: Arkitekthøgskolen i Oslo, 1973).
"Kineserne og økologien," *(snm) nytt*, 7 (Sept. 1977), 20–2.
Amble, Erling, and Henning Hansen, *Det kapitalistiske boligproblemet* (Oslo: Arkitekthøgskolen i Oslo, 1970).
Amnesty International, *Annual Report 1972–1973* (London: Amnesty International, 1973).
Annual Report 1973–1974 (London: Amnesty International, 1974).
Andersen, David, et al., "How the System Dynamics Society came to be: A collective memoir," *System Dynamics Review*, 23, no. 2/3 (2007), 219–27.
Andersen, Finn Mørch, et al., *Om olje, vett og vern* (Trondehim: NTH, 1974).
Andersen, Gisle, *Parlamentets natur: Utviklingen av norsk miljø- og petroliumspolitikk* (Oslo: Universitetsforlaget, 2017).
Andersen, J. A.,"Våre jordressurser: Dagens vekstkurve tilsier termisk ubalanse om 50 år," *Teknisk ukeblad*, 118, no. 36 (1971), 15–18, 23.
Andersen, Rune Frank, and Tom-Olaf Norheim Kjær, *Esso-Raffineriene ved Slagentangen og Valløy og deres betydning for Tønsberg-distriktet* (Bergen: Norges Handelshøyskole, 1976).
Andersen, Willy, Hans Christian Bugge, Dag Meier-Hansen, Oscar Wergeland Branck, and Ståle Eskeland, *Bravoutblåsningen: Aksjonsledelsens rapport*, NOU 57 (Oslo: Universitetsforlaget, 1977).
Anderson, Roy M., Raymond J. H. Beverton, Arne Semb-Johansson, and Lars Walløe, *The State of the Northeast Atlantic Minke Whale Stock: Report of the Group of Scientists Appointed by the Norwegian Government to Review the Basis for Norway's Harvesting of Minke Whales* (Ås: Økoforsk, 1987).
Andersson, Axel, *A Hero for the Atomic Age: Thor Heyerdahl and the Kon-Tiki Expedition* (Oxford: Peter Lang, 2010).
Anker, Peder, "Arne Næss sett utenfra," *Samtiden*, 4 (2002), 4–19.
"Buckminster Fuller as Captain of Spaceship Earth," *Minerva*, 45 (2007), 417–34.
"Den store økologiske vekkelsen som har hjemsøkt vårt land," in *Universitetet i Oslos historie*, vol. 7 (Oslo: Unipub, 2011), pp. 103–71, 461–79.
Imperial Ecology: Environmental Order in the British Empire, 1895–1945 (Cambridge, MA: Harvard University Press, 2001).
"Science as a vacation: A history of ecology in Norway," *History of Science*, 45 (2007), 455–79.

"The call for a new EcoTheology in Norway," *Journal for the Study of Religion, Nature and Culture*, 7, no. 2 (2013), 187–207.
Anker, Peder, and Nina Witoszek, "The dream of the biocentric community and the structure of utopias," *Worldviews*, 2 (1998), 239–56.
Anonymous, "Alle prater naturvern ... Disse gjør noe," *Teknisk ukeblad*, 118, no. 40 (1971), 17–18.
"'Aksjon Hardangervidda' i gang," *Norsk natur*, 6 (1970), 122–4.
CICERO senter for klimaforskning: en evaluering (Oslo: Norges forskningsråd, 2000).
"Executive summary," in Jostein Mykletun (ed.), *Sustainable Development, Science Policy: The Conference Report* (Oslo: Norwegian Research Council for Science and the Humanities, 1990), pp. 5–16.
"Fifth Assembly: Notes for sections," *Study Encounter*, 10, no.1 (1974), 1–16.
"Forurensningene kan bringes under rimelig kontroll," *Teknisk ukeblad*, 119, no. 18 (1972), 3–4.
"Gandhi and the nuclear age," *Choice*, 3 (1967), 364.
Genetics and the Quality of Life: Report of a Consultation Church and Society, June 1973 (Geneva: Christian Medical Commission, 1974).
"Miljøteknologiske prosjekt," *(snm) nytt*, 6 (1977), 22.
"Natur og menneske," *Forskningsnytt*, 18, no. 6 (1973), 24.
"Norway is angry about film on acid rain," *New Scientist*, 1418 (Oct. 31, 1985), 13.
"Og etter oss," *Norsk Natur*, 5 (1969), 34–9.
Oljen og vi (Oslo: Norske Esso, 1973).
Petroleumsvirksomhetens plass i det norske samfunn, St. meld. no. 25 (Oslo: Finansdepartementet, 1974).
"Too High a Price?" *Times Literary Supplement*, June 5 (1969), 616.
Working Meeting on Analysis of Ecosystems: Tundra Zone (Ustaoset: IBP Norway, 1968).
"Økopolitisk samarbeidsring ('Ringen') i stutte ordlag," *Ringen*, 1 (1978), 3–5.
Anonymous (ed.), *Og etter oss ...* (Oslo: Norges Naturvernforbund, 1970).
Tirich Mir: The Norwegian Himalaya Expedition, Sölvi and Richard Bateson (trs.) (London: Hodder and Stoughton, 1952).
Apostol, Pavel, "English summary," in *Calitatea vieţii şi explorarea viitorului* (Bucharest: Editura politică, 1975), pp. 258–69.
Ariansen, Per, *Miljøfilosofi: En innføring* (Oslo: Universitetsforlaget, 1992).
Arnason, Thorvaldur, *Olje eller fisk? En vurdering av forurensningsfaren som mulig konflikt mellom oljeaktiviteten og fiskeriene på vår kontinentalsokkel* (Trondheim: Kommit, 1973).
Asdal, Kristin, *Knappe ressurser? Økonomenes grep om miljøfeltet* (Oslo: Universitetsforlaget, 1998).
Politikkens natur – naturens politikk (Oslo: Universitetsforlaget, 2011).
Aubert, Karl Egil, "En del elementære logiske emner," *Journal of Symbolic Logic*, 17 (1952), 288.
Aune, Egil, "Sur nedbørs følger for skogbruket," *Teknisk ukeblad*, 119, no. 24 (1972), 29–30.

Ausland, John C., *Norway, Oil, and Foreign Policy* (Colorado: Westview Press, 1979).
Austad, Torleiv, "Kirkens medansvar for den rådende sosiale praksis," in Per Voksø (ed.), *Mennesket og miljøet* (Oslo: Kirkerådets utvalg for forsking og utredning, Luther forlag, 1975), pp. 36–49.
Austgulen, Odd Rune, et al., *Ressurser, befolkning: en kommentar til NOU 1974:55* (Bergen: Norges handelshøyskole, 1975).
Bardi, Ugo, *The Limits to Growth Revisited* (New York: Springer, 2011).
Barth, Fredrik, "Ecologic relationships of ethnic groups in Swat, North Pakistan," *American Anthropologist, New Series*, 58, no. 6 (Dec. 1956), 1079–89.
"Moral og miljøkrise," in Svein Gjerdåker, Lars Gule, and Bernt Hagtvet (eds.), *Den uoverstigelige grense* (Oslo: Cappelen, 1991), pp. 149–53.
"Preface," in Fredrik Barth (ed.), *The Role of the Entrepreneur in Social Change in Northern Norway* (Bergen: Universitetsforlaget, 1963), 3.
Barth, Fredrik, and Colin Turnbull, "On responsibility and humanity: Calling a colleague to account," *Current Anthropology*, 15, no. 1 (1974), 99–103.
Barth, Thomas Fredrik Weiby, "Innledning" and "Geologiske randbemerkninger," in Jens Evensen, *Muligheter og rettigheter på havbunnen: Dyphavet – et nytt ekspansjonsfelt?* (Oslo: Elingaard Forlag, 1970), pp. 9–11, 47–52.
Bastiansen, Otto, "Forord," in John D. Bernal, *Vitenskapens historie* (Oslo: Pax, 1978), pp. 11–12.
Bates, Marston, *Menneskets plass i naturen*, Brynjulf Valum (trs.) (Oslo: Cappelen, 1966).
Benestad, Olav, *Kurs om energi og energisparing* (Oslo: Rådet for natur- og miljøfag, 1978).
Berg Eriksen, Trond, "Naturen som appellinstans," *Kirke og kultur*, 79 (1974), 293–6.
Berge, Erling, "Befolkning og befolkningspolitikk," *Kirke og kultur*, 80 (1975), 102–10.
Bernal, John D., "The physical basis of life," *The Proceedings of the Physical Society*, 62, no. 10 (1949), 597–618.
The Social Function of Science (London: Routledge, 1939, 1946).
Berner, Mia, "Min debut," *Prosa*, 1 (2006), 48.
Berntsen, Bredo, "Nasjonalparker," *Naturen*, 96 (1972), 195–204.
Naturvernets historie i Norge: Fra klassisk naturvern til økopolitikk (Oslo: Grøndahl, 1977).
"Radikal, liberal, konservativ – en grenseoppgang," *Samtiden*, 81 (1972), 178–85.
"Sett Rosenqvist i gapestokken!" *Orientering*, 11 (1974), 10.
Berntsen, Lars Viggo, "Menneskesynet i biologilærebøker i skolen," in Peder Borgen (ed.), *Mennesket og naturen i kristendom og naturvitenskap* (Trondheim: Tapir, 1980), pp. 58–104.
Beyer-Brock, Harald, "Den økologiske harmonimodell," in *Natur og menneske: artikkelsamling* (Oslo: Rådet for natur og miljøfag, 1979), pp. 243–8.
"Den økologiske 'harmonimodell' sett i lys av jegere og sankere, eller de såkalte naturfolk," *Naturen*, 3 (1977), 99–103.

Biersdorf, John E., *Elements of Research Design for a Study of Value Change in Religion in American Society* (New York: Working Paper from the National Council of Churches, 1972).
Birch, Charles, *Regaining Compassion for Humanity and Nature* (Kensington: New South Wales University Press, 1993).
Bjørklund, Tor, *Mot strømmen: Kampen mot EF 1961–1972* (Oslo: Universitetsforlaget, 1982).
Bjørnstad, Åsmund, "Økologi, etikk og religion – ein samtale med Rolf Edbergs forfatterskap," *Kirke og kultur*, 88 (1975), 206–15.
Black, John N., *The Dominion of Man: The Search for Ecological Responsibility* (Edinburgh: Edinburgh University Press, 1970).
Blekastad, Milada, "Poesi og økologi – to sider av same sak?" *Forskningsnytt*, 19, no. 5 (1974), 19–23.
Bock, Paul, *In Search of a Responsible World Society: The Social Teachings of the World Council of Churches* (Philadelphia: Westminster Press, 1974).
Bolin, Bert, *A History of the Science and Politics of Climate Change* (Cambridge: Cambridge University Press, 2007).
Bolin, Bert, et al., *The Greenhouse Effect: Climatic Change and Ecosystems* (Chichester: John Wiley, 1986).
Bookchin, Murray, "Social ecology versus deep ecology," *Green Perspectives*, 4/5 (1987), 1–23.
Borchgrevink, Nils, "Naturfølelse og naturvern," *Samtiden*, 77 (1968), 360–6.
Borgen, Peder, "Helbredelsesundere i det Nye Testemente: Noen synspunkter," in *Mennesket og naturen i kristendom og naturvitenskap* (Trondheim: Tapir, 1980), pp. 43–64.
Borgen, Peder, (ed.), *Miljøkrise og verdivalg: miljøkrisen i kristent perspektiv og som utfordring i samfunn og skole* (Trondheim: Tapir, 1991).
Borgstrøm, George, *Mat for milliarder* (Oslo: Gyldendal, 1968).
"World food scarcity and the struggle for human survival," *Anticipation*, 18 (1974), 17–19.
Borowy, Iris, *Defining Sustainable Development for Our Common Future: A History of the World Commission on Environment and Development (Brundtland Commission)* (London: Routledge, 2014).
Borring, Jan, "En tallmagiker refser romantikerne," *Orientering*, 11 (1974), 10.
"På tide med aksjoner mot demninger og maskiner," *Miljømagasinet*, 2 (1981), 4–5, 36.
Borring, Jan, and Per Houge, *Den økologiske krisen i Sahel* (Oslo: Rådet for Natur og Miljøfag, 1975).
Botkin, James W., Mahdi Elmandjra, and Mircea Malitza, *No Limits to Learning: Bridging the Human Gap: A Report to the Club of Rome* (Oxford: Pergamon Press, 1979).
Boulding, Kenneth E., *Beyond Economics* (Ann Arbor: University of Michigan Press, 1968).
"The Economics of the Coming Spaceship Earth," in Henry Jarrett (ed.), *Environmental Quality in a Growing Economy* (Baltimore: John Hopkins University Press, 1966), pp. 3–14.

Braathen, Geir O., *Sluttrapport fra forskningsprogram om klima- og ozon spørsmål 1989-1998* (Oslo: Norwegian Institute for Air Research, 2000).
Bradford, George, *How Deep Is Deep Ecology* (Hadley: Themes Change, 1989).
Brand, Stewart (ed.), *The Whole Earth Catalogue* (San Francisco: Point Foundation, 1968).
Brandtzæg, Brita, et al., *Vil vi sprelle med? En bok om kvinner og olje* (Oslo: Pax, 1975).
Bravo, Michael, *North Pole: Nature and Culture* (London: Reaction Books, 2019).
Bravo, Michael, and Sverker Sörlin (eds.), *Narrating the Arctic: A Cultural History of Nordic Scientific Practices* (Canton, MA: Science History Pub., 2002).
Breirem, Knut, *Norges ressurssituasjon i global sammenheng: utdrag og kommentarer til NOU 1974:55* (Ås: Norsk Institutt for Næringsmiddelforskning, 1974).
Breivik, Gunnar, "Biografiske opplysninger," in Vegard Fusche Moe and Sigmund Loland (eds.), *I bevegelse: et festskrift til Gunnar Breivik på hans 60-årsdag* (Oslo: Gyldendal, 2003), pp. 231–40.
"Forurensning og naturvern," in Lars Østnor (ed.), *Nestekjærlighet i samfunnet: Sosialetisk spørsmål i kristent lys* (Oslo: Luther Forlag, 1975), pp. 120–32.
"Friluftsliv: en vei til et nytt samfunn," *Mestre fjellet*, 6 (1973), 23, 39.
Friluftsliv: noen filosofiske og pedagogiske aspekter (Oslo: Norges idrettshøyskole, 1979).
"Heidegger og teologien," *Ung teologi*, 3 (1970), 81–92.
Idrettens filosofi, MA Thesis (Oslo: The Norwegian School of Sport Sciences, 1975).
"Kristen tro og natur-forståelse," *Kirke og kultur*, 84 (1979), 345–52.
"Likevektssamfunnet – et teologisk vurdering," in Harald Olsen (ed.), *Mot et samfunn i likevekt* (Oslo: Land og Kirke, 1978), pp. 108–23.
"Læren om Gud og det store huset: (teo-logi og øko-logi)," in Paul Hofseth (ed.), *Økofilosofisk lesebok*, vol. 2. (Oslo: Samarbeidsgruppa for natur og miljøvern, 1974), ms. 1–17.
"Menneskets plass og funksjon i naturen i følge kristendommen og den økologiske tenkning: en sammenlignende og kritisk analyse," in *Mennesket og naturen i kristendom og naturvitenskap* (Trondheim: Tapir, 1980), pp. 105–27.
"Om teologiens opprinnelse," *Norsk teologisk tidsskrift*, 71 (1970), 176–91.
"Religion, livsform og natur," in Paul Hofseth and Arne Vinje (eds.), *Økologi: Økofilosofi* (Oslo: Gyldendal, 1975), pp. 82–95.
"Teologi og politikk," in Pål Repstad (ed.), *Kirken og samfunnet* (Stavanger: Nomi Forlag, 1970), pp. 108–20.
"Teologi og økologi," *Prismet*, 31 (1980), 4–7.
Breivik, Gunnar, and Haakon Løymo (eds.), *Friluftsliv fra Fridtjof Nansen til våre dager* (Oslo: Universitetsforlaget, 1978).
Brochmann, Dybwad Bertram, *Mentalitet og livsskjæbne* (Bergen: Det frie samfunds forlag, 1929).
Brox, Ottar, *Hva skjer i Nord-Norge?* (Oslo: Pax, 1966).

Newfoundland Fishermen in the Age of Industry (Newfoundland: Memorial University of Newfoundland, 1972).
"Three types of North Norwegian entrepreneurship," in Fredrik Barth (ed.), *The Role of the Entrepreneur in Social Change in Northern Norway* (Oslo: Universitetsforlaget, 1963), pp. 19–32.
Brown, Lester R., *Building a Sustainable Society* (New York: Norton, 1981).
Brown, Lester R., and Pamela Shaw, *Six Steps to a Sustainable Society* (Washington: Worldwatch Institute Report 48, 1982).
Brundtland, Gro Harlem, "Energiforsyning i Norge i framtida," in *Stortingsforhandlinger 1974/1975*, May 13, 1975, p. 4163.
"Forskning, forvaltning og politikk," *Ting*, 2 (1977), 24–31, 28.
Madam Prime Minister: A Life in Power and Politics (New York: Farrar, Straus and Giroux, 2002).
Mitt liv 1939–1986 (Oslo: Gyldendal, 1997).
"Også rapporter kan være bærekraftige," *U-nytt*, 3 (1990), 30–1.
"The politics of oil: A view from Norway," *Energy Policy*, April 1988, 102–9.
"The test of our civilization" (interview), *New Perspectives Quarterly*, 6 (1989), 4–7.
Brundtland, Gro Harlem, and Knut Liestøl, "Seasonal variations in menarche in Oslo," *Annals of Human Biology*, 9 (1982), 35–43.
Brundtland, Gro Harlem, and Lars Walløe, "Menarcheal age in Norway in the 19th century: A re-evaluation of historical sources," *Annals of Human Biology*, 3 (1976), 363–74.
Bryhni, Inge, and Ivan Th. Rosenqvist, "De geologiske vitenskaper og menneskene," in Ivan Th. Rosenqvist (ed.), *Geologien og mennesket* (Oslo: Gyldendal, 1973), pp. 9–21.
Bryn, Knut, et al., *Oljen og det norske samfunn* (Oslo: Tanum, 1976).
Buchen, Irving H., "Futuristic Conference in Romania," *The Futurist*, 7 (Feb. 1973), 31–2.
Buckminster Fuller, Richard, *Operating Manual for Spaceship Earth* (Edwardsville: Southern Illinois University Press, 1969).
Burnett, D. Graham, *The Sounding of the Whale: Science and Cetaceans in the Twentieth Century* (Chicago: University of Chicago Press, 2012).
Bush, Vannevar, *Science the Endless Frontier: A Report to the President*, July 1945 (Washington: National Science Foundation, reprint 1960).
Bøckman, Nils, *Olje: hovedbegrepene i petroleumsteknologien: kortfattet oversikt over norsk oljepolitikk* (Oslo: Hartmark, 1972).
Bøckman, Peter Wilhelm, *Liv, fellesskap, tjeneste: en kristen etikk* (Oslo: Universitetsforlaget, 1970).
"Synet på mennesket og naturen i kristen systematikk," in *Mennesket og naturen i kristendom og naturvitenskap* (Trondheim: Tapir, 1980), pp. 65–84.
Callicott, J. Baird, "Whaling in Sand County: A dialectical hunt for land-ethical answers to questions about the morality of Norwegian minke-whale catching," *Colorado Journal of International Environmental Law and Policy*, 8 (1997), 1–30.
Caradonna, Jeremy L., *Sustainability: A History* (Oxford: Oxford University Press, 2014).

Carpenter, Richard (ed.), *Assessing Tropical Forest Lands: Their Suitability for Sustainable Uses* (Dublin: Tycooly International, 1981).
Carson, Rachel, *Den tause våren*, Torolf Elster (trs.) (Oslo: Tiden, 1962).
Silent Spring (Greenwich: Fawcett Crest, 1962).
Ceaușescu, Nicolae, "Opening remarks," in "Management Science and Futures Studies in Socialist Romania," *Viitorul Social* (Bucharest: Meridiane Pub. House, 1972), pp. 7–18.
Christiansen, Per Fredrik, and Helge Vold, *Kampen om universitetet: Boken fra filosofistudentenes aksjonsuke* (Oslo: Pax, 1969).
Christie, Helge, "Kina," *(snm) nytt*, 9 (Dec. 1976), 22–3.
Christie, Helge, Erling Amble, and Erik Steineger, "To linjer i miljøvern arbeidet," *Miljømagasinet*, 8 (1974), 10–11, 22.
Christoffersen, Svein Aage, "Biologi og kristendom," *Norsk teologisk tidsskrift*, 74 (1973), 182.
Ciplea, Licinius, "The technological parameters of long range ecological politics" (abstract), in Helen Seidler and Cristina Krikorian (eds.), *3rd World Future Research Conference: Abstracts* (Bucharest: Centre of Information and Documentation in Social and Political Sciences, 1972), pp. 21–2.
Cittadino, Eugene, "A 'marvelous cosmopolitan preserve': The dunes, Chicago, and dynamics ecology of Henry Cowles," *Perspectives on Science*, 1 (1993), 520–59.
"The failed promise of human ecology," in Michael Shortland (ed.), *Science and Nature* (Oxford: BSHS Monographs, 1993), pp. 252–83.
Clark, Stephen R. L., "The rights of wild things," *Inquiry*, 22 (1979), 171–88.
Clines, Francis X., "Oslo Journal: New Age of Norse Goddess?" *The New York Times*, Jan. 6, 1987, A4.
Cobb, John B., *Sustainability: Economics, Ecology, and Justice* (New York: Orbis Books, 1992).
Coen, Deborah R., *Climate in Motion: Science, Empire, and the Problem of Scale* (Chicago: University of Chicago Press, 2018).
Cohen, L. Jonathan, "Democracy, ideology and objectivity," *Mind*, 67 (1958), 411–13.
Cole, H. S. D., Christopher Freeman, Marie Jahoda, and K. L. R. Pavitt, *Thinking about the Future: A Critique of The Limits to Growth* (London: Sussex University Press, 1973).
Collett, John Peter, *Historien om Universitetet i Oslo* (Oslo: Universitetsforlaget, 1999).
Connelly, Matthew, *Fatal Misconception: The Struggle to Control World Population* (Cambridge, MA: Harvard University Press, 2008).
Conner, Daniel, "Is AIDS the answer to and environmentalist's prayer?" *Earth First!* Dec. 22, 1987, 14–16.
Coomer, James C. (ed.), *Quest for a Sustainable Society* (New York: Pergamon, 1979).
Cooper, Anderson, "Alexandria Ocasio-Cortez on 60 Minutes," *CBS*, Jan. 6, 2019.
Cousteau, Jacques-Yves, "Er klokken blitt tolv?" *Naturen*, 94 (1970), 411–20.

Dahl, Eilif, "Bemerkninger om refugieproblemet og de kvartærgeologiske metodene," *Norsk Geologisk Tidsskrift*, 43 (1963), 260–5.
Forelesninger i økologi (Ås: Norges Landbrukshøgskole, 1967).
"Globale ressursproblemer," *Samtiden*, 82 (1973), 257–67.
"Kostnader ved utslipp av svoveldioksyder i atmosfæren," *Teknisk ukeblad*, 118, no. 50 (1971), M1–2.
"Kostnader ved utslipp av svoveloksyder i atmosfæren" *Teknisk ukeblad*, 119, no. 22 (1972), 3–5.
"Omkring nedbørens forsuring og plantenes næringstilgang," *Vann*, 4, no. 3 (1969), 120–3.
"Refugieproblemet og de kvartærgeologiske metodene," *Svensk naturvitenskap*, 14 (1961), 81–96.
Økologi for ingeniører og arkitekter (Oslo: Universitetsforlaget, 1969).
Økopolitikk og økologi (Oslo: The Royal Norwegian Society for Development, 1971).
Dahl, Eilif, and Oddvar Skre, *En undersøkelse av virkningen av sur nedbør på produktiviteten i landbruket* (Stockholm: Nordforsk, Miljøvårdssekretariatet, 1971).
En vurdering av mulige eller sannsynlige skader for landbruket ved utslipp av røyk fra et planlagt varmekraftverk på Slagentangen (Oslo: Røykskaderådet, 1971).
Dahl, Helmer, "Forurensning, forskere og politikere," *Teknisk ukeblad*, 118, no. 9 (1971), 22–5.
Dahmén, Erik, *Set pris på miljøet* (Oslo: Det Norske Samlaget, 1970).
Dale, Eivind, Hilde Jervan, Atle Midttun, Jan Eivind Myhre, and Dag Namtvedt, *Ressursforvaltningens historie* (Oslo: Resource Policy Group, 1984), pp. 35–84.
Dalkey, Norman C. with Daniel L. Rourke, Ralph Lewis, and David Snyder, *Studies in the Quality of Life* (Lexington, MA: Lexington Books, 1972).
Daly, Herman E., "Toward a stationary-state economy," in J. Harte and R. Socolow (eds.),*The Patient Earth* (New York: Holt, Rinehart, and Winston, 1971), pp. 226–244.
(ed.), *Toward a Steady-State Economy* (San Francisco: Freeman, 1973).
Dalton, D., "Gandhi and the nuclear age," *Political Studies*, 15 (1967), 251–2.
Dammann, Erik, *Med fire barn i palmehytte* (Oslo: Aschehoug, 1968).
Ny livsstil – og hva så?: Om samfunnsutviklingen fra en ny og bedre livsstil til en ny og bedre verden (Oslo: Gyldendal, 1976).
Darnton, John, "Norwegians Claim their Whaling Rights," *New York Times*, Aug. 7, 1993, 1.
Daston, Lorraine, and Peter Galison, *Objectivity* (New York: Zone Books, 2007).
Dator, Jim, "The WFSF and I," *Futures*, 37 (2005), 371–85.
Dawkins, Richard, *The God Delusion* (London: Black Swan, 2006).
The Selfish Gene (Oxford: Oxford University Press, 1976).
Derr, Thomas Sieger, *Ecology and Human Liberation: A Theological Critique of the Use and Abuse of Our Birthright* (Geneva: World Council of Churches, 1973).

Devall, Bill, "The deep ecology movement," *Natural Resources Journal*, 20 (1980), 299–322.
Devall, Bill, and George Sessions, *Deep Ecology: Living as if Nature Mattered* (Salt Lake City: Gibbs Smith, 1985).
Dokk Holm, Erling, "Rosenqvist saken," *F.eks*, 3 (1994), 22, 24.
Dordick, Herbert S., and Jack Lyle, *Access by Local Political Candidates to Cable Television: A Report of an Experiment* (Santa Monica, CA: Rand, 1971).
Dordick, Herbert S., and Georgette Wang, *The Information Society: A Retrospective View* (Newberry Park: Sage Publications, 1993).
Drengson, Alan R., *The Practice of Technology: Exploring Technology, Ecophilosophy, and Spiritual Disciplines for Vital Links* (New York: State University of New York Press, 1995).
Dresner, Simon, *The Principles of Sustainability* (London: Earthscan, 2002).
Drivenes, Einar-Arne, and Harald Dag Jølle (eds.), *Norsk polarhistorie*, vol. 2. (Oslo: Gyldendal, 2004).
Dumas, André, "The ecological crisis and the doctrine of creation," *The Ecumenical Review*, 27 (1975), 24–35.
Dybdahl, Knut, "Lite imponerende" (interview with Ivar Giæver), *Teknisk ukeblad*, 140, no. 45 (Dec. 9, 1993), 16.
Eckholm, Erik, *The Dispossessed of the Earth: Land Reform and Sustainable Development* (Washington: Worldwatch Institute Report 30, 1979).
Edberg, Rolf, *Brev till Columbus* (Stockholm: Norstedt, 1974).
   Et støvgrann som glimter: Ødelegger vi mulighetene for fortsatt liv på jorden? Hans Heiberg (trs.) (Oslo: Aschehoug, 1967).
   "Jordens resurser och den tekniska människan," *Kirke og kultur*, 72 (1967), 195–211.
   Spillran av ett moln: Anteckningar i färdaboken (Stockholm, Norstedt, 1966).
   The Dream of Kilimanjaro (New York: Pantheon Books, 1976).
   Tomorrow Will Be Too Late: Dialogue on the Threshold of the Third Millennium (Moscow: Progress Publishers, 1989).
   Vid trädets fot: Lekmannafunderingar mot höstlig bakgrund (Stockholm, Norstedt, 1971).
Edwards, Paul N., "The world in a machine: Origins and impacts of early computerized global systems," in Agatha C. Hughes and Thomas P. Hughes (eds.), *Systems, Experts, and Computers* (Cambridge, MA: The MIT Press, 2000), pp. 221–54.
Efstathiou, Sophia, and Bjørn K. Myskja, "Appreciation through use: How industrial technology articulates an ecology of values around Norwegian seaweed," *Philosophy and Technology* (2018), 1–20.
Einarson, Oddvar, *Kampen om Mardøla*, 90 minutes (Oslo: Elinor Film, April 1972).
Elder, Frederick, *Crisis in Eden: A Religious Study of Man and Environment* (Nashville: Abingdon Press, 1970).
   Prophecy Concerning Man and Environment, MA thesis (Cambridge, MA: Harvard Divinity School, 1968).
   "Two modern doctrines of nature," in Donald R. Cutler (ed.), *The World Year Book of Religion: The Religious Situation*, vol. 2. (London: Evans Brothers, 1969), pp. 367–94.

Elders, Fons (ed.), *Reflexive Water: The Basic Concerns of Mankind* (London: Souvenir Press, 1974).
Elf Norge, *Om olje* (Stavanger: Elf Aquitaine A/S, 1976).
Elliot, Robert, "Faking nature," *Inquiry*, 25 (1982), 81–93.
Enebakk, Vidar, "The three Merton theses," *Journal of Classical Sociology*, 7 (2007), 221–38.
"UNESCO og vitenskapshistoriens relevans," in John Peter Collett, Jan Eivind Myhre, and Jon Skeie (eds.), *Kunnskapens betingelser. Festskrift til Edgeir Benum* (Oslo: Vidarforlaget, 2009), pp. 124–45.
Engelskjøn, Torstein, *Biologisk forskning i Norge: En analyse med spesiell vekt på grunnforskningens ressurser, organisasjon og innhold* (Oslo: Institute for Studies in Research and Higher Education, 1972).
Enger, Per S., "Hva nå med norsk biologi?" in Nils Roll-Hansen og Hans Skoie (eds.), *Forskningspolitiske spørsmål i norsk biologi* (Oslo: Institute for Studies in Research and Higher Education, 1974), pp. 86–96.
Enzensberger, Hans Magnus, "Den politiske økologi – en kritikk," *Vardøger*, 9 (1977), 15–46.
"Norwegische Anachronismen." Published as *Norsk utakt*, Lasse Tømte (trs.) (Oslo: Universitetsforlaget, 1984).
"Zur Kritik der Politischen Ökologie," *Kursbuch*, 33 (Oct. 1973), 1–42.
Eriksen, Reidar, Per Halvorsen, and Steve I. Johansen, *Aluminiumsindustriens framtid* (Trondheim: Universitetet i Trondheim, 1977).
Eriksen, Thomas Hylland, *Fredrik Barth: En intellektuell biografi* (Oslo: Universitetsforlaget, 2013).
Evensberget, Snorre, *Thor Heyerdahl: The Explorer* (Oslo: Stenersens Forlag, 1994).
Evensen, Jens, *Oversikt over Oljepolitiske Spørsmål: bl.a. på bakgrunn av utenlandsk oljelovgivning og utenlandsk konsesjonspolitikk* (Oslo: Industridepartementet, 1971).
Executive Committee of the World Council of Churches, "The global environment, responsible choice and social justice," *The Ecumenical Review*, 23 (1971), 438–42.
Eyerman, Ron, "Intellectuals and popular movements: The Alta confrontation in Norway," *Praxis International*, 3 (1983), 185–98.
F., G., "Third World Future Research Conference," *Futures*, 4 (1972), 381–2.
Faarlund, Nils, "Bidrag til en ekspedisjonssosiologi," *Mestre fjellet*, 13 (1972), 11–14.
"Expertokrati eller demokrati," *Mestre fjellet*, 1 (1971), 3.
"Friluftsliv – A way home," in Børge Dahle (ed.), *Nature: The True Home of Culture* (Oslo, 1994), pp. 21–6.
Friluftsliv: hva – hvorfor – hvordan (Oslo: Norges idrettshøyskole, 1974).
"Friluftsliv i barne- og ungdomsskolen," *Vår skole*, 61 (1975), 196–209.
"Glimt fra klatringen på eggen," *Mestre fjellet*, 13 (1972), 9–10.
"Hva mener vi med friluftsliv?" *Mestre fjellet*, 15 (1973), 4–6.
"Hvorfor," *Mestre fjellet*, 13 (1972), 6–7.
"Jorden – et lite romskip i det golde universet," *Mestre fjellet*, 1 (1970), 5–6.
"Om økoliv," *Mestre fjellet*, 15 (1973), 7–9.

"Peter Wessel Zapffe 70 år," *Mestre fjellet*, 1 (1970), 19.
"Sigmund 70 år!" *Tindeposten*, 4 (2004), 16–19.
"Vi må lære å bruke naturen – uten å forbruke den," *Mestre fjellet*, 1 (1968), 5–8.
Farjeon, Eleanor, "Morning has broken," in *Norske salmebok* (Bergen: Eide forlag, 2013), p. 920.
Feyerabend, Paul, "Remarks on *Interpretation and Preciseness*," in Nina Witoszek and Andrew Brennan (eds.), *Philosophical Dialogues: Arne Næss and the Progress of Ecophilosophy* (Lanham: Rowman and Littlefield, 1999), pp. 50–6.
"'Science:' The myth and its role in society," *Inquiry*, 18 (1975), 167–81.
Findlay, James F., *Church People in the Struggle: The National Council of Churches and the Black Freedom Movement, 1950–1970* (New York: Oxford University Press, 1993).
Fitjar, Magne, *Økologi og verdi hos Arne Næss og Ole Jensen: semesteroppgave i miljøfag* (Bergen: Department of Geography, 1983).
Fleming, James Rodger, *The Callendar Effect* (Boston: American Meteorological Society, 2007).
Fluge, Frithjof, "Interpretation and preciseness," *Journal of Philosophy*, 45 (1948), 502–3.
Fløistad, Guttorm (ed.), *Peter Wessel Zapffe* (Oslo: Pax, 1969).
Fløistad, Guttorm, and Per Fredrik Christiansen (eds.), *Peter Wessel Zapffe: Dikt og drama* (Oslo: Universitetsforlaget, 1970).
Folkebevegelsen mot Norsk medlemskap i Fellesmarkedet, *Folkebevegelsens melding om Norges forhold til De Europeiske Felleskap (EF)* (Oslo: Folkebevegelsen mot Norsk medlemskap i Fellesmarkedet, 1972).
Foreman, Dave, and Bill Heywood (eds.), *Ecodefence: A Field Guide to Monkeywrenching* (Tucson, AZ: Ned Ludd Book, 1985).
Forrester, Jay W., *World Dynamics* (Cambridge: Wright-Allen Press, 1971).
Fox, Warwick, *Toward a Transpersonal Ecology; Developing new Foundations for Environmentalism* (Boston: Shambhala, 1990).
Friedman, Robert Marc, *Appropriating the Weather: Vilhelm Bjerknes and the Construction of a Modern Meteorology* (Ithaca: Cornell University Press, 1989).
Frislid, Ragnar, Paul Hofseth, and Johan Støyva (eds.), *Miljøleksikon: Økologi, natur- og miljøvern* (Oslo: Stiftelsen NKI, 1976).
Fægri, Knut, "Den klassiske biologis stilling i moderne naturvitenskap," *Naturen*, 90 (1966), 528–546.
Føllesdal, Dagfinn, "Økologi og økonomi," *Kirke og kultur*, 80 (1975), 231–2.
Gaare, Odd, "Hartvig Sætra: Økopolitisk sosialist," *Prosa*, 2 (2019), 50–7.
Galtung, Johan, "'The limits to growth' and class politics," *Journal of Peace Research*, 10, no. 1/2 (1973), 101–14.
"Økologi og klassekamp," *Samtiden*, 82 (1973), 65–83.
Økologi og klassepolitik, Therese Henrichsen (trs.) (Copenhagen: Christian Ejlers' Forlag, 1972).
Galtung, Johan, and Fumiko Nishimura, *Kan vi lære av Kineserne?* (Oslo: Gyldendal, 1975).

Galtung, Johan, and Arne Næss, *Gandhis politiske etikk* (Oslo: Tanum, 1955).
Garnåsjordet, Per Arild, "Forskerutdanning i natur- og miljøfag," in Lars Emmelin (ed.), *Miljöverdsutbildning vid universitet och högskoler* (Oslo: Nordisk ministerråd, 1977), pp. 71–80.
Geelmuyden, Niels Chr., *Grepet i Ord* (Tjøme: eBokNorden, 2014).
Gillette, Robert, "The limits to growth: Hard sell for a computer view of doomsday," *Science*, 175, no. 4026 (March 10, 1972), 1088–1092.
Gjefsen, Truls, *Arne Næss: Et liv* (Oslo: Cappelen Damm, 2011).
Gjessing, Guttorm, "Ecology and peace research," *Journal of Peace Research*, 4 (1967), 125–39.
Gjærevoll, Olav, "Forord," in Nalle Valtiala, *Mennesket – et skadedyr?* Brynjulf Valum (trs.) (Oslo: Cappelen, 1970), pp. 7–8.
Mine memoarer (Trondheim: Arbeiderbevegelsens historielag, 1998).
Naturvern i Norge (Oslo: Hygea, 1967).
Glacken, Clarence J., *Traces on the Rhodian Shore: Nature and Culture in Western Thought from Ancient Times to the End of the Eighteenth Century* (Berkeley, CA: University of California Press, 1967).
Gleditsch, Nils Petter, Åke Hartmann, and Jon Naustalslid, *Mardøla-aksjonen* (Oslo: Institute for Peace Research, 1971).
Glesne, Ola, "Noen økologiske grunnbegreper," in *Natur og menneske: artikkelsamling* (Oslo: Rådet for natur og miljøfag, [1979]), pp. 13–27.
Glesne, Ola, and Rasmus Hansson, "Har miljørørsla glemt naturen?" *Miljømagasinet*, 7 (1983), 4–5.
Godal, Jon, "Litt om Ressurser," in Paul Hofseth (ed.), *Økofilosofisk lesebok*, vol. 1. (Oslo: Samarbeidsgruppa for natur og miljøvern, 1974), ms. 16 pages.
"Mardøla-aksjonen og norske bønders vandring til Kongen i København," *Kirke og kultur*, 76 (1971), 494–8.
"Om hardingfele og naturvern," *Kirke og kultur*, 77 (1972), 406–8.
Graf, Karl, "Solen bestemmer klimaet," *Teknisk ukeblad*, 138, no. 29 (Aug. 22, 1991), 12–13.
Grepstad, Jon (ed.), *Mardøla: Dokumentasjon og Perspektiv* (Oslo: Samarbeidsgruppa for natur og miljøvern, 1971).
Grimeland, Geir, *En historie om klatring I Norge: 1900–2000* (Oslo: Fagbokforlaget, 2004).
Grober, Ulrich, *Sustainability: A Cultural History* (Cambridge: UIT Cambridge, 2012).
Guha, Ramachandra, "Radical American environmentalism and wilderness preservation: A Third World critique," *Environmental Ethics*, 11 (1989), 73–83.
Gulowsen, Jon, et al., *Loppemarked: Humørfylt handel hvor alle tjener og ingen blir snytt* (Oslo: Stiftelsen miljøforskning, 1985).
Gundersen, Frode, "Utviklingstrekk ved miljøbevegelsen i Norge," *Sosiologi i dag*, 2 (1991), 12–35.
Gundersen, Geir, "Lekmannsrørsla og klassekampen," *Ung teologi*, 5 (1971), 47–61.
Gunleiksrud, Gaute, "Kristne perspektiver på økologi: Om skapertro, menneskesyn og forvalteransvar," in Per Voksø (ed.), *Mennesket og miljøet* (Oslo: Kirkerådets utvalg for forsking og utredning, Luther forlag, 1975), pp. 97–111.

"Om å være kristen i et i-land i en u- og øko-tid," *Kirke og kultur*, 80 (1975), 193–205.
"Vektsamfunnets krise og kirkens evangelium," in Harald Olsen (ed.), *Mot et samfunn i likevekt* (Oslo: Land og Kirke, 1978), pp. 138–54.
Haagensen, Kjell, and Atle Midttun (eds.), *Kraftutbygging, konflikt og aksjoner* (Oslo: Universitetsforlaget, 1984).
Haarstad, Kjetil, "Ingen dramatisk drivhuseffekt," *Teknisk ukeblad*, 136, no. 10 (March 9, 1989), 24.
Haave, Jørgen, *Naken under kosmos: Peter Wessel Zapffe, en biografi* (Oslo: Pax, 1999).
Hafsten, Ulf, *Naturvernets århundre* (Oslo: Norges Naturvernforbund, 1977).
Hagemann, Fredrik, "Muligheter for å finne olje på den norske kontinentalsokkel," in Mimi Lønnum (ed.), *Norsk oljepolitikk* (Oslo: Elingaard forlag, 1972), pp. 11–33.
Hagen, Anders, "Fra Hardangerviddas historie," *Forskningsnytt*, 15 (1970), 31–5.
Hagtvet, Bernt (ed.), *Den vanskelige ulydigheten* (Oslo: Pax, 1981).
Haldane, John B. S., "The origin of life," *The Rationalist Annual*, 1929, 3–10.
Hale, Julian, *Ceauşescu's Romania: A Political Documentary* (London: George G. Harrap, 1971).
Hanisch, Ted, "Økokrise – fra viten til handling," in Svein Gjerdåker, Lars Gule, and Bernt Hagtvet (eds.), *Den uoverstigelige grense* (Oslo: Cappelen, 1991), pp. 165–73.
Hanisch, Tore Jørgen, and Gunnar Nerheim, *Norsk oljehistorie: Fra vantro til overmot?* Vol. 1 (Oslo: Leseselskapet, 1992).
Hansson, Steinar, and Ingolf Håkon Teigene, *Makt og mannefall: Historien om Gro Harlem Brundtland* (Oslo: Cappelen, 1992).
Haug, Hermod, "Bioteknologi – selger biologene sjela si?" *Bio*, 2 (1987), 4–5.
Hauge, Anton, "Dommedagsprofetiene," *Forskningsnytt*, 19, no. 5 (1974), 31.
Hauge, Jens Gabriel, *Gud og naturen: Om vitenskap og kristen tro* (Oslo: Genesis forlag, 1999).
  "Kirkens engasjement i økokrisen: Oljeuttalelsen som vedlegg," in Per Voksø (ed.), *Mennesket og miljøet* (Oslo: Kirkerådets utvalg for forsking og utredning, Luther forlag, 1975), pp. 113–20.
  "Kirkens Verdensråd og befolkningsproblemene," *Kirke og kultur*, 80 (1975), 76–85.
  "Mennesket og naturen fra naturvitenskaplig syn," in *Mennesket og naturen i kristendom og naturvitenskap* (Trondheim: Tapir, 1980), pp. 9–28.
Haukeland, Per Ingvar, *Himmeljorden: Om det av Gud i Naturen* (Oslo: Kvekerforlaget, 2009).
Hegge, Hjalmar, "Human-økologi eller sosial-darwinisme: Veier og avveier i økofilosofien," *Norsk filosofisk tidsskrift*, 12, no. 1 (1977), 1–24.
  "Jürgen Habermas og erkjennelsesteoriens dilemma," *Norsk filosofisk tidsskrift*, 4 (1969), 133–58.
  "Livskvalitet og levestandard," in Paul Hofseth (ed.), *Økofilosofisk lesebok*, vol. 2. (Oslo: Samarbeidsgruppa for natur og miljøvern, 1974), ms. 7 pages.

Mennesket og naturen: Naturforståelsen gjennom tidene – med særlig henblikk på vår tids miljøkrise (Oslo: Universitetsforlaget, 1978).
"Theory of science in the light of Goethe's science of nature," *Inquiry*, 15 (1972), 363–86.
"Økologi og filosofi," *Forskningsnytt*, 4 (1973), 54–6.
"Økonomisk vekst eller økologisk likevekt," *Samtiden*, 81 (1972), 74–81.
Hegseth, Bjørn L., *Miljøkunnskap – miljøvern: Forsøk på en oversikt* (Trondheim: NTH-trykk, 1970).
Heiberg, Inger, "Energibruk – et etisk problem?" *Kirke og kultur*, 83 (1978), 445.
Helsvig, Kim Gunnar, *Elitisme på Norsk: Det Norske Videnskaps-Akademi 1945–2007* (Oslo: Novus forlag, 2007).
Hemleben, Johannes, *Biologi og kristendom* (Copenhagen: Borgens forlag, 1972).
Hempel, Carl G., "Toward a theory of interpretation and preciseness," *Journal of Symbolic Logic*, 15 (1950), 154.
Henriksen, Jan-Olav, *Mennesket og naturen: etiske og religionsfilosofiske perspektiver på naturen og økokrisen* (Oslo: Menighetsfakultetet, 1991).
Henriksen Olav G. (ed.), *Kvinner i fjellet* (Lom: Norsk fjellmuseum, 2002).
Hermens, Ferdinand A., "Democracy in a World of Tensions," *Review of Politics*, 13 (1951), 375–81.
Hervik, Arild, et al., *Energianalyser: energiforbruket ved framstilling og distribusjon av matvarer* (Oslo: Rådet for natur og miljøfag, 1977).
Hessen, Dag, *Landskap i endring* (Oslo: Pax, 2016).
Hestmark, Geir, *Vitenskap og nasjon – Waldemar Christopher Brøgger 1851–1905* (Oslo, Aschehoug, 1999).
Heyerdahl, Thor, "Altademningen og norsk dyreliv," *Norsk natur*, 1 (1987), 28.
"Atlantic Ocean pollution observed by Expedition Ra," *Biological Conservation*, 2, no. 3 (April 1970), 221–2.
"Atlantic Ocean pollution and biota observed by the 'Ra' expeditions," *Biological Conservation*, 3, no. 3 (April 1971), 164–7.
Early Man and the Ocean (Carden City, NY: Doubleday, 1979).
Fatu-Hiva: Back to Nature (Garden City, New York: Doubleday, 1974).
Green was the Earth on the Seventh Day (New York: Random House, 1996).
"How vulnerable is the ocean?" in Barbara Ward, et al. (eds.), *Who Speaks for Earth?* (New York: Norton, 1973), pp. 45–63.
I Adams fotspor: En erindringsreise (Oslo: Gyldendal, 2006).
"Isolationist or diffusionist?" in Geoffrey Ashe (ed.) *The Quest for America* (New York: Praeger, 1971), 115–54.
"Mennesker og miljø i romfartsalderen," in Arne Fjørtoft, Jahn Otto Johansen, Thor Heyerdahl (eds.), *Befolkningsbomben: overbefolkning, krig og fred* (Oslo: Cappelen, 1985), pp. 89–110.
På jakt efter paradiset: Et år på en sydhavsø (Oslo: Gyldendal, 1938).
"The creative wilderness," in Børge Dahle (ed.), *Nature: The True Home of Culture* (Oslo: NIH, 1994), pp. 9–13.
Heyerdahl, Thor, and Per Lilliestrøm, *Jakten på Odin: På sporet av vår tapte fortid* (Oslo: Stenersen, 2001).

Hille, John, *Miljøtrusler for døve ører* (Oslo: Fremtiden i våre henders forskningsinstitutt, 2001).
Hjorthol, Lars Martin, *Alta: Kraftkampen som utfordret statens makt* (Oslo: Gyldendal, 2006).
Hofseth, Paul, "Biologer i forvaltninger," *Bio*, 1/2 (1984), 5–11.
"Fra estetikk til økopolitikk," in Bredo Berntsen (ed.), *Fra blomsterfredning til økopolitikk: Østlandske Naturvernforening 1914–1974* (Oslo: Østlandske Naturvernforening, 1975), pp. 44–50.
Rådet for natur- og miljøfag: Rapport fra virksomheten 1972–75 (Oslo: Rådet for natur- og miljøfag, 1975).
Rådet for natur- og miljøfag: Rapport fra virksomheten 1972–78 (Oslo: Rådet for natur- og miljøfag, 1978).
"Voksenopplæring og desentralisert miljøfagundervisning," in Lars Emmelin (ed.), *Miljöverdsutbildning vid universitet och högskoler* (Oslo: Nordisk ministerråd, 1977), pp. 62–70.
Hofseth, Paul, and Harald Celius, *Sosiale konsekvenser av oljevirksomhet i Skottland* (Oslo: Rådet for natur og miljøfag, 1975).
Hofseth, Paul, Ola Hole, and Sigmund Kvaløy, *Logikkoppgaver til Arne Næss: en del elementære logiske emner* (Oslo: Universitetsforlaget, 1968–1973).
Hofseth, Paul, and Arne Vinje (eds.), *Økologi Økofilosofi* (Oslo, Gyldendal, 1975).
Hofstad, Knut, "Energibruk – et etisk problem?" *Kirke og kultur*, 83 (1978), 297–300.
Holm, Berit G., "Ikkevold – teori og praksis," *Kirke og kultur*, 76 (1971), 411–29.
Holm, Kjell Gunnar, and Knut Sørensen, "Økologi og økopolitikk: Noen trekk ved økobevegelsen i Norge," *Vardøger*, 9 (1977), 47–69.
Holst, Per A., "Svein Rosseland and the Oslo Analyzer," *IEEE Annals of the History of Computing*, 18, no. 4 (1996), 16–26.
Holsworth, Robert D., *Public Interest Liberalism and the Crisis of Affluence: Reflections on Nader, Environmentalism, and the Politics of a Sustainable Society* (Boston: G. K. Hall, 1980).
Hughes, J. Donald, "Ecology in ancient Greece," *Inquiry*, 18, no. 2 (1975), 115–25.
Huse, Sigmund, "Naturvern på økologisk grunnlag," *Norsk natur*, 1 (1965), 4–7.
Høibraaten, Helge, "Norway in 1968 and its aftermath; Maoism, the power of the periphery and the cultural upper class of the sixty-eighters," in Guri Hjeltnes (ed.), *Universitetet og studentene* (Oslo: Forum for universitetshistorie, 1998), pp. 184–91.
Høivik, Tord (ed.), *År 2000* (Oslo: Pax, 1969).
Høivik, Tord (ed.), "Framtidsforsking – et urovekkende fenomen?" *Forskningsnytt*, 18, no. 6 (1973), 21–4.
Ingstad, Benedicte, *Oppdagelsen: En biografi om Anne Stine og Helge Ingstad* (Oslo: Gyldendal, 2009).
Ingstad, Helge, *Apache-indianerne: jakten på den tapte stamme* (Oslo: Gyldendal, 1939).
East of the Great Glacier (New York: Knopf, 1937).

Land of Feast and Famine (London: V. Gollancz, 1933).
Land under the Pole Star (New York: St. Martin's Press, 1966).
"Norse explorers," in Geoffrey Ashe (ed.), *The Quest for America* (New York: Praeger, 1971), pp. 96–112.
Pelsjegerliv blandt Nord-Kanadas Indianere (Oslo: Gyldendal, 1931).
Westward to Vinland (New York: St. Martin's Press, 1969).
Øst for den store bre (Oslo: Gyldendal, 1935).
International Union for Conservation of Nature and Natural Resources, the United Nations Environmental Programme, and World Wildlife Fund, *World Conservation Strategy: Living Resource Conservation for Sustainable Development* (New York: IUCN-UNEP-WWF, 1980).
Jacobsen, Roy, *The Invisible* (London: MacLehose, 2017).
Jacobsen, Terje (ed.), *Olje: fra kilde til forbruker* (Oslo: Schibsteds Forlag, 1973).
Jacobsen, Trond Gansmo, *Økofilosofi* (Oslo: Fagbokforlaget, 2007).
Jansen, Alf-Inge, *Makt og miljø: En studie av utformingen av den statlige natur og miljøvernpolitikken* (Oslo: Universitetsforlaget, 1989), pp. 51–101.
Jarving, Stein, *Grønt liv: Økologisk strategi – populistisk virkelighet: Om jordbrukskollektiv i praksis* (Oslo: Gyldendal, 1974).
Jaworowski, Zbigniew, Tom Segalstad, and V. Hisdal, *Atmospheric CO_2 and Global Warming: A Critical Review*, 2nd ed. (Oslo: Norsk Polarinsitutt, 1992).
Jaworowski, Zbigniew, Tom V. Segalstad, and N. Ono, "Do glaciers tell a true atmospheric CO_2 story?" *The Science of the Total Environment*, 114 (1992), 227–84.
Jensen, Ole, *I vækstens vold: økologi og religion* (Copenhagen: Fremda, 1976).
"Teologisk argumentasjon for tesen: Forurensning er blasfemi," *Kirke og kultur*, 77 (1972), 385–96.
Jenssen, Ingebrigt, and Ivan Th. Rosenqvist, "Kalsiumutvasking og syrenedfall," *Teknisk ukeblad*, 119, no. 25 (1972), 27.
Johansen, Arne B., "Hardangervidda skal utforskes: Et prosjekt for tverrvitenskaplig kulturforskning i gang fra 1970," *Forskningsnytt*, 14 (1969), 26–9.
Johnson, Lawrence E., *A Morally Deep World; An Essay on Moral Significance and Environmental Ethics* (Cambridge: Cambridge University Press, 1991).
Jonson, Jonas O., "Skapelsen: Frelsens sakrament," in Harald Olsen (ed.), *Mot et samfunn i likevekt* (Oslo: Land og Kirke, 1978), pp. 124–37.
Jørgensen, Per M. (ed.), *Botanikkens historie i Norge* (Oslo: Fagbokforlaget, 2007).
Jørstad, Finn R., *Historien om Finse* (Bergen: Nord 4, 1998).
Kaltenborn, Karl F., "Miljøvern – globale løsninger for globale problemer," *Teknisk ukeblad*, 119, no. 28 (1972), 4.
Kaplan, Sylivan J. and Evelyn Kivy-Rosenberg (eds.), *Ecology and the Quality of Life* (Springfield, IL: Charles C. Thomas, 1973).
Karlsen, Håken Torfinn, *The Cost of Participating in the Greenhouse Gas Emission Permit Marked* (Oslo: Statistics Norway, 2014).
Kaul, Dagny, "Dilemmaet i moderne naturoppfatning," *Norsk teologisk tidsskrift*, 74 (1973), 163–81.
"Ecofeminism in the Nordic countries," *Journal of the European Society of Women in Theological Research*, 2 (1994), 102–9.

Keller, J. Chr., "Naturfilosofi – en omvurdering av moral," *Mestre fjellet*, 4 (1970), 4.
Kindingstad, Torbjørn, and Fredrik Hagemann, *Norges oljehistorie* (Stavanger: Wigestrand, 2002).
Kirk, Andrew G., *Counterculture Green: The Whole Earth Catalog and American Environmentalism* (Lawrence: University Of Kansas Press, 2007).
Kirkpatrick, Sale, "The cutting edge: Deep ecology and its critics," *The Nation*, 246, no. 19 (May 1988), 670–4.
Klein, David R., *The Making of an Ecologist*, Karen Brewster (ed.) (Fairbanks, Alaska: University of Alaska Press, 2019).
Kleivan, Helge, "Økologisk endring i Labrador," *Naturen*, 86 (1962), 200–13.
Klingberg, Frank K., "Democracy in a world of tensions," *Western Political Quarterly*, 4 (1951), 337–8.
Knorr, Dietrich (ed.), *Sustainable Food Systems* (Chichester, UK: Ellis Horwood, 1983).
Knudsen, Trond, Karen Johanne Baalsrud, and Paul Hofseth, *Miljøfagundervisning utover videregående skole: en oversikt over undervisningsopplegg og litteratur* (Oslo: Rådet for natur- og miljøfag, 1978).
Koertge, Noretta, "The pluralist and possibilist aspect," *British Journal for the Philosophy of Science*, 24 (1973), 313–16.
Kofoed, Jan-Erik, "Nok ein sigar for kraftfantastane?" *(snm) nytt*, 1 (Jan. 1978), 3.
Kohler, Robert E., *All Creatures: Naturalists, Collectors, and Biodiversity, 1850–1950* (Princeton: Princeton University Press, 2006).
Kopp, Lore L., "Gandhi and the nuclear age," *Kyklos*, 19 (1966), 764–5.
Kvaløy Setreng, Sigmund, "Å dyrke tobakken sjøl," *Natur og Samfunn*, 4/5 (1990), 12.
 "Buddisme-økologi. Et tanke slektskap," in *Natur og menneske: artikkelsamling* (Oslo: Rådet for natur og miljøfag, [1979]), p. 249.
 "Demokrati," *(snm) nytt* 7 (Sept. 1976), 7–9.
 "Ecophilosophy and ecopolitics: Thinking and acting in response to the threats of ecocatastrophe," *The North American Review*, 259 (Summer 1974), 16–28.
 "Eikesdal-Grytten i naturvernåret – utbyggernes glansnummer," *Norsk natur*, 6 (1970), 69.
 "Forord," in Stein Jarving, *Likevektssamfunn* (Karlsøy: Regnbuetrykk, 1976), 6–7.
 "Gaia versus Servoglobe," in Roy Bhaskar, et al. (eds.), *Ecophilosophy in a World Crisis* (London: Routledge, 2012), pp. 99–114.
 "Gjenforeningen med det Ene som gjennomstrømmer all natur" (drawing), in Gunnar Breivik and Haakon Løymo (eds.), *Friluftsliv fra Fridtjof Nansen til våre dager* (Oslo: Universitetsforlaget, 1978), p. 193.
 "Inside nature," in Børge Dahle (ed.), *Nature: The true home of culture* (Oslo, 1994), pp. 29–37.
 "Ivar Mysterud, inspirator og medarbeider – hvordan økofilosofien ble til," in *Med lua i hånden* (Oslo: Department of Biosciences, 2008), pp. 37–9.
 "Klatring og naturopplevelse," *Mestre fjellet*, 2 (1968), 11–12.

"Kommersiell turisme – informasjonsmengde null?" *Mestre fjellet*, 3–4 (1968), 29.
"Mangfold er livsstyrke!" *Byggekunst*, 53 (1971), 1268.
Mangfold og tid (Trondheim: NTNU Department of Music, 2001).
"Mardøla, Masi: Vår egen tid" (interview), in Magnar Mikkelsen, *Masi, Norge* (Oslo: Cappelen, 1971), pp. 97–111.
"Mardøla, miljøvern og maktspel," *Senit*, 3 (1970), 4–11.
"Mardøla, miljøvern og maktspill," in Brunjulf Valum (ed.), *Øko-katastrofe* (Oslo: Grøndahl, 1971), pp. 153–162.
"Mardøla – samvær som kampform" *Mestre fjellet*, 1 (1971), 5–13.
"Mother Earth's treasures and their revealers," in Padma Tshewang, Phuntsok Tashi, Chris Butters, and Sigmund Sætreng (eds.), *The Treasure Revealers of Bhutan* (Kathmandu: Bibliothecha Himalayica, 1995), pp. 139–58.
Musikk-kritikk og kommunikasjon, MA thesis (Oslo: Department of Philosophy, University of Oslo, 1965).
"Nagarkot og Damavand – to pilgrumsturer vinteren 1969," *Mestre fjellet*, 2 (1969), 5–6, 16.
"Norwegian ecophilosophy and ecopolitics and their influence from Buddhism," in Klas Sandell (ed.), *Buddhist Perspectives on the Ecocrisis* (Kandy, Sri Lanka: Buddhist Publication Society, 1987), pp. 49–72.
"Peter Wessel Zapffe og verdien av utemmet natur," in Guttorm Fløistad and Per Fredrik Christiansen (eds.), *P. W. Zapffe: Dikt og drama* (Oslo: Universitetsforlaget, 1970), pp. 252–65.
"Rolwaling – et livssamfunn i likevekt," *Mestre fjellet*, 15 (1973), 11–12.
"Samarbeidsgruppen for Natur og Miljøvern: Mini historikk og aktualia," *Mestre fjellet*, 1 (1970), 7–8, 17.
"To økosofier i Norge; deres begynnelse og en del til," *Norsk filosofisk tidsskrift*, 37 (2002), 117–25.
"Trenger mennesket uberørt natur?" *Kvekeren*, 1 (1973), 6–7.
"Tseringma-hymnen og det hellige fjell Tseringma," in Sven Erik Skønberg (ed.), *Grønn pepper i turbinene* (Oslo: Universitetsforlaget, 1985), pp. 81–4.
Øko-filosofi: Litteraturliste og orientering til studenter og andre interesserte (Oslo: Samarbeidsgruppa for natur og miljøvern, May 1971).
Øko-filosofisk fragment: Kompleksitet og komplikasjon (Oslo: Samarbeidsgruppa for natur og miljøvern, 1972–1973).
"Økofilosofi som forståelsesnøkkel," in Paul Hofseth (ed.), *Økofilosofisk lesebok*, vol. 1. (Oslo: Samarbeidsgruppa for natur og miljøvern, 1974), ms. 16 pages.
"Økologi – vannkraft – samfunn," *Norsk natur*, 6 (1970), 150–62.
"Økokrise – glimt fra det norske økofilosofiske forsøket," in *Den uoverstigelige grense* (Oslo: Cappelen, 1991), pp. 102–16.
Økokrise, natur og menneske (Oslo: Samarbeidsgruppa for natur og miljøvern, 1973).
"Økokrise, natur og menneske," in *Natur og menneske: artikkelsamling* (Oslo: Rådet for natur og miljøfag, 1979), pp. 82–119.
Kvam, Ragnar, *Mannen og havet* (Oslo: Gyldendal, 2005).
Kvendseth, Stig S., *Giant Discovery: A History of Ekofisk through the first 20 years* (Stavanger: Phillips, 1988).

Kvinnsland, Ole-Jacob, "The Norwegian experience," in Maurice Scarlett (ed.), *Consequences of Offshore Oil and Gas* (St. John's: Memorial University of Newfoundland, 1977), pp. 85–105.

Kvåle, Nils, "Flytende naturgass – vårt fremtidige drivstoff?" *Teknisk ukeblad*, 118, no. 7 (1971), 19–22.

Kwa, Chunglin, "Representations of nature mediating between ecology and science policy: The case of the International Biological Programme," *Social Studies of Science*, 17 (1987), 413–42.

Landberg, Arthur, "Kraftverk basert på naturgass," *Teknisk ukeblad*, 119, no. 25 (1972), 27–8.

"Naturgasskraft i et optimalt sammensatt kraftsystem." *Teknisk ukeblad*, 119, no. 13 (1972), 4–5.

"Naturgasskraftverk – alternativ til olje/atomkraftverk?" *Teknisk ukeblad*, 118, no. 25 (1971), 28, 32.

"Naturgasskraftverk i elektrisitetsforsyningen," *Teknisk ukeblad*, 119, no. 1 (1972), 11, 15.

Larsen, Guttorm, "Naturvern og ikkevold," *Mestre fjellet*, 3–4 (1969), 11, 16.

Larsen, Thor, "Økologi og sunn fornuft," *Norsk natur*, 7 (1971), 40–1.

Larsen, Tryggen, "En samtale om verden: Vi står overfor bestemte begrensninger med store konsekvenser," *Forbrukerrapporten*, 10 (1972), 4–10.

Laszlo, Ervin, "The pluralist and possibilist aspect," *Philosophical and Phenomenological Research*, 34 (1973), 279–80.

Lavik, Nils Johan, and Jardar Seim (eds.), *Deilig er jorden? Ti innlegg om demokrati, revolusjon og kristendom* (Oslo: Pax, 1969).

Leach, Edmund, *A Runaway World?* (New York: Oxford University Press, 1968).

Lee, Martha F., *Earth First! Environmental Apocalypse* (New York: Syracuse University Press, 1995).

Lehland, Ketil, "Mardøla etc., især det siste," *Samtiden*, 79 (1970), 517–22.

Linden, Eugene, "Sharpening the Harpoons" and "Sustainable Follies," *Time*, May 24, 1993, 56–7.

Lenin, Vladimir, *Collected Works* (Moscow: Progress Publishers, 1966).

Lerøen, Bjørn Vidar, *From Groningen to Troll: Norske Shell – 25 Years on the Norwegian Continental Shelf* (Oslo: Norske Shell, 1990).

Troll over Troubled Water (Oslo: Statoil, 2003).

Letnes, Odd, "Virkeligheten som simuleringspill," *Apollon*, 1 (1999), 9–11.

Levi, Lars, and Lars Andersson, *Population, Environment and Quality of Life: A Contribution to the United Nations World Population Conference* (Stockholm: Allmänna Förlaget, 1974).

Lid, Gunnar, "Om dyrelivet i den foreslåtte nasjonalparken på Hardangervidda," *Norsk natur*, 1 (1966), 66–71.

Lieberg, Sigmund, *Environmental Education in Nordic Compulsory Schools* (Copenhagen: Nordisk ministerråd, 1976).

Lied, Finn, et al., *Norges ressurssituasjon i global sammenheng*, NOU 1974: 55 (Oslo: Universitetsforlaget, 1974).

Social Difficulties versus Social Problems, GRS-76 (Oslo: Gruppen for Ressursstudier, 1976).

Lindhjem-Godal, Anders, "'Kjernefamilien er en sosial sjukdom': Kollektivliv på Karlsøy i Troms," in Tor Egil Frøland and Trine Rogg Korsvik (eds.), *1968: Opprør og motkultur på norsk* (Oslo: Pax, 2006), pp. 93–118.

Lindqvist, Martti, *Economic Growth and the Quality of Life: An Analysis of the Debate within the World Council of Churches 1966–1974* (Helsinki: The Finnish Society for Missiology and Ecumenics, 1975).

The Biological Manipulation of Man and the Quality of Life (Helsinki: Research Institute of Lutheran Church, 1972).

Lloyd, Genevieve, "Spinoza's environmental ethics," *Inquiry*, 23 (1980), 293–311.

Longcope, Kay, "Norway's Prime Minister of Equality Gro Harlem Brundtland lets her voice be heard." *Boston Globe*, Sept. 22, 1987, p. 69.

Lousley, Cheryl, "Narrating a global future: Our common future and the public hearings of the World Commission on Environment and Development," in Elizabeth DeLoughrey, Jill Didur, and Anthony Carrigan (eds.), *Global Ecologies and the Environmental Humanities: Postcolonial Approaches* (New York: Routledge, 2015), pp. 245–67.

Lovelock, James, *Gaia: The Practical Science of Planetary Medicine* (London: Gaia Books Limited, 1991).

Lurås, Gunhild, *Kamerater? Striden i Norges Kommunistiske Parti 1963–1967*, MA thesis (Oslo: University of Oslo, 2002).

Lydersen, Aksel, "Kostnader ved utslipp av svoveloksyder i atmosfæren," *Teknisk ukeblad*, 119, no. 9 (1972), 19.

Lydersen, Aksel, and Dagfin Lydersen, "Kostnader ved utslipp av svovel i atmosfæren," *Teknisk ukeblad*, 119, no. 25 (1972), 27.

Lyngnes, Rasmus, "Kan biologisk kunnskap gjeve dei unge mål og meining med livet?" *Naturen*, 96 (1972), 392–8.

Løddesøl, Leif T., "Norske regler om oljeutvinning," *Lov og rett* (1965), 154–60.

Lønning, Inge, "Teologien som økofilosofiens tjenestepike?" *Kirke og kultur*, 80 (1975), 237–8.

M., R. P., "The pluralist and possibilist aspect," *Review of Metaphysics*, 27 (1974), 804–5.

Magnus, Anders, and Tor Selstad, "Massenes skaperkraft er uendelig," *Miljømagasinet*, 1 (1974), 24–7.

Malitza, Mircea, "Technological development and the future of Man in a socialist society," *Anticipation*, 18 (1974), 23–5.

Mancilla, Alejandra, "The moral limits of territorial claims in Antarctica," *Ethics and International Affairs*, 32, no. 3 (2018), 339–60.

Manes, Christopher, *Green Rage: Radical Environmentalism and the Unmaking of Civilization* (Boston: Little, Brown and Comp., 1990).

"Population and AIDS" (pseudonym Miss Ann Trophy), *Earth First!* May 1, 1987, 32.

Manum, Svein B., "Institutt for Geologi og geologibygningen 1958–1993" *Institutt for Geologi: Rapport*, 65 (1993), 1–6.

Marcuse, Herbert, *Det en-dimensjonale menneske: Studier i det avanserte industrielle samfunns ideologi*, Thomas Krogh (trs.) (Oslo: Pax, 1968).

One Dimensional Man: Studies in the Ideology of Advanced Industrial Society (London: Routledge, 1964).

Martiniussen, Erik, *Drivhuseffekten: Klimapolitikken som forsvant* (Oslo: Manifest, 2013).

Marx, Karl, "Theses on Feuerbach" (1888), in D. McLellan (ed.), *Karl Marx: Selected writings* (New York: Oxford University Press, 1977).

Mates, Benson, "Interpretation and preciseness," *Philosophical Review*, 67 (1958), 546–53.

Maud, Ralph, *The Man Who Discovered America* (Montreal: National Film Board of Canada, 1981).

Meyer, Niels, Helveg Petersen, and Villy Sørensen, *Oprør fra midten* (Copenhagen: Gyldendal, 1978).

McCutcheon, Robert, *Limits of a Modern World: A Study of the 'Limits to Growth' Debate* (London: Butterworths, 1979).

McGinn, Colin, "Evolution, animals, and the basis of morality," *Inquiry*, 22 (1979), 81–99.

McHale, John, "Future research: Some integrative and communicative aspects," in Robert Jungk and Johan Galtung (eds.), *Mankind 2000* (Oslo: Universitetsforlaget, 1970), pp. 256–63.

The Future of the Future (New York: George Baziller, 1969).

McKeon, Richard (ed.), *Democracy in a World of Tensions* (Chicago: University of Chicago Press, 1951).

McKibben, Bill, *Falter: Has the Human Game Begun to Play Itself Out?* (New York: Henry Holt and Co., 2019).

Meadows, Dennis L., and Jørgen Randers, "Adding the time dimension to environmental policy," *International Organization*, 26, no. 2 (1972), 213–33.

Meadows, Donella H., Dennis L. Meadows, Jørgen Randers, and William W. Behrens III, *Hvor går grensen? MITs forskningsrapport om verdens fortsatte vekst*, Leif Bakke (trs.) (Oslo: Cappelen, 1972).

The Limits to Growth: A Report for the Club of Rome's Project on the Predicament of Mankind (New York: Signet, 1972).

Mellgren, Doug, "'Doomsday' Seed Vault Opens in Arctic," *NBC News*, Feb. 27, 2008.

Ministry of Foreign Affairs and Ministry of Agriculture, *Air Pollution across National Boundaries: The Impact on the Environment of Sulfur in Air and Precipitation: Sweden's Case Study for the United Nations Conference on the Human Environment* (Stockholm: Bocktrykeriet, 1971).

Ministry of the Environment, *Bruken av Hardangervidda* (Oslo: Universitetsforlaget, 1974).

Internasjonale tiltak for bekjempelse av sur nedbør (Oslo: Miljøverndepartementet, Sept. 1974).

Miljø og utvikling: Norges oppfølging av Verdenskommisjonens rapport, St. meld. no. 46 (1988–1989) (Oslo: Government Printing, 1989).

Sur nedbør og dens virkninger i Norge (Oslo: Miljøverndepartementet, July 1974).

Mitman, Gregg, *The State of Nature: Ecology, Community, and American Social Thought, 1900–1950* (Chicago: The University of Chicago Press, 1992).

Mitroff, Ian I., "The myth of objectivity or why science needs a new psychology of science," *Management Science*, 18, no. 10 (June 1972), 613–18.
Mjelva, Roar, "Termodynamikkens 2. hovedsetning som etisk motivasjon," *Kirke og kultur*, 83 (1978), 445–6.
Moe, Fredrik H., et al. (eds.), *Miljøvern og kraftutbygging* (Oslo: Aschehoug, 1970).
Myrås, Harald, et al., *Kritiske og supplerende kommentarer til NOU 1974:55* (Trondheim: Komiteen for miljøvern, 1975).
Mysterud, Ivar, "En kommentar til økologisk forskning," *Forskningsnytt*, 14 (1969), 18–25.
"Endringer i miljø og fauna," in Ragnar Fris Lid and Arne Semb-Johansson (eds.), *Norske dyr*, vol. 5. (Oslo: Cappelen, 1971), pp. 412–28.
Noen økologiske grunnbegreper (Oslo: Universitetet i Oslo, 1973).
"Noen økologiske grunnbegreper," in Paul Hofseth (ed.), *Økofilosofisk lesebok*, vol. 1. (Oslo: Samarbeidsgruppa for natur og miljøvern, 1974), ms. 48 pages.
"Økopolitikk, biologi og klassekamp," *Norsk natur*, 7 (1971), 123–7.
(ed.), *Forurensning og biologisk miljøvern* (Oslo: Universitetsforlaget, 1971).
Mysterud, Ivar, and Iver Mysterud, "Reviving the ghost of broad ecology," *Journal of Social and Evolutionary Systems*, 17 (1994), 167–95.
Mysterud, Ivar, and Magnar Norderhaug, "Koblingen mellom økologi og politikk," *Norsk natur*, 8 (1972), 6–11.
"Mirakeløkonomi og vekstsyke i Japan," *Norsk natur*, 8 (1972), 4–6.
"Teknisk-økonomiske løsninger på den økologiske krise?" *Norsk natur*, 8 (1972), 12–16.
"Økopolitikk – naturvernets nye dimensjon," *Norsk natur*, 7 (1970), 24–7.
Mysterud, Ivar, and Eivind Østbye, "The future of Hardangervidda," *Research in Norway*, 1 (1973), 57–68.
"Vitenskapelige interesser og vassdragsreguleringer på Hardangervidda," *Forskningsnytt*, 1 (1972), 35–45.
Mytting, Ivar, and Rasmus Hansson, *Friluftsliv i konsesjonsbehandling av vassdragssaker* (Oslo: Rådet for natur- og miljøfag, approx.1980).
Mytting, Lars, *Norwegian Wood: Chopping, Stacking, and Drying Wood the Scandinavian Way* (New York: Abrams Image, 2015).
Nesje, Øystein, "Økofilosofisk lesebok," *Miljømagasinet*, 6 (1974), 30.
Nesje, Øystein, and Sven Erik Skønberg, "Forord," in *Natur og menneske: artikkelsamling* (Oslo: Rådet for natur og miljøfag, 1980–82), pp. 1–12.
"Økokrisen, Norge, og vi: Intervju med Sigmund Kvaløy," *Miljømagasinet*, 6 (1974), pp. 20–2, 28.
Nesse, Øystein, "Økofilosofisk lesebok," *Miljømagasinet*, 5 (1974), 31.
"Økofilosofisk lesebok," *Miljømagasinet*, 6 (1974), 30.
Neurath, Paul, *From Malthus to the Club of Rome and Back: Problems of Limits to Growth, Population Control, and Migrations* (London: Sharpe, 1994).
Nielsen, Torben Hviid, Arve Monsen, and Tore Tennøe, *Livets tre og kodenes kode: Fra genetikk til bioteknologi, Norge 1900–2000* (Oslo: Gyldendal Akademisk, 2000).

Nilsen, Kåre Andre, "Jorden har ressurser til fortsatt vekst," *Friheten*, Oct. 1974, 7–12.
Nilsen, Yngve, *En felles plattform? Norsk oljeindustri og klimadebatten i Norge fram til 1998* (Oslo: TIK Senter, 2001).
En sterk stilling? Norsk Forskerforbunds historie 1955–2005 (Oslo: Vigmostad, 2005).
"Ideologi eller kompleksitet? Motstand mot vannkraftutbygging i Norge i 1970-årene," *Historisk tidsskrift*, 87 (2008), 61–84.
Nilsen, Yngve, and Magnus Vollset, *Vinden dreier: meteorologiens historie i Norge* (Oslo: Scandinavian Academic Press, 2016).
Nilsson, Jan-Evert, and Jørgen Randers, *Den unødvendige arbeidsløsheten*, GRS-217 (Oslo: Gruppen for Ressursstudier, 1979).
Njølstad, Olav, *Strålende forskning: Institutt for Energiteknikk 1948–1998* (Oslo: Tano Aschehoug, 1999).
Nord, Erik, "Underutvikling og utvikling," in *Natur og menneske: artikkelsamling* (Oslo: Rådet for natur og miljøfag, 1979), pp. 189–229.
"Økokrisens internasjonale perspektiver," in Per Voksø (ed.), *Mennesket og miljøet* (Oslo: Kirkerådets utvalg for forsking og utredning, Luther forlag, 1975), pp. 50–5.
Norderhaug, Ann, and Magnar Norderhaug, "Norge og overbefolkningen," in *Natur og menneske: artikkelsamling* (Oslo: Rådet for natur og miljøfag, 1979), pp. 156–88.
Noreng, Øystein, "Norwegian oil industry on the continental shelf – social impact, possibilities, problems and policies," in Maurice Scarlett (ed.), *Consequences of Offshore Oil and Gas* (St. John's: Memorial University of Newfoundland, 1977), pp. 59–84.
The Oil Industry and the Government Strategy in the North Sea (Boulder, CO: Croom Helm, 1980).
Norgaard, Kari Marie, *Living in Denial: Climate Change, Emotions and Everyday Life* (Cambridge, MA: MIT Press, 2011).
Norheim, Olav, "Det gløymde folket," *Syn og segn*, 123, no. 3 (2017), 47–53.
Nwosu, Benjamin C. W., "Quality of life on the technological options: The African perspective," *Anticipation*, 17 (May 1974), 31–5.
Næss, Arne, *Anklagene mot vitenskapen* (Oslo: Universitetsforlaget, 1980).
"Blodigle og menneske," *Mestre fjellet*, 13 (1972), 18.
"Bærekraftig utvikling: En begrepsavklaring," *U-Nytt*, 3 (1990), 8–9.
"'Conquest of mountains': A contradiction?" *Mestre fjellet*, 1 (1970), 13, 17.
"De forskjellige holdningene til fjell opp gjennom tidene," *Mestre fjellet*, 2–3 (1970), 19, 22.
"Deep ecology and ultimate premises," *The Ecologist*, 18, no. 4/5 (1988), 128–31.
Det gode lange livs far (Oslo: Damm, 1995).
Ecology, Community and Lifestyle: Outline of an Ecosophy, David Rothenberg (trs.) (Cambridge: Cambridge University Press, 1989).
En del elementære logiske emner (Oslo: Universitetsforlaget, 1941–1985).
"Environmental ethics and Spinoza's ethics," *Inquiry*, 23 (1980), 313–25.

Erkenntnis und wissenschaftliches Verhalten (Oslo: Vitenskapsakademiet, 1936).
Filosofiens historie, 2 vol., various editions (Oslo: Universitetsforlaget, 1961–2001).
"Forskerens ansvar i miljøkrisen," *Forskningsnytt*, 17 (1972), 48–51.
Freedom, Emotion and Self-subsistence: The Structure of a Central Part of Spinoza's Ethics (Oslo: Universitetsforlaget, 1975).
Gandhi and the Nuclear Age, Alistair Hannay (trs.) (Totowa, NJ: Bedminster Press, 1965).
Gandhi og atomalderen (Oslo: Universitetsforlaget, 1960).
"Gandhis lære og situasjonen i dag," *Forskningsnytt*, 5 (1960), 2–4.
"Grønn sosialisme," *Kvekeren*, 5 (1972), 71–2.
Interpretation and Preciseness (Oslo: Dybwad, 1953).
"Klatrefilosofiske og biografiske betraktninger," *Mestre fjellet*, 17, no. 16 (1975), 17–16.
"Letter to Dave Foreman, 23 June 1988," in Nina Witoszek and Andrew Brennan (eds.), *Philosophical Dialogues* (New York: Rowman and Littlefield, 1999), pp. 227–31.
Mao Tsetung: massene filosoferer (Oslo: Universitetsforlaget, 1974).
"Miscarea ecolgică superficială si profundă," in Mihai Botez and Mircea Ioanid (eds.), *Viitorul comun al oamenilor: comunicări prezentate la cea de-a III-a Conferintă mondială de cercetare a viitorului, Bucuresti, septembrie 1972* (Bucharest: Editura politică, 1976), pp. 275–83.
"Mountains," *The Trumpeter*, 21 (2005), 51–4.
"Naturen ebber ut," in *Innerdalen bør bli nasjonalpark* (Oslo: Grøndahl, 1965), pp. 8–9.
Notes on the Foundation of Psychology as a Science (Oslo: Universitetets studentkontor, 1948).
"Om høsting av hval," *Natur og Miljø Bullettin*, July 27, 1992.
Opp stupet: til østtoppen av Tirich Mir (Oslo: Gyldendal, 1964).
Oppgavesamling i logikk med kommentarer (Oslo: Universitetets studentkontor, 1943).
"Paul Feyerabend: A green hero?" in G. Munevar (ed.), *Beyond Reason* (Dordrecht: Kluwer, 1991), pp. 403–16.
"Self-realization in mixed communities of humans, bears, sheep, and wolves," *Inquiry*, 22 (1979), 231–41.
"Skytsgudinnen Gauri Shankar: Appell om fredning," *Mestre fjellet*, 13 (1972), 15.
Symbolsk logikk (Oslo: Univeristetets studentkontor, 1948).
"The case against science," in C. I. Dessaur, et al. (eds.), *Science between Culture and Counter-Culture* (Nijmegen: Dekker and van de Vegt, 1975), pp. 25–48.
The Pluralist and Possibilist Aspect of the Scientific Enterprise (London: George Allen and Unwin, 1972).
"The Norwegian roots of deep ecology," *The Trumpeter* 21, no. 2 (2005), 38–41.

"The shallow and the deep ecology movement," Erling Schøller (trs.), *The Trumpeter*, 24, no. 1 (2008), 59–66.
"The shallow and the deep, long-range ecology movements: A summary," *Inquiry*, 16 (1973), 95–100.
"The shallow and the deep, long-range ecology movements: A summary," in Nina Witoszek and Andrew Brennan (eds.), *Philosophical Dialogues* (Boston; Rowman and Littlefield, 1999), pp. 3–7.
"Truth" as Conceived by Those Who are Not Professional Philosophers (Oslo: Vitenskapsakademiet, 1938).
"Why not science for anarchists too? A reply to Feyerabend," *Inquiry*, 18 (1975), 183–94.
Økologi og filosofi 1 (Oslo: Department of Philosophy, 1971).
Økologi og filosofi: Et økosofisk arbeidsutkast, preliminary 3rd. ed. (Oslo: Department of Philosophy, 1972).
Økologi, samfunn og livsstil, 4th ed. (Oslo: Universitetsforlaget, 1974).
Økologi, samfunn og livsstil, 5th ed. (Oslo: Universitetsforlaget, 1976).
Næss, Arne with Per Ariansen, Thomas Krogh, and Hans Eirik Aarek, *Vitenskapsfilosofi: en innføring*, 2nd preliminary ed. (Oslo: Universitetsforlaget, 1973).
Næss, Arne, and Inga Bostad, *Inn i filosofien: Arne Næss' ungdomsår* (Oslo: Universitetsforlaget, 2002).
Næss, Arne, Jans A. Christophersen, and Kjell Kvaløe, *Democracy, Ideology and Objectivity: Studies in Semantics and Cognitive Analysis of Ideological Controversy* (Oslo: Oslo University Press, 1956).
Næss, Arne with Thomas Krogh, *Vitenskapsfilosofi: utvalgte emner til innledning* (Oslo: Universitetsforlaget, 1971).
Næss, Arne, and Ivar Mysterud, "Philosophy of wolf policies I: General principles and preliminary exploration of selected norms," *Conservation Biology*, 1, no. 1 (May 1987), 22–34.
Næss, Arne Jr., *Drangnag-Ri: Det hellige fjellet* (Oslo: Orion, 1995).
Næss, Erling Dekke, *Autobiography of a Shipping Man* (Colchester, UK: Seatrade Publications, 1977).
Nørhøj, Henning, *Moder jord: om kristendom og økologi* (Copenhagen: Nyt Nordisk forlag, 1977).
Nøttestad, Øyvind, *SFT: Fra forkynner til forvalter* (Oslo: SFT, 1994).
Odell, Peter R., *Olje og makt* (Oslo: Gyldendal, 1972).
Oden, Svante, *Aspects of the Atmospheric Corrosion Climate* (Stockholm: IVA's Korrosionsnämnd, 1965).
"Regionala aspekter på miljöstörningar," *Vann*, 4, no. 3 (1969), 93–112.
Odum, Eugene P., *Fundamentals of Ecology* (Philadelphia: Saunders Co., 1953).
Fundamentals of Ecology, 2nd ed. (Philadelphia: Saunders Co., 1959).
Fundamentals of Ecology, 3rd. ed. (Philadelphia: Saunders Co., 1971).
Odum, Howard, *Environment, Power and Society* (New York: Wiley, 1971).
Oftedahl, Christoffer, "Gode muligheter for olje- eller gassfunn på kontinentalsokkelen," *Forskningsnytt*, 4 (1965), 56–7.
Olsen, Haakon, "Fysikermøtet i Bergen 16–18 juni 1971: System dynamics," *Fra fysikkens verden*, 33, no. 4 (1971), 69–72.

Olsen, Harald, "Forord," in Harald Olsen (ed.), *Mot et samfunn i likevekt: fra de nordiske kirkers arbeid med ressurs- og miljøspørsmål* (Oslo: Land og Kirke, 1978), pp. 7-9.

"Mot en økopolitisk enhetsfront?" *Kirke og kultur*, 77 (1972), 397-405.

"Utkast til et økopolitisk program," in Per Voksø (ed.), *Mennesket og miljøet* (Oslo: Kirkerådets utvalg for forsking og utredning, Luther forlag, 1975), pp. 78-96.

(ed.), *Mot et samfunn i likevekt: Fra de nordiske kirkers arbeid med ressurs- og miljøspørsmål* (Oslo: Gyldendal, 1978).

Omholt, Anders, "Naturessursene i samfunnspolitisk perspektiv," *Teknisk ukeblad*, 119, no. 20 (1972), 15-16, 32.

Oparin, Alexander I., *The Origin of Life* (New York: Macmillan, 1938).

Ore, Aadne, and Ove Arbo Høeg, "Universitetets geologiske institusjoner," in *Universitetet i Oslo:1911-1961*, vol. 1 (Oslo: Universitetsforlaget, 1961), pp. 561-91.

Oreskes, Naomi, and Erik M. Conway, *Merchants of Doubt* (New York: Bloomsbury, 2010).

Orvis, Pat, "International pact sought on acid rain." *Winnipeg Free Press*, Mar. 14. 1984, 27.

Osland, Lidvin M., "Olje- og oljegeologi," in Odd Harbek (ed.), *Nordsjøoljen: Ny norsk naturressurs* (Oslo: Minerva Forlag, 1970), pp. 18-31.

Ottar, Brynjulf, "OECD/Nordforsk-projektet tar sikte på å klarlegge spredningsmønster for sur nedbør i Europa," *Teknisk ukeblad*, 119, no. 24 (1972), 15-16.

Ottosen, Kristian, *Liv og død: Historien om Sachsenhausenfagene* (Oslo: Aschehoug, 1990).

Ottesen, Nils, "Håpløshetens evangelium," *Orientering*, 11 (1974), 10.

Paine, Robert, *Dam a River, Damn a People?* (Copenhagen: IWGIA, 1992).

Parmar, Samuel L., "Foreward," in David M. Gill (ed.), *From Here to Where? Technology, Faith and the Future of Man* (Geneva: World Council of Churches, 1970), pp. 5-8.

"Ethical guidelines and social options after the Limits to Growth debate," *Anticipation*, 18 (1974), 20-2.

Paulsen, Gard, et al., *Building Trust: The History of DNV, 1864-2014* (Oslo: Dinamo Forlag, 2014).

Pharo, Helge, "Norway's peace tradition spanning 100 years," *Scandinavian Review*, 93 (2005), 15-23.

Phillipsgruppen, *Ekofisk: olje fra Nordsjøen* (Oslo: Phillipsgruppen, ca. 1973).

Pirages, Dennis (ed.), *The Sustainable Society: Implications for Limited Growth* (New York: Praeger, 1977).

Ponnamperuma, Cyril, Akira Shimoyama, and Elaine Friebele, "Clay and the origin of life," *Origins of Life and Evolution of Biospheres*, 12 (1982), 9-40.

Pos, Hendrik Josephus, "Erkenntnis und wissenschaftliches Verhalten," *Theoria*, 3 (1937), 117-24.

Power, P. F., "Gandhi and the nuclear age," *Annals of American Academics*, 368 (1967), 201.

Pratt, Henry J., *The Liberalization of American Protestantism* (Detroit: Wayne State University Press, 1972).
Quine, Willard Van Orman, "Methodological Reflections on Current Linguistic Theory," *Synthese*, 21 (1970), 386–98.
Qvenild, Marte, "Svalbard Global Seed Vault: A 'Noah's Ark' for the world's seeds," *Development in Practice*, 18, no.1 (2008), 110–16.
Randalls, Samuel, "Optimal climate change: Economics and climate science policy histories (from heuristic to normative)," *Osiris*, 26 (2011), 224–42.
Randers, Gunnar, *Atomenergi som industriell kraftkilde* (Kjeller: Institutt for Atomenergi, 1953).
  Atomer og sunn fornuft (Oslo: Aschehoug, 1950).
  Atomkraften: verdens håp eller undergang (Oslo: Cappelen, 1946).
  Lysår (Oslo: Gyldendal, 1975).
  "Norges stilling til Euratom," *Teknisk ukeblad*, 109 (1962), 773.
Randers, Jørgen, *Conceptualizing Dynamic Models of Social Systems: Lessons from a Study of Social Change*, PhD thesis (Cambridge, MA: A. P. Sloan School of Management, MIT, 1973).
  "DDT movement in the global environment," in Dennis L. Meadows and Donella H. Meadows (eds.), *Toward Global Equilibrium* (Cambridge, MA: Wright-Allen Press, 1973), pp. 49–83.
  En ramme for norsk utenrikspolitikk, GRS-56 (Oslo: Gruppen for Ressursstudier, 1975).
  En undersøkelse av spinnsystemet i α-Fe_2O_3 ved uelastisk neutronspredning, MA thesis (Kjeller: Institutt for Atomenergi, 1969).
  "From limits to growth to sustainable development *or* SD (sustainable development) in a SD (system dynamics) perspective," *Systems Dynamics Review*, 16, no. 3 (2000), 213–24.
  "How to stop industrial growth with minimal pain?" *Technological Forecasting and Social Change*, 11, no. 4 (1978), 371–82.
  "Industripolitikk i Norge," *Kontrast* 18 (1982), 44–9.
  "System simulation to test environmental policy: DDT," *International Journal of Environmental Studies*, 4, no. 1 (1972), 51–61.
  "The carrying capacity of our global environment – A look at the ethical alternatives," *Anticipation*, 8 (1971), 2–11.
  The Quest for a Sustainable Society, GRS-9 (Oslo: Gruppen for Ressursstudier, 1975).
  "Utopier og lønnssystem," *Samtiden*, 87 (1978), 349–51.
Randers, Jørgen (ed.), *Elements of the System Dynamics Method* (Cambridge, MA: MIT Press, 1980).
Randers, Jørgen, and Dennis L. Meadows, "The dynamics of solid waste," *Technology Review*, 75 (March/April 1972), 20–32.
  "The dynamics of solid waste," in Dennis L. Meadows and Donella H. Meadows (eds.), *Toward Global Equilibrium* (Cambridge, MA: Wright-Allen Press, 1973), pp. 165–211.
Randers, Jørgen with Donella Meadows, "The carrying capacity of the globe," *Sloan Management Review*, 13, no. 2 (1972), 11–27.

"The carrying capacity of our global environment: A look at the ethical alternatives," in Herman E. Daly (ed.), *Toward a Steady State Economy* (San Francisco: Freeman, 1973), pp. 283–306.

Randers, Jørgen and Leif K. Ervik (eds.), *The System Dynamics Method: Proceedings of the 5. International Systems Dynamics Conference* (Oslo: Gruppen for Ressursstudier, 1976).

Reed, Peter, "Man apart: An alternative to the self-realization approach, *Environmental Ethics*, 11 (1989), 53–69.

Regan, Tom, "An examination and defense of one argument concerning animal rights," *Inquiry*, 22 (1979), 189–219.

Reimers, Eigil, David R. Klein, and Rolf Sørumgård, "Calving time, growth rate, and body size of Norwegian reindeer on different ranges," *Arctic and Alpine Research*, 15 (1983), 107–18.

Reinertsen, Maria, *Ligningen for lykke* (Oslo: Cappelen, 2010).

Repp, Gunnar, "Norwegian relationships to nature through outdoor life," in Jan Neuman, Ivar Mytting and Jiri Brtnik (eds.), *Outdoor Activities* (Lüneburg: Edition Erlebnispädagogik, 1996), pp. 32–42.

Repstad, Pål (ed.), *Kirken og samfunnet* (Stavanger: Nomi Forlag, 1970).

Rian, Dagfinn, "Mennesket og naturen i det Gamle Testamentet," in *Mennesket og naturen i kristendom og naturvitenskap* (Trondheim: Tapir, 1980), pp. 29–42.

Riksrevisjonen, *The Office of the Auditor General of Norway's Investigation of Norway's International Climate and Forest Initiative* (Bergen: Fagbokforlaget, 2019).

Ringdal, Nils Johan, *Georg Valentin von Munthe af Morgenstiernes forunderlige liv og reiser* (Oslo: Aschehoug, 2008).

Riste, Olav, *Norway's Foreign Relations: A History*, 2nd ed. (Oslo: Universitetsforlaget, 2005).

Rodman, John, "The Liberation of Nature?" *Inquiry*, 20 (1977), 83–131.

Rokkones, Ola, "Behovet for en norsk befolkningspolitikk," *Kirke og kultur*, 80 (1975), 92–101.

Roll-Hansen, Nils, *Det Internasjonale Biologiske Program (IBP) i Norge* (Oslo: Institute for Studies in Research and Higher Education, 1982).

"Hva slags natur ønsker vi?" *Samtiden*, 82 (1973), 285–95.

Ideological Obstacles to Scientific Advice in Politics? The Case of 'Forest Rain' from 'Acid Rain' (Oslo: Makt og demokratiutredningen, 2002).

"Science, politics, and the mass media: On biased communication of environmental issues," *Science, Technology and Human Values*, 19 (1994), 324–41.

Sur nedbør – et storprosjekt i norsk miljøforskning (Oslo; NAVF, 1986).

Roll-Hansen, Nils, and Geir Hestmark, *Miljøforskning mellom vitenskap og politikk* (Oslo: NAVF, 1990).

Romøren, Tor Inge, "Økologi, samfunn og livsstil," *Norsk filosofisk tidsskrift*, 9, no. 4 (1975), 179–80.

Rosenqvist, Ivan Th., "Atomenergi, atomkapprustning og keiserens nye klær," *Samtiden*, 81, no. 3 (1972), 129–34.

"Den store miljøbløffen," *Vegviseren*, 16 (1989), 8–9.

"Energi og andre ressurser," *Årbok 1976* (Trondheim: Norges Teknisk Vitenskapsakademi, 1976), pp. 1–12.
Et bidrag til analyse av geologiske materialers bufferegenskaper mot sterke syrer i nedbørsvann (Oslo: NAVF, 1976).
"Har vi nok ressurser?" in Mauritz Sundt Mortensen (ed.), *I forskningens lys* (Oslo: NAVF, 1974), pp. 343–58.
"Hvorfor bokføre gasskraft, vasskraft og uran efter ulike prinsipper," *Teknisk ukeblad*, 119, no. 48 (1972), 31.
"Jordens energireserver i geokjemisk lys," *Teknisk ukeblad*, 109 (1962), 1077–80.
"Jordens undergang," *Kirke og kultur*, 71 (1966), 468–79.
"Kraftverk basert på naturgass," *Teknisk ukeblad*, 119 , no. 24 (1972), 19.
"Muligheter for kjemisk intelligensindustri i Norge," *Tidskrift for kjemi, bergvesen og metallurgi*, 8/9 (1967), 142–6.
"Norges stilling til Euratom," *Teknisk ukeblad*, 109, no 29 (1962), 1–3.
"Norges stilling til Euratom," *Teknisk ukeblad* 118, no. 8 (1971), 18.
Numedalsprosjektet – en tverr-geovitenskapelig undersøkelse (Oslo: Department of Geology, University of Oslo, 1970).
"Om de Norske kvikkleirers egenskaper og mineralogiske sammensetning," *Teknisk ukeblad*, 93 (Oct. 1946), 571–6.
"Om leires kvikkagtighet," *Særtrykk av meddelelser fra vegdirektøren*, 799 (1946), 5–12.
"Om leires plastisitet," *Særtrykk av meddelelser fra vegdirektøren*, 799 (1946), 12–16.
"Origin and mineralogy glacial and interglacial clays of southern Norway," *Clays and Clay Minerals*, 23 (1972), 153–9.
"Refugieproblemet og de kvartærgeologiske metodene," *Norsk Geologisk Tidsskrift*, 41 (1961), 319–21.
"Skal internasjonal kapital bestemme over våre ressurser?" *Friheten*, 6 (1973), 7.
"Sub-Moraine Deposits in Numedal," *Bulletin of the Geological Institutions of the University of Uppsala*, 5 (1973), 7–12.
Sur jord surt vann (Oslo: Ingeniørforlaget, 1977).
"Svar til Eilif Dahl," *Norsk Geologisk Tidsskrift*, 43 (1963), 266.
"Tanker over verdens råstoffreserver og Norge," *Forskningsnytt*, 12 (1967), 8–12.
"Vasskraft, naturvern og varmekraft," *Syn og segn*, 79 (1973), 110–12.
"Verden i år 2000," *Forskningsnytt*, 13, no.1 (1968), 13–15.
"Verdens mineralressurser er enorme," *Teknisk ukeblad*, 122, no. 43 (Oct. 1975), 18–19.
"Verdifullt korrketiv til dommedagsprofetiene," *Forskningsnytt*, 19 (1974), 35.
"Vett eller vasskraft?" *Syn og segn*, 62, no. 9 (1966), 1–5.
"World energy resources," in M. W. Thring and R. J. Crookes (eds.), *Energy and Humanity* (Stevenage: Peter Peregrinus, 1974), pp. 8–18.
Rothenberg, David, "A platform of deep ecology," *The Environmentalist*, 7 (1987), 185–90.
Arne Næss: Gjør det vondt å tenke? (Oslo: Grøndahl, 1992).

Is It Painful to Think? Conversations with Arne Naess (Minneapolis: University of Minnesota Press, 1992).
Rothenberg, David, and Peter Reed (trs. eds.), *Wisdom of the Open Air: The Norwegian Roots of Deep Ecology* (Minneapolis: University of Minnesota Press, 1992).
Rothschild, Rachel E., *Poisonous Skies: Acid Rain and the Globalization of Pollution* (Chicago: University of Chicago Press, 2019).
Roucek, Joseph S., "Democracy in a world of tensions," *American Sociological Review*, 16 (1951), 425–6.
Routley, Richard, "Alleged problems in attributing beliefs, and intentionality, to animals," *Inquiry*, 24 (1981), 385–417.
Rowland, Wade, *The Plot to Save the World: The Life and Times of the Stockholm Conference on the Human Environment* (Toronto: Clarke, Irwin, 1973).
Rubin, Charles T., *The Green Crusade: Rethinking the Roots of Environmentalism* (New York: The Free Press, 1994).
Rudie, Ingrid, *Visible Women in East Coast Malay Society* (Oxford: Oxford University Press, 1994).
"Økologi og kultur," in Paul Hofseth (ed.), *Økofilosofisk lesebok*, vol. 1. (Oslo: Samarbeidsgruppa for natur og miljøvern, 1974), pp. 110–31.
Rønnild, Arne, "Gud og naturvitenskapen," *Tidsskrift for teologi og kirke*, 48 (1977), 193–203.
Rønnow, Tarjei, *Saving Nature: Religion as Environmentalism, Environmentalism as Religion* (Munich: LIT Verlag, 2011).
"Takk gode Gud for moder jord, hun gjør oss ett med alt som gror: Religiøsitet og miljøengasjement i Norge," *Norsk antropologisk tidsskrift*, 15 (2004), 18–31.
Rørvik, Thor Inge, *Historien om examen philosophicum 1675–1983* (Oslo: Forum for University History, 1999).
Sabin, Paul, *The Bet: Paul Ehrlich, Julian Simon, and Our Gamble over Earth's Future* (New Haven: Yale University Press, 2013).
Sahlins, Marshal, "Primitiv økonomi," in *Natur og menneske: artikkelsamling* (Oslo: Rådet for natur og miljøfag, 1979), pp. 37–46.
Said, Edward W., "How do you spell Apartheid? O-s-l-o," *Ha'aretz*, Oct. 11, 1998.
Salleh, Ariel Kay, "Deeper than deep ecology: The eco-feminist connection," *Environmental Ethics*, 6, no. 4 (1984), 340–5.
Samarbeidsgruppa for natur og miljøvern, *Dette bør du vite om EF* (Oslo: Pax, 1972).
Håndbok i miljøvern: Økopolitisk strategi og taktikk (Oslo: Cappelen, 1973).
Schmidt, Karl Patterson, *Warder Allee 1885–1955* (Washington: National Academy of Sciences, 1957).
Schneider, Stephen H., and Starley L. Thompson, "Future changes in the atmosphere," in Robert Repetto (ed.), *The Global Possible: Resources, Development, and the New Century* (New Haven: Yale University Press, 1985), pp. 397–430.
Schou, Axel, *Olje: Oljegeografi i motoralderen* (Oslo: Aschehoug, 1965).

Schrumpf, Ellen, *Abortsakens historie* (Oslo: Tiden, 1984).
Schumacher, Ernst F., "Small is beautiful," *Study Encounter*, 9, no. 4 (1973), 13–16.
Seierstad, Atle, *Norge og oljen* (Oslo: Pax, 1970).
Seim, Jardar, "Miljøvern utan politiske følgjer?" *Syn og segn*, 78 (1972), 515–24.
Seip, Jens Arup, *Fra embedsmannsstat til ettpartistat og andre essays* (Oslo: Universitetsforlaget, 1963).
Sem Fure, Jorunn, *Inni forskningsalderen, Universitetet i Oslos 1911–1940* (Oslo: Unipub, 2011).
Universitetet i kamp, in *Universitetet i Oslos historie*, vol. 4 (Oslo: Unipub, 2011).
Semb-Johansson, Arne, *Relation of Nutrition to Endocrine-Reproductive Functions in the Milkweed Bug Oncopeltus fasciatus (Dallas) (Heteroptera: Lygaeidae)*, PhD thesis (Oslo: University of Oslo, 1958).
"Samspillet i nature," in Ragnar Frislid and Aren Semb-Johansson (eds.), *Norges Dyr* (Oslo: Cappelen, 1971), vol. 5, pp. 44–58.
"Stockholm-konferansen kan få stor betydning," *Forskningsnytt*, 17 (1972), 7–10.
Semb-Johansson, Arne, Jon Lund Hansen, and Ivar Mysterud, *Bred Økologi: En tverrfaglig utfordring* (Oslo: Cappelen, 1993).
Serafimova, Silviya, "Whose mountaineering? Which rationality? The role of philosophy of climbing in the establishment of 20th century Norwegian ecophilosophies," *Balkan Journal of Philosophy*, 8, no. 1 (2016), 61–70.
Shapiro, Judith, *Mao's War against Nature: Politics and the Environment in Revolutionary China* (Cambridge: Cambridge University Press, 2001).
Sibley, Mulford Q., "Gandhi and the nuclear age," *Political Science Quarterly*, 82 (1967), 144–5.
Singer, Peter, "Killing humans and killing animals," *Inquiry*, 22 (1979), 145–56.
Sivertsen, Bjarne, *Beregning av midlere belastning gjennom lengere tid som resultat av utslippene fra varmekraftverk på Slagentangen* (Kjeller: Norwegian Institute for Air Research, May 1971).
Skage, Olav R., *Hardangervidda: Naturvern – Kraftutbygging* (Oslo: Universitetsforlaget, 1971).
Skarstein, Frode, *Helge Ingstad: En biografi* (Oslo: Spartacus, 2010).
Skartvet, Andreas (ed.), *Revolusjon i Guds namn?* (Oslo: Samlaget, 1968).
Skirbekk, Gunnar, "Distrikshøgskolar, mot-ekspertise og populisme," in Rolf Vik (ed.), *Vassdrag og samfunn* (Oslo: Universitetsforlaget, 1971), pp. 213–34.
Eco-Philosophical Manuscripts (Bergen: Ariadne, 1992).
Økologi og politikk (Bergen: Universitetet i Bergen, 1972).
Skjelsbæk, Kjell, "Økokrisen som en utfordring til velferdssamfunnets ideologi og struktur," in Per Voksø (ed.), *Mennesket og miljøet* (Oslo: Kirkerådets utvalg for forsking og utredning, Luther forlag, 1975), pp. 56–70.
Skjervheim, Hans, "Naturvern og politick," in Rolf Vik (ed.), *Vassdrag og samfunn* (Oslo: Universitetsforlaget, 1971), pp. 180–8.
Objectivism and the Study of Man (Oslo: Universitetsforlaget, 1959).
"Økologi og normalpolitikk,." in Svein Gjerdåker, Lars Gule, and Bernt Hagtvet (eds.), *Den uoverstigelige grense* (Oslo: Cappelen, 1991), pp. 85–101.

Skjeseth, Jon, *Mennesket og biosfæren: Biologi for Gymnasets Grunnkurs* (Oslo: Fabritius, 1972).
Slagstad, Rune, *Positivisme og vitenskapsteori* (Oslo: Universitetsforlaget, 1979).
Skre, Oddvar, "Mennesket og naturmiljøet: Ressursfordeling og ressursbehov i dag og i morgen," in Per Voksø (ed.), *Mennesket og miljøet* (Oslo: Kirkerådets utvalg for forsking og utredning, Luther forlag, 1975), pp. 11–35.
Sur nedbør: Årsaker og verknader (Oslo: Norges Naturvernforbund, 1972).
Skønberg, Sven Erik, "Norsk økofilosofi," in *Natur og menneske: artikkelsamling* (Oslo: Rådet for natur og miljøfag, 1979), pp. 63–81.
Smith, Cliff, "Economist urges tax boost," *Medina County Gazette*, Aug. 28, 1974, 18.
Smith, J. Maynard, and E. Szathmáry, *The Origins of Life: From the Birth of Life to the Origin of Language* (Oxford: Oxford University Press, 1999).
Snow, Charles P., *The Two Cultures and the Scientific Revolution* (Cambridge: Cambridge University Press, 1959).
Solem, Jon, "Naturverner for vår tid?" *Harvest* (blog, Sept. 21, 2014).
Solenes, Oskar, "Friluftsliv og klassekamp: To sider av samme sak?" *Arbeiderhistorie*, 21 (2007), 7–25.
Somby, Niillas A., "Et lysglimt," in Sven Erik Skønberg (ed.), *Grønn pepper i turbinene* (Oslo: Universitetsforlaget, 1985), pp. 112–22.
Spengler, Oswald, *The Decline of the West* (New York: Oxford University Press, 1991).
Spinoza, Benedict de, *Ethics*, in *Works of Spinoza*, vol. 1, R. H. M. Elwes (trs.) (New York: Dover Pub., 1955).
Stahl Johannsessen, Kjell, "Oljesommer," in Odd Harbek (ed.), *Nordsjøoljen: Ny norsk naturressurs* (Oslo: Minerva Forlag, 1970), pp. 7–17.
Stanley, Matthew, *Practical Mystic: Religion, Science, and A. S. Eddington* (Chicago: Chicago University Press, 2007).
Statens Oljeråd, *Innstilling nr. 6 fra Statens Oljeråd om endringer i Kgl. Res. av 9 april 1965 om utforskning og utnyttelse av undersjøiske petroliumsforekomster* (Oslo: Statens Oljeråd, May 5, 1972).
Statistics Norway, *Holiday House Survey* (Oslo: Statistics Norway, 1970).
Holiday Survey (Oslo: Statistics Norway, 1968).
Outdoor Life (Oslo: Statistics Norway, 1974).
Steenbergen, Bart van, "The first fifteen years: A personal view of the early history of the WFSF," *Futures*, 37 (2005), 355–60.
Steineger, Erik, *Etnobotaniske undersøkelser i et sherpasamfunn i Rolwalingdalen, Nepal*, MA thesis (Oslo: Matematisk-naturvitenskapelig fakultet, 1977).
Steiner, H. Arthur, "Gandhi and the nuclear age," *Western Political Quarterly*, 19 (1966), 547–8.
Stenberg, Lennart, *Longterm Development in the Scandinavian Forest Sector: A Study of Transition Problems Using the System Dynamics Approach*, GRS-88 (Oslo: Gruppen for Ressursstudier, 1977).
Stenseth, Nils Chr., "En oppfordring til biologene om å utforme en økopolitikk," *Naturen*, 96 (1972), 118–26.

"Matematisk modellbygging i økologisk forskning," *Forskningsnytt*, 19 (1974), 28–34.
Theoretical Studies on Fluctuating Populations: An Evolutionary Approach, PhD thesis (Oslo: Zoological Institute, 1977).
Stigen, Anfinn, "En del hovedpunkter i forelesning 'mennesket og naturen' holdt for examen philosophicum studenter september 1973," in Paul Hofseth (ed.), *Økofilosofisk lesebok*, vol. 2. (Oslo: Samarbeidsgruppa for natur og miljøvern, 1974), ms. 7 pages.
Tenkningens historie, 2 vol. (Oslo: Gyldendal, 1983).
Stivers, Robert, *The Sustainable Society: Ethics and Economic Growth* (Philadelphia: Westminster Press, 1976).
Stoll, Mark S., *Inherit the Holy Mountain: Religion and the Rise of American Environmentalism* (Oxford: Oxford University Press, 2015).
Stoltenberg, Jens, *Makroøkonomisk planlegging under usikkerhet – en empirisk analyse* (Oslo: Statistics Norway, 1985).
Stridbeck, Bolof, *Ekosofi och etik* (Göteborg: Bokskogen, 1994).
Strøksnes, Morten A., *Shark Drunk: The Art of Catching a Large Shark from a Tiny Rubber Dinghy in a Big Ocean* (New York: Knopf, 2017).
Strømme, Roar, "Teologien i møte med øko-krisa," *Ung teologi*, 12 (1979), 1–11.
Økologi og teologi: tankar om ei kristen naturforståing innfor den økologiske krisa, MA thesis (Oslo: Menighetsfakultetet, 1978).
Stubberud, Juel, "Rolf Edberg og Norge," in *Rolf heter jag* (Karlsatd: Föreningen för Värmlandslitteratur, 2000), pp. 119–26.
Sundby, Ragnhild, "Globalforgiftning," *Naturen*, 89 (1965), 3–11.
Svarstad, Hanne, and Shivcharn S. Dhillion (eds.), *Responding to Bioprospecting* (Oslo: Spartacus, 2000).
Sæter, Einar, and Svein Sæter, *XU – i hemmeleg teneste 1940–1945* (Oslo: Det Norske Samlaget, 1995).
Sæther, Anne Karin, *De beste intensjoner: Oljelandet i klimakampen* (Oslo: Cappelen, 2017).
Sætra, Hartvig, *Den Økopolitiske Sosialismen*, 3rd ed. (Oslo: Pax, 1973).
Jamvektssamfunnet er ikkje noko urtete-selskap (Oslo: Samlaget, 1990).
Sørensen, Nils Andreas, "Kostnader ved utslipp av svoveloksyder i atmosfæren," *Teknisk ukeblad*, 119, no. 16 (1972), 46.
Takle, Svein, "Momenter for et kirkelig handlingsprogram," in Harald Olsen (ed.), *Mot et samfunn i likevekt* (Oslo: Land og Kirke, 1978), pp. 155–63.
Tangaard, Per, *Energi over alle grenser: kristent livssyn og forvaltning av ressurser* (Oslo: Credo, 1983).
Thamdrup, Harald M., *Naturens husholdning* (Oslo: Aschehoug, 1966).
Thue, Fredrik W., *Empirisme og demokrati* (Oslo: Universitetsforlaget, 1997).
Thue, Fredrik W., and Kim G. Helsvig, *1946–1975 Den store transformasjonen*, vol. 5, *Universitetet i Oslo 1811–2011* (Oslo: Unipub, 2011), 331–42.
Tobias, Michael (ed.), *Deep Ecology* (San Marcos, CA: Avant Books, 1984).
Toffler, Alvin, *Future Shock* (New York: Random House, 1970).
Toulmin, Stephen, "An Empirical Study," *Philosophical Review*, 65 (1956), 116–18.

Try, Jakob, "Befolkningsproblem, matvaresituasjon og kortsynthet," *Kirke og kultur*, 73 (1968), 326–38.
Tsetung, Mao, *Mao Tsetungs dikt*, Kjell Heggelund and Tor Obrestad (trs.) (Oslo: Gyldendal, 1971).
The Poems of Mao Tse-tung (New York: Harper and Row, 1972).
Tvedt, Terje, *Angels of Mercy or Development Diplomats?* (Oxford: James Curry, 1998).
Det internasjonale gjennombruddet (Oslo: Dreyer, 2017).
Tveit, Odd Karsten, *Nordsjøoljen* (Oslo: Grøndahl, 1973).
Vår olje og vår kraft (Oslo: Grøndahl, 1973).
Ulstein, Ragnar, *Etterretningstjenesten i Norge 1940–45* (Oslo: Cappelen, 1989–1990).
United Nations, *Report of the United Nations Conference on the Human Environment* (New York: United Nations, 1973).
United Nations Environmental Programme, *Environment and Development in Africa* (New York: UNEP, 1981).
Unneberg, Bjørn, *Grønn sosialisme for utkantproletarer* (Oslo: Cultura Forlag, 1971).
Vaa, Mariken, "Samtaler i samtiden: Mellom olje og sol," *Samtiden*, 89 (1980), 9–13.
Veen, Tor Dagfinn, *Oljen i Nordsjøen* (Stavanger: Rogalandsbanken, 1973).
Vetlesen, Arne Johan, *The Denial of Nature: Environmental Philosophy in the Era of Global Capitalism* (London: Taylor and Francis, 2015).
Vetlesen, Vesla, *Kvinner i olje-Norge* (Oslo: Folkets brevskole, 1975).
Vik, Rolf, "Forord," in Rolf Vik (ed.), *Vassdrag og samfunn* (Oslo: Universitetsforlaget, 1971), 11.
"Hvor står biologene i teknikkens århundre?" *Naturen*, 91 (1967), 259–69.
International Biological Programme, IBP i Norge: Årsrapport (Oslo: IBP, 1968–1974).
International Biological Programme: Final Report Scandinavian Countries (Oslo: Scandinavian National Committees of the International Biological Programme, 1975).
"Kjenner vi vårt miljø? – Tar vi vare på det?" In anonymous (ed.), *Fem på tolv: En bok av vitenskapsmenn om vår mulige fremtid* (Oslo: Gyldendal, 1968), pp. 125–54.
"Naturvern er menneskevern," *Naturen*, 90 (1966), 195–205.
"Trusselen mot miljøet," in Anonymous (ed.),*Verden i dag* (Oslo: Gyldendal, 1969), pp. 79–92.
"Vårt miljø og biologenes ansvar," *Samtiden*, 78 (1969), 67–79.
Vik, Rolf, and Frans-Emil Wielgolaski, "Det Internasjonale Biologiske Program i 1969," *Forskingsnytt*, 15 (1970), 14–20.
Viksveen, Thor, *Jens Stoltenberg: Et portrett* (Oslo: Pax, 2011).
Vinje, Arne, "Distriktsnedbygging eller auka sjølberging?" *Miljømagasinet*, 5 (1973), 32–4.
"Norsk økopolitikk: Fram for auka sjølberging," *Miljømagasinet*, 4 (1973), 30–2.

Vischer, Lukas, "Climate change, sustainability and Christian witness," *Ecumenical Review*, 49 (1997), 142-61.
Voksø, Per, "Innledning," in Per Voksø (ed.), *Mennesket og miljøet* (Oslo: Kirkerådets utvalg for forsking og utredning, Luther forlag, 1975), pp. 7-10.
Vollset, Magnus, Rune Hornnes, and Gunnar Ellingsen, *Calculating the World: The History of Geophysics as Seen from Bergen* (Oslo: Fagbokforlaget, 2018).
Walløe, Lars, "Whale numbers in dispute," *Nature*, 362 (April 1, 1993), 389.
Ward, Barbara, and René Dubos, *Only One Earth: The Care and Maintenance of a Small Planet* (New York: Norton, 1972).
Warde, Paul, *The Invention of Sustainability: Nature and Destiny, c. 1500-1870* (Cambridge: Cambridge University Press, 2018).
Watts, Jonathan, "Norway's Push for Arctic Oil and Gas Threatens Paris Climate Goals," *The Guardian*, Aug. 10, 2017.
Weart, Spencer R., *The Discovery of Global Warming* (Cambridge, MA: Harvard University Press, 2003).
Wedberg, Anders, "Interpretation and preciseness," *Journal of Symbolic Logic*, 14 (1949), 54-5.
  "Interpretation and preciseness," *Journal of Symbolic Logic*, 15 (1950), 73-4.
  "Interpretation and preciseness," *Journal of Symbolic Logic*, 15 (1950), 204.
Wendelbo, Per, "Plants from Tirich Mir: A contribution to the flora of Hindukush," *Nytt magasin for botanikk*, 1 (1952), 1-70.
Werskey, Gary, *The Visible College: A Collective Biography of British Scientists and Socialists of the 1930s* (London: Free Association Books, 1988).
Westermoen, Toralf, in *Forhandlinger i Stortinget*, 538 (May 13, 1975), 4172.
Wetlesen, Jon, "Value in nature: Intrinsic or inherent?" in Nina Witoszek and Andrew Brennan (eds.), *Philosophical Dialogues: Arne Næss and the Progress of Ecophilosophy* (Boston: Rowman and Littlefield, 1999), pp. 405-17.
White, Lynn T., "The historical roots of our ecologic crisis," *Science*, 155, no. 3767 (Mar. 10, 1967), 1203-7.
  "Den økologiske krises historiske røtter," *Naturen*, 95 (1971), 77-92.
Wielgolaski, Frans-Emil, "Fenologi, produksjonsøkologi og andre kjente eller ukjente økologiske begreper," *Naturen*, 92 (1968), 179-84.
Wiggen, Birgit, *Debatten omkring populisme/økopolitikk i Norge 1966-1976*, MA thesis (Oslo: The Norwegian Library School, 1976).
Wilson, Edward, *Sociobiology: The New Synthesis* (Cambridge, MA: Harvard University Press, 1975).
Wisløff, Jens, "Utkast til et økopolitisk program," in Per Voksø (ed.), *Mennesket og miljøet* (Oslo: Kirkerådets utvalg for forsking og utredning, Luther forlag, 1975), pp. 71-7.
Witoszek, Nina, "Marx, Næss, og Gaia: Hva skal vi gjøre med kulturen?" *Kontrast*, 122, no. 3/4 (1990), 4-10.
  Norske naturmytologier: fra Edda til økofilosofi (Oslo: Pax, 1998).
Witoszek, Nina, and Andrew Brennan (eds.), *Philosophical Dialogues* (New York: Rowman and Littlefield, 1999).
World Commission on Environment and Development, *Our Common Future* (Oxford: Oxford University Press, 1987).

World Council of Churches, "Report of the Advisory Committee on 'The search for a just, participatory and sustainable society'," in Koson Srisang (ed.), *Perspectives on Political Ethics: An Ecumenical Enquiry* (Geneva: WCC, 1979), pp. 174-93.
"Science and technology for human development: The ambiguous future and the Christian hope: Report," *Anticipation*, 19 (1974), 1-43.
"Selected preparatory papers," *Anticipation* 17 (May 1974), 1-61.
World Council of Churches Central Committee and David E. Johnson (eds.), *Uppsala to Nairobi, 1968-1975: Report of the Central Committee to the Fifth Assembly of the World Council of Churches* (New York: Friendship Press, 1975).
World Population Conference, *The Population Debate: Dimensions and Perspectives: Papers of the World Population Conference, Bucharest, 1974*, 2 vol. (New York: United Nations, 1975).
Worster, Donald, *Nature's Economy: The Roots of Ecology* (San Francisco: Sierra Club Books, 1977).
Worthington, Edgar B., *The Ecological Century: A Personal Appraisal* (Oxford: Oxford University Press, 1983).
(ed.), *The Evolution of IBP* (Cambridge: Cambridge University Press, 1975).
Wright, Georg Henrik von, "Essays om naturen, mennesket og den vitenskapelig-tekniske revolusjon," *Naturen*, 91 (1967), 155-80.
"Symbolsk logikk," *Journal of Symbolic Logic*, 14 (1949), 185.
Wyller, Kari Bruun, and Thomas Chr. Wyller (eds.), *Norsk oljepolitikk* (Oslo: Gyldendal, 1975).
Ydegaard, Torbjørn, *Sherpa – folket under Everest* (Holte: Skarv, 1988).
Ytreberg, Pål, "Diktat fra Høyer, Kvaløy m.fl.," *(snm) nytt*, 5 (May 1976), 9-11.
Zapffe, Peter W., "Avskjed med Gausta," in *Barske glæder og andre temaer fra et liv under åpen himmel*, Sigmund Kvaløy (ed.) (Oslo: Cappelen Damm, 2012), pp. 127-8.
Zapffe, Peter W., *Barske glæder og andre temaer fra et liv under åpen himmel*, Sigmund Kvaløy (ed.) (Oslo: Gyldendal, 1969).
"Biosofisk perspektiv," in Jan Brage Gundersen (ed.), *Essays* (Oslo: Aventura, 1992), pp. 141-68.
Den logiske sandkasse: elementær logikk for universitet og selvstudium (Oslo: Pax, 1966).
Essays og epistler (Oslo: Gyldendal, 1967).
"Farvell Norge," in *Barske glæder og andre temaer fra et liv under åpen himmel*, Sigmund Kvaløy (ed.) (Oslo: Cappelen Damm, 2012), pp. 129-35.
Om det tragiske (Oslo: Gyldendal, 1941).
"The Last Messiah," in Peter Reed and David Rothenberg (eds. trs.), *Wisdom in the Open Air* (Minneapolis: University of Minnesota Press, 1993), pp. 40-52.
Zelko, Frank, "Blood on the ice: The Greenpeace campaign against the harp seal slaughter," in Marco Armiero and Lise Sedrez (eds.), *A History of Environmentalism: Local Struggles, Global Histories* (London: Bloomsbury, 2014), pp. 107-27.

Øfsti, Audun (ed.), *Ecology and Ethics: A Report from the Melbu Conference, 18–23 July 1990* (Trondheim: Nordland Akademi for Kunst og Vitenskap, 1992).
Økland, Jan, "Naturviten og naturbruk: Om dyreliv og miljøforhold I norske vassdrag," *Naturen*, 91 (1967), 387–97.
Østbye, Eivind, "Aktuell forskning i enkle økosystemer, med særlig henblikk på høyfjellsforskning i Norge," *Forskningsnytt*, 4 (1967), 70–3.
Bibliography of the Finse Area 1781–1996 (Finse: The High Mountain Ecology Research Station, 1997).
En undersøkelse over nivale carabiders økologi, særlig innen slekten Nebria Latr, MA thesis (Oslo: University of Oslo, 1963).
"Høyfjellsøkologisk forskningsstasjons historie," in Lauritz Sømme og Eivind Østbye (eds.), *Finse: Et senter for høyfjellsforskning* (Finse: Høyfjellsøkologisk forskningsstasjon, 1997), pp. 3–9.
Østbye, Eivind, et al., "Hardangervidda, Norway," *Ecological Bulletins*, 20 (1975), 225–64.
Østerud, Øyvind, *Konflikt og administrasjon: en studie i norsk kraftutbygging*, MA thesis (Oslo: Department of Political Science, University of Oslo, 1970).
"Lite land som humanitær stormakt?" *Nytt norsk tidsskrift*, 4 (2006), 303–16.
"Naturverdier og samfunn – en ideologisk skisse," in Rolf Vik (ed.), *Vassdrag og samfunn* (Oslo: Universitetsforlaget, 1971), 189–210.
Øverland, Per, *Kristen etikk* (Oslo: Lunde, 1970).
Øygard, Olav, *Preken i møte med den økologiske krise*, MA thesis (Oslo: Menighetsfakultetet, 1981).

Index

Aarek, Hans Eirik, 102, 109
Acid Precipitation Program, 196–7, 224
acid rain, 175, 192, 196, 198–200, 216, 218, 221, 235–6
Ager-Hanssen, Henrik, 224
Allee, Warder Clyde, 23
Alnæs, Finn, 66, 69
Alta-Kautokeino, 20, 22, 91, 93, 138, 202–4, 236
Amble, Erling, 80, 89, 111
Amundsen, Roal, 14
Andenæs, Johannes, 81, 84
Andersen, Gisle, 227
Andersson, Axel, 15, 17
Apel, Karl-Otto, 100, 209
Archer, Colin, 14
Ariansen, Per, 102, 209
Austad, Torleiv, 132
Ayer, Alfred J., 107

Barroso, José Manuel, 1
Barth, Fredrik, 5, 14, 23–6, 111, 231
   Swat, North Pakistan, 24
Barth, Thomas, 23, 179
Bates, Marston, 33
Behrens, William W., 147
Benestad, Olav, 105
Bernal, John, 71, 177–8, 181
Berner, Mia, 55
Berntsen, Bredo, 187
Berntsen, Thorbjørn, 225
Biersdorf, John E., 153–4
biocentric vs. anthropocentric, 129

Birch, Charles, 162
Bjerknes, Vilhelm, 219
Bjørnebye, Anne, 84, 93
Black, John N., 123
Bolin, Bert, 218, 220
Bonnevie, Kristine, 14
Bookchin, Murray, 213
Borgström, George, 109, 161
Boulding, Kenneth, 43, 161, 164
Brand, Stewart, 7
Bratteli, Trygve, 193, 195
Bravo, Michael, 4
Breivik, Birgir, 133
Breivik, Gunnar, 133–6, 139, 141
Brennan, Andrew, 88
Broch, Hjalmar, 14
Brostigen, Gunnar, 84, 93
Brown, Lester, 217
Brox, Ottar, 26–7, 29, 43
   Hva skjer i Nord Norge?, 27
   Torsken, 26
Brundtland, Gro Harlem, 6, 143, 170, 172, 195–6, 199–203, 205–6, 214, 216–18, 220–1, 223–5, 227, 235–7
   Chair of the World Commission, 217
   Director-General World Health Organization, 6
   Prime Minister, 206, 214, 220–1
Bryn, Kåre, 228
Brøgger, Waldemar Chr., 177
Bucharest, 85, 87, 122, 159–60, 166, 210
Buckminster Fuller, Richard, 149
Buddhism, 122, 124

Bugge, Hans Christian, 217, 223
Bush, Vannevar, 145–7

Callicott, J. Baird, 214
Carson, Rachel, 5, 32–3, 38, 147, 232
Ceaușescu, Nicolae, 87, 160–1
Center for International Climate Environmental Research, Oslo, 223–4, 227
Center Party, 89
Centre for Development and the Environment, 222–3
Christian Democratic Party, 129, 133
Ciplea, Licinius, 86–7
Cittadino, Eugene, 23
Clark, Stephen R. L., 99
Clean Development Mechanism, 228, 238
climate change, 1, 28, 174, 176, 203, 218–19, 222, 224–7, 229, 235–7, 239
Club of Rome, 85–6, 147, 150–1, 159, 161, 166, 172
Coen, Deborah, 197
Cold War, 3, 5, 15, 18–19, 27, 57, 65, 81, 84–5, 89, 92, 101, 122, 128, 138, 145, 150, 160, 164, 172, 182, 184, 203–4, 226–7, 230, 236, 240
Commoner, Barry, 73
Communist Party, 160, 177
Conservative Party, 136
Convention on Biological Diversity, 228
Cousteau, Jacques-Yves, 34
cross-country skiing, 10, 12, 61, 118

Dahl, Eilif, 34–6, 38–40, 55, 82, 167, 189–91, 193, 196–7, 199, 201, 217
 acid buffer capacity, 191
 acid rain, 191
 Rondane, 36
Dammann, Erik, 17
Davidson, Donald, 99
Dawkins, Richard, 115, 144
DDT pollution, 33, 147, 193
Deep Ecologists, 6, 64, 75, 80, 82, 85, 88–9, 91–2, 94, 99–100, 103–4, 107, 111, 119–20, 122, 146, 167–8, 187, 197, 203–5, 207, 209, 212–13, 215–16, 219–20, 224, 226, 230, 234–5, 237
 Samarbeidsgruppa for natur- og miljøvern, 64

Deep Ecology, 5, 74, 77, 85, 87–8, 90, 97–9, 115, 120–1, 123–4, 142, 206, 209–12, 216, 223, 233–4, 236
Derr, Thomas Sieger, 130, 159
Det Norske Veritas, 228
Devall, Bill, 210
Dordick, Herbert, 155
Douglas, Neil, 154
Dovland, Harlad, 228
Drengson, Alan R., 211, 216
Dubos, René, 19
Dunker, Henning, 109

Earth First!, 203, 210–12, 236
Earth Summit, 5, 202, 224, 228, 236
ecology, 5–6, 16, 23–5, 31–3, 35, 37–8, 41–2, 49, 51–2, 60, 64, 69–71, 78, 80, 88–9, 96–7, 101–2, 104, 106, 111–14, 122–4, 128–9, 131–2, 135, 141, 164, 166, 182, 185, 189, 193, 205, 209–10, 213, 215, 223, 231–2, 236
ecophilosophy, 3, 46, 50–1, 80, 88, 93–4, 96, 100, 105, 111, 124, 126, 128, 130, 134, 204, 212
Ecophilosophy Group, 65, 69, 72–3, 93, 98, 102, 107, 109, 112, 211, 232
Ecopolitical Cooperation Ring, 91, 203
eco-politics, 3, 43, 111, 135
ecoreligion, 3, 88, 125, 133, 135, 137, 140–1
eco-theology, 131, 138, 141
Edberg, Rolf, 129
Eden, 16–18, 20, 117, 127, 152, 218, 235–6
Ehrlich, Paul, 74
Ekofisk, 174–5
Elder, Frederic, 129
Elliot, Robert, 99
Environmental Studies, 83–4, 92–4, 99, 101–2, 104, 106–7, 111–12, 114–17, 206–7, 211, 217, 221, 223, 234
 Environmental Research Foundation, 207
 Environmental Studies Seminar, 116
Enzensberger, Hans Magnus, 28, 89
 Tjøme, 28
Eriksen, Reidar, 69, 106
Euratom, 145, 183, 188
European Community, 22, 79, 81, 83–5, 89, 92, 96, 100, 106, 109, 111, 113, 145, 165, 171, 182, 188, 197, 204, 206, 233, 235
European Science Foundation, 224

Index

European Year for Conservation of Nature, 42
Examen philosophicum, 57, 59, 71, 107, 112, 133, 135-6
Exxon, 175, 185
   acid rain, 176

Faarlund, Nils, 44, 52, 60-1, 69, 75, 77-8, 92, 109, 115, 122, 134, 137, 139
   Beding (Nepal), 75, 77, 122
   free-air-person, 61
   Gauri Shankar, 122
   Hemsedal, 44, 61
   Norwegian Mountaineering School, 44, 61
Feyerabend, Paul, 103
Finse, 29-30, 32, 41, 44, 78, 84, 232, 234, 236
fishermen-peasants, 13, 27-8, 70, 78, 106, 214, 230-1, 233, 239
Fleicher, Carl A., 82
Foreman, Dave, 210-12, 216
Forrester, Jay W., 146-7, 149, 154, 156, 171
Fox, Warwick, 216
free-air-life, 10, 61, 78, 230
Freud, Sigmund, 54
Friedman, Milton, 226
Fægri, Knut, 38
Føllesdal, Dagfinn, 58

Galtung, Johan, 6, 57, 62, 65, 85-6, 91, 118, 122, 150, 166, 169, 173
   on Gandhi, 57, 65
   Peace Research Institute, 85, 91, 122, 150
Garder, Per, 69
George, Poikail, 154
Giæver, Ivar, 222
Gjærevoll, Olav, 40, 165, 194
Glacken, Clarence, 112, 123
Glesne, Ola, 207
Godal, Jon Boyer, 69, 90, 109, 114
Golden Age, 149, 152, 158, 171, 235
Government Pension Fund of Norway, 226, 240
Green New Deal, 4, 240
Green Party, 239
Greenpeace, 214
Grepstad, Jon, 69
Gunleiksrud, Gaute, 132, 138

Habermas, Jürgen, 52, 99, 113
Hafslund, 175, 181-2, 189, 192
Haldane, John B. S., 178
Hamsun, Knut, 232
Hanisch, Ted, 224, 227
Hardangervidda, 41, 43, 92, 192, 232, 234
Hare, Kenneth, 219
Harlem, Gudmund, 191, 196
Hauge, Jens Gabriel, 132, 141, 161, 169
Haukeland, Per Ingvar, 119
Hegge, Hjalmar, 67, 69, 82, 109, 113
   on Goethe, 113
Heidegger, Martin, 134
Helland, Botolv, 80
Hessen, Dag, 231
Heyerdahl, Liv, 15
Heyerdahl, Thor, 5, 14-17, 19-20, 231
   Fatu-Hiva, 14-16, 231
   Kon-Tiki expedition, 15
   Larvik fjord, 14
   Motane, 16-17
   oceanic pollution, 18
   World Federalist Movement, 19
   World Wilderness Congress, 20
   World Wildlife Fund, 20
High Mountain Ecology Research Station, 29-30, 84, 232
Hitschmann, Edward, 54
Hoel, Adolf, 177
Hofseth, Paul, 69, 93, 103, 106-7, 109, 116, 217, 221
Hole, Ola, 93
Hollås, Oddmund, 69
Hughes, J. Donald, 99
Huxley, Julian, 56
   UNESCO, 56
Hylland, Aanund, 84, 93
Høibraaten, Helge, xii, 13
Høyer, Karl Georg, 69, 80, 91

Ingstad, Anne Stine, 5, 22
   L'Anse aux Meadows, 22
Ingstad, Helge, 5, 14, 20-2, 27, 231
   Apache Indian Reservation, 21
   Chipewyan First Nation, 20
   Governor of East Greenland, 21
   Land of Feast and Famine, 21
   Vinland Colony, 22
Institute of Energy Technology, 144
International Biological Program, 6, 31, 37-40, 102, 121, 232

International Climate and Forest Initiative, 239
International Institute for Environmental Affairs, 19

Jacobsen, Roy, 232
Jarving, Stein, 63, 90
Jensen, Ole, 128
Johnson, Lawrence E., 216
Jonas, Hans, 100

Kant, Immanuel, 113
Kaul, Dagny, 129
Kettener, Matthias, 100
Keynes, John Maynard, 226
Klein, David, 123–6
Kohler, Robert E., 32
Kroepelin, Bjarne, 15
Krogh, Thomas, 71, 102
Kvaløy Setreng, Sigmund, 52, 60–3, 65–70, 74–8, 80, 82, 84, 88–91, 93, 99–101, 104, 109, 111, 113, 115, 122–6, 128, 139, 185, 204, 207–9, 221, 232
   Beding (Nepal), 75–6, 79, 90, 115, 122, 124
   Bhutan, 208
   Budalen, 207
   Gauri Shankar, 122, 124
   Industrial Growth Society, 77, 100, 204, 208, 233
   Life Necessities Society, 77, 100–1, 204, 207–8, 233
   Nagarkot, 63
   Øko-filosofisk fragment, 99

Labor Party, 11–12, 34, 36, 145, 166, 169, 172, 175, 179, 182–4, 188–9, 191, 193, 195–6, 200, 202–3, 216, 221, 223–6, 229, 235–6
   power-socialism, 12, 60, 175, 177, 182, 189, 191, 194, 200
Leach, Edmund, 6, 25
Leifsen, Esben, 211
Leiro, Jostein, 228
Lenin, Vladimir, 60, 177
Leopold, Aldo, 74, 210
Lewin, Kurt, 55
Lied, Finn, 169, 172, 217
Lind, Terje, 93
Lindholm, Magne, 80
Lloyd, Genevieve, 99

Lønning, Inge, 136
Lousley, Cheryl, 220
Lovelock, James, 212, 216
Lutheranism, 6–7, 11, 101, 119–20, 130, 133, 139, 141, 143–4, 233–4

Maathai, Wangari, 1
Malitza, Mircea, 161
Maoism, 28, 59, 72–3, 78, 90–1, 167
Marcuse, Herbert, 34, 52, 70
Mardøla, 65, 67–70, 74, 79, 82, 100, 109, 120, 124, 126–7, 193, 204, 233
Marstrander, Johan, 69
Martiniussen, Erik, 227
Marx, Karl, xi, 11, 28, 121, 209
Mates, Benson, 56
McGinn, Colin, 99
McHale, John, 86
McKibben, Bill, 4, 240
Mead, Margaret, 150
Meadows, Dennis L., 147
Meadows, Donella H., 147
Ministry of the Environment, 193, 197, 201, 207, 221, 226
Miró, Carmen, 19
Mitman, Gregg, 23
Morgenstierne, Georg, 24
Müller, Paul, 33
Myrdal, Gunnar, 19
Mysterud, Ivar, 42–3, 62, 64, 69, 72, 89, 109, 111, 123–4, 126, 185, 215

Nansen, Fridtjof, 14, 177, 185
NATO, 6, 53, 111, 145, 166, 182, 184, 188
Nature and Humans (seminar), 62, 64, 69, 72, 107–9, 111–12, 114–16, 135–6, 211, 223
Nepal, 63, 75, 78–9, 88, 90, 100, 115, 122, 124, 204, 207–8, 230, 233, 238
Nilsen, Yngve, 227
Nobel Peace Prize, 1, 3
Norderhaug, Magnar, 42–3, 82, 109, 115
Norgaard, Kari Marie, 239
Norling, Dag, 80
Norsk Hydro, 238
North Sea, 106, 146, 174, 180, 184, 192, 234–5
Norwegian Academy of Science and Letters, 35–6, 173, 177
Norwegian Agricultural College, 34, 36

Norwegian Alpine Club, 24, 48–9, 53, 57, 60, 64, 71, 78
Norwegian Geographical Society, 48
Norwegian Institute of International Affairs, 37
Norwegian Pollution Council Authority, 189
Norwegian Research Council, 38, 224
Norwegian School of Management, 173
Norwegian School of Sport Sciences, 61, 134, 139
Norwegian School of Theology, 131, 133
Norwegian Society for the Conservation of Nature, 63
Norwegian Trekking Association, 30–1
Norwegian Veterinary School, 132
Næss, Arne, 6, 24, 36, 44–55, 57–62, 64, 66–9, 71–2, 74–5, 77–8, 85, 87–8, 91, 94–9, 101–4, 107, 109, 111–13, 115, 118, 122–6, 129, 136, 139, 166, 169, 173, 185–6, 200, 208–12, 214–16, 221, 223–4, 232
  Beding (Nepal), 75, 122
  Bhutan, 208–9
  on Gandhi, 57, 63, 65, 74, 78, 122
  Gauri Shankar, 122
  Hallingskarvet Mountain, 44–5, 47, 94, 118, 232
  Interpretation and Preciseness, 55
  Nagarkot, 63
  Økologi, samfunn og lifsstil, 98
  Skarveredet, 45–6, 48–9
  T = G2/(LS + Ås), 49, 95
  Tirich Mir, 48–9, 78, 95
  Tvergastein, 46–9, 54, 59–60, 63, 94, 97–8, 211
  Vienna Circle, 54, 59
Næss, Else, 47, 54, 59
Næss, Erling, 76
  Royal Nepal Shipping, 76
Næss, Siri, 59

Ocasio-Cortez, Alexandria, 4
Odum, Eugene P., 34, 102
Olsen, Harald, 121
Oparin, Alexander, 178
Oslo School of Architecture, 63
  Og etter oss ..., 63
Ottar, Brynjulf, 196
  acid rain, 196
outdoor life, 10, 20, 23, 29, 32, 40–1, 44, 51, 53, 59, 61, 105, 111, 120, 127, 134, 230

Paradise, 15, 135
Parmar, Samuel L., 161
PCB pollution, 33
Peccei, Aurelio, 19, 148
  Volkswagen Foundation, 148
periphery, 3–4, 6, 25, 40, 46, 70, 75, 92, 131, 134, 230, 232–3, 236, 239–40
Perry, Everett, 154
Phillips Petroleum, 174
pioneer country, 6, 220–1, 223, 225, 229, 236–7
pollution, 9, 17–19, 28, 33, 42, 67, 71, 80, 87, 91, 93, 102, 106, 120, 137, 147, 151, 162, 166, 175–6, 183, 189–90, 196, 200, 207, 212, 234, 236–8
Promised Land, 164, 218, 229

Quine, Willard Van Orman, 54, 58

Randers, Gunnar, 144–6, 166, 168–9, 183
Randers, Jørgen, 6, 85, 87, 114, 143–7, 149, 151–2, 154, 156, 158, 160, 162, 164, 166–72, 183, 194, 213, 234–6
  Conservative Student Union, 146
  Resource Policy Group, 167, 169–72
  The Limits to Growth, 6, 85–6, 114, 143–4, 148–9, 153–6, 159, 161–2, 165–6, 168, 170–1, 194, 234
Reed, Peter, 211, 223
Regan, Tom, 99
Reimers, Eigil, 123–4
Riste, Olav, 3
Rodman, John, 99
Rokkan, Stein, 56
Roll-Hansen, Nils, 42, 65
Rosenqvist, Ivan Th., 36, 55, 111, 146, 168, 173, 176–8, 180–1, 183, 186–8, 191–3, 197, 199–201, 222, 235, 237
Roseland, Svein, 144
Roszak, Theodore, 150
Rothenberg, David, 211, 223
Rothschild, Rachel, 196, 198
Royal Swedish Academy of Sciences, 33
Rudie, Ingrid, 111
Rudolf Steiner School, 129
Rønnow, Tarjei, 7, 119

Sámi people, 12, 22–3, 202–5, 216, 220, 236
Scharrer, Berta, 35
Schei, Peter Johan, 221

Schlick, Moritz, 54
scholar-activists, 4, 6–8, 41, 102, 230, 232–3, 239
Schumacher, Ernst F., 159, 210
Sea Shepherd, 214
Seeger, Pete, 81
Semb-Johansson, Arne, 30, 34–5, 37–9, 213
Sessions, George, 210
Shepard, Paul, 210
Sherpa people, 75–8, 88, 90, 95, 122, 204, 233, 236
Singer, Peter, 99
Skattebøl, Lars, 83
Skirbekk, Gunnar, 42, 60, 166, 209
Skjervheim, Hans, 60
Skre, Oddvar, 131, 189–90
   acid rain, 131
Skønberg, Sven Erik, 69, 102, 114–15
Slagentangen, 175, 181, 183, 185, 189–91
   acid rain, 191
Sletelid, Ragnhild, 69
Sloan School of Management MIT, 146, 157, 169, 234
Smelvær, Svein, 70
Snow, Charles P., 5
Snyder, Gary, 210
Somby, Niillas A., 202, 204–5
Sörlin, Sverker, 4
Spengler, Oswald, 52
Stalin, Joseph, 60, 178
Standing Rock Indian Reservation, 203
Stanley, Matthew, 144
Statoil, 169, 224, 238
   Great Australian Bight, 238
steady-state, 27–8, 41–3, 63, 70–1, 76–7, 79, 90, 102, 114, 121, 152, 204, 206, 232–3
Steineger, Erik, 89–90
Stene, Erna, 70
Stenseth, Nils Christian, 43
Stigen, Anfinn, 111–12
Stivers, Robert, 164
Stoll, Mark S., 119
Stoltenberg, Jens, 1–2, 6, 225–8, 237
   Secretary General of NATO, 6
   Svalbard Global Seed Vault, 1
   United Nations Special Envoy on Climate Change, 6, 237
Stoltenberg, Thorvald, 227
Stone Age, 29, 231
Stridbeck, Bolof, 216
Strøksnes, Morten A., 231
sustainability, 3, 142, 144, 149, 158, 164, 170–1, 218, 221, 224, 237
sustainable development, 3, 5, 158, 171, 202, 214, 218, 223, 228–9, 235–6
sustainable effort, 156, 171
sustainable society, 143–4, 147, 162–4, 171, 217, 221, 235–6
Svalbard, 1–2, 36, 179
Svalbard Global Seed Vault, 1
Sylivan Routley, Richard, 99
Sæther, Anne Karin, 227
Sætra, Hartvig, 27–9, 43
   Den økopolitiske sosialismen, 27
   eco-politics, 27
   Gratangen, 28

Tansley, Arthur G., 35
Taylor, Charles, 99
Thant, U, 18–19
Toffler, Alvin, 153
Tolman, Edward C., 54
Treholt, Thorstein, 196
Tvedt, Terje, 3, 237
Tømte Gård, 123

Uexküll, Jakob von, 52
United Nations, 3, 6, 18–20, 159, 219, 229, 231, 236
United Nations Conference on the Human Environment, 18, 33, 130, 148, 159, 189
United Nations Convention on the Law of the Sea, 18
United Nations Environment Programme, 217–18
United Nations Framework Convention on Climate Change, 228
University of Bergen, 25, 38, 132, 209
University of Oslo, 24, 30, 34–6, 38–9, 47, 55, 58, 64, 81, 88, 92–4, 98, 102, 108, 121, 123, 128, 133–6, 145, 161, 167, 169, 176, 178, 181, 184, 186, 195, 206, 209, 214, 226, 232
   Department of Biology, 39, 105
   Department of Philosophy, 59, 68, 111, 186, 209
University of Tromsø, 20, 72
University of Trondheim, 209
Ustaoset, 46, 50, 54, 97, 103

Vetlesen, Arne Johan, 237
Viestad, Haftor, 109
Vik, Rolf, 38-9, 41, 60, 63, 194
Vinje, Arne, 70, 80, 94, 100, 106, 116
Voksø, Per, 130
Vøringsfossen Waterfall, 127

Walløe, Lars, 213, 217
Ward, Barbara, 19
Watson, Paul, 214
Weart, Spencer R., 175
Wendelbo, Per, 48
Westermoen, Toralf, 129
Wetlesen, Jon, 70, 72, 109
whales – hunting of, 76, 213-14, 233
White, Frank, 154
White, Lynn, 120-1, 123-4, 126, 128-9, 132, 135, 152, 161
Willie, Nordal, 34
Wilson, Edward O., 114
Wisløff, Jens, 132
Witoszek, Nina, 8, 88, 209
wolves – hunting of, 185, 215, 237
World Commission on Environment and Development, 6, 143, 171, 202, 217, 236
  Our Common Future, 143, 220, 224-5, 236

World Council of Churches, 119, 130, 142, 150, 159, 165, 170-1, 221, 235-6
World Population Conference, 164
World Population Year, 159
World Resource Institute, 218
World Student Christian Federation, 130
Worldwatch Institute, 217
Worster, Donald, 210
Worthington, Edgar, 37
Wright, Georg Henrik von, 33, 38, 56

XU, 36, 55, 189

Ytreberg, Pål, 90

Zapffe, Berit, 67
Zapffe, Peter Wessel, 48, 50-3, 60, 62, 67, 111, 211, 230
  Barske glæder, 51, 67
  Gaustad Mountain, 53
  Stetind Mountain, 51, 230
Zuckerman, Solly, 19

Øfsti, Audun, 100
Østbye, Eivind, 30, 35, 123-4, 126
Østerud, Øyvind, 60

Studies in Environment and History (*continued from page ii*)

Kieko Matteson *Forests in Revolutionary France: Conservation, Community, and Conflict, 1669–1848*
Micah S. Muscolino *The Ecology of War in China: Henan Province, the Yellow River, and Beyond, 1938–1950*
George Colpitts *Pemmican Empire: Food, Trade, and the Last Bison Hunts in the North American Plains, 1780–1882*
John L. Brooke *Climate Change and the Course of Global History: A Rough Journey*
Paul Josephson et al. *An Environmental History of Russia*
Emmanuel Kreike *Environmental Infrastructure in African History: Examining the Myth of Natural Resource Management*
Gregory T. Cushman *Guano and the Opening of the Pacific World: A Global Ecological History*
Sam White *The Climate of Rebellion in the Early Modern Ottoman Empire*
Edmund Russell *Evolutionary History: Uniting History and Biology to Understand Life on Earth*
Alan Mikhail *Nature and Empire in Ottoman Egypt: An Environmental History*
Richard W. Judd *The Untilled Garden: Natural History and the Spirit of Conservation in America, 1740–1840*
James L. A. Webb, Jr. *Humanity's Burden: A Global History of Malaria*
Myrna I. Santiago *The Ecology of Oil: Environment, Labor, and the Mexican Revolution, 1900–1938*
Frank Uekoetter *The Green and the Brown: A History of Conservation in Nazi Germany*
Matthew D. Evenden *Fish versus Power: An Environmental History of the Fraser River*
Alfred W. Crosby *Ecological Imperialism: The Biological Expansion of Europe, 900–1900, second edition*
Nancy J. Jacobs *Environment, Power, and Injustice: A South African History*
Edmund Russell *War and Nature: Fighting Humans and Insects with Chemicals from World War I to Silent Spring*
Adam Rome *The Bulldozer in the Countryside: Suburban Sprawl and the Rise of American Environmentalism*
Judith Shapiro *Mao's War against Nature: Politics and the Environment in Revolutionary China*
Andrew Isenberg *The Destruction of the Bison: An Environmental History*
Thomas Dunlap *Nature and the English Diaspora*
Robert B. Marks *Tigers, Rice, Silk, and Silt: Environment and Economy in Late Imperial South China*
Mark Elvin and Tsui'jung Liu *Sediments of Time: Environment and Society in Chinese History*
Richard H. Grove *Green Imperialism: Colonial Expansion, Tropical Island Edens and the Origins of Environmentalism, 1600–1860*
Thorkild Kjærgaard *The Danish Revolution, 1500–1800: An Ecohistorical Interpretation*

Donald Worster *Nature's Economy: A History of Ecological Ideas, second edition*
Elinor G. K. Melville *A Plague of Sheep: Environmental Consequences of the Conquest of Mexico*
J. R. McNeill *The Mountains of the Mediterranean World: An Environmental History*
Theodore Steinberg *Nature Incorporated: Industrialization and the Waters of New England*
Timothy Silver *A New Face on the Countryside: Indians, Colonists, and Slaves in the South Atlantic Forests, 1500–1800*
Michael Williams *Americans and Their Forests: A Historical Geography*
Donald Worster *The Ends of the Earth: Perspectives on Modern Environmental History*
Robert Harms *Games against Nature: An Eco-Cultural History of the Nunu of Equatorial Africa*
Warren Dean *Brazil and the Struggle for Rubber: A Study in Environmental History*
Samuel P. Hays *Beauty, Health, and Permanence: Environmental Politics in the United States, 1955–1985*
Arthur F. McEvoy *The Fisherman's Problem: Ecology and Law in the California Fisheries, 1850–1980*
Kenneth F. Kiple *The Caribbean Slave: A Biological History*

CPSIA information can be obtained
at www.ICGtesting.com
Printed in the USA
LVHW011616270721
693842LV00002B/180